D0553567

God's Work In Our Lives

VOLUME II

True Stories
of God's Touch

A GUIDEPOSTS BOOK

God's Work in Our Lives—Volume II. Copyright © 2002 by Guideposts, Carmel, New York 10512. All rights reserved.

No part of this publication may be reproduced, stored in a retrieval system or transmitted in any form or by any means, electronic, mechanical, photocopying, recording or otherwise, without the written permission of the publisher. Inquiries should be addressed to the Rights & Permissions Department, Guideposts, 16 E. 34th St., New York, NY 10016.

Every attempt has been made to credit the sources of copyrighted material used in this book. If any such acknowledgment has been inadvertently omitted or miscredited, receipt of such information would be appreciated.

Acknowledgments

All material that originally appeared in *Guideposts* magazine is reprinted with permission.

All Scripture quotations, unless otherwise noted, are taken from *The King James Version of the Bible*.

Scripture quotations marked (NIV) are taken from *The Holy Bible, New International Version*. Copyright © 1973, 1978, 1984 International Bible Society. Used by permission of Zondervan Bible Publishers.

Scripture quotations marked (NRSV) are taken from the *New Revised Standard Version Bible*. Copyright © 1989 by the Division of Christian Education of the National Council of the Churches of Christ in the U.S.A. Used by permission. All rights reserved.

Scripture quotations marked (RSV) are taken from the *Revised Standard Version of the Bible*. Copyright © 1946, 1952, 1971 by Division of Christian Education of the National Council of Churches of Christ in the U.S.A. Used by permission.

Scripture quotations marked (TLB) are taken from *The Living Bible*. Copyright © 1971 by Tyndale House Publishers, Wheaton, IL 60187. All rights reserved.

"Friends Angelical" by Amy Carmichael is from *Toward Jerusalem*. Christian Literature Crusade, Fort Washington, PA.

"The Man on the Rock" by Patsy Ruth Miller is adapted from *My Hollywood: When Both of Us Were Young*. Copyright © 1988 by Patsy Ruth Miller.

"My Sailor Boy" by Ada Adams, as told to Phyllis Sjoblom is reprinted by permission of Phyllis Sjoblom and *The Pentecostal Evangel*. Copyright © 1985 by the General Council of the Assemblies of God.

"When I am Sore Behest" by Antoinette Goetschius is from *Decision* magazine.

www.guidepostsbooks.com
Guideposts Books & Inspirational Media Division
Compiled by Evelyn Bence
Designed by David Matt
Cover photo by V.C.L./Getty Images
Artwork by Celia Johnson
Typeset by Westchester Book Composition
Printed in the United States of America

God's Work
In Our Lives VOLUME II

Contents

Chapter 3 | God Preserves Our Lives

Chapter 4 | God Prepares Us in Dreams and Visions

Chapter 5 | God Shines His Light

Chapter 6 | God Sends a Message

Chapter 7 | God Gives Help and Strength

Chapter 8 | God Removes the Sting of Death

Chapter 9 | God Orders His Angels

This book

continues in the format of the first volume of *God's Work in Our Lives,* celebrating God's care and concern for us by showing examples of the surprising and mysterious ways in which He directs our lives. He can arrange a whole series of events, involving many people, to bring the answers to our prayers, or He can meet a need through a seemingly insignificant pair of shoelaces. As in biblical times, God speaks to us today in whispers and dreams, in shouts and intuition. In His planning, there are no coincidences, just the working out of His purposes in ways that often defy explanation. ¶ One chapter of this volume deals with death; how God occasionally takes people to the brink and then indicates that their time to "cross over" is not yet come; how He sometimes gives special comfort to those who must let go of a loved one whose life on earth is complete. ¶ And the last chapter features stories of mysterious messengers who give strength, help, or comfort— strangers who are best described by the poet Amy Carmichael's phrase at the end of this volume: "Friends Angelical." ¶ As you read these pages, we hope not only that you will be inspired by the stories, but that you also will be on the lookout for the mysterious ways in which God works His wonders in your life. We also hope you are inspired to listen to God's voice and look for opportunities to become God's messenger to someone else in need of graceful care.

God's Work In Our Lives

VOLUME II

Trust in the Lord with all thine heart. . . . In all thy ways
acknowledge him, and he shall direct thy paths.
—Proverbs 3:5–6

CHAPTER ONE

God Directs
Our Paths

The Acts of the Apostles, chapter 8, tells of a dramatic story of God directing the Apostle Philip to travel a certain desert road, on which Philip met an Ethiopian who was clearly asking for an explanation of an Old Testament passage. Proverbs 3 promises that God will direct the paths of those who trust in Him. That promise was realized by the writers in this section, who testify to the guiding hand of God. May their stories increase your own confidence in God.

Stopped on the Stairs

M Y HUSBAND, RAY, had not returned from his first hemodialysis at the medical center. It was 7:00 P.M. He knew I had an important meeting at eight and had insisted that I not wait for him.

I grabbed my car keys and left our apartment at 7:30. Taking the hall steps at a fast clip, I was stopped on the second step—physically stopped. An insistent feeling made me go back to the apartment.

After fifteen minutes of pacing, I began to feel foolish. I put on my coat and started down the steps. Again I was stopped. It was as though a hand held me back. I retreated, unlocked the door and reentered the apartment. I sat down in a chair by the telephone and waited.

At eight o'clock I heard fumbling at the door. When I opened it, Ray stood there ashen-faced and shivering. Helping him inside, I wrapped him in a comforter and took his temperature. Ninety degrees! After he'd had some hot soup and coffee, the color began to seep back into his face.

Later I found out what had happened at the center. Apparently the fluid levels on the machine had been set incorrectly. Too much fluid had been pulled from Ray's body, and he went into shock. He had been treated and released when he said he was okay. But during the forty-minute drive home in a car with a heater that didn't work, he had had a relapse.

"Thank God you were home," he said. "Honey, I prayed you'd be here." —*Carol M. Anderson*

The Security Guard

W E WERE SITTING at the table in our Florida home and talking to our next-door neighbors. This young couple had helped us a lot in the past year and a half, after my stroke and my husband's leg injury.

Unexpectedly, the husband began telling us the story of his troubled past. At age sixteen he'd fallen in with the wrong crowd in his home-town of Greenwood, South Carolina, and had spent a year in a refor-matory. When he was released he'd had good intentions, but because of his record, he couldn't find a job.

He became desperate and decided to rob a local service station so he could have enough money to leave the state. He stole his father's car and gun and just before closing time drove up to the service window of a gasoline station. He was about to demand all the money from the woman manager.

"But just then," he explained, "I looked up and saw the sign overhead. It read, 'GOD IS OUR SECURITY GUARD—ALWAYS ON THE JOB.' And I knew I couldn't rob that place. I then rushed home and prayed all night. I was determined to get my life straightened out. And with God's help, I did."

As he finished, I looked at my husband. Both of us remembered a night thirteen years ago when I sat at our kitchen table in the same town of Greenwood, South Carolina, trying to make a sign for our business. I had scribbled down several words. Then finally it came, the slogan that my husband put on the sign that stood on the roof of the small service station that we managed:

GOD IS OUR SECURITY GUARD—ALWAYS ON THE JOB.

—DOROTHY NICHOLAS

The Driver

THERE WAS A STORM on its way that December night of 1986, but I didn't know it. Warnings were flashed on TV screens all across the state, but I didn't see them. The radio said not to leave your house unless you absolutely had to, but I didn't hear it. That night I was sitting in my apartment in Rochester, reading, and feeling overwhelmed. I had an impulsive urge to get away and the farm seemed the only place I could go. Feeling lonesome for my mother, I said to Mealie, my dog, "Come on, let's go see Grandma."

Wearing just the clothes I had on, but no hat or boots, I walked out the door with Mealie at my heels. We climbed into my Datsun and headed toward Lyndonville, New York, where I had grown up. I'd left home when I was nineteen. I'd married and lived all over the United States, but always I'd returned. The farm reminded me of the stability I longed for, the security I'd lost.

After a bad marriage, I thought I'd finally made peace with being alone. I had a nice apartment and a steady job waiting tables, but I was lonely and unsure of the future. I'd always thought God had meant me to do more with my life. At thirty-six, I still felt that I hadn't accomplished anything.

The snow was coming down fast as I drove north through Chester on Interstate 390, heading toward the Lake Ontario State Parkway. That was the most direct route west to Lyndonville, and I could avoid the traffic on the other roads.

There was a problem, though, when I reached the parkway. It hadn't been touched by snowplows and the snow was already inches deep. I turned around at the first exit and drove back to Route 104, a much-traveled, well-maintained highway eight miles south.

"Guess I should have gone this way from the beginning," I told Mealie. "Now we're already twenty miles out of our way."

The snow on 104 looked bad too, but I didn't want to turn back. And I didn't want to admit I was scared. Mealie and I pushed on, driving very slowly, following the red taillights of the car ahead. The wind howled around us and the snow swirled so fiercely that I could see nothing else but those red taillights. It seemed pointless to turn back. After all, the weather would be just as bad going east as it was going west and I wouldn't have any taillights to follow. In two hours of driving, not a vehicle had passed me going in the opposite direction.

Suddenly the red taillights stopped. A man stepped out and fought against the wind. As I rolled down my window to talk to him, the wind gushed in so hard that I could barely breathe.

He leaned down to me. "I'm stopping," he said. "I can't see anything at all now."

"Where are we?"

"Somewhere near Albion."

Albion! I had been driving two hours and was only as far as Albion! That's usually only a thirty-five-minute trip.

Trying to sound calm, I said, "I guess I'll keep going. There's no sense for me to stop here. I'm only going to Lyndonville."

"Okay," he said. "Good luck."

Within moments of leaving him, I had second thoughts. It was obvious that we had been the only two cars on the road. Now I was alone. Maybe I should go back, but why? I only had fifteen more miles to go.

I drove on. I was traveling alone in a vast expanse of whiteness, a sort of no-man's-land. The only way I stayed on course was by making out the mailboxes along the road. Now and again I veered toward one, and shaking with fear, I'd have to stop and maneuver my way onto the road again. Sometimes a glimpse of light beckoned from a faraway house. I was tempted to stop and try to make it on foot to the light. But wearing only jeans, a sweater and sneakers, I was not prepared for a difficult walk through a blizzard. And if I stopped the car and stayed in it, the snow was coming down so fast that we would soon be buried under it.

Minute by minute, second by second, my mind raced along. My hands ached, locked around the steering wheel in a vicelike grip of fear and concentration. My body was so tense that it felt as though it were ready to break into pieces.

Now most of the windshield was covered with ice. The buildup on the wiper blades was so great that their rubber surfaces couldn't even make contact with the glass. Visibility was so poor that everything looked the same—a surreal landscape of stark white.

I could only inch forward. Suddenly the car jolted to a stop and in the split second it took for me to realize that I'd plowed into a snowbank, I screamed. Frantic, wild with fear, I began to argue with myself. "You fool, now you've done it. You'll never get out."

Calmly, something inside me said, *Just back out slowly. Drive out the way you came in.*

"No, you're stuck. You'll stay there and freeze to death. Mom won't even find out for days. Poor Mealie. She's afraid."

Back out slowly. It can be done.

Finally I took my mind's advice. Trying to calm Mealie in the seat beside me, I backed out slowly. My body sagged with relief. I straightened the car out and we started moving forward again. But what was the use? I peered desperately out the windshield. There was nothing but snow. No road, no lights, no mailboxes, just snow.

Shaking my head in disbelief, my eyes flooding with tears, I cried out, "Lord, help me. Please, Lord, I can't drive anymore. I can't go on. Take over. Please, Lord, drive this car for me."

No sooner were those words out of my mouth than something wondrous began to happen. Ahead, where moments before all had been white, a tiny spot of clear highway shone in my headlights. I drove toward it and then there was another little clearing in the road. And then another and another. To my astonishment we kept moving forward, foot by foot, yard by yard.

"Thank You, Jesus," I prayed. In my desperation I had called out to Him and He answered. He was with me in the blizzard. Wouldn't He be with me always?

I drove on—or should I say the Lord drove. I sat in the driver's seat with my hands on the wheel, but I knew I wasn't driving. Gradually my courage returned and my tears disappeared. He was showing me I wasn't alone. I never had been.

Suddenly a set of tire tracks appeared from nowhere. I followed them until I was only three miles from the farm. At that point, after almost three and a half hours of driving, I finally saw a snowplow coming toward me in the opposite direction. Passing it, I switched lanes, taking advantage of the road it had cleared.

When at last I made it to the farm, Mealie jumped out of the car, and we both hurried into the warmth of the house. But now I felt secure. Like the psalmist, I knew for a fact that the Lord is my shepherd. He had brought me home. —LYNN ERICE

Flowers in Time

SPEAK TO ME, LORD, and speak through me." It was my daily prayer and I said it that Sunday at St. Luke's. On the altar, red roses glowed, roses I'd provided in memory of my mother. When the service was over, I turned to my son, Bob. "After we have dinner, let's take the altar flowers to Miss Marie."

"Good idea," he agreed. Mother and Miss Marie, now in her eighties, had been close friends.

Driving home, humming the recessional hymn together, we broke off at the same moment. "Let's take the flowers to Miss Marie right now." The identical thought had occurred to both of us.

"What made you change your mind?" I asked as Bob turned the car toward Miss Marie's house.

"I don't know," was all he could say.

"I don't either." I hesitated. "But let's not waste any time."

Miss Marie's daughter, Alice, answered the doorbell. "How nice!" she said as I handed her the roses. "I've been in bed with the flu." She gestured vaguely. "Mother was resting in her room. Let me see if she's awake now."

Then, a sharp cry.

Bob and I raced down the hall. Miss Marie lay unconscious on the floor, Bob lifted her to her bed. I dialed the emergency ambulance. Alice began sponging Miss Marie's forehead with cool water. Her eyes fluttered.

"Lucky you got to her in time," the medic told us. "When it's a little stroke they can't call for help."

"Couldn't speak," Miss Marie murmured. "Prayed to God in my heart."

That made two prayers. He'd answered loud and clear.

—ELLEN ST. JOHN BARNWELL

Prayer for Tomorrow

Beyond today will be tomorrow,
But what it will bring of joy or sorrow
I cannot know. I only pray
Your guidance, Lord, each hour, each day,
Your strength to bear whatever may be
Your loving wisdom has for me.
So sweet or bitter, sad or gay,
Be with me, Lord, beyond today.

—CARLENE A. WALLACE

The Picture in Aunt Lana's Mind

PACIFIC BEACH, WASHINGTON, where Grandma and Aunt Lana lived for many years, is a very small town in a very bleak part of the world. Forlorn, one could call it. Not many people want to live there, or go there, for it rains incessantly, the people are poor, and the Pacific's waves are much too rough for surfing or swimming. Still, I loved my visits there, and never more than during the summer of 1973, when Aunt Lana included me in one of her spiritual "adventures." It was an adventure in blind trust.

Aunt Lana and Grandma went to live in Pacific Beach because that's the only place where Aunt Lana could find employment. She's a teacher. She is also handicapped. In 1949, she was struck down by polio, and this robust, six-foot-two woman has been in a wheelchair ever since. Aunt Lana is a triumphant woman, however, with a hard, practical hold on life and a bold grip on the life of the spirit. I think she's especially attuned to spiritual things *because* she's handicapped and not running around wastefully the way most of us are.

On the last day of my summer visit in 1973, when I was fourteen, I realized that something was troubling Aunt Lana. The sun was dancing across the surf when I went down to the kitchen that lovely morning. But as we breakfasted on apricots, toast and hard-boiled eggs, Aunt Lana was silent. Not so Grandma. "The sun always shines over a day in Pacific Beach," she said cheerily. "But for the rest of the day you'd better keep your coat on."

We cleared the table, and just as I was about to go back upstairs, I saw Aunt Lana sitting in her room, just staring.

"Anything I can do?" I said, concerned. She shook her head. Then as I was about to leave, she changed her mind.

"Well, maybe there *is* something you can do. I'm stymied."

She told me a strange story about a picture that had come into her mind a few days before. She hadn't paid much attention to it at first, for it was simply a scene that had flashed into her consciousness—some sand and some rocks and a body of water, that's all. But the scene kept coming back, persistently intruding on her prayers and thoughts.

"I have a feeling that the picture comes from the Lord, that He's trying to tell me something," Aunt Lana said. "But what?"

To me, this was pretty deep spiritual stuff. I felt a little timid about presuming to advise Aunt Lana in this special area of hers, but I was soon deeply involved—and fascinated. We talked for a while, and then, remembering that Aunt Lana loved stories, I said, "What do you think one of your detectives would do?" That started Aunt Lana taking the picture apart piece by piece, as though each held a clue.

"All right," she said, closing her eyes and summoning the picture into view. "The sun is shining. There's water on the left, sand on the right, a bluff of rock hovering over that—so that must be north. And if that's so, then this is very likely a beach on the West Coast."

"Maybe one here in Washington?"

"Yes, it looks like our shoreline," Aunt Lana replied, "but there's nothing to distinguish it, no man-made thing." She was silent now, her eyes still closed. "But the water," she said so suddenly that I jumped, "look at the water! It's smooth, no ripples. That could mean a cove of some sort." Then a little sadly, "But not on this wild coast of ours."

Aunt Lana and I wrestled with these meager facts for a little while, and then we had to admit that we could make nothing of them. Still, Aunt Lana couldn't shake the conviction that the picture had some special meaning for her.

At noon we were just getting ready to dry the luncheon dishes and Aunt Lana was reaching for the dish towel when her hand stopped in mid-air. "Bobby," she said, "there's some quiet water up north of here, up in the Indian reservation. I feel sure I've seen some."

"Let's try to find it," I said, and with a flurry of excitement we made plans for the search. We were about ready to leave when Grandma suggested that as long as we were heading up near the Quinault reservation, we might drop off some old clothes she'd been saving to give away. Aunt

Lana thought that a good idea. One of her students lived up in Taholah with an aged grandmother. Maybe they'd have some use for them.

With Aunt Lana at the wheel of her white Impala—with the hand brake she'd designed herself and had someone weld—we headed north. The road paralleled the ocean, winding over hills and through creek canyons. We passed storm-sculptured rocks where sea birds took shelter from the turbulent breakers. Bizarre pillars of stone dotted the beaches like human forms in windblown garments. "The Indians say that those pillars are women waiting for the men to return from the sea," Aunt Lana said, filling me with wonderful facts about the Quinault Indians who once had earned their livelihood from whaling.

We traveled on. The road narrowed and threatened to become gravel, though it never quite did. Soon we crossed into the Quinault reservation. About a mile or so deeper in, she stopped the car. "Point Grenville!" she shouted. "Quick, Bob, over there! Run to the beach. See what's there." I was out of the car lickety-split, and in a few minutes came panting back.

"It's there!" I called. I described the cove with the ocean on the left and the beach with the looming rocks on the right, and the sun's rays glistening on the water's quiet ripples.

Aunt Lana threw up her arms in a wild expression of joy. She reached over and hugged me and kissed me on the forehead. Then she became serious. "Now tell me what else you saw."

"I didn't see anything else, Aunt Lana."

"Nobody was there?"

"Nobody."

"You didn't see anything odd?" I shook my head. Aunt Lana's face darkened. She put her head down on the steering wheel; I knew she was praying.

"Well," she said finally, "I don't know what it means. Stymied again."

It seemed a shame to give up now. We discussed the possibility of our just staying there and waiting for something to happen, and for a while that's what we did. As time passed, I guess we both felt disillusioned. At one point I looked into the back seat and saw the boxes of clothes Grandma had given us; I suggested that we bring them to the Indian family.

"What clothes?" Aunt Lana said. She'd forgotten about them. My idea prevailed, however, and we started up again and drove toward the little town huddled in a small valley by a river. In Taholah, Aunt Lana drove up to the fish cannery and sent me in with instructions to buy a fish for dinner. I bought a small salmon, wrapped it in three layers of the *Aberdeen World,* and put it in the trunk. Fishing meant jobs, and the noble salmon provided for the needs of many of the town's families, most of whom were desperately poor.

After that we drove to Second Street and turned down it. The houses we passed were blank-walled—the Indians thought that a house facing the street would be haunted and bring bad luck. We drove to the house on the corner, the only one that was painted—a bright canary yellow with a blue stripe around the middle. Aunt Lana honked the horn and presently small child toddled out, squinted at us, and ran back inside.

"The grandmother is very old," Aunt Lana explained to me. "I am told that she has eighteen children of her own, and who knows how many grandchildren."

Soon the old grandmother appeared. By the time she shuffled up to Aunt Lana's door, I was out of the car and waiting with a box of clothes. The old Indian reached out to touch Aunt Lana's outstretched hand. "You've come," she said. "I've been expecting you."

Aunt Lana and I looked at each other. Then we both looked at the grandmother. Perhaps we hadn't heard her correctly.

"You were expecting us?"

"Yes, yes," she said, and gradually, in stops and starts, fumbling for words, she told us about the trouble in the family, the people out of work, someone in jail, the hunger, the lack of warm clothing, the ever-pervasive need. Then one day, she continued, when her feeling of help-lessness was at its worst, she had wandered down to the beach.

As the old woman mentioned the word "beach," I saw a glimmer come into Aunt Lana's eyes. "And then?" Aunt Lana said.

"I walk along the edge of the water. A long time." As she talked I pictured her moving aimlessly among the rocks while the great waves thundered and splashed. "Then I come to a place where the ocean is more quiet and the wind is very kind . . ."

A cove, I wanted to say. *You came to a cove.*

". . . and there I talk to God. 'Please, God,' I say, 'tell someone to bring help. Not for me, God—for the little ones.'"

It was almost unnecessary to ask her when she had prayed in the quiet cove. I knew, Aunt Lana knew, that the old woman had been talking to her God three days before, the very day, the very hour, when the picture first came into Aunt Lana's mind. And so it proved to be.

I carried the boxes of clothes into the house while Aunt Lana sat in the car making arrangements for help. Then we left. The old grandmother, surrounded now by a crowd of children, waved good-bye. "God is taking care," I heard her say. "God is taking care."

At the end of the day, just before leaving Aunt Lana's home for my own, I took a last walk on the beach. I wore a coat to shield me from the windblown rain. The beginning of a storm from the southwest brought waves that washed my rubber boots. It had been a day like no other, a day in which Aunt Lana had helped me learn what she had known for a long time: that God has countless ways of letting us know that He is there, taking care. —ROBERT J. FOSS

The Column of Smoke

I WAS WAITING FOR THE BUS to take me down from the Janiculum Hill into the city of Rome when I turned and saw black smoke rising into the sky. It seemed to be coming from my studio, a small, cabinlike study built up against the ancient Roman wall that bounded the grounds of the American Academy. I'd arrived there three weeks before with my most precious possession: the first draft of my new novel.

The smoke—I thought of the electric coil I'd been using to heat water for the endless cups of tea I need to fuel my writing. What if I had started heating water and forgotten? Suppose the coil had slipped from the cup and started a fire that would not only destroy the studio committed to my care for a year but the pages and pages of work I could never duplicate?

I hurried back, but soon saw that the smoke came from a bonfire in the adjoining orchard. I felt relieved, and even a little foolish. But since I was now so close, I went into my studio anyway.

The electric coil *was* still plugged in, and the water I'd meant to use for tea before I left had all boiled out of a cup that had tipped over— and the red-hot coil had toppled onto the desk and was charring the wood. Manuscript pages that would have flared up in a second were only inches away.

Drawn by that column of smoke, I'd come back just in time. "Thank God," I said.

Of course, thank God. —JOSEPH CALDWELL

The Skunk

I T WAS A RUSTLING in the woods that made me glance out the window beside my word processor. At the edge of the trees I caught sight of a skunk, his black-and-white pattern echoing the dappled light. He seemed to be furiously busy—burrowing maybe? My knowledge of skunks began and ended with that appalling odor.

Next moment, though, the animal emerged from beneath the trees and ran zigzagging across the lawn: plumelike tail, striped back and . . . where his head should have been, a bizarre-looking yellow helmet. As he came closer I saw what the "helmet" was. A six-ounce plastic yogurt container.

The carton struck a rock, and the creature whirled in another direction, only to bump up against our picnic table. For a second he stood still, shaking his head frantically. But the yogurt carton was cone-shaped, the narrow mouth wedged fast about his neck. The skunk charged blindly back into the woods.

I stared after him in dismay. How long since he had forced his head into that carton to reach some bit of food on the bottom? How long had he been running in darkness and terror?

It would be the work of a second for me, I thought, to pull that thing off. But the idea of pursuing a skunk through the undergrowth kept me immobilized at the window. How would I ever catch him? And then what? In his panic wouldn't he be certain to spray me?

I sat down and tried to pick up the thread of the story was writing that I had to finish today. But I could think only of an animal running till he dropped from exhaustion. Mustn't this sort of thing have happened before? Might animal experts know what to do?

From the kitchen telephone I dialed the local ASPCA. "We only handle domestic animals," the woman told me. "You want the State Conservation Department." She gave me a number in New Paltz, New York.

New Paltz meant a toll call. Anyhow, by now the skunk would be a long way off. Maybe someone else would see him. Someone braver and more athletic.

I dialed the number in New Paltz. A man in the Department of Wildlife listened to my story, then held a muffled conversation. "As long as skunks can't see you," he said into the phone, "they don't spray."

Well . . . that sounded all right, as long as the skunk's head was inside the container. "What happens after the carton comes off?" I asked.

"Just make sure," the man advised, "that he doesn't feel threatened."

I wondered how one went about reassuring a terrified skunk.

"You could throw a blanket over him," Wildlife suggested. "Then run while he's finding his way out."

"That might work," I said, but I must have sounded as unsure as I felt, because the man asked where I was calling from and began looking up names of conservation officers in my area.

How long would it take, I wondered, for someone to get here? Where would the skunk be by then? Standing there in the kitchen, I was gripped by a sudden strange urgency. I thanked the man, hung up, and ran outside. Without stopping to change out of my next-to-best slacks (*does skunk scent ever wash out?*), and forgetting about the blanket theory, I ran up our driveway to the road.

Of course the skunk wasn't there. Nor did I know why I was. In his frenzy, when I'd seen him last, the animal had been heading the opposite way, straight down the hill into the woods.

But my feet never slowed. I turned left and dashed down the street as though rushing to a long-ordained appointment. I'd run perhaps a hundred yards when a black-and-white streak emerged from the bushes beside the road and ran straight at me, the carton bumping the pavement with each step. I stooped down and grabbed hold of the yogurt carton before the astonishment of finding the skunk hit me.

The animal was tugging and twisting, unexpectedly strong, to get away. *If they can't see you they won't spray.* His front claws scrabbled against the slippery yellow plastic, his body strained backward, and still he could not wrench free of the carton's viselike neck. It took both of my hands tugging the other way to hold on—until a small black head suddenly popped free.

And there we stood, facing each other, two feet apart.

I don't know what *he* saw, and how threatening or not the apparition was, but what *I* saw was a sharp quivering nose, two small round ears, and alert black eyes that stared straight into mine.

For fully ten seconds we held each other's gaze. Then the skunk turned, ran a few yards, and vanished into the mouth of a culvert that runs beneath the road.

For a moment more I stood there, looking after him. Three minutes could not have passed since I hung up the telephone in the kitchen.

But a timeless parable had played itself out, I thought, as I headed back down the drive. The skunk was all those needs I hesitate to get involved in: *Involvement takes time and I have deadlines to meet. I probably can't do anything anyway. Somebody else can handle it better. Besides, involvement can be ugly, and the stench may rub off on me.*

And all these things, of course, may be true. But I've got a yellow pencil-holder on my desk, a rather scratched and battered one, to remind me that every now and then God's answer to a need is me.

—*Elizabeth Sherrill*

The Whistle

I WAS PACKING THAT MORNING when I heard a shrill whistle. I rushed into the living room only to discover it came from the TV. We were preparing to go from Boulder to Montrose, Colorado, with our ten-week-old baby, Leslie.

As we drove through the mountains that afternoon, big sleety drops of rain turned into heavy wet flakes of snow. Near the top of Fremont Pass, traffic slowed and we could barely see. I nursed Leslie and then Neil pulled over and held her. "Is something wrong?" I asked when Leslie's cry suddenly became low and husky.

Neil handed her back to me in a panic. She was coughing and gasping. I patted her on the back, but she turned bluish gray and seemed to stop breathing. I began to administer mouth-to-mouth resuscitation, but without oxygen she could go into respiratory arrest. "Lord," I prayed, "save my baby."

Just then the shrill sound of a whistle pierced the swirling snow. "That's a mine over there," I called to Neil. "Someone will have oxygen there."

Neil started the car and crossed the road to the gate of a molybdenum mine. We flagged a guard, told him our problem, then raced down the drive, where two nurses met us with an oxygen tank. I put the huge mask over Leslie's ashen face and, slowly, she began breathing again.

Later we went to a hospital, where tests confirmed that Leslie was all right. The doctor there had one question: "How did you know there would be oxygen at the mine?"

The shrill sound I had heard that morning was a mine whistle blowing in an episode of *The Waltons.* I watched just long enough to see a miner revived—with oxygen.

—*Kerri Tillquist*

Mission to the Strangest Place

LOOKING BACK ON IT, I can see how people viewed me as a religious crackpot. I got off the plane in Caracas, Venezuela, that hot August day back in 1962 with only seventy-two dollars in my pocket, nineteen years old, alone, unable to speak Spanish, but convinced that the Lord had told me to go to South America and preach His word to the Indians.

It had all started four years earlier, back in St. Paul, Minnesota, when Jesus Christ became very real to me. My relationship with Him deepened in college, where my aim was to become a professor of languages. However, I began to feel this inner nudge to share His life with those who had never known Him.

"But where, Lord?" I found myself asking.

Then over a period of time, I became interested in South America, particularly Venezuela and Colombia.

I applied to a well-known mission board in Venezuela. They informed me that I didn't have the educational requirements. I was relieved and returned to my dream of becoming a language professor.

Yet God still nudged me.

"But, Lord, I was turned down. I have no contacts, no money, no mission board. You want me to go down there by myself without anyone to take care of me?"

And ever so gently in my mind, the words came, "Bruce, I'm in South America too."

Then came that wonderful feeling of reassurance. Suddenly I knew that with Him by my side I could do anything. But I soon discovered the big difference between plunging ahead on your own power and waiting for His guidance. The Lord knew how inadequate I was. And His preparation came in a series of remarkable incidents.

Soon after I arrived in Caracas, so alone and so ill-equipped, a Venezuelan college student noticed me wandering about the city. We struck up a friendship and I moved into his house where I began to learn the language.

When he learned of my interest in the Indians, he introduced me to a doctor with the government's Indian Commission. Doctor Christian invited me to accompany him by canoe up the muddy Orinoco River. For three weeks I lived with a semicivilized tribe and learned their ways.

After this trip, the doctor referred me to an American-Venezuelan cultural exchange program in Caracas where I met a man with the Ministry of Health. He asked me to teach English to some university students preparing to attend Harvard University's school of tropical medicine. I did, and at the same time I learned the rudiments of tropical medicine.

One day my superior and I were talking about Indians. "Have you ever heard of the Motilone tribe?" he asked. He described a legendary Stone Age tribe that had resisted civilization since time began. No one had ever learned their language, since few entering their territory ever returned.

These fierce savages, he said, lived in a wild jungle area on the border between Venezuela and Colombia.

Venezuela and Colombia!

I sank back in awe. I knew then that those were the people to whom God wanted me to go.

Within a week I was on a bus headed for the foothills of the Andes Mountains. Then I set off into the jungle alone. Three days later I stumbled half-starved into a settlement of Yucco Indians, a semiprimitive tribe. For eight months I lived with them, learning their language. Finally three Yucco braves reluctantly agreed to take me to a trail that led to the Motilones.

We chopped our way through the jungle for seven days. Suddenly an arrow pierced my thigh. I fell to the ground: my companions fled.

Out of the ferns stepped five squat brown men, eyes glittering under short-cropped hair. I had met the Motilones.

They dragged me to my feet and I limped with them to their settlement. I was thrust into a communal hut where I lay on a palm mat. Days went by; my wound festered. I developed amoebic dysentery and began hemorrhaging blood.

The period that followed was a nightmare of pain and trial. However, I continued to try to bring God's love to those people. Finally, some of them took pity on me and one in particular, a man called Bobarishora, became my friend. As they tried to pronounce my name, "Bruce" became "Bruchko," which has stayed with me ever since.

Meanwhile a powerful chieftain who lived in a distant village heard of me and wanted to kill me. Now I felt impelled to visit this chieftain. If I could gain his friendship, I could travel safely throughout all Motilone territory. My native friends shook their heads but I insisted. However, during the trip to see this chief, I became terribly fatigued.

Suddenly Bobarishora looked at me and gasped, "Bruchko, your eyes have turned yellow!"

I had hepatitis. My only hope was to continue on and trust in God.

The chief was waiting in a frenzy. "Why have you not killed him?"

My friends argued that I was dying already. Later I learned that to a Motilone the worst thing is to die outside your own land. Then your soul is doomed to wander forever.

The chief agreed this would be a fitting end for me. For two weeks I lay in a hut slowly dying. There was little sound except the low murmur of women as they worked.

Suddenly the voices rose in alarm. I heard the distant drone of a helicopter. My friend, Bobarishora, rushed to my side. "Bruchko, the cannibal flute is coming."

The Motilones felt that airplanes were droning flutes of the white-skins who, they believed, were cannibals who ate Motilones. "Bobby," I pleaded, "carry me out and put a red cloth next to me." He pulled me to a clearing, then fled.

Now I could hear the helicopter land and soon I was looking up into the amazed face of a doctor I had met when I first traveled up the Orinoco River. He explained that he had been visiting an oil company camp. On impulse he asked their pilot to fly him over Motilone territory to take pictures.

I was taken to Maracaibo where I was told it would be six months before I would recover and that I could never return to a jungle climate. But I had a deepening peace in my heart. God had brought me to the Motilones; He would help me to continue. Within three weeks I was back up the river, well supplied with medicines given me by an oil company.

The Motilone chief received me with awe. To him the helicopter had been a sacred vulture sent to take my body. Now I had returned with supernatural prestige. I lived with the Motilones, learning their language, their customs.

But the witch doctors watched me with suspicion. I knew that Motilones believed that evil spirits lived in rocks, trees, and rivers. So one day I placed a smear of river mud under my microscope and showed it to a witch doctor.

"There," I said, referring to the wriggling microbes, "are your evil spirits."

She shrank back in terror. Then I showed her how disinfectant left them lifeless. This is how I first introduced the Motilones to medical science. It was also how their witch doctors became my close allies.

I lived with them for four years, but when I felt ready to give the Motilones the word of God I felt confused and frustrated. They had a vague belief in an entity "who lived somewhere," but where they did not know. Yet how could I introduce God as He really was, independent of my own personality and culture?

I searched for some illustration as a key in introducing the Bible; to them a book was meaningless. I prayed that God would speak through me, that He would show me the right time to do it.

One afternoon the answer came. As Bobarishora, some other men, and I were out walking, we heard agonizing cries echoing through the valley. We looked for their source and found Atabadora, a powerful tribal leader. He had dug a deep pit and was now calling into it for their god to reveal himself. Atabadora's brother had died in a strange territory and he wanted assurance that his brother's spirit would be brought back.

Another man perched in the top of a tall tree was shouting for the great spirit "to come from the horizon." The two had been screaming since sunrise, and as evening shadows crept over them, their voices had dwindled to a croak.

I now found it possible to start a lively discussion. The man in the tree came down and joined us. He reminded us of the tribal legend about the tall man who one day would walk through the tribe carrying a banana stalk out of which God would come.

"Why look for God in a banana stalk?" I asked in puzzlement.

They couldn't explain it. Bobarishora walked over to a banana tree, cut off a cross section, and tossed it to us. "This is the kind of banana stalk our god can come from."

In a mirthful mood, one of the other men struck at the stalk with his machete, hitting it lengthwise.

I gasped.

As it split open, the pale unborn banana leaves unpeeled from within it like the pages of a book.

And now I understood the reason for each step God had had me take in the four years of getting to know the Motilones, of mastering each nuance of their strange and beautiful tongue, of learning how they thought, their hopes and dreams.

I grabbed up my pack and took out my Bible. Flipping open the pages, I pointed to its leaves and said, "This is it. God's language is here. This is God's banana stalk!"
—*BRUCE E. OLSON*

What to Pray For

I asked for bread and got a stone;
I used the stone to grind the grain

That made the flour to form the bread
That I could not obtain.

Instead of asking Him to give
The things for which we pray,
All that we need to ask from God
Is this: show us the way.
—James A. Bowman

His Broad Shoulders

L ean on the lord," friends in our prayer group urged us. "His shoulders are broad."

At the time, my husband and I needed a shoulder to lean on. Our business had turned sour, our savings were dwindling, and at retirement age, we were scrounging for jobs. In the midst of this, my ninety-four-year-old mother experienced a mental and physical breakdown. Living with my sister in southwestern Arizona, she required twenty-four-hour care, and now it looked as if she needed to be put into a nursing home.

One Sunday night I was praying about our problems as I drove home alone from my sister's after a week spent helping with Mom's care. The narrow two-lane road was heavy with traffic coming from Las Vegas, the headlights blinding my eyes. Three different times I came over hills to find a driver coming at me in my lane, and I had to pull off the side of the road to avoid a collision. I don't mind telling you I was thankful that *those* broad shoulders were there.

Two weeks later I made the same trip with my husband. In full daylight we reached the road just north of Kingman, Arizona. "This was the stretch," I told him, "where I had to pull off."

We looked and looked, and grew quieter and quieter.

For that entire forty-mile section of Highway 93, cactus and greasewood and mesquite grow close to the roadside. There were no shoulders—only His to lean on. —Helene Lewis Coffer

The Miracle Mattress

W e kept our newest baby in an egg carton—not one of those Styrofoam ones with pockets for a dozen eggs, naturally, but the large cardboard box that hundreds of eggs come in. My resourceful wife had covered the box with some flannel material printed in nursery scenes, and this makeshift arrangement served well enough as a bassinet. But now the baby was five months old and too big to sleep in the egg carton anymore.

I was struggling through school while working nights, collecting and counting mosquitoes for the City Health Department in Jacksonville, Florida. If I'd been paid a penny for each mosquito in the traps, instead of by the hour, I could have afforded all sorts of luxuries, such as a crib for our third baby. But supporting a family of five on a part-time job imposes quite a few financial limitations, so the baby slept in the egg carton.

One night in family devotions, my wife explained the whole situation to our Lord. "Dear Jesus," Ginny prayed, "we've just got to have a new crib mattress. Eve is too big for her little box, and she needs a bed. You know we have that old crib in the storeroom, but it was secondhand when we got it. And after Jennifer and Donald outgrew it, that mattress was in tatters, so we need a new mattress. Soon, please. Amen."

Ginny's prayers made me mad. I felt frustrated because I was trying to live as I thought God wanted, and I felt He had let me down. I attended school because I thought He wanted me there. My job seemed to be the place He had for me, and I was trying to raise my family right. But I couldn't even afford a mattress for a secondhand baby crib. It just didn't seem fair.

Another thing complicated our situation. Early in our marriage Ginny and I had decided to attempt to live without buying anything on credit, without ever borrowing money and without ever telling anyone except God about our needs. We have not always stayed within these guidelines, but they represent part of a standard of faith we acknowledge. I suspect the real reason we first aspired to this life-style was that we were too hard-headed, proud, and stubborn to admit how poor we actually were. At any rate, the baby slept in a box, Ginny prayed, and I was mad at God.

One afternoon during the week after Ginny's prayer, one of my fellow students needed a ride to work after school, so I gave him a lift. We had to cross the Main Street Bridge over the St. Johns River. This bridge spans nearly a mile of river and is about a hundred feet above the water. It carries traffic for U.S. Highways 1 and 17 and is one of the most heavily traveled bridges in the city. A huge metal grating in the center of the bridge rises to allow ships to pass underneath in the main channel of the river. As we drove across that metal grating, something lay right in the center of the roadway—it looked like a brand-new crib mattress.

Since a truck was following me closely, I couldn't stop to check. I had to follow the flow of traffic into downtown Jacksonville, where one-way streets forced me to make an eight-block loop before I could head north over the bridge again. All this maneuvering took close to thirty minutes, but when I returned, incredibly, the crib mattress still lay on the grate, untouched by the busy traffic. Right then and there, I stopped being mad at the Lord.

I paused on the center span. My friend leaped out, threw the crib mattress in the backseat, and jumped in the car again as traffic honked behind us. The mattress probably had fallen from the back of a truck or something, and there was no way for me to locate its original owner. Except for a scuffed place at one corner, it appeared to be in perfect condition.

That night as Ginny and I put together our old crib to receive its new mattress, I hesitated. "Suppose it's not the right size for our crib?"

"Hand me the screwdriver," Ginny replied. "God wouldn't send us a mattress that doesn't fit."

She was right.

—*John W. Cowart*

The Long Leap

FIFTY YEARS OF TRAVELING around the world as a U.S. merchant marine should be enough adventure for anyone. But not until I was an old man living alone in New York City did I experience the most terrifying night of my life.

I was living in a little room in a men's hotel on 34th Street. Recently released from a veterans' hospital after four months of treatment, I was blind in one eye, with only partial vision in the other. I was worried. How would I get along? I had always been an independent person. But now, to be almost blind? Still, I was grateful to be back on my own and, with a cane, could get around somewhat.

One March night in 1972 I went down to the street for a paper and chatted a bit with the news vendor. As I headed back to the lobby, I could just about see the neon cross of the mission down the street glowing through the mist. It made me feel good. As the elevator took me to the seventh floor where my room was, I thought back on how God had helped me through my seventy-two years. As a young soldier in Guatemala, about to drown in a raging river, I turned to Him, and the torrent swept me to safety. Some years later I was aboard a ship wallowing helplessly in a hurricane. Again, He was there.

As I settled in bed, I offered my nightly prayer. "O Father, thank You for this room. Thank You for still being able to read the paper." I relaxed and then fell into a sound sleep.

Dimly, I heard shouting. *It's probably some young men quarreling in the alley,* I thought. I turned over. But the noise increased. Then I began to hear bells, like fire bells. I crawled out of bed, fumbling for my glasses. I checked my watch; it was nearly eleven o'clock. I picked up the phone to call the desk and find out what was going on. No answer. I jiggled the hook, but the phone was dead. Apprehension began to build in me. This was an unfamiliar building; I didn't know my way around it. Now I could hear sirens wailing from far below.

Fire? Could the building be on fire? I had to find out.

I opened the door to the hall and fell back as thick black smoke billowed into the room. I slammed the door.

"O God, I've got to get out of here!"

I remembered a metal fire-escape door down the hall. I pulled on my pants, donned a raincoat, hat and winter gloves, then wrapped a wet towel around my face. I could hold my breath for two minutes. Within that time, I knew, I had to get out that fire door.

When I pulled open my door again, thick, hot, asphyxiating smoke swallowed me. I groped along the walls, sensing through my gloves the paint bubbling on the plaster, hearing the crackle of flames, feeling the searing heat.

Ah, the fire door! I grabbed the hot metal handle and pulled. Nothing. It was swollen tight into its frame by the heat! I yanked at it. Now my lungs were bursting. "Don't breathe!" my mind screamed. But I couldn't hold my breath anymore. My chest surged as I gasped for air.

There was no air—only a hot, swirling pitch that burned my nostrils, choked me, filled me with sickness. My legs crumpled and I seemed to be dizzily whirling into a black vortex, dimmer, dimmer....

And then I seemed to hear a voice, strong, powerful, commanding: "Run to the window! Fast! Run!"

It shocked me. And then, perhaps from years of instantly obeying commands at sea, I rose and began running blindly, twisting, turning through the labyrinth of corridors.

And then I saw it. A dim light. I rushed to it and found myself in front of a small window. I lifted it. Surprisingly it slid up easily, unlike the usual paint-sealed windows of old buildings. I leaned out, gasping, filling my lungs with fresh, cold air.

As my head cleared, I looked down to the street at the end of the alley far below. It was alive with the activity of fire pumpers and the clamor of the crowd. In the garish brilliance of floodlights, tiny faces looked up to the front of the building. Would anyone see me there at the side in the dark?

I leaned farther out the window. Behind me the inferno roared as timbers exploded into flames and walls buckled and cracked. Now heat seared my back. My coat began to smolder.

I had to get out.

In the dark, about six feet from the window, was a large round chimney pipe. But I saw no hope of a handhold on its wide, sooty girth.

But wait. What was that? Farther down an iron brace-bar extended from the chimney to the building wall. It looked much too far for me to reach, but in desperation I reached for it anyway.

I remember nothing more until I found myself clinging to the brace. "Thank You, Lord." I breathed, as I got a firmer grip. I looked down to the street. No one could possibly see me up here.

Then I remembered the little flashlight I always carry in my coat. Anchoring myself with one arm, I carefully reached into my pocket. I waved the flashlight. No one seemed to notice. About ten minutes passed. I rested. Fifteen minutes. I began to tire. Twenty minutes. My body ached in the cold night air. Slowly I waved my flashlight. Still no one seemed to notice. Twenty-five minutes. My muscles cramped and I began to shake in pain. I looked at my hand: it was white from clutching the bar. Was it a part of me anymore? I wasn't sure.

Below me infinity stretched seven stories to the concrete pavement. As I feebly swung the light, an insidious feeling came over me. How relaxing it would be just to let go, just rest my tired muscles. And then I remembered. God had brought me this far. I could not let Him down now. I waved the flashlight again.

A thin cry floated up: "Don't jump!" Had someone seen me? And then other voices rose, encouraging voices: "Don't jump." "We're coming . . . hold on!"

New strength flowed through me. I felt I had won a battle with something far darker than the smoke pouring out of the window above me.

And now I was bathed in light. As the fire ladder reached toward me, I could hear cheers from the street. The ladder halted just below me, trembling as a fireman scrambled up. "Here," he called. "I'll help you down."

"No, thank you," I said as my feet felt for the step. "I can make it." *An old man can still have dignity,* I thought, as I eased down the ladder to safety.

The next day a TV cameraman and I walked through the charred halls to the window I had escaped from. He looked down at the iron brace and whistled. "That's quite a distance. How did you do it?"

So I told him. I told him God had shown me the way to that window and that I was sure He had helped me reach that brace.

He stared at me for a moment, then turned to set up his equipment. Whether he believed me is something I don't know. But I do know without a doubt that I couldn't possibly have escaped that burning building without God's help.

I know too that I don't have to worry anymore about how I will get along with my limited eyesight. The Lord has shown me that He will always be with me.
—*Jose M. Sandoval*

The Little Brown Church

THE WORLD SEEMED VERY GOOD to William Pitts that June day in 1857 as he gazed out of the stagecoach window, watching Iowa's flat farmland whirl by. Pitts, a schoolteacher, was on his way to see pretty Ann Warren, the young woman who would soon be his bride.

The stagecoach clattered to a stop in a swirl of dust at the prairie town of Bradford. While the sweating horses were changed, Pitts strolled down Cedar Street to stretch his legs. He paused at a peaceful glade where the forest thinned to merge with the prairie.

Standing there in the quiet, Pitts thought, *What a magnificent spot this would be for a country church.* Mentally, he could almost see it.

Later, when he returned to his Wisconsin home the schoolteacher, still haunted by the vision of that peaceful, lovely vale, wrote a hymn. Then he put his work away in a drawer. For six years it collected dust, forgotten.

In the fall of 1863, Pitts was called to Bradford Academy to teach a singing class. Riding horseback, he again entered the peaceful Iowa town.

There, on Cedar Street, at the exact spot where Pitts had stopped six years earlier, a clapboard, square-belfried church was being built.

Amazed, Pitts remembered the hymn he'd written and then tossed aside, a hymn entitled "The Little Brown Church in the Vale." Blinking now, to be sure he wasn't dreaming, the elated young teacher noticed that the one-room church was painted the exact color he had envisioned.

The song that William Pitts wrote was to become one of the most loved of the traditional Protestant hymns; but what meant most to the schoolteacher and sustained him throughout the years was his realization that God can, indeed, work wonders.　　　　　　—BILL NELSON

An Unusual Year for Poinsettias

IN MAY OF 1971, our first shipment of poinsettia starter shoots was delivered to our greenhouse. As I helped unload the flats, I wondered if I had ordered more than my customers would need.

I finally managed to submerge that concern with faith in God's guidance. He had led Margaret and me into this work when we had nothing. After several years' struggle we finally had developed our own wholesale flower business. Margaret, our two children and I all loved working with plants. And the flowers used to celebrate the Christian holidays, especially the poinsettias, gave us the most joy.

Poinsettias are sensitive tropical plants that need love in nurturing. The problem lies in growing the right amount, for they are in demand only a few weeks each year. Grow too few and you have disappointed florists who can't satisfy their customers. Too many and you find that poinsettias, as beautiful as they are, do not make good eating. So we depend on intuition.

We began nurturing the fragile four-inch-high sprigs by repotting them in sterilized soil. Then, keeping them at seventy degrees and misting them regularly, we watched them grow into bushy mother plants. In about a month we took cuttings from each plant.

If we were fortunate, they'd take root and become mother plants themselves. As we repeated the process, the poinsettias began to move across the greenhouse racks like a vast green carpet.

Summer cooled into fall and now, as November clouds scurried above, we knew we must make our final decision. Did we have enough plants to satisfy our customers? An inner guidance told me we needed more. From a local grower I ordered a load of a thousand plants. They looked so nice I ordered a thousand more. A few days later he phoned and offered me a third load at an attractive price. On impulse I told him to send them on.

We moved plants to make room. Then I began to worry. One load would be enough. Two was stretching our luck. But three?

I fought those fears by keeping busy. Now we had to be very watchful. The poinsettias would soon bloom as the top leaves, called bracts, slowly turned red. It's vital that they reach full bloom at Christmas. So we control their development by lowering the temperature to hold them back, or raising it to develop them faster.

Then it happened. Out in the greenhouse one morning, a winter's sun warmed my neck as I bent in the rich heady fragrance.

"Chris!" It was Margaret; she had a strange expression on her face. "The phone."

I walked to the phone. On the line was a large Southern grower.

"Your shipment of poinsettias should reach you in a few hours," he said. "Will someone be there?"

I stared dumbly into the phone. Suddenly it all rushed back. Last spring I had decided to try this man's stock and placed a sizable order over the phone. I had completely forgotten it!

Sweat beaded on my forehead. "No! No!" I wanted to shout. "I already have too many!" A battle raged within me. I had a legal right to refuse them. I hadn't signed anything. But I had given my word.

The huge trailer truck strained into our little driveway. By more squeezing and reorganizing, we finally found room. I signed the slip, the truck thundered off, and Margaret and I stood looking at all the poinsettias.

What had I done? I remembered something from the Bible about a man must "keep a promise even if it ruins him" (Psalm 15:4, TLB). My forgetfulness now threatened to wash out all our work. Panic welled within me.

A leaf brushed my hand. I looked down at it. A blush of crimson was on the leaf. And I thought of the legend of this flower—how a poor Mexican boy on his way to the shrine of the Nativity had no gift to offer the Christ Child, nothing but a graceful weed he had found in the forest. But as he placed his gift before the altar with all his love, the top leaves miraculously turned flame red, making it a dazzling flower.

These were His flowers, each one a reminder of His presence.

"Margaret," I said, "we'd better raise the temperature for this batch if they're going to bloom in time."

Two weeks passed and then it was time for florists to phone in their orders. They came in the usual trickle at first. Joe, who always seemed to call early, asked for his usual hundred.

Then, as Christmas shopping picked up, more orders came in. Joe phoned for another load. Now repeat orders began to flow in from everywhere.

It turned out to be an unusual year for poinsettias.

By Christmas Eve our greenhouse was bare. Aching with fatigue, I walked into our living room and slumped into a chair by the Christmas tree to dream into its lights—and to thank God again for His Son who taught us to have faith and to remember that "a man's heart deviseth his way: but the Lord directeth his steps" (Proverbs 16:9).

—CHRISTIAN DORNBIERER

"Follow Me"

Will not our hearts within us burn
    On the darkening road,
If a White Presence we can discern—
    Despite an ancient load?

Whither goest thou, pilgrim Friend?
    Lone Figure far ahead,
Wilt thou not tarry until the end—
    And break our bread?

Follow we must amid sun or shade,
    Our faith to complete,
Journeying where no path is made—
    Save by His feet!

—JOSEPH FORT NEWTON

The Guitar Lesson

WHEN OUR SON DAVID WAS TWELVE we took him to a symphony concert featuring a classical guitarist. After that his one great goal in life was to play classical guitar.

He practiced constantly. He idolized the Spanish master Andrés Segovia and dreamed of meeting him. He wanted to own a fine Ramirez guitar—far too expensive for us. He aspired to become a professional musician. I was proud of him, but also worried. His dreams were so big. "Lord," I prayed, "don't let him down."

In 1974, when David was thirteen, I found out that Segovia was coming to Chicago's Orchestra Hall. From Lansing, Michigan, where we live, I sent away for tickets, requesting one seat near the stage for our young aficionado. We received four tickets in the back balcony and one front-row center!

The concert was the thrill of a lifetime. From our balcony seats I could look down through my opera glasses and see David in the front row. His eyes never left the stage. Afterward he rushed backstage to meet the eighty-year-old maestro. A short time later David joined us in the lobby, empty-handed.

"I was next in line, Mom," he said, "when his secretary said Segovia was tired and wouldn't be signing any more programs."

I was crushed. *How could You do this to him, God?* I wondered.

The next day, we toured the Sears Tower and browsed through the shops on Michigan Avenue. All the while I couldn't get over the disappointment of the night before.

Finally, we drove to an outlet where Ramirez guitars were sold just so David could see one. At the correct address we couldn't find a sign for the store—just a rickety staircase. I waited in the car while David and his father went up.

Minutes later, David came rushing down. "Give me the program from last night!" he said, breathless.

I gave him the program and followed him inside. There was the maestro, shaking David's hand! For several minutes the two talked about David's music, and then the owner of the store asked our son, "Could you walk Mr. Segovia down the stairs?"

As he watched the two of them leave, the owner said to me: "This is the first time Segovia has been to the store in years. Usually we send our instruments to him."

That was the day I learned to trust God with the big dreams of my guitarist son, who later played in a master class with Segovia, and eventually performed at Orchestra Hall—with a Ramirez guitar.

—*JEANNE BREAUGH*

In the Right Direction

I HAVE ALWAYS LOVED THE SNOW. I'm eighty-five and legally blind, but I can see light and some shapes—and I still get excited by fluffy flakes. That's why I ventured out of my house in Marion, Michigan, late one snowy afternoon last winter.

I shuffled down my long driveway to my favorite Douglas fir. I went from tree to tree, shaking snow from the boughs. Soon I noticed that I was surrounded by vague unfamiliar shapes. I'd gone too far into the woods! I turned and started walking back toward my driveway. But which way had I come? Everything was so white. And cold. The snow fell harder. Wiping tears from my eyes, I rushed forward in a panic. "God," I cried, "please help me."

Abruptly I stopped in my tracks.

I stood perfectly still as a feeling of relief broke through my fear. Then I turned completely around and struck out in a new direction. Finally I came to a fence. It was my boundary line! I followed that fence, just hung to it, until I reached my gate. "Thank You, God," I said.

The next morning, Dan, the young man who shovels snow for me, came rushing in, alarmed by the footsteps he had seen on the snow-covered property. "Don't worry," I quickly explained, "they're mine."

"Mrs. Leavy," Dan said, "I followed those footsteps. They lead up to the edge of the riverbank, right to where the drop-off is steepest. If you'd taken even one more step forward . . ."

But that was where I had stopped and called out—to the One who always leads in the right direction. —*THELMA LEAVY*

We Had to Stop

T HE RAIN HAD BEEN COMING DOWN since dawn in northern Mississippi, when my husband, Ewart, and I drove twenty-six miles to the church where he preached. It hadn't let up by the time we were ready to head back home that night.

As we arranged our wet umbrellas in the car and buckled up I heard myself humming an old spiritual, "Angels watchin' over me . . ." My husband squinted to see the road as the headlamps became coated with muck. But we were used to flooding in our area. The swishing windshield wipers and purring motor lulled me to sleep.

"Stop!" I screamed, waking suddenly.

Ewart's foot immediately hit the brakes. Then he looked at me, astonished. "Why?" he asked.

I was as bewildered as he. "I just know we *had* to stop," I said.

We were about halfway home, somewhere near the bridge into Hickory Flat. Taking the flashlight from the glove compartment, my husband sloshed out into the two inches of water covering the road. He moved to the front of the car to see if things looked okay and shrugged his shoulders at me. With one hand on the hood, he stepped back with his right foot to wipe off the muddy headlamps. Suddenly he lost his balance and lunged forward, grabbing for the hood with both hands. He held on, looking down over his shoulder.

Less than six inches separated us from a twenty-foot-deep channel of raging water. The bridge had washed away. —*LOLA M. AUTRY*

A Man with a View

M Y WIFE, FERNE, AND I STOOD IN FRONT of the small, thirty-room hotel that summer morning in 1954, so taken by its potential that we didn't see the drawbacks. The Alta Mira was already a hundred years old and looked it, with its peeling beige stucco façade, its three acres of weeds, its too-steep driveway and limited parking. "Just think, Ferne," I said, "what this place will be like with a little work."

I said the words while looking out over the waterside village of Sausalito and farther out over San Francisco Bay. It was the view that grabbed my attention. If caution did creep into my thinking, it was my age. At fifty-six I should have been thinking about retirement, not about refurbishing some run-down old hotel.

But I took Ferne's elbow and steered her up the hotel's rickety steps, exclaiming about the terrace I would build here someday. My terrace would be attached to a first-class hotel, like the places I had known in my childhood. Known *about*, that is. When I was a youngster, my family rarely visited such establishments. My father was a glazier in Berlin; men who installed windows for a living didn't stay in fancy hotels.

Ferne and I picked our way through the lobby. I could tell why its owners were anxious to sell. The lobby was dark; tiny windows defied you to enjoy the view. From somewhere in the building came gurgling and knocking sounds as water struggled to negotiate ancient pipes. Few people wanted to stay in this bathroom-down-the-hall place.

"But we'd make a go of it, Ferne. We'd knock down the walls, open up the view. Thousands of people would stream up here. Thousands."

Whatever I decided to do, Ferne said, she was with me. We drove back to the Fairmont Hotel in San Francisco, where I was catering manager and where friends had told me about the Alta Mira. "The hotel's a bargain, Bill. With your experience, you could make something out of it."

Experience I had, all right; I'd earned it through turning my back on an old European tradition. In the ordinary course of things at the turn of the century when I was born, a dutiful son in Germany was supposed to follow his father into the family business. But as I grew up I dreamed of going into hotel management, where I could work with people instead of with a putty knife. My father slapped his trousers leg and looked away when he heard this news. But eventually he let me go. I completed a fifteen-year apprenticeship, beginning with the Adlon Hotel in Berlin, and in time managed every phase of some of the finest hotels in Europe and America.

Now at last I was about to put these decades of experience to work with a hotel of my own. Ferne and I and two partners bought the Alta Mira for $100,000. Already I was sketching plans for my terrace, where people could eat outdoors under umbrellas during the day and by candlelight at night.

But those dreams seemed unattainable. One of my partners died shortly after we acquired the hotel. I bought out his interest, and there went the money for the plumbing system. The occasional guest who struggled up the hill didn't appreciate being awakened at 4:00 A.M. by clanging pipes. "I wouldn't stay in this boiler shop another night if it were *you* paying *me* for the room!" one man said as he made his escape.

And in trying to keep the kitchen open we put our purchases on the cuff. One morning I came into the dim lobby and was pleased to see six gentlemen waiting there. "Customers!" I whispered to Ferne as I stepped behind the front desk.

"Look again, Bill," Ferne said. "Those are our suppliers wanting their money." Day after day the same purveyors waited in the lobby, bills in hand. We paid what we could.

After a year of limping along like this my other partner wanted out. With the very last of our resources we bought the final interest. The place was ours now, but what good was that? More months passed with less and less money for cleaning up the grounds and upgrading the kitchen. We had exhausted our funds and the patience of our creditors.

"Ferne, my dear, there is no hope left," I said one night in the fall of 1958, after four years of struggle. "You might as well pack our things."

Ferne agreed. I went down to the front desk from our apartment in the hotel to close the accounts of our two guests. Now and then I stopped to doodle on the plans for the terrace that would never come to pass. At eleven o'clock I decided to take a walk, the last ever as a hotel owner.

In the dark I headed up the path toward the rear of the grounds. Then, as I was ambling along, someone began speaking to me. The quiet voice seemed to come from inside the bushes. I looked, but couldn't see a soul, so I started walking again.

There. Again! I made out the words now: "If you follow me, I can help."

Who would be out this late, and why wasn't he showing his face? "Who's there?" I whispered. Then, more loudly, "Show yourself! I'm not going to talk to anyone who's hiding." Nothing.

I took another step forward, searching. Then the voice, again: "If you follow Me, I can help you."

This time I began to suspect. "God?" I whispered.

What should I do? "Lord?" I said, using the name Ferne sometimes used. Ferne was the one who went to church, not I. "Lord?" my voice trembled. Nothing more.

I ran back to the hotel and stumbled upstairs and opened the door, calling, "Ferne!" The light in our bedroom went on immediately. Half-packed suitcases sat on their baggage racks. "Something's happened."

I told my wife that maybe, just maybe, I had heard God speak. Actual words. About following and helping. Ferne was nodding her head up and down, saying yes, yes, even when I went on to put it more strongly: "I've met the Lord, my dear!"

The light of morning didn't quell our excitement even in the face of the same empty breakfast tables. That noon we unpacked our bags.

Over the next few days I occasionally wandered to the back of the property, where I'd met Him. What did God mean when He said He'd help? And what was the right and honorable thing to do about our debts when we had no money? These weren't exactly musings—it was more like I was talking to God, asking questions. And amazingly, it also seemed I was getting answers.

The first thing I thought the Lord told me to do was to call each of the purveyors who had been sitting in our lobby. I was to tell them I still had no money but appreciated their patience and that if I prospered they would be our suppliers for as long as I owned the hotel. Sounded like stall talk to me, but I followed Him.

Next morning there was not one bill collector waiting in the lobby.

On the third day a gentleman came to the front desk. He was not one of the purveyors, but I figured he must have been from some other creditor because he said he wanted to talk about money. I barely looked up. What more could I say to these bill collectors? "You are wasting your time, sir. I have no money."

"Banks are in the business of lending money," the man said.

"That doesn't do me any good. I have no credit."

"I think we can work something out through an insurance policy."

Slowly I began to pay attention. This man was selling life insurance. He told me he had convinced the local bank that under special circumstances the Alta Mira deserved a loan, even now. All the ingredients for success were there except capital and time. Capital, for improvements. And time, for my top experience to pay off. That's where insurance came in. The bank would lend me money for improvements; the hotel would take out a policy on my life, with the bank as beneficiary; if I died early, before the bank could be repaid from profits at the hotel, the loan would be repaid from death benefits.

One week later the bank president called me and said, "Mr. Wachter, we have the privilege of offering you a loan for one hundred thousand dollars."

Ferne and I were singing with joy. We began putting our new capital to work, asking for God's guidance at each step. First we were to pay off the banker and fishmonger and butcher and greengrocer. Then bit by bit we were to landscape, and get rid of those thumping pipes.

Most exciting of all was the day we hired the contractor to start work on the terrace. I'd been right. That terrace wasn't even finished before people started flocking in. News passed by word of mouth that the Alta Mira had a wonderful outdoor area with umbrellas and flowers and a terrific view. Before we knew it we were swamped. We had to call the contractor again with plans for expanding the terrace. With the money that now started to flow through our books we refurbished the hotel itself, three rooms at a time, each with its own bath. All of the suppliers who had kept faith with us flourished too.

Nearly thirty-four years have passed since I heard the voice on our hotel grounds. Our hotel is so successful that we get dozens of offers every year to buy us out.

But at ninety-three, where would I go and what would I do? Our church and our staff and customers are our very lives. Ferne and I thank God for this by making every effort to follow Him. Each morning over coffee we read the Bible and pray for individuals among the fifty-member hotel staff. And we pray for our guests, those who come back every year and those who are about to become our friends. Above all we thank God for the privilege of following Him in these times when every day brings some new risk.

It's interesting how, when I was twenty, my father became upset when I did not follow him down the safe and known way. Years later my heavenly Father also told me to follow Him. But He added the words which have let me see risk as adventure: "Follow Me," He said, "and I will help you." —WILLIAM WACHTER

God Makes a Path

God makes a path, provides a guide,
    And feeds a wilderness;
His glorious name, while breath remains,
    O that I may confess.

Lost many a time, I have had no guide,
    No house but a hollow tree!
In stormy winter night no fire,
    No food, no company;

In Him I found a house, a bed,
    A table, company;
No cup so bitter but's made sweet,
    Where God shall sweetening be.
                —ROGER WILLIAMS

But my God shall supply all your need according to his riches in glory by Christ Jesus. —Philippians 4:19

CHAPTER TWO

God Supplies Our Needs

In Psalm 34:10, David says that "those who seek the Lord lack no good thing" (RSV). David's faith was strong enough that he could write this when he was in the custody of an enemy king. The stories in this section show how God supplied physical needs—fuel, food, even shoelaces—sometimes by unexplained mysterious means and sometimes by prompting generous human acts of kindness and mercy.

Brown Shoelaces

Hurrying through the supermarket, I accidentally knocked over a display of shoelaces. Impulsively, in my embarrassment, I flung a packet of men's shoelaces into the shopping cart and, after paying for them, tossed the shoelaces into my purse.

Then I was off to the rehabilitation hospital where I'd been visiting daily with Donald, a man whose arms and legs were paralyzed after he'd fallen from a ladder.

That day I found Donald unusually despondent. "Brenda," he said to me after we'd finished our physical therapy session, "I've tried to be cheerful about all this, but sometimes I feel as though God simply doesn't care any more about what happens to me."

"You *know* He cares," I began. But I had no real answer for him. We sat in silence.

"Oh, by the way," Donald said to me later as I started to leave, "no big deal, but the nurse broke one of my shoestrings this morning. Could you get me a new pair?"

Shoestrings! I opened my purse and took out the brown pair from the supermarket. We stared at them in amazement. I bent down and laced the strings into Donald's shoes.

Shoestrings. For a pair of shoes on feet that could not move to wear them out. For a set of hands that couldn't even tie the bow.

"Donald, if God cares enough to supply you with shoestrings before you even ask," I said, "I'm certain He cares enough about you in more important ways."

A smile broke onto his face. "Yes, you're right," Donald said. "I'm sure, too."

Shoestrings. Whenever I'm discouraged, I think of them. Then I know that God cares for me, too, meticulously, intimately. Right down to the laces in my shoes.

—*Brenda Minner*

Our Refuge

Whenever you come to the Lord
    with an earnest prayer,
He is there.
When you come with a contrite heart
    or a human fear,
He will hear.

Though you may have little to give,
bring Him your best;
He supplies the rest.
—NINA WILLIS WALTER

Those Fish!

IF YOU COME TO OUR HOUSE THESE DAYS, you'll find a fish mobile dangling over our kitchen table. Those fish swinging in the air always remind me of the *real* fish that insisted on entering our lives. And I never fail to remember the dreary night that I reluctantly took that first batch of fish from the freezer . . .

"This is the last straw," I muttered angrily as I slapped at the hot grease that had just spattered my arm. The pungent odor of fish frying permeated my kitchen, and I had been battling waves of nausea already.

Those fish had been in the freezer for a month, the meager results of the last fishing trip the boys had with their father. The four intervening weeks since then had been the worst of my life. Now, looking at those fish I was about to serve, I thought grimly, *I'm not that hungry.*

Well, I *was* that hungry, for with the exception of a pound of ground meat, designated for Sunday's dinner, we had nothing else to eat. Monday was payday, so we had survived the month, but no one in his right mind would term this victorious living. What about God's promises to meet our needs? Philippians 4:19, for instance? "But my God shall supply all your need according to his riches in glory by Christ Jesus." *Probably another fairy story, like living happily ever after,* I thought bitterly. I was fool enough to believe that one too.

Fred and I had such high ideals and dreams when we married, but his habit of taking a "social drink" had gradually developed into a real drinking problem, and we'd finally lost everything we owned. I'd taught school before our three sons were born, and when our youngest entered kindergarten, I returned to teaching to provide a stable income. But Fred's drinking became even more intense, culminating in full-scale alcoholism that tore our family apart. Reluctantly I filed for divorce. And one month ago my marriage of thirteen years was declared null and void.

Now my sons and I were left with the choice between these unappetizing fish—or nothing at all. Worse, it seemed indicative of a future that didn't promise anything better. So the boys came in, and eat those fish we did.

After dinner I was left alone with my worries, staring at the months ahead. Almost unconsciously my thoughts turned into a grumbled prayer: *Lord, if You don't help us, there's no way we're going to make it.*

Suddenly I was aware of an unearthly stillness that filled the kitchen. The presence of Jesus was very real, and I seemed to hear clearly the command: *Make a list of all the things you're so worried about.*

"That's easy," I replied. I grabbed a pencil and paper and wrote: House payment, new glasses for Grady, gym shoes for Woody, jeans for David, groceries...

Then the same Presence brought to mind the verse from Matthew: "Take no thought for your life, what ye shall eat, or what ye shall drink; nor yet for your body, what ye shall put on ... But seek ye first the kingdom of God, and his righteousness; and all these things shall be added unto you" (6:25, 33).

I looked at the list. Every item fell neatly into one of these categories.

"Lord, that's easy to believe when things are going all right," I protested. "But I'm alone now, scratching to make ends meet. Like tonight. We had nothing left to eat."

And then I thought, *We did have those fish.*

A few months later soft autumn sunlight warmed our church pew where I sat, insides churning, palms sweaty. The choir was singing heartily, but I couldn't concentrate on the music or the words. I could only concentrate on that offering plate, coming closer and closer. We were broke. Although Fred was legally responsible for child support, he never contributed any money at all, which left my sons and me a monthly income of five hundred dollars. After the bills, we were left with exactly one hundred. And if I gave my tithe of fifty dollars... that would leave me the choice of getting shoes that two of the boys desperately needed—or buying food. I held the check in my hand as the plate got closer and closer. How could God want me to have to make this choice?

Take no thought for your life, came the whisper again.

"But my boys," I protested.

Take no thought...

The usher handed me the plate. I dropped in the check.

I didn't feel relieved or virtuous. In fact, when we got home, I was a portrait of self-pity. I stopped again in the kitchen, staring at a can of tomatoes, wondering how to turn it into a meal, when there was a knock on the door. There stood my friend Betty Jean, and in her hands was a pan of fish. "Carolyn and I cooked fish together and had these left over. I can't refreeze them. Can you and the boys use them?"

Those fish. We had a wonderful meal. More than we could eat.

That year, for the first time in my life, I dreaded Christmas. Every carol, every holiday symbol brought bittersweet memories of happier times. Of course, our budget was stretched to the limit, but we'd get by. Then, without warning, I had a blowout on the old station wagon. I got the car home and put on the spare.

Dejected already, I couldn't bear to stay in the house just then, surrounded by ghosts of Christmases past. I absentmindedly got in the car and drove to the supermarket. I got a cart and walked the aisles without purpose. I thought it would help to be surrounded by piped-in carols and bustle and people, but it just made me feel more alone. So alone.

I felt a touch on my shoulder and heard a friendly voice behind me.

"Why, Peggy, it's so good to see you! How in the world are you and those boys? By the way, do they like fish? Ed just came home with another catch, and I have no more room in my freezer. I was just wondering what to do with them."

Those fish. I had to smile. I knew the spare would be okay until I could afford a new tire. I also realized that, regardless of what I felt, I was *not* alone.

For over two years we got along all right; just barely, but we got along. My frustration and self-pity abated a little at a time. And then— *whop!* I got the worst case of mumps on record. Never had I been so sick! I would see the boys off to school, then collapse on the sofa for the rest of the day. My fellow teachers took turns bringing in our supper, but my convalescence seemed to go on forever. Discouragement enveloped me again. And then my co-worker Mary put a pot of chili on the stove and came out to the den where I was resting miserably.

"Peggy," she said, "I know this sounds awful right now, but if you'll tell me where your freezer is, I'd like to leave a catch of fish that you can cook up when you're feeling better."

Those fish!

I'm sure she thought I was delirious as I began to laugh joyfully. Now I couldn't help but remember the many times Jesus used fish to minister to the needs of people as He walked this earth. He fed the multitude of five thousand with five loaves and two fish, and again the four thousand with seven loaves and a few fish. After His resurrection, to reassure His faithful followers, He asked for some fish, and ate with them. Later, at the Sea of Galilee, He cooked fish for His disciples and called Peter back into service. And He'd never forgotten *us* in our time of need.

I looked at Mary, where she still stood, amazed. "Thanks a lot for the fish," I told her. "As a matter of fact, I'm feeling better already." And do you know, I really *was* feeling better.

Fish in the freezer. This was exactly where I'd started, grumbling, those years before, so alone and bitter. Again the freezer was stocked. We'd come full circle. But how much I'd changed.

I wasn't the only one. Soon after, three years following our divorce, I received a letter from Fred. God had taken care of him, too. He told how he had spent the past fifteen months at The Anchorage, a Christian rehabilitation center for alcoholics. While there, he'd come to rely on God, and his life had been changed. He asked our forgiveness and sent us some money. From that day on, he began to help with our financial needs.

Eventually Fred and I were remarried in the little chapel at The Anchorage. I had prayed that the Lord would be faithful and save our marriage. Instead, he was faithful to save *us,* and made a new marriage with new people. The hopeless end for us was God's beginning.

Indeed, if you come to see us these days, you'll find that fish mobile over our kitchen table, a reminder that if we seek God first, everything else really will be provided. And when visitors like you notice it, as they usually do, I have a wonderful chance to tell them how God once again used fish to minister to the needs of His people.

—*Peggy Wood Stewart*

A Load of Coal

O**N CHRISTMAS EVE 1948, THE SNOW** was coming down hard, blowing and swirling around my old two-ton dump truck as I drove across the West Virginia mountains. It had been snowing for hours and had accumulated eight to ten inches deep. My job at that time was delivering coal to the miners who lived in the coal camp. I had finished early and was looking forward to getting home.

As I neared the road that led to my home, I was flagged down by my stepfather. He told me about a mother with three children who lived about six miles up in the mountains. Her husband had died several months previously, leaving her and the children destitute. In the tradition of taking care of our own, the miners had assembled several boxes of food, clothing and gifts that they wanted me to deliver, along with a load of coal, to the family.

Now believe me, I didn't want to go. Let's face it, I had worked hard all day, it was Christmas Eve, and I wanted to get home to my family. But that was just it—it was Christmas Eve, the time of giving and goodwill. With this thought in mind, I turned the truck around and drove back to the coal tipple, where I filled the truck. When I returned, I loaded boxes in the front seat and in every nook and cranny I could find in the back. Then I set off.

Back in the hills of West Virginia, folks had built homes in some pretty out-of-the-way places. This woman's place was really out of the way. I had to travel on a road that had not been cleared by the highway department, nor had any path been made by traffic. I drove up the valley as I had been directed, and turned off the road into a hollow called Lick Fork. The "road" was actually a snow-filled creek bed. When I saw that, I began to have doubts that I could make it. Nevertheless, I shifted into first gear and crept ahead.

When I came to the place a mile farther on where I was supposed to turn into the mountain to get to the woman's house, my heart dropped. There before me was a winding path that had been hand-cut up the side of the mountain. I still could not see her house. I pulled the truck up to the path and got out. After looking the situation over, I decided there was no way I could get that two-ton dump truck up through that path.

What am I to do? I wondered. *Maybe I can just dump the coal and ask the family to come down for the food and clothes.* So I got out and walked up the path. It was near dusk, the temperature had dropped, and the blowing snow was beginning to drift.

The path was about six feet wide, overhung with snow-covered branches and littered with stumps and limbs. Finally I reached the clearing where the house stood, a little shack with thin walls and cracks you could see through. I called the woman out of the house, explained why I was there, and asked if she had any way to carry the food and coal. She showed me a homemade wagon with wheelbarrow wheels.

Here I was in ten inches of snow, with a truck I had to empty before dark, an impassable path and a wagon with wheelbarrow wheels. The only solution, as I could see it, was to turn the truck around, back it in as far as I could, dump the coal and set the boxes off.

As I returned to the truck, I kept asking, "Lord, what am I doing here?"

I started up the engine, turned my old truck around and went into reverse. Foot by foot that old truck backed up along that mountain path. I kept telling myself, "I'll just keep going until I can't go any farther."

However, the truck seemed to have a mind of its own. All at once, I was sitting there in the dark with my taillights reflecting through the snow on that little shack. I was dumbfounded. That old truck had not slipped one inch or got stuck one time. And standing on the porch were four of the happiest people I had ever seen.

I unloaded the boxes and then dumped the coal, shoveling as much as I could under the sagging porch. As I worked, the thin, ill-clothed children dragged and pushed the boxes into the shack. When I had finished, the woman grasped my hand and thanked me over and over.

After the good-byes, I got into the truck and started back. Darkness had overtaken me. However, upon reaching the "road," I stopped the truck and looked back at the path. "There is no way," I said to myself, "that I could have maneuvered this truck up that mountain, through all that snow, in the dark, without help from somewhere."

I had been raised to worship God. I believed in the birth of Christ. And that Christmas Eve, in the hills of West Virginia, I knew I had been an instrument of what Christmas is all about.

—*H. N. Cook, as told to his daughter Patsy C. Godsey*

Sudden Increase

I HAD ONLY TWO ONE-DOLLAR BILLS in my wallet and they had to last until payday, ten days away. My husband was away on business, and I was at home with our two children conserving every cent.

On Monday my father called to say he needed to attend a union meeting on Friday afternoon. Would I come and stay with Mother? She was bedridden with brain cancer and had to have someone help her with her medicine. I didn't hesitate to say yes. Back then, in 1970, one dollar would buy enough gas to get there and back, and I would still have an "emergency" dollar left.

All week long my five-year-old kept asking for a treat from the ice cream truck. And each time, I would open my wallet, show her the two one-dollar bills, and explain why we couldn't afford such a luxury.

When we arrived on Friday, Daddy's parting words were, "Don't forget to give Mom her Dilantin," her anticonvulsant medicine. But after he'd gone I discovered the bottle was empty. I was terrified that if Mother didn't get her medicine on time, she'd go into convulsions.

Mother told me to check her purse and a couple of other places for loose change, but that was all I found—loose change. I telephoned my sisters, but no one was home. The prescription cost over eight dollars. Where would I get that money?

"God will take care of it," Mother said.

At my wit's end, I decided to go to the pharmacist's with my lone dollar and beg him to trust me for the rest. But when I looked in my wallet again, I was stunned.

That single was a ten-dollar bill.   —ESTHER MCINTOSH

The Little Red Hen

A T ONE POINT DURING THE WINTER of 1940, my husband, a house painter, was temporarily unemployed because of the weather, and the textile plant where I worked was closed due to a seasonal lay-off. We literally had no money. To make matters worse, our eighteen-month-old daughter, Rachel, was recovering poorly from pneumonia, and the doctor insisted we feed her a boiled egg each day. Even that was beyond our means.

"Why not pray for an egg?" suggested our baby-sitter, who was staying on without pay to help us. We were a churchgoing family, but this teenager's depth of faith was something new to us at the time. All the same, she and I got on our knees and told the Lord that Rachel needed an egg each morning. We left the problem in His hands.

About ten o'clock that morning we heard some cackling coming from the hedge fence in front of our house. There among the bare branches sat a fat red hen. We had no idea where she had come from. We just watched in amazement as she laid an egg and then proceeded down the road, out of sight.

The little red hen that first day was a surprise, and we thanked God for it, but can you imagine how startled we were when we heard the hen cackling in the hedge the next morning? And the morning after that, and the morning after that? Every day for over a week, Rachel had a fresh boiled egg.

Rachel grew better and better, and at last the weather turned and my husband went back to work. The next morning I waited by the window and watched. But our prayers had been answered—precisely.

The little red hen did not come back. Ever.   —JOSEPHINE M. KUNTZ

A Strange Place to Hope

R ANK UPON RANK WE STOOD that hot September morning in 1944, more than a thousand women lining the railroad siding, one unspoken thought among us: *Not Germany.*

Beside me my sister Betsie swayed. I was fifty-two, Betsie fifty-nine. These eight months in a concentration camp since we had been caught concealing Jews in our home had been harder on her. But prisoners though we were, at least till now we had remained in Holland. And now when liberation must come any day, where were they taking us?

Behind us guards were shouting, prodding us with their guns. Instinctively my hand went to the string around my neck. From it, hanging down my back between my shoulder blades, was the small cloth bag that held our Bible, that forbidden book which had not only sustained Betsie and me throughout these months, but given us strength to share with our fellow prisoners. So far we had kept it hidden. But if we should go to Germany . . . We had heard tales of the prison inspections there.

A long line of empty boxcars was rolling slowly past. Now it clanged to a halt and a gaping freight door loomed in front of us. I helped Betsie over the steep side. The dark boxcar grew quickly crowded. We were pressed against the wall. It was a small European freight car, thirty or forty people jammed it. And still the guards drove women in, pushing, jabbing with their guns. It was only when eighty women were packed inside that the heavy door slid shut and we heard the iron bolts driven into place outside.

Women were sobbing and many fainted, although in the tight-wedged crowd they remained upright. The sun beat down on the motionless train, the temperature in the packed car rose. It was hours before the train gave a sudden lurch and began to move. Almost at once it stopped again, then again crawled forward. The rest of that day and all night long it was the same, stopping, starting, slamming, jerking. Once through a slit in the side of the car I saw trainmen carrying a length of twisted rail. Maybe the tracks ahead were destroyed. Maybe we would still be in Holland when liberation came.

But at dawn we rolled through the Dutch border town of Emmerich. We were in Germany.

For two more incredible days and two more nights we were carried deeper and deeper into the land of our fears. Worse than the crush of bodies and the filth was the thirst. Two or three times when the train was stopped the door was slid open a few inches and a pail of water passed in. But we had become animals, incapable of plan. Those near the door got it all.

At last, on the morning of the fourth day, the door was hauled open its full width. Only a few very young soldiers were there to order us out and march us off. No more were needed. We could scarcely walk, let alone resist. From the crest of a small hill we saw it, the end of our journey, a vast gray barracks city surrounded by double concrete walls.

"Ravensbrück!"

Like a whispered curse, the word passed back through the line. This was the notorious women's death camp itself, the very symbol to Dutch hearts of all that was evil. As we stumbled down the hill, I felt the Bible bumping on my back. As long as we had that, I thought, we could face even hell itself. But how could we conceal it through the inspection I knew lay ahead?

It was the middle of the night when Betsie and I reached the processing barracks. And there under the harsh ceiling lights we saw a dismaying sight. As each woman reached the head of the line she had to strip off every scrap of clothes, throw them all onto a pile guarded by soldiers, and walk naked past the scrutiny of a dozen guards into the shower room. Coming out of the shower room, she wore only the thin regulation prison dress and a pair of shoes.

Our Bible! How could we take it past so many watchful eyes?

"Oh, Betsie!" I began—and then stopped at the sight of her pain-whitened face. As a guard strode by I begged him in German to show us the toilets. He jerked his head in the direction of the shower room. "Use the drain holes!" he snapped.

Timidly Betsie and I stepped out of line and walked forward to the huge room with its row on row of overhead spigots. It was empty, waiting for the next batch of fifty naked and shivering women.

A few minutes later we would return here stripped of everything we possessed. And then we saw them, stacked in a corner, a pile of old wooden benches crawling with cockroaches, but to us the furniture of heaven itself.

In an instant I had slipped the little bag over my head and stuffed it behind the benches.

And so it was that when we were herded into that room ten minutes later, we were not poor, but rich. Rich in the care of Him who was God even of Ravensbrück.

Of course when I put on the flimsy prison dress, the Bible bulged beneath it. But that was His business, not mine. At the exit, guards were feeling every prisoner, front, back and sides. The woman ahead of me was searched. Behind me, Betsie was searched. They did not touch or even look at me.

Outside the building was a second ordeal, another line of guards examining each prisoner again. I slowed down as I reached them, but the captain shoved me roughly by the shoulder. "Move along! You're holding up the line!"

So Betsie and I came to our barracks at Ravensbrück. Before long we were holding clandestine Bible study groups for an ever-growing group of believers, and Barracks 28 became known throughout the camp as "the crazy place, where they hope."

Yes, hoped, in spite of all that human madness could do. We had learned that a stronger power had the final word, even here.

—*Corrie ten Boom*

The Sudden Freeze

WHEN MY HUSBAND, QUINCY, and I bought a farm and moved to Gallatin Gateway in April 1964, I couldn't wait to get unpacked. I had to plant my vegetable garden by May.

I needed some extra confidence this time, since I had never planted a garden so close to the mountains before and I wasn't "onto" the sudden nighttime temperature changes that wreak havoc on plants.

I enjoyed planting a big garden, but I also felt it was a necessity. With thirteen growing children to feed, I had to make my contribution to our family's health and finances. My garden would provide us with enough vegetables for canning to see us through the next winter.

Quincy and the boys worked hard on our five hundred acres, tending the beef and milk cows, chickens and pigs. The girls and I cultivated the garden, planted seeds, weeded, and watered. There was hardly a vegetable in a seed catalog for our altitude that I didn't have in my garden.

Our new home abutted the foot hills of snowcapped peaks seventy miles from Yellowstone National Park. I looked forward to a family outing there to see the roaring waterfalls, the hot spouting geysers, the cold sparkling rivers and the antelope, elk and other wildlife.

We were now also only ten miles from my mom and dad. Their deep faith had rubbed off on me, and when I poked a tiny carrot seed in the soft earth, I felt the Lord was kneeling right beside me, getting His knees and hands dirty too. I thought I had a no-fail crop-insurance policy.

True, I put in long hours, and when canning season arrived, I'd often be working till midnight canning tomatoes, beans, or whatever was ripe at the time. But I really enjoyed it, and I knew that when winter came, I'd be able to go down to the cellar to get three or four quarts of vegetables for supper. I'd linger and feast my eyes on the thousand-plus quarts of ruby red beets, green beans, golden corn, peas, carrots, and strawberries, to name a few, that I had provided for my family.

By August I knew my garden would be a winner again; one hundred fifty quarts of green beans were already canned and on the shelves. We always did the beans "assembly line"—I'd pick the tender vines, and the girls would cut and snap, joking and talking nonstop under the old willow tree in the yard. The deep satisfaction I felt packing the jars and processing made the hot, steamy job worth every bead of sweat.

Making pickles was next, and *that* job was a real labor of love. Our kids insisted I pack a pickle in their school lunches, and if I forgot, I'd hear about it. Deep down, I was flattered. That summer, though, the dill came up poorly, yellowish and unfit for pickling. I blamed it on the black gumbo soil. But Mom and Dad had plenty of "volunteer" dill that had resown itself, so by late August I placed an SOS phone call.

"Mom, I have a terrific crop of cucumbers! Can you spare some dill for pickles?"

They drove up before I had a chance to pick the cucumbers. The kids had already scattered to the pasture, well into their usual after-supper baseball game. Mom carried in a big brown paper bag full to bulging with the most beautiful green dill I had ever seen. She set it down in the entryway, and we visited and watched the kids in the field. At dusk the folks drove off.

"I'll pick the cukes first thing in the morning," I yawned at Quincy. "It's too dark out in the garden now."

But I never did get to pick them. The next morning as I neared the garden, I stopped in my tracks when I saw the devastation before me. A hard freeze had stolen in during the night. Yesterday's firm, perky cucumber leaves were like limp, wet rags, hiding soft, mushy cucumbers below. The patch was a total loss.

I hurried to the staked-up tomatoes. Yesterday they were green and some were turning, ready to be brought inside to ripen. Today they too were mushy, black and glassy.

I was heartsick. This was a tremendous loss to our food supply. And all that time and effort wasted! I felt I had let the family and myself down. If only I'd stayed up and listened to the weather report on the late news. Truth is, even if I had remembered, I had been too tired.

I berated myself all day for not having gone out and picked the cucumbers by flashlight. And that night, I tossed and turned, feeling quite alone, though Quincy was sleeping peacefully beside me. Despite my carefully nurtured faith in the Lord, I wasn't accepting this disappointment gracefully. The Lord knew how hard I had worked to do the right thing by my family.

Like a broken record, I was tormenting myself with if-onlys when I heard a gentle voice saying, "Agnes, who feeds you and your family?" Was I hearing things? Everyone else was asleep. Then I decided it could be only one Person speaking to me.

I paused before whispering weakly, "Well, God, You do." Then I added as if to affirm my faith, "I know it all comes from You."

It was a while before the voice continued, "Does it really matter if it comes out of *your* garden or not?"

That question took me by surprise and I giggled. "God, I guess it doesn't really matter whether or not it comes from my garden. I know it all comes from You." With that I was given total peace, and I fell asleep.

The next day I was still puzzled by the Lord's question. For days I hoped someone in the valley would have a bumper crop of cucumbers and I'd be able to fill the pickle jars. But no cucumbers, much less tomatoes, came my way.

Eventually I got tired of looking at the bag of dill mocking me in the entryway. One day I jammed another bag over the top and placed the dill out of sight on a roughed-in ledge by the stairs leading to the cellar.

The following winter brought a bitter cold snap that hung over the valley. By the end of February, the temperature hovered at twenty below, snow lay frozen on the ground, and driving was treacherous on the mountain curves. The days were short, so it was dark when we sat down for our evening meals.

Late one afternoon I went down cellar to get vegetables for supper and noted with dismay how bare the shelves looked. The corn, beans, and peas were going fast. And where there should have been tomatoes and pickles was row after row of empty, dusty jars. Going back upstairs, I shook my head as I passed the bag of dill. Then I busied myself at the stove.

Suppertime was my family's favorite time of the day. All fifteen of us sat around a huge oblong table that had been Quincy's mother's. I always spread the table with the prettiest oilcloth I could find. Quincy had made two long padded benches, covered in a cheerful orange, the color of glowing embers. Our oversize kitchen was warm and cozy from the old Monarch wood-and-coal stove that I cooked on.

We were having a delightful meal, the kids recounting what happened at school, when someone pounded hard on the door. I pushed my chair back, mumbling, "Who in the world would be out in this bitter cold—and in the dark too?"

Standing in the entryway was one of our neighbors, a man in his late thirties with a full dark beard that was glazed and white with frost. He looked like Santa Claus.

"Mrs. Huyser," he said as he stepped into the warm kitchen, "how many fresh cucumbers and tomatoes can you use?"

The clatter of knives and forks ceased. All eyes fastened on our bearded visitor. With my mouth agape, I thought, *Did I hear right? Fresh cucumbers and tomatoes in February?* I was speechless.

"I have a two-ton truck outside more than half full with cucumbers, tomatoes, green beans—even eggplant." Quincy and I zipped up our winter jackets, tugged on mittens, and trudged out to look.

Our neighbor's teeth were on the verge of chattering, but his soft voice was steady and clear. "The produce was on its way from Mexico, but the road coming down the canyon was so icy that the truck slid into the Gallatin River."

"How come it didn't freeze?" I blurted.

"All the boxes that landed on the bank did freeze, but the ones that went in the river were okay. The insurance company hired me to get the truck out and let me keep whatever I wanted. So I salvaged this stuff." He thumped the side of the truck. "I figured you could use some of this with your big family. The only thing is," he added somewhat apologetically, "my wife will want the green beans since she didn't get to can any last summer."

I managed to say, "That's one thing I *did* can."

We packed in nine big boxes of beautiful Beefsteak-size tomatoes and box after box of firm, green, perfect-for-pickling cucumbers, and the next day I prepared for canning.

I was surprised that some of the dill was still green, and the rest revived in a warm water bath. By early March I had canned ninety-two quarts of ice pickles, bread-and-butter pickles, and, of course, crisp dills. It was the only time I had ever been able to "play" at pickling, not pressured to can everything at once, as I was at harvesttime.

I was putting up the pickles when I remembered what the Lord had said to me seven months before: "Does it really matter if it comes out of *your* garden or not?" And when I answered, "I know it all comes from You," I didn't dream it would come from an ice-cold, fast-flowing mountain river.

But then I don't even *try* to fathom His ways. I simply don't have the imagination.   *—AGNES HUYSER*

Snowflakes in September

IN SEPTEMBER LAST YEAR Sister Grace began forming a picture of a Christmas tree in her mind. As the director of pastoral care at Charleston's St. Francis Xavier Hospital, Sister Grace had been asked to decorate the tree that would be placed in the lobby of the Omni Hotel. The tree would have angels on it and snowflakes—lots of snowflakes, exquisite ones crocheted by hand. By Thanksgiving Sister Grace had acquired the angels, but the snowflakes were not to be found. On the day before Thanksgiving, Doris Hartvig was admitted to the hospital for tests. Doris detested idleness, and she was soon busy at work with needles and yarn.

"Could you do a snowflake?" one of the nuns, Sister Mary Joseph, asked her.

"I can," Doris replied. In fact, not long ago she had bought a book that described how to crochet snowflakes. They weren't easy to do, and each one required a lot of time.

With renewed hope, Sister Grace went to see Doris. She described in detail the Christmas tree she had her heart set on: a blue bow on top, angels clinging to the branches, and lacy snowflakes hanging from the boughs.

"How many snowflakes do you need?" Doris finally asked. "We should have sixty," Sister Grace replied, "but there's no time to make that many."

Doris smiled. She reached under her bed and took out a bag of needlework, and then drew out one beautiful crocheted snowflake after another—forty, fifty, over sixty of them! They were ironed, starched, and ready to be hung.

In September Doris Hartvig had felt a great urge to crochet snowflakes. Now she knew why.   *—ROBERT HAWKINS*

There Was Plenty!

I'VE ALWAYS HAD A STRONG FAITH in God, but I had never looked for miracles in my life. Until a few years ago . . .

When our family of four lived in Muskogee, Oklahoma, our income was so small we could barely pay for necessities. Sometimes it was cornflakes and milk for a week. On one such occasion, friends traveling through town stopped in, and to my amazement, my husband invited them for dinner.

I fidgeted, then went into my bedroom, knelt down, and asked God how I was to cook a dinner with no food in the house.

"But you have," came the answer that formed in my head. "You have meat in the freezer." (I didn't believe it.) "You have vegetables." (Maybe a can of beans.) "Make a stew. And you have flour. Make biscuits." (That I could do. I'm a good biscuit builder.)

I went to the kitchen to prove my inner voice wrong, but there in the freezer lay a small amount of hamburger, in the crisper lay half an onion and a carrot, and in the bin under the sink were two small potatoes.

I made the stew. Hadn't I asked God for help? What could I do but follow the directions that seemed to come to me? I put the flimsy fare in a pot, mixed up the biscuits, then set the table.

When I took up the stew there was barely enough to fill a medium-size serving bowl; I thought my husband and I would eat only biscuits and milk. But when I passed the stew around, behold, there was plenty. I served us and passed the bowl around again!

When our dinner was over, the guests thanked me for the delicious meal. And I gathered up leftovers.

We had *leftovers*. We did, we really did! —ADELE HOOKER

"Prove Me Now"

BRING YE ALL THE TITHES into the storehouse, that there may be meat in mine house, and prove me now herewith, saith the Lord of hosts."

Prove God? Put Him to the test? At first the idea seemed utterly presumptuous that a young Oklahoma housewife and mother like me should dare to dare God to prove Himself. Yet that is what Malachi 3:10 was suggesting, and that very verse became the springboard to one of the most profound spiritual experiences of my life.

The year was 1934, one of the terrible Depression years. My husband, Corwin, was fortunate: he had a job. Corwin was an automotive electrician, a mechanic, and he received nine dollars for a week's work; a week being seventy-two hours in six days. We had two children, Betty Ellen and David, and though we felt ourselves fortunate to have food on the table, there was no money, none whatsoever, left over for extras.

Our living conditions were meager, even by 1934 standards. In our little three-room house we used kerosene for cooking and lights, coal for heat, and borrowed a neighbor's telephone in emergencies. Our one luxury was running water and bathroom facilities.

Our lives revolved completely around our church, University Baptist at Sixth and Columbia in Tulsa, not because we had acquired a deeper love for the Lord—that love was always there—but because there was no money for amusements or other social outlets. It bothered me, however, that I could not do more for the church.

From the time that I had accepted Christ as my personal Savior until the Depression hit us hard, I had believed in—and practiced—tithing. This had not been difficult when there was money for the necessities of life with a little left over. But now, when pennies were counted as dollars, we had to stop. I felt that God would understand.

Then something happened. One evening as I was studying my Sunday school lesson I found my entire mind and spirit suddenly come alive as I read that passage in Malachi about tithing that said "and prove me now herewith, saith the Lord of hosts."

God knows that I love Him, I thought. *He knows I am doing all I can to serve Him. He knows that nine dollars a week, thirty-six dollars a month for a family of four is not a living, just a bare existence.* Prove God by reducing that amount by three dollars and sixty cents a month? Would God require that from the small, inadequate amount that I had for my family?

I just couldn't understand why I was so torn apart by that verse of Scripture. I spent a long night searching my soul and praying. How unrealistic it seemed for God to ask me to surrender a part of the very little I had when He could provide so very much for us—indeed He had told us of the abundance He intended for us: "Give and it shall be given unto you; good measure, pressed down, shaken together and running over" (Luke 6:38).

The first thing He did say was "give." Even the widow with her mite had done that—she had given everything—yet I was asked to give but a tenth. In my mind I saw Him taking a small amount and multiplying it, the way He took a few loaves and fed thousands of people. I wondered what He might do with my tithe.

By morning, when that long night was over, I knew that He was not asking me to *test* Him; what He was asking me to do was *trust* Him.

On Saturday, as I did each week, I took my husband's salary of nine dollars and carefully allocated it for the following week's needs. With new determination I put first on my list: tithe, ninety cents. When I came to the end of my absolute needs I was twenty cents short of having enough for the children's milk. Milk was five cents a quart and they must have a quart a day to be properly fed. I went over my list again. Each item had been cut to the minimum. There was only one thing I could do—reduce the tithe by twenty cents. Surely God would understand. I started to change the nine to a seven, but in that instant I felt as though someone had slapped my hand. I could not do it. The words "Prove me! Prove me!" kept burning through my mind. I closed my eyes and said, "All right, God. I will."

The following morning when I dropped God's ninety cents into the offering plate, a wonderful peace came over me. I knew that somehow God was going to take care of everything.

On the following Tuesday morning my last five cents had been spent for milk. My children faced four days without, and yet I found myself going about my work with a joyful anticipation that I could neither describe nor understand.

About eleven o'clock there was a knock on my front door. Answering it, I was confronted by a pleasant, smiling man who introduced himself as Ralph Gibson. He said he had worked with my husband about six years before and had come by to pay back a long overdue loan that he owed Corwin. With that he pressed a bill into my hand and started to leave.

It was a five-dollar bill, and I was so stunned I'm not sure I even said, "Thank you." The only thing I remember clearly was standing on my porch, holding a five-dollar bill in my hand, watching a stranger walk out of my yard as I said, "Thank You, God!

An hour later when my husband came home for lunch, he kissed me and asked the reason for my radiant face.

When I told him, he said: "Honey, there just has to be some mistake. I just barely remember Ralph Gibson, and I'm sure I never lent him money. There just has to be some mistake."

"Ralph Gibson may have made a mistake in thinking he owed you five dollars," I said. "You may be making a mistake in having lent it to him and forgotten it. But the fact that this is a genuine five-dollar bill and I have it in my possession is not a mistake. Neither is it a mistake that the children will have not only milk for the rest of the week, but some badly needed clothing as well. And the most wonderful truth of all is that I did not make a mistake in obeying God when He asked me to believe Him, trust Him and prove Him."

Many times and in many ways since then God has taught me many things through His word, and through the personal touch of His Holy Spirit. But this one lesson will always be, for me, one of the great forward steps in faith. Faith in not only God's goodness, but in His loving, caring providence for all who will dare to trust Him.

—*Alice A. Lindsay*

God's Demands

He never asks me to go anywhere He has not gone,
To face anything He has not faced,
To love anyone He does not love,
Or to give anything He has not given.

—*Author Unknown*

Car Trouble

THE OTHER DAY THE WIFE and I were talking with a neighbor, and the subject of feeling close to God came up. Immediately I thought of one time in particular, a time of great uncertainty for Carolyn and me. It was the spring of 1955, early in our marriage. Carolyn was eighteen, I was twenty-two, and our first child, Karen, was a year old. I had just finished my tour of duty with the Navy in San Diego, and we were heading home to Tacoma, Washington.

Packing and getting on the road had worn us out. We had only enough money for gas and groceries. My separation check from the Navy would be mailed to my folks' home in Tacoma. And then what? we wondered. I had no trade, no job. How would we get by? This was in our minds and in our conversation on the road back home. Frankly, there weren't any answers, and that was scary.

"I'm exhausted," I said to Carolyn.

"Me too," she replied wearily as she tried to soothe our fretting baby girl.

Dusk had fallen in the Siskiyou Mountains. Pulling our eight-year-old business coupe into a clearing by the roadside, we camped for the night in the twenty-one-foot trailer hitched behind the car. The trailer had been our home in California, and we were pulling it to Tacoma with us.

We were miles from any town, along a two-lane road that led through the mountains of northern California. Not much traffic passed along this stretch except for an occasional truck whizzing—a little too fast, I thought—around the curves.

Early the next morning, just after breakfast, I noticed it: a big black 1937 Buick sedan stopped right at the bend of the road. "What a strange place for anyone to stop," I said to Carolyn. "You'd think the driver would know better."

The car was half on, half off the road. No one could pass without going into the opposite lane. And one of those big trucks might be coming around the bend . . .

"Carolyn, I'm going to go up and speak to those people about moving their car." I had seen a man get out and go to the back of the car, then a woman. As I approached, they both looked frustrated. Hopeless, you might say. A boy of about six was looking out of the window.

"This is a dangerous stopping point," I called out.

"I can't get it to move," the man said to me. "It just locked up. I think it's this back wheel. But I tell you, it won't move."

"Well, maybe you should try pushing it off the road."

"It won't move," he said again helplessly.

"Got any tools?" I asked the man.

"Well, no, ah . . . I'm not very mechanical, I'm afraid. We're on our way to Oregon, where I have a job prospect. This couldn't have happened at a worse time."

All of their possessions were inside the car and strapped on top of it. It was clear that this young family had been struggling. Everything about them spoke of their need. The old car. Well-worn clothes. Belongings that most people would yard-sale today. That job prospect was their only hope, and now, with barely enough money for gas, they were faced with car trouble.

I directed the man to go up the road and the woman to go down the road to warn approaching traffic. Then I got my tools, jacked up the Buick and took off the rear wheel.

The brake linings had wedged over one another and had forced the round drum into an ellipse that was locked in place. I forced off the brake drum with a pry bar and hammer. Brake drum, brake shoes, lining—all useless. Then I bolted the wheel back on, and we coasted the car down to our trailer so that I could work on it.

It would take some sort of invention to put this family, desperate to get to that job interview, back on the road. "The best I can do," I said to the man and his wife, "is to pinch off the brake tube to this wheel so you won't lose fluid when you press the brake pedal. That means you'll have three wheels with brakes and one without. That will get you to the nearest town, but you must stop there and replace the drum and brake shoes."

I could see the worried looks cross their faces. I figured the reason—they didn't have the money for parts or repairs. "Do you have any relatives or friends in this part of the country?" I asked.

"No," said the man. "No one."

Carolyn and I didn't have much either, but at least we were heading toward family.

"Well, on this mountain road you can't drive very far with only three working brakes. It's just too dangerous . . ." I still hadn't figured how I would close off the brake tube to that one wheel. Maybe I could make something to cap it. Or pinch it shut. As I was considering possibilities, the couple's little boy ran up. He'd been playing just down the bank.

"Daddy, Daddy—" In his excitement he could hardly get his breath. "There's a car down the bank, and it's just like ours!"

"Oh, Son," said his father, a bit wearily, "it may look like ours, but it isn't." His mind was far away, somewhere up the road, at the next town, wondering how he was going to buy the parts he needed to get them to Oregon.

"Son, you just think it looks like ours. Now you run and play. We've got to fix this car somehow."

"But Daddy, it *is* just like ours!"

He was so positive that I said to the man, "Why don't we just have a look? It couldn't hurt."

The car was overturned about sixty feet down the embankment, and as we climbed down I could see that it had landed near some large boulders near a river. The engine and transmission were missing—taken by scavengers. So were the wheels.

But as I inspected it, the man and I looked at each other. Our curiosity turned to wonder. The car was *identical* to his. Same model, same year, same color. And though the wheels were missing, the brake drums were still intact.

I had brought my pry bar and hammer and some wrenches, and I busied myself in taking off the brake drum that was closest. I was balancing on the rocks and working with the wrenches while the man and his son poked around the car.

"Could I borrow that pry bar?" the man asked.

"Sure," I said and handed it over.

Intent on my work and still thinking about the coincidence of an identical wreck being at the exact spot in the road where this man's car broke down, I heard the two working with the pry bar to open the trunk of this old hulk. Still locked, or rusted shut after all these years . . .

Then I heard the creaking sounds of the trunk hinges opening. "Hey, there's a lug wrench!" shouted the man. "I could sure use that . . . and there's a paper bag." I heard the rustling of paper. And then silence.

The man came around to where I was working. He stared at me for a moment. I could tell it was difficult for him to speak. He held a brown paper sack.

"Do you have any idea what's in this sack?" he asked finally.

He stood there swallowing hard, trying not to cry. "Here . . . see? New brake shoes!"

With the necessary parts provided, I repaired their car, Carolyn fixed them a meal, and they started off down the road, waving. Alone? Helpless? Not at all. You see, I knew that Somebody upstairs cared very much for those three, and He was providing for their every need.

Right then and there, things no longer seemed so uncertain for Carolyn and me and Karen, either. For I also knew that if God could provide for those people, He could provide for us.

And as I was telling my neighbor the other day, for thirty-five years He has done just that.

—Ron Bailey

The Penny Gift

IN 1987 WHILE MY WIFE AND I were on a sixteen-month, freelance writing stint in Europe, I had one more reminder that God does provide, even in unexpected ways. It was the year of the dollar devaluation. Week after week we watched the money we'd brought with us shrink against other currencies. As our cost of living soared, so did my anxiety.

I was at my most anxious one morning when I pulled into a self-service gas station just off one of the autobahns in Germany. The dollar's latest plunge had brought fuel to the equivalent of three dollars a gallon, and I was muttering to myself as I turned on the pump and watched the "amount due" dial spin faster than my eye could follow.

At that moment I noticed a young man ambling up the street in my direction. Wearing stained corduroy trousers and a torn sweater, he had the childlike look that so often goes with mental retardation. He stopped and stood watching me fill the tank.

As I withdrew the nozzle the young man edged closer and at first I thought he wanted a ride. But he had drawn a small purse from his pocket and was fumbling with the clasp. He emptied a few coins into his hand and with clumsy fingers selected one of them.

"Fur dich," he said. *For you.* He held out a one-pfennig piece, worth less than half a U.S. cent.

"For me? But I don't need..."

I stopped short. In fact I had just been feeling very much in need. I stood there with the gasoline hose in one hand, the little copper in the other, watching God's spokesman wander off up the street.

—*John Sherrill*

In Full Supply

YEARS AND YEARS AGO, MY GRANDMOTHER told me a story out of her past that I always think of at gift-giving time, especially at Christmas. I remember sitting in her lap as dark-eyed little Sue Belle Johnson, my grandmother, explained how, shortly after the turn of the century, at remote and often lonely stations across the United States and overseas, missionaries and their families lived lives of hardship, privation, and isolation in their efforts to carry the gospel to people most of us would never know or see.

Probably at no time of the year were their feelings of isolation and loneliness more keenly felt than at Christmas. To remember them at this season, the custom in those days was for churches to send what were called "missionary barrels" to missionaries in remote locations.

The missionary and his wife would sit down with their children and make a list of things they wanted for Christmas. The list would include articles of clothing, toys, perhaps books or household utensils— whatever they especially needed but could not afford or could not find to buy. The list also included the ages of the children and their clothing sizes.

When completed, the list was sent to the missionary organization that helped sponsor them. The organization in turn sent it to a church, whose members would then take it upon themselves to acquire the items on the list.

My grandmother's church in Hattiesburg, Mississippi, was one of the churches that received such a Christmas list. That particular year, the list came from a missionary family in what was then called Indian Territory. The women of Grandmother's church, many of them, saw it as a holy task to choose an item and either buy it, make it, or donate money for its purchase.

On an appointed day all the requested items would be brought to the church, and the women would check the items against the list, wrap them, and pack them into a big wooden-staved, double-ended barrel. The barrel would then be shipped in time for the family to receive it by Christmas.

Not everybody in Grandmother's church cooperated. While the women were packing the missionary barrel, one of the more well-to-do women of the church walked into the room carrying a coat. "I've got this coat of my husband's that I want to give to you," she announced offhandedly. "I'm going to buy him a new one."

Grandmother was appalled. She didn't say anything, but she was thinking plenty: *These other people have worked hard to get these articles, some have sacrificed to get them, and here this woman is in effect bragging, "I'm so rich I can go out and buy another coat."*

The more she thought about the woman's haughtiness, the more irritated Grandmother became. *She's just ridding herself of an unwanted castoff,* Grandmother said to herself. *What kind of Christmas attitude is that?* Grandmother was furious—about the coat and with the woman.

A coat was not on the missionary family's list, and the women packing the barrel had no intention of putting the coat in it. But after all the requested items had been carefully placed in the barrel, there was still room left.

"Well," one of the women said, "let's put that coat in. It might help keep the other articles tight, keep them from bouncing around and maybe breaking."

So, they folded the coat, packed it in, and closed the barrel. Then they shipped it to the family out in the Indian Territory.

Weeks passed. Christmas came and went. Then a letter arrived at the church: the family's thank-you, written by the missionary's wife. "Dear Friends," it began, "we want to thank you for the barrel."

She then recounted how her husband and their three children had driven to the railhead to pick up the barrel, had brought it home and placed it upright in the middle of the living room floor in their little cabin, waiting for Christmas. The children were so excited they danced around it in gleeful anticipation.

Then on the day before Christmas a fierce winter storm blew in. It quickly developed into a blizzard, with snow so thick and winds so furious that the entire outdoors seemed a blowing, blinding mass of white. Shortly before suppertime, as the blizzard raged, there was a banging on the front door, and when the missionary opened the door to see what the banging was, there stood an old man, grizzled, ill clad for the freezing temperature, shivering and covered with snow.

"I'm lost," the man said. "Could I come in for a while?"

The missionary opened the door wider and said, "Of course. Come on in."

After supper, it was all but impossible to contain the children, they were so excited and eager to open the barrel. But their mother managed to get them bedded down, explaining that they would have to wait a little longer, since it would be terribly impolite to open the barrel, pull out the presents, and distribute them with the old man there. "There's nothing for him," the mother said. "It's just the things we put on our list. We'll have to wait till the man leaves."

The next morning, Christmas morning, the family arose and found that the storm had not abated; the winds were as wild as the night before. The mother fixed a special breakfast for everyone, and when breakfast was over, they watched and waited for the storm to end so that the old man could be on his way and they could break open the barrel.

Afternoon came and the storm was still raging, but the children just couldn't wait any longer. So the missionary and his wife explained to the old man that the barrel had been packed many weeks earlier and contained Christmas presents for the family only. They apologized profusely, and when the old man nodded and said he understood, the missionary turned to the barrel and began to break open the uppermost end of it.

The family then began pulling out, one by one, the items they had asked for on their Christmas list. Each item was clearly marked so that they all knew whose present it was. Everyone was excited. The clothes, the toys, everything, were exactly what the family had requested. Everyone was happy and pleased, while the old man sat and watched.

Finally they reached the bottom of the barrel. There on the bottom, at the end of the barrel that had been uppermost when the women packed it, was an item the family didn't recognize. It was nothing they had asked for. When the missionary reached deep into the barrel to pull out the object, he could see it was a man's coat. He held it up. It looked to be about the size of the old man. "Try it on." The man took it and slipped it on. It fit perfectly. "It must be for you," the missionary told him, smiling.

"How did you ever know," the missionary wife's letter concluded, "that we would need a man's coat for Christmas? Thank you all so very much."

By the time she finished reading the letter, my grandmother said, she was nearly overcome with awe. The cast-off coat that had needed a new owner had found one. An old man who had needed a warm coat had been given one. A family who had taken in a lost stranger and needed a special present for him had been provided with one. It was all too marvelous to comprehend, my grandmother said. Surely God, in His wondrous omniscience, she said, had wrought a miracle with a gift she had thought unworthy.

When she finished her story, grandmother took my hands in hers and said, "I learned that day that I had been wrong—and that I should never despise a gift that God can use."

As Christmas approaches again, I'm remembering once more my grandmother's words. As I choose presents to give this Christmas, I am hoping that they will be gifts that will make the recipients happy and me proud to give. But most of all I am praying that, whatever they are, whomever they're for, they will be exactly the gifts that God can use.

—Jacqueline Hewitt Allen

Manna

Out of despair hope is dawning;
After the darkness comes light.
His mercies are new every morning,
He scatters His manna each night,

Scatters it freely as hoarfrost.
Then use it as freely, nor hoard
In fear of tomorrow's privation.
It pleases our bountiful Lord

To give these good gifts to His children.
His promise is faithful and true,
That He will provide on the morrow
Enough for tomorrow's need too.
 —*MARTHA SNELL NICHOLSON*

Jehovah himself is caring for you! He . . . preserves your life.
—Psalm 121:1, 7, TLB

CHAPTER THREE

God Preserves Our Lives

When we look at our lives, there's no way to know about *all* the "near misses" when disaster has been averted. But the writers of these stories were given a glimpse of what might have been—if God's hand had not intervened to prevent a mishap and preserve life: their own or that of their children, loved ones, or comrades.

The Missing Shoes

O F ALL TIMES to have the airline lose my luggage! It was only my toiletries case with my one pair of good shoes, but of all places to wind up without them!

I'd flown out to Farmington, New Mexico, for a one-day seminar sponsored by the Southwest Christian Writers' Association. "No one will care about your shoes," Margaret, the group's president, assured me.

Doubtless Margaret was right, but *of all times.* Even as I said it, a phrase came to mind: "... we should at all times, and in all places, give thanks unto Thee." At *all* times.

We met at the First Presbyterian Church. At the seminar's close, several writers came up to the speaker's stand. Suddenly there was a terrifying *crack.* Then a woman shouted, "Lie down! Every one!"

Two men were outside, one of them brandishing a gun. The sound of exploding glass had come from the window. Later we learned that the men had been drinking and shooting at telephone poles. From the wall beyond the speaker's stand the police recovered the tip of an electric screwdriver fired from a homeade pistol.

While Margaret filled out the police report, the rest of us said goodbye, each no doubt recalling a step forward or a delay that had kept him or her out of the line of fire.

For my part, I was tracing a trajectory, from the window to the wall, an inch over the spot where I'd been standing. I was thinking of a pair of two-and-a-half-inch heels in a missing bag, and echoing a prayer: "... we should at all times, and in all places, give thanks to Thee, O Lord."

—*ELIZABETH SHERRILL*

Caught in the Train Tracks

I T WAS 5:30 WHEN MY THREE CHILDREN and I left the grocery store, so in order to be home before dark, we took the shortcut. A cold mist fell—the dreariness of a February dusk in Michigan.

When we came to the train tracks, my six-year-old, Lynda, tripped and fell, and her right foot became wedged between the wooden tie and the steel track.

"Untie your shoe, honey, and slip your foot out," I said. But Lynda had already pulled her shoelace into a tight knot. I tried to unravel the knot with my house key, then a hairpin. Still it held fast. I tried yanking

Lynda's foot free of the shoe, but it wouldn't come. I had to get the knot untied.

Starting to worry, I scooted my other two children down the embankment, then dropped my bag of groceries and ran back to Lynda.

Just then I felt a faint vibration. An approaching train! I dug at the knot—ripping my nails, bloodying my fingers. Lynda and I both broke into fearful sobbing.

"O God," I cried, "help us. Please, God."

Two little faces stared up at me from the ditch, terror-stricken. My eyes then strayed to the spilled bag of groceries.

"The ham! The ham!" I screamed in a strange fit of revelation. I grabbed the canned ham, ripped the key from its bottom and peeled off the lid. Using the sharp edge of the lid, I severed the shoelace and pulled Lynda out of her shoe. In the glare and roar of the oncoming train we tumbled into the ditch. Safe.

Now, I've heard it said that God gives us what we need when we need it. But I've since wondered, what did the Lord give me just then? The sharp lid on a can of ham, or an imagination sharpened to the quick? —*HELEN S. MCCUTCHEON*

The Voice on the Phone

W HEN A TORNADO STRUCK LOUISVILLE, KENTUCKY, in April 1974, our family was at home—all but our youngest son, Collyn. He was in kindergarten at Southern Baptist Theological Seminary a few miles away.

Huddled together in our basement, we heard the rain pounding and the storm's violent roar. When the noise abated, we went upstairs, relieved to find our neighborhood untouched. But the radio said the storm had headed toward the seminary.

My husband went for Collyn and I stayed at home with our two older boys. I tried to call the kindergarten. The number did not ring. Instead I heard clicks and then the phone went dead.

"Mama," my son Chris reported, "the radio just said the tornado went through the Baptist seminary and took the roof off."

Both children began to cry. With my own fear, how could I comfort them? I thought: *Only God can help me now. He's in charge.* "Boys," I said, "we're in God's hands."

Again I tried to phone. Dead. I was about to hang up when the number rang.

"Don't worry," said the woman who answered. "The children were taken to another building before the storm. They're fine." We hugged and shouted for joy.

The area around the seminary had been devastated. Huge trees lay twisted on the ground; live electrical wires sparked on the wet sidewalks; homeless people wandered in a daze. But my husband found Collyn safe, just as the woman had said.

Later, when I went to thank the woman who'd comforted me on the phone, Collyn's teacher said, "But Mrs. Coates, you couldn't have spoken with anyone. Our phone lines were destroyed. Besides, there was no one in the building when you called."   —LYNNE COATES

The Holdup

IT WAS 9:00 P.M., FEBRUARY 6, 1981—closing time at the self-service Husky Gas Station in Albuquerque, New Mexico, where I'd been employed for about two months. As I counted out the day's receipts and put the money into a bank bag, I thought again how lucky I'd been to get this job. In the two years since I'd graduated from high school, I'd had a hard time finding good, steady work.

My mother, however, had not been pleased when I'd told her about my new job.

"Steve, I'm scared," she'd admitted. "I read all the time about robberies at those self-service stations. What if you get hurt?"

"Don't worry, Mom, I'll be fine," I'd reassured her. "Nothing is going to happen."

Now, looking forward to the dinner waiting for me at home, I slipped my fleece-lined denim jacket over my white T-shirt and blue corduroy pants, tucked the bag under one arm, and left the cashier's booth near the pumps to cross the parking lot to the storage shed where the safe was located. En route, I passed a man wearing a black windbreaker and black pants. He mumbled something to me, but I just nodded and went on. People on foot often cut across that parking lot, so I felt no alarm.

I stashed the money in the safe, then hurried outside and locked the shed. I'd started to turn back toward the booth when the same man I'd seen five minutes before stepped around from behind the shed and stopped me. A shock flashed through me at the sight of the black ski mask he'd pulled down over his face. The thing that turned my knees to Jell-O, though, was the gun he held in his black-gloved hand.

"Oh, my God," I gasped.

"That's right," he responded coolly.

Meaning, I knew, that he was about to hold me up, and he could see that I realized it. He motioned with the gun toward the booth, which was still unlocked and brightly lighted.

"Give me your money," he said.

He hadn't seen that bag under my arm, then. He didn't know I'd locked the money in the shed.

"I don't have any money," I told him.

He snorted in disbelief. "Don't give me that! Get in there and open that cash register!"

I moved toward the booth, trying to control my rubbery legs, which threatened to pitch me forward onto the asphalt.

"I'm telling you the truth," I insisted. "All I've got left are some rolls of change." And then, realizing I'd have to explain that, I did tell a lie: "The manager came by just a while ago and picked up the rest of the money. You're too late."

"Oh yeah? I'll have to see for myself."

He followed me into the booth. I glanced out toward the empty street, usually so busy. Surely someone would drive by and see what was happening, I told myself. All I had to do was try to stay calm until help arrived. Calm? My hands trembled as I groped for the lever on the register. The drawer slid open.

"Look, just change," I told him.

He began to curse. His eyes glared ferociously at me through the holes in the mask. He looked insane. Or high on dope. Still holding the gun on me, he began rummaging through the shelves in the booth with his other hand, hunting for the bag of money he seemed convinced was there.

"Pull the phone off the wall," he told me shortly.

The hole in the barrel of the gun, pointed at my chest, looked as big to me as the hole in the end of a car's tailpipe. I grabbed the phone with both hands and yanked. It didn't budge. I tried again, but my arms had all the strength of wet spaghetti. Finally, I picked up a small knife and cut through the cord.

He's just making sure I won't call the police. I said to myself. *Now he'll leave, and I can go home.*

That's all I wanted right then—just to go home, to the safety of my own four walls, to the love and support of my parents. I'd tell my younger brother about the attempted robbery. He'd be surprised, maybe not even believe me at first. Home . . .

The man peered through the window of the booth toward my 1973 Chevy Impala parked nearby.

"The money must be in your car," he snapped. "Get moving."

And he motioned again with the gun.

We left the booth and walked across the parking lot to the car. He searched me there, looking for rolls of money in my pockets. All he found was my wallet, which he kept. Then he told me to open the car. Still keeping the gun pointed in my direction, he felt around under the empty seats.

"Get in," he demanded. "You drive. Pretty soon I'll have you drop me off somewhere."

I wanted to believe him. After all, I argued to myself, I had nothing to give him. Sooner or later, he'd have to let me go.

We headed down the street in the car. When the man noticed that the gas tank registered almost empty, he went into a rage. He began to taunt me about making minimum wage at a gas station and not being able to afford gas for my own car.

"Look at me, I can get plenty of money any time I want it," he boasted, "and I don't have to work for no crummy minimum wage."

Then he told me that he was the man who had murdered Phil Chacon, a popular Albuquerque policeman who had been shot to death several months before. That murder was still unsolved.

My heart began to pound. My hands, damp with perspiration, slipped on the surface of the steering wheel. For the first time I looked at the fact that this man might kill me.

I needed help. I wanted to reach out to someone, anyone, but only God knew the danger I was in. Somehow my grandmother's face appeared in my mind, smiling at me the way she had when I was little. She'd been the one in our family with a strong belief in God. I'd wanted to believe in God, too—but for me, now as then, He seemed far away, out of reach. I just couldn't get in contact with Him, not the way she could.

Maybe it was because I'd always felt shy and insecure. Despite my parents' encouragement. Despite my grandmother's love. For I'd had some physical problems as a child that had kept me from developing as fast as my friends. While they shot up to become basketball and football stars, I remained slight of build. When they all began talking in deep voices and shaving every morning, I still looked, with my baby face, like a twelve-year-old. I gradually drew away from others at school, staying in my own corner, never speaking up in class. Even though I finally grew to be over six feet tall in my last two years of high school, my habit of staying in the background continued. That's another reason I'd never called on God—I thought someone as unimportant as I was didn't stand a chance of being heard.

Now, with this masked gunman sitting beside me, I *wanted* to be noticed. I kept hoping that someone would glance into our car at an intersection and see what was happening. One man in a car did pull up beside us, but then the light changed, and he took off, leaving me once more alone. Or was I alone?

Desperately, I began to pray: "God, if You're listening, I sure do need help. Maybe I am a nobody—maybe I've never done anything important—but I still don't want to die. Please—please, can You do something?"

The gunman told me what streets to take and where to turn. I saw at last that we were headed toward the airport near the south edge of town.

I said, "Look, I'll just let you out, and I'll go away, and you'll never hear from me again. You've only taken about fifteen dollars in change. I'll make that up out of my own pocket, and no one will ever know . . ."

The old coward bit. I'd fantasized, when I was younger, about all the brave things I'd do if I were ever in a jam. But actually looking into the barrel of a gun had sent my once-imagined courage right down the tubes.

"I haven't decided yet what to do with you. Just keep driving," he told me flatly.

When we came to a fork where the road circled to the left, into a loading area in front of the airport terminal building, the man had me veer instead to the right, down a winding dirt road that led out into the deserted dunes beyond the west end of the runways. In the glow of the headlights, I saw clumps of dead *chimisa* and trash-draped tumbleweeds. The rocky dunes rolled away on either side, bleak as the surface of the moon.

My chest felt constricted. My breathing had become fast and shallow.

"Lord, this really looks bad," I prayed silently. "Are You here? Are You with me?"

At the same time, a part of me kept rationalizing—maybe the man really didn't intend to kill me. Why should he, what would he gain? Maybe he'd just let me out and then steal my car. It would take me a while to get back to the main road where I could flag down a ride. But at least I'd be safe—the nightmare would be over, and I could go home . . .

"Stop," the man suddenly barked.

I pulled over toward the side of the road and turned off the key.

"Now get out. Leave the key in the ignition," he instructed.

I felt greatly relieved. *Good,* I thought, *he'll soon be gone.*

I climbed out and moved a few steps away, into the sand and tumbleweeds. The man slid over and got out too, coming to stand directly in front of me. Without saying another word, he brought the gun up, pointing it at my face.

It's amazing the number of thoughts that can flash through a person's mind in just one split second. I knew that I was going to die right then, and there was nothing I could do. I felt no sorrow for myself, but I grieved for my parents and what they would have to go through, trying to deal with such a terrible memory for the rest of their lives.

Well, Lord, this is it, I thought, becoming strangely calm.

All that, in the brief time it took the man to level the gun and pull the trigger.

I saw the flash, I heard the explosion. I waited to fall. Nothing happened. I stood on my feet, staring straight into the barrel. Had he missed? He couldn't have missed . . .

He pulled the trigger again. Again, I saw the flash and heard the explosion. Again, incredibly, I found myself still on my feet, facing that gun.

It misfired. I thought . . . but in that case, there would just have been a click, no flash or loud noise. Blanks? Even with those, there should have been a blast of some kind, powder burns, at that close range . . .

Where had those bullets gone?

I stared at the man, he stared at me. Then he looked in a puzzled way at the gun. He started to pull the trigger again, but seemed to change his mind. Instead, he taunted me about how close I'd come to death.

"You're lucky this time," he concluded, motioning toward the road. "Start walking."

I took off at once, stumbling through the sand and gravel. I couldn't believe that I was still alive. My mind reeled as I tried to take it in. To have the gun fail once seemed to me to be a miracle. But *twice* . . .

I snapped back to the present with a new shock of alarm, realizing that the car was rocketing up behind me like a race car roaring off the starting line. Before I could dive out of the way, the front bumper slammed into the backs of my legs. The car continued to speed forward as my body catapulted into the air and crashed headfirst onto the hood. With arms and legs flailing, I bounced over the windshield to the top of the car. From somewhere came the sound of breaking glass as my body careened about, somersaulting onto the trunk and then smacking face down into the road.

The car roared off. I lay there, stunned, with sand in my mouth. *But I was still alive!* Broken and helpless, no doubt, but alive . . .

Gingerly, carefully, I began to stir, testing for broken bones. I thought my legs would surely be fractured from the impact of the bumper, or my skull cracked and my neck snapped from the crash onto the hood. But all my joints worked with no trouble. I pushed to my knees, blinking against the sting of gravel in my left eye. Getting my feet under me, I rose to my full height under the brilliant glitter of the desert stars.

Broken bones? Not one! Only a few skinned places on my face and chest, a knot on my head, and the gravel in my eye. I'd been shot at twice and run down with my own car—and there I stood, virtually unhurt.

I heard myself saying aloud, "Thank You, thank You, thank You," over and over. And I knew that I was thanking God. Because to come out whole through three attempts on my life seems to me to be more than just coincidence. I really think the hand of God had to be at work in there somewhere.

I headed through the dunes toward the distant glow of lights in the fifteen-story hotel at the airport. With my clothes torn and dirty, with blood from the skinned places seeping through my T-shirt, I finally stumbled into the lobby and asked the startled desk clerk to phone for the police.

Later, the police and I found my car abandoned near the airport with two blue imprints from my pant legs ground into the bumper, a big dent in the hood where my head had hit, and a broken right window, which I must have kicked with one foot in my tumble over the car. Although the person who kidnapped me was never identified, there was a man of the same height and build convicted a few months later, along with another man, for the murder of policeman Phil Chacon. When I looked at the eyes of that man in a newspaper picture, I felt a shock jar my nerves. He might well have been the man in the ski mask, although I can't say for sure.

But one thing I do know for sure: my old sense of worthlessness is gone. It doesn't matter that I was never a big football star or a straight "A" student—when I called to God, He heard me. To Him, I was not unimportant. Now that my life has been spared, I'm determined to make the most of the talents I do have, whatever they may be.

Because of that resolve, I reported to work on time the day after I'd been kidnapped. The people in charge were impressed by that and soon promoted me, making me the youngest person in the city ever to become a Husky station manager.

I'm pleased by the promotion, of course. But even if that hadn't happened, I know God would still care for me anyway, no matter what I look like or what kind of so-called "crummy" salary I might be drawing.

I haven't yet been able to forgive the man who tried to kill me, but I'm working on it. Meanwhile—with God's help—I have a station to run.

—*Steve Akers*

Courage

Give to the winds thy fears;
    Hope and be undismayed;
God hears thy sighs and counts thy tears,
    God shall lift up thy head.

Through waves and clouds and storms
    He gently clears thy way;
Wait thou His time; so shall this night
    Soon end in joyous day.

Leave to His sovereign sway
    To choose and to command;
So shalt thou wondering own, His way
    How wise, how strong His hand!

Far, far above thy thought
    His counsel shall appear,
When fully He the work hath wrought
    That caused thy needless fear.

Let us in life, in death,
    Thy steadfast truth declare,

And publish with our latest breath,
Thy love and guardian care.
—PAUL GERHARDT, TRANSLATED BY JOHN WESLEY

On a Rock

I WAS GOING SNORKELING in the Palm Beach inlet with my fourteen-year-old son, Don, and our diving instructor, Jerry. We were to swim out past the jetty, then float into the channel with the tide. Yet I hesitated. The breakers were enormous.

I put on the foam rubber wet-vest and Jerry's weight belt to offset the vest's buoyancy. Actually, I knew that the weight should be adjusted for each diver, I just didn't think about that at the time.

We dove in, Jerry and Don paddling along in front, with me right behind. As we swam out, the distance between us grew. *Better swim harder*, I thought. But I was swimming as hard as I could. Halfway out I saw Jerry and Don clear the end of the jetty.

The next instant, a wave slammed me against the rocks. Then another and another. The barnacles on the boulders lashed my arms and legs. The heavy weight around my waist was dragging me down. I tried to grab on to the rocks, but they were too large, too slippery, too sheer.

Exhausted, battered, I knew right then that I was going to die. I was pleasantly surprised that I felt prepared for it. I imagined myself standing in the presence of God, and the thought gave me great peace. I looked up and said quietly, "I'm ready, Father..."

Needless to say, I did not die. I'm still mystified by the way I was saved. To this day I'm drawn often to Psalm 27:5: "For in the time of trouble, he shall hide me in his pavilion: ... he shall set me up upon a rock."

In my time of trouble, a huge wave suddenly crashed into the jetty and a swirling column of water lifted me up, up, up, six feet in the air, spun me around in a sitting position, and placed me safely on top of a rock.

—RON CHAMBERS

In Danger

When I was growing up, I always liked to hear my father tell the story of a strange premonition he'd had as a young missionary in China. Dad's superior, a Mr. Sinton, had just left Luchow for an extended journey to outlying missions, when Dad was overwhelmed with the feeling that Mr. Sinton was in mortal danger. Every night, Dad prayed for his safety.

When Mr. Sinton returned, he told about having retired one night in a guest house where a tiny charcoal brazier burned. Later that evening Mr. Sinton had heard a loud mysterious pounding. Getting up, he went to the window, pushed it open, and looked out. No one was there. He started toward the door, but the next thing he knew, he was waking up flat on the floor. He had been overcome by toxic fumes from the brazier. Opening the window had saved his life!

Several years ago, when Dad was eighty-two, he called me at the office. "I had such a vivid dream early this morning," he said, "that I had to call you. I dreamed you were in danger. Is your house okay?"

I didn't want to do it, but remembering Dad and Mr. Sinton, I actually went home—only to discover my sick cat sleeping in front of the electric heater. No fire. No danger. I turned off the heater and, feeling foolish, returned to the office.

At home that night, I turned on the heater again, and fifteen minutes later the lights in the kitchen sizzled and flickered out. The motor on the heater had burned out, blowing the fuses and filling the kitchen with acrid smoke . . . —*MARY RUTH HOWES*

Call Roy Stanley

I T WAS ALMOST DARK when I went into the kitchen to fix some supper. I didn't feel a bit hungry, but there are two rules we insulin-dependent diabetics must adhere to: take insulin regularly and don't skip meals.

So I shook some oatmeal into a pan of water, and set it to cooking on a front burner of my electric stove. I started across the kitchen to get milk from the refrigerator, but I never made it. My feet slipped out from under me and I fell hard, flat on my back, on the floor.

Oh, you've done it now, old girl.

I pushed and stretched and made every effort to get up, but I couldn't even sit up. Nothing I could do was going to get this over-weight seventy-year-old body off the floor. I needed help. I thought about screaming, but who would hear me? I was a widow who lived alone and had already closed and locked all the windows and doors.

The telephone! I could call my sister, Martha. The telephone hung high on the wall, over near my bedroom door. Next to it was my broom, propped against the wall.

I dug my elbows into the rough texture of the floor covering and managed to slide on my back a couple of inches. Six or seven more shoves and a lot of panting put me near the phone. Using the broom, I gave it a *whack* that sent the handset banging to the floor. But to my dismay, I couldn't make a call. The dial was up on the phone.

Fear was beginning to gnaw at me. The burner under my oatmeal was glowing brightly. What would happen if the water boiled out? Would the metal pan melt and ruin my stove? Would it set my house on fire?

But there was nothing I could do. I was locked in my house with no way to contact the outside world, and no light except the glow from the electric burner.

Finally I whispered, "Lord Jesus, I'm so alone and I'm afraid. Please come and be here with me. Quiet me, Jesus, and protect me, and please take care of my pan of oatmeal."

The air began to chill as the evening grew longer. I hugged my arms about me and wished for a blanket. I dragged myself into the bedroom and looked longingly at the heavy spread on my bed. I could never pull that down. But there were some clothes lying on the cedar chest. Again I dug my elbows into the rug, and I pulled down a sweater and skirt to cover myself.

As the night grew blacker, I thought of the insulin shot I normally took after supper. What condition would I be in by morning? Was I going to die? My back was beginning to ache. I had no idea what damage I had done to myself. Panic began to smother me.

"Lord," I prayed, "don't leave me. Please stay with me and comfort me." Then I began to recite Scripture verses, mostly those I'd learned in Sunday school, one verse after another, until I slipped into a fitful sleep.

When the light of morning roused me, I thanked God that the long night was over and my house was not burned.

I said my morning prayers and made another attempt to get up from the floor. I could not move. My throat was dry and I was hungry. And how long could I go without insulin?

Surely a neighbor would telephone. Oh, no! The phone was off the hook. But then, maybe someone would come and knock on the door.

All morning I listened carefully but no knock came. I kept praying, "Jesus, please help me."

Around noon a thought flashed through my mind: *Call someone.*

Another thought: *Call your friends.*

"But the phone . . ." I said aloud.

I began to call out names. I started with my sister; I knew she'd be at work. Then I called my neighbors, one by one, pausing after each, listening for a knock.

I had run out of names to call when another sudden thought invaded my tired mind: *Call Roy Stanley.* Roy had stopped by two days earlier to pray with me, but he lived so far away.

Still the thought persisted: *Call Roy.*

So I began calling, "Roy, please come to me. I need you." I said it aloud, over and over without stopping.

It was about two o'clock when I heard a loud knocking on the back door. I yelled, "Come and help me. I need you."

Then I heard a series of heavy blows and a splintering of wood. Footsteps . . . and Roy was standing over me.

"Christine!" he exclaimed. "What are you doing on the floor?"

I told him.

Roy went to the kitchen to get some water for my parched throat. He phoned my sister and called for an ambulance. Then as we waited he told me how he happened to be there.

Roy and his wife were at home when he felt a strong urge to check on me. He told his wife, "I have to go to Christine. Something has happened to her."

When he knocked on my door, he got no answer, but something seemed to urge him, *Don't leave. Go to the back and knock again.* So he went around to the back door, knocked harder, and finally heard me calling, "Come and help me. I need you."

As the ambulance arrived, I felt a strange sense of elation. Jesus *had* been with me through the night. He'd brought Roy to rescue me. He'd answered every single one of my prayers. Even the one about the oatmeal. For when I finally thought about that burner, I said to Roy, "Will you please check on a pan of oatmeal I put on to cook last night? It must be burned black by now."

A strange expression crossed Roy's face. "I turned that burner off when I got the water for you," he said. "Did you say you put it on *last night?* Christine, that oatmeal is not burned. In fact, it's just ready to eat now!"

—CHRISTINE SKILLERN

Her Mother's Voice

THE YEAR IS 1939. The place is an eighty-acre dairy farm outside the small town of Chehalis, Washington, sixteen miles from the nearest doctor or hospital. A little girl, an eighteen-month-old toddler dressed in overalls, slams the screen door as she ambles out onto the back porch to play in the sunshine. Her mother is inside the house, cleaning.

Outdoors on this warm spring morning the world is full of delights to explore. The youngster runs through the dewy grass, picks dandelions, and carries them back to the house. On the porch an old enameled kettle sitting in the sun catches her eye. It is filled with peas soaking in an arsenic solution, something that will prevent them from rotting when planted. Back then, seeds weren't pretreated as most are today.

The little girl is fascinated with the liquid in the kettle. Taking a battered tin cup, she dips it in the pot, fills it with the liquid, then lifts it.

Just then her mother hears a voice calling her, "Ella, Ella, come quick!" She follows the voice through the house and out the back door where she spots the little girl, the cup at her lips. Frantic, she grabs the toddler and empties the cup. She wipes the little girl's lips, but, no, the youngster hasn't had a drop of the poison. The mother arrived just in time.

I know this story well because I was that little girl, and the woman who rescued me was my mother. And as for the voice, Mother recognized it right away. It belonged to her mother, my grandmother. The mystery? My grandmother had died the year before, six months after I was born.

—Lois Bunker Woods

That Old Pickup Truck

Back that winter of 1950, I wouldn't have said I knew much about praying, but I guess I knew where to turn when I needed help. At the time, Joe Spurgin and I were baching on the Nielson Ranch south of Cody, Wyoming. He was a ranch hand and I was a cowboy, and we were left in charge of feeding and caring for the livestock while the ranch manager, Bill Hill, was away.

When I woke up one February morning it must have been twenty below zero. I know I had to chop ice for the cows' drinking water. I spent most of the day doctoring the animals that were sickly. Then, while Joe stayed back at the bunkhouse, I rode my horse into an area called Oregon Basin to check on the cattle there. Toward evening I headed home, eager for the hot supper Joe would have ready to eat.

I wasn't far from the ranch when I knew something was wrong. No smoke was coming out of the chimney, no sign of Joe. I put up my horse in the barn. Walking away from the stall, I saw blood frozen on the ground. I thought Joe must have butchered a beef. Then in the tack room I saw Joe Spurgin himself, lying on his back with a rifle next to his right arm. I knelt down to check his pulse. It was real weak, but Joe was still alive. *I've got to get him to the hospital,* I thought, *and quick!*

On the ranch we had an old Chevrolet pickup truck. Trouble was, it was hard to start. In the middle of summer we had to push and pull it to get it running, but in the below-zero winter, I could never tell what it would do. I rushed outside, panting in the cold air, and as I ran I said to God, "Please help me start it so I can save Joe Spurgin."

I slid onto the cold leather seat, slammed the door, blew on my hands for warmth, put my foot on the gas pedal and turned the key in the ignition. I couldn't believe my ears. No sputter, no cough! The engine started with one turn of the key.

"Thank You, God," I whispered. "Just keep the engine running." I jumped out, lowered the tailgate and ran back to get my wounded partner.

Now, Joe was a big man, six feet tall and over two hundred pounds. With his long johns, wool shirt, jeans, cowboy boots, overshoes, coveralls and a heavy sheepskin coat, add another twenty-five. How was a man of my size, five feet seven and one hundred forty pounds, going to move this body? "Lord," I prayed, "You helped me get that old pickup started. Now I have another favor to ask. Help me move my friend."

Before I tried to lift Joe's body, I saw he was frozen down in his own blood. I picked up a shovel, slipped it under where the blood had frozen his clothing to the barn's wooden floor and pried him loose. Joe was still unconscious. "Don't die on me," I said, and then somehow I managed to hoist him on my shoulders.

I slipped him into the back of the truck, shut the tailgate and drove wild and fast to the Cody hospital. It was dark by the time I got there.

I backed up to the emergency room door, ran into the hospital, and was met by a doctor I knew well, Dewitt Dominick. I told him in an excited tone of voice that I had a man in my truck who was shot with a .25 caliber Winchester rifle.

Two helpers took a gurney out to the truck and loaded what I feared was a dead man onto it. Then the doctor looked him over and said, "Yep, he's alive. Just barely."

Joe's clothing was cut off him and the doctor found that Joe had been shot in the back of his right knee. The bullet came out of his ankle. Joe was still pale and unconscious, but I had to leave him at the hospital and get back to look after the ranch.

I put in a sleepless night. Next morning I got up early, fed the cattle, and took care of the ranch chores. I cleaned up, shaved, grabbed a cup of strong black coffee and went outside to the pickup. Once again I slid onto the leather seat, slammed the door, put my foot down on the accelerator, and turned the key in the ignition.

Nothing. I sat there for a minute, then smiled. *Lord,* I thought, *You helped me when I needed it most. I can get to the hospital just fine without this old pickup. You just keep old Joe alive.*

I went out to the road to hitchhike and in a few minutes caught a ride that took me straight to the hospital. Joe was sitting up in bed, smiling. He'd had several pints of blood pumped into him and now a shade of color was back in his face.

"How'd it happen?" I asked.

"Don, after you rode off yesterday I saw a coyote near the sheep pen. I ran to the barn and grabbed the rifle that hangs in the tack room. And that's all I remember. I must have fainted dead away when I saw all that blood." He shook my hand and thanked me for saving his life.

Joe got well, but after that he never came back to the ranch to work. I lost track of him for a while, then heard that he went to Cañon City, Colorado, where he was employed at the state prison. He retired after twenty years and moved back to Billings, Montana, where he had a sister nearby. In 1980 the sister called me and asked if I could come see Joe. He was dying and had asked for me.

I drove up to Billings and found Joe looking as gray as he did when I discovered him on the barn floor. Again Joe shook my hand and thanked me for saving his life. He gave me his hat, his silver belt-buckle, and all the money he had left in the world, $150.

"No," I said, "I don't want your money, Joe."

"Take it, partner," he said. "I'm going to die tonight. I'm going to see God, and when I get there I'm going to thank Him for giving me thirty more years to live."

Joe died that night, and all these years I've kept his hat and buckle. They remind me of an old friend and an old Chevy pickup truck, and they remind me that God gives you help just when you need it most.

—DON BELL

Seconds Away from Death

WHEN I WAS A COLLEGE YOUNGSTER I was much interested in crew racing. Mostly I rowed in an eight-oared shell that competed in various regattas. Now and then I would also try rowing alone in a single scull, a fragile splinter about twelve feet long, barely a foot wide, very light, very fast and very unstable—any awkward or sudden movement could easily tip it over.

On this weekend our crew was competing at a college where the rowing took place on a broad smooth river. In our practice outing we had rowed upstream from the boathouse, as did the other crews, not downstream. But I gave no particular thought to this.

Early in the morning, with time to kill, I went down to the boathouse and took out a single scull. It was a beautiful day, sunny and warm. For a change of scenery I decided to row downstream. In a single scull, unless you turn your head, you can't see where you're going; you guide yourself by watching the shoreline as it slides past. With the current and a breeze aiding me, I seemed to fly across the burnished water. In almost no time I had covered a mile, keeping to the middle of the river with no thought of danger.

But suddenly something made me look over my shoulder, and when I did my heart seemed to stop. Fifty yards farther on *the river disappeared*. It simply vanished, because it was pouring over a dam or breakwater at least twenty feet high. Now I could hear the muffled roar it made as it plunged into the gorge below. In that terrifying moment, I knew that I was only seconds away from death. I stopped rowing and sat there, frozen, but the current carried me on.

To turn a single scull you back with one oar and pull with the other, but gently, gently, not too hard. You're supposed to take your time, but I had no time. Two words flashed through my mind: *Don't panic*. To this day I don't know how I did it, but I whirled the scull around, hooked the racing water with both blades, drove my shoulders back and my legs down, and felt the scull leap like a waterbug away from the dam and back upstream into safety.

Just lucky? Too many questions remain. What made me look around just in time? Why did I *not* panic? How did I manage to spin the scull around, keep my balance, and start moving back upstream? Today, more than half a century later, the old familiar phrase still echoes in my mind. Just six words: *But for the grace of God. . . .*

—ARTHUR GORDON

CHAPTER THREE

Out of the Night

Christmas Day
1944

Dear Mom,

This is a very different Christmas Day than I have ever spent in my life. Right now I'm living in the hayloft of a farmer's barn, and I'm very glad to be here rather than out in a foxhole somewhere . . .

The Battle of the Bulge. The final desperate attempt of the Germans to break through Allied lines in Belgium and dash to Antwerp and the sea. For six days our 84th Infantry Division had been diverted from the Ninth Army in the north to the beleaguered First Army area in the Ardennes forest. The fiercest fighting of the war, and I, a nineteen-year-old private, was in the middle of it.

My letter home to Pennsylvania was written on a Christmas morning that was sunny and quiet—deceptively quiet. "The barn I slept in last night," I wrote, "made me think of the place where Jesus came into the world." Then I began reminiscing to Mom about the good Christmases we'd had as I was growing up—always starting with the traditional dawn service at St. John's Lutheran in Boyertown. Church had always been an important part of my life. I'd started college thinking I might go into the ministry.

The letter home was upbeat all the way. I didn't mention anything about the things that had been troubling me. How I had become disillusioned with organized religion because I saw so few Christians either at home or in the combat zone—certainly not Christians trying to live the way Jesus had taught. Or how the weather had been so miserable and the fighting so blazing that I feared I'd never live to see Pennsylvania again.

The last straw was my being sent to these snow-covered hills and woods where we might be attacked at any moment from out there, somewhere. I was beginning to think that God had forsaken me.

Still, even though we'd spent the last five days floundering around trying to stop the Germans, even though our supply trucks had been captured, at least we'd had a barn for shelter on Christmas Eve, and our cooks were promising us a hot meal for Christmas Day.

"Let's go, men," Sergeant Presto, our squad leader, shouted. "Collect your gear and fall out. We're going on a mission."

I groaned. We all groaned. There went our first hot meal in a week!

We drove for about ten miles and then the trucks dropped us and sped away. It was dusk. Troops were strung out all along a dirt road that circled through some hills. When Presto came back from a meeting with the platoon leader, he gathered the ten of us—we were one man short in the squad—around him.

"Okay, men, here's what we're going to do. This won't take long and we're going to travel light. Leave your packs and entrenching tools here." He made it sound so simple. Intelligence had said that some German infantry were dug into a nearby hill and were causing havoc by shooting down on the roads in the area. Our battalion's job was to go up and flush them out.

Single file on each side of the winding road, we moved up the hill. We moved quietly, warily. At the top, we were surprised to find, not Germans, but an abandoned château in the middle of a clearing. Our squad went into the building. We found a billiard table and the tension broke as we played an imaginary game of pool using our rifles as cues.

Then Presto came stalking in. The Germans, he said, were in the woods beyond the clearing. Our orders were to chase them out into the waiting arms of another battalion positioned at the other end of the woods.

"There'll be three companies in this deal," Presto said. "Two of us will stretch out along the edge of the forest while the other hangs back in reserve. Now, as soon as we push into the woods, everybody fires, got it?"

We spread out, walked through the darkness to the forest's edge, then, at a signal, we burst in, opening up with everything we had. We kept up a brisk pace, keeping contact with our buddies along the moving line, walking and firing for about a mile. But the forest was empty. There was no movement anywhere...

The trees in front of us exploded. Suddenly, the night went bright with every kind of firing I'd ever seen or heard of—rifles, rifle-launched grenades, mortars, machine guns, tracers over our heads, bullets at our thighs. But worst of all, Tiger tanks. At least six of them, opening up point-blank with 88-millimeter cannons. Their projectiles whined and crashed all up and down our line.

Our intelligence was wrong, I thought angrily, as I flung myself down on my stomach. *They told us there were no tanks up here. Now we're really in for it.*

Within seconds men were screaming in pain all around me. I saw a tree with a big trunk and made a sudden lunge to get behind it, but I wasn't quick enough. Something tore into my thigh. There was hot, searing pain.

We were completely pinned down. The Tiger tanks kept scanning their turrets and firing on every yard of our line. The German ground troops sent their small arms fire into anything that moved.

The minutes went by. Five. Ten. Fifteen. Then came a lull in the barrage. I called over to my best buddy, Kane. We called him "Killer." He was the gentlest guy in our platoon, but we'd nicknamed him that after the popular comic strip character, "Killer Kane."

"Are you hurt, Killer?"

"Naw. But I think everybody else over here is. Presto's hit bad."

I called to Cruz on my right. He was our squad's B.A.R. man. There was no answer. Then I barely heard him whispering, "I'm hurt. Real bad. Floyd's dead. Corporal John's hit bad."

Well, I thought, if Presto's out and the Corporal, too, we don't have a leader.

The pounding started again, this time with flares so they could spot us better. We did some firing back and then the action subsided into another lull.

Down along the rear of our line came a figure, crawling. It was our platoon runner. "Captain says we're getting nowhere," he whispered to Killer and me. "We're pulling back in five minutes. Move out when you hear our covering fire."

I crawled over to Killer. "We've got to get our guys out of here," I said. "You go up your side and I'll go down mine, and we'll drag as many as possible to that big tree back there."

"How're we going to get them out of here, though?"

"I don't know," I said. "But we can't leave them lying here."

We were trapped. I lay there on the cold ground feeling helpless, that forsaken feeling again. Where was the God that I had prayed to during all those years of church and Sunday school back home in Pennsylvania? "And whatsoever ye shall ask in my name, that will I do," the Bible had said to me clearly (John 14:13). Was it necessary, when I needed help so badly, to ask?

"O Lord," I mumbled, "help us. We're trying to get our wounded buddies out of here. Show us the way."

I had no sooner started dragging Corporal John toward the meeting tree when the firing started up in the center of our line. *There's the sig-*

nal for pulling back, I thought frantically, *but we can't do it. The Germans will sweep in on us; they'll mop us up before we can pull back.*

Just as I got to the tree, I saw that Killer had brought back three wounded squad members. So we had six in all to get back. I closed my eyes and in desperation said: "In Your name, Lord, help us."

I opened my eyes. In the black of night, moving mysteriously among the shattered trees, a giant hulk came toward us. *The Germans,* my heart thumped, *they've broken out of the brush. They're bearing down on us.* No, it was something else, something unbelievable. It now came into full view and stopped beside our tree.

A horse.

A big, docile, shaggy chestnut, standing there without harness, as though awaiting our bidding.

Killer and I looked at each other in disbelief. We didn question then where the horse came from, or how, or why; we just got to work. Moving swiftly, we draped Cruz and the Corporal on the chestnut's broad back, then Mike and Presto. Then, with Killer carrying one of our buddies and me carrying the other, we led the horse out of the woods. At the clearing the horse trotted on ahead of us, straight to the château, and by the time Killer and I got there, our wounded were already on medical stretchers. The two men we carried in were cared for; the medics gave a quick look at my shrapnel wound; and then, as fast as we could, Killer and I went to find the horse. We wanted to pat him, give him some sugar, anything to make him sense our gratitude.

But he wasn't there. We looked everywhere, asked everyone we saw, but no one could tell us anything about him. He had simply vanished—gone from us as mysteriously as he had come.

The next morning at the aid station the shrapnel was removed from my leg, and at noon Killer and I lined up for our belated Christmas dinner. The day before, one hundred ninety men in our company would have answered the chow call; today there were thirty-five of us. All the wounded men in our squad had survived, however, though some were never to see action again.

Killer and I looked at the turkey and sweet potatoes in our mess kits. Hot and savory and long-awaited as this food was, we had no appetite. We were still too full of our emotions: the sorrow for lost buddies; the shock of our own survival; the strange, deeply affecting arrival and departure of the horse. We could not get the horse out of our minds then, nor have I since, for that noble creature did more than just save our lives; he reaffirmed my faith. I have always believed that on that

Christmas night forty-four years ago, God sent that horse to reassure a doubting soldier of His presence, even as He had sent His Son for that purpose on a Christmas night twenty centuries ago.   —JACK HARING

Doubt

He who doubts from what he sees
Will ne'er believe, do what you please.
If the sun and moon should doubt,
They'd immediately go out.

—WILLIAM BLAKE
FROM AUGURIES OF INNOCENCE

Adrift

NOTHING, IT SEEMED, could spoil that hot, windy day in June. At 10:00 A.M. my husband, Joe, and I pulled out of the driveway of our apartment in Gainesville, Florida, where Joe was getting his master's degree in architecture. Trailing behind our camper-truck was our sixteen-and-a-half-foot sailboat. We were headed for Cedar Key on Florida's Gulf coast.

"Just think, a whole afternoon of sailing," I said. Gringo, our big cinnamon-brown dog, wagged his tail. Joe whistled. It was starting so perfectly.

If anything at all threatened to mar the day it was the problem we'd wrestled with for weeks. Joe would finish graduate school in a couple of months, and after that, life curled up into big question marks: Where should we settle? Which job should we take? I'd worried till I was in knots. But now, as we bounced along the highway, I shoved aside my anxieties about the future. They could wait till I returned.

We arrived at the marina with the sun burning at high noon. As I stepped from the truck, a strong gust of wind squalled through the parking lot. I gazed out at the choppy blue water. A few emerald islands dotted the bay. And beyond that, the Gulf stretched to the horizon, immense and awesome. A peculiar feeling swept through me. Not really foreboding, just uneasiness.

We threw a twelve-ounce bottle of water in the boat, strapped on bright orange life jackets, and slid our sailboat into the water. "Hop on, Gringo," I called. Within minutes the three of us were careening out into the bay. I leaned over the side of our little turquoise boat to steady it against a fresh wind howling from the northeast.

Suddenly we slammed aground on a sandbar. I listened as the sand grated against the boat, hoping the centerboard wouldn't be damaged. Without that slim three-foot stabilizer that serves as a keel, we would lose practically all control.

"I'll shove us off" Joe yelled, pushing with an oar. Suddenly we broke free. Joe struggled to tack to the deeper channel waters. But something was wrong. The boat side-slipped through the blue-green swells like a car without a driver. The centerboard was obviously damaged. I wondered how badly. We were sliding sideways out of the bay! There was only one last island between us and open sea. The shoreline was shrinking to a green strip in the distance.

"Joe! We're passing the last island!"

"Don't worry, we'll make it," he said. Joe . . . always the optimist.

But around the island, the wind was even wilder. With windswept water slashing over our boat's sides, we were being pitched from wave to wave. I grabbed for terrified Gringo. "Lord," I whispered, "I think we're going to need Your help." But the gale seemed to tear the words away from my mouth.

Joe seized the anchor and threw it over. "Oh, no!" I screamed as the anchor line tore from its cleat. The rope snaked overboard and disappeared forever.

"Got to get the sails down," Joe shouted over the wind, "or we'll be blown out to sea!" In our haste we did lower them, but we knocked a fitting loose and lost the halyard that we'd need to raise the sail later.

We looked at each other in horrified silence. The only way we could hoist the sail again would be to lower the hinged mast to the deck and re-rig the line from its top. And that required a calm sea and no wind at all.

In desperation, Joe fitted oars into the oarlocks and tried to row. It was hopeless. We reeled on like a toothpick in a torrent. Now the sun was sinking into a fading orange haze. Night was coming . . . darkness on the ocean. I looked back toward land. It was gone. We were lost, blown into the open sea.

Soon darkness surrounded us. Black waves crashed against the boat, showering us with cold water. I shivered in the night wind. Joe helped me wrap up in the sails and we huddled in the cramped, decked-over cockpit area beneath the mast. The boat pitched so violently that we had to lash ourselves down with ropes to keep from going overboard. My body pounded the hard hull of the boat till I ached.

Then seasickness struck. All night as we slid through the dark, twisted labyrinth of water, I lay in agonizing nausea. I wondered... was anyone, anywhere, looking for us?

As dawn filtered into a Sunday sky and the relentless wind still blew, I looked out at the most terrifying sight of my life. Water. Everywhere. Like a jagged gray blanket, it stretched on forever.

"Joe, where are we?" I asked.

"We're a long way out," he said grimly. "We were blown southwest."

The sun became a white-hot laser. I licked my parched lips. "We'll have to save our water," Joe said, as he measured out a few sips. I drank, watching Gringo lick the salt water on the boat. How long could we last on twelve ounces of water in this heat?

Hours went by. I craned my neck, searching for an airplane. Not even a sea gull flew this far out. Our boat became a tiny floating island of hopelessness. I remembered the anxieties of yesterday. What to do after Joe finished graduate school suddenly seemed such a small, petty uncertainty.

The waves rolled by like the years of my life. Unconsciously, I laid my hand on Gringo's head. He turned his huge brown eyes up to mine. As I stared down into Gringo's eyes, something profound, yet simple, took place. I saw the look of trust. Trust that, despite everything, I was taking care of him, as always. And like an arrow, a thought came to my mind. *Why shouldn't I trust God just as Gringo was trusting me?*

Across the boat Joe was saying, "We're helpless. If only we could raise the sails again, but it's impossible with the wind and waves this rough."

The thought returned: *Trust.*

I spoke slowly, hesitantly. "Do you remember in the Bible when the disciples were caught in a storm on the Sea of Galilee?"

Joe looked at me strangely. "Go on."

"Jesus calmed the wind and waves for them," I said. "If He did it for the disciples, wouldn't He do it for us?"

So while the sun glowed low and golden on the ocean, we joined hands and prayed. "Please, Lord, we're trusting You to still the wind and water. Amen." Three minutes passed. Four. Five. And then, in a moment so awesome I can still scarcely believe it, the six-foot swells melted into a sheet of still water. The wind stopped abruptly. There wasn't a ripple or a sound.

Frantically we lowered the hinged mast to the deck and retrieved the line for hoisting the mainsail. "It'll work now," Joe said, raising the mast.

Our sails slatted in the still air. "Lord," I said, "we're ready. Please give us wind to blow us back east to shore."

As if the Creator's hand were moving across the sea, a steady wind began to blow. The sun hovered on the water. We were sailing away from it, east toward land! "Praise God," I rasped.

The moon rose in front of us. Since the wind was from the west, we could run before it with no need for our useless centerboard. For twelve hours, Joe clutched the rudder and the line controlling the mainsail. We guessed we'd been blown over a hundred miles out to sea. Yet, if this wind held, we could make land again.

As daylight approached, Joe neared complete exhaustion. We both collapsed in the tiny cockpit to sleep. When we awoke, the sea was a mirror of glass, the world an eerie vacuum of silence. The sails hung limp. What had happened to our east wind?"

"What does it mean?" I asked. Joe shook his head. Gringo paced nervously. Fear mounted in me like a tidal wave. Was this the calm before the storm I'd always heard about?

O God, I thought, You've brought us this far. Why have You left us here?

Trust Me, came the silent assurance. Trust? Stranded, without land in sight, our water gone, our bodies near collapse, and maybe a storm coming. Suddenly, it seemed too much to ask.

Joe crawled into the cockpit in despair. Even he, the eternal optimist, knew. We had reached the end.

I stared at the sea, too desolate to cry. "God," I whispered, "I was counting on You..." I stopped, my breath suspended. For in the distance, coming over the horizon was a cross. I rubbed my eyes and looked again. It was still there. A breath-taking white cross! It seemed to be rising straight out of the water. Was I hallucinating? Seconds later a boat rose beneath the cross. It was a cross-shaped mast. Dear God! It was real! My breath came back in muffled little gasps. A dazzling white boat was plowing right at us.

"Joe," I called, hardly able to find my voice. "A boat!" Joe leaped up, his eyes incredulous. As it churned closer, Joe raised his life jacket to the top of the mast. I waved my arms wildly.

Soon, a fifty-one-foot yacht was before us. Up on deck, an astonished boy peered down at us. "What in the world are you doing way out here?" he called.

I burst into tears as a vacationing doctor and his family appeared on deck and helped us aboard. We gathered around their table below, while the doctor checked his charts. He returned, shaking his head. "The course I set this morning on automatic pilot was eighteen miles off. An eighteen-mile deviation. I can't explain it."

But I could. There in the safe, solid cabin of the doctor's boat, it all ran together. The calming of the ocean, the sudden east wind, then its abrupt ceasing, an eighteen-mile alteration on sophisticated electronic navigation equipment—all this had made their big yacht and our little sailboat intersect exactly in the midst of endless time and water. God— a powerful, ingenious, caring God—had been there through every uncertain hour. And now I knew I could trust Him with very uncertainty . . . including those small, worrisome anxieties about the future still waiting for us at home.

A few hours later a storm smashed into the Gulf, twisting the sea into savage ten-foot waves. But I leaned back, enveloped in the thundering sound of the storm, at peace. My future, like the sea, rested in very good hands.

—SANDY FEATHERS-BARKER

The Tractor Moved

"Ask, and it shall be given you," Jesus said (Matthew 7:7). I've always believed this, but never so totally as the day of the accident in 1978.

The grass on our 121-acre dairy farm needed cutting, so I hitched a set of mower blades to my tractor and went to work. The tractor was huge, and for added traction on our up-and-down Maryland terrain, its rear wheels were filled with five hundred pounds of fluid, and a two hundred-pound weight hung from each hub.

When I finished the job, I was on a slight uphill grade near our chicken house. I switched off the ignition and climbed down from the high seat. I was unfastening the mower blades when the tractor started moving backward.

I tried to twist around and jump up on the seat, but I didn't make it. The tractor's drawbar hit me in the knees, knocking me flat, and the seven hundred-pound left wheel rolled over my chest and stopped on top of it. I struggled for breath. The pain was agonizing. I knew I was facing death, and I made my request.

"Please, God," I begged, "release me."

At that moment the tractor began to move.

It went forward enough to free my chest, and—to my astonishment—it moved *uphill!*

My dog, and then a farmhand, found me; and after six broken ribs, two fractures and twelve days in the hospital I was back home, talking with the Maryland state trooper called to investigate the accident. "I won't try to explain it officially," he told me. "Why, a dozen men couldn't have moved that tractor off you."

Twelve men or twelve hundred, it didn't matter. Asking God's help did.

—*LLOYD B. WILHIDE*

Explosion over Little Rock

THE HUGE STRATEGIC AIR COMMAND BOMBER swung into position for takeoff. The six jet engines whined with power as they lifted the giant aircraft off the runway into the gray light of dawn. Climbing slowly, since it was fully loaded with highly volatile fuel (the equivalent of three large tank truckloads), the B-47 turned on a heading that would put it over the heart of nearby Little Rock, Arkansas, in less than five minutes, at an altitude of eighteen thousand feet. The date was March 31, 1960.

In the copilot's seat, 1st Lt. Tom Smoak, a native of Richmond, Virginia, let his thoughts run back to the hours before takeoff. The alarm had gone off at 3:15 A.M. and he had slipped quietly out of bed to keep from waking his wife, Betsy. He followed his usual custom of spending those first few moments reading his Bible, communing with God in a "quiet time."

Tom picked up a card on which he had written a Bible verse he intended to memorize on this particular flight. It read: "The steps of a good man are ordered by the Lord: and he delighteth in his way. Though he fall, he shall not be utterly cast down: for the Lord upholdeth him with his hand" (Psalm 37:23–24).

Opening the closet he looked at the two flight suits that hung before him. One was the light, comfortable nylon suit which pilots prefer to wear. The other was the heavy, bulky, fire-resistant suit which he seldom wore because of its awkwardness. Tom reached for the heavy flight suit. He didn't question the decision, simply having a deep feeling that God intended it to be that way. The morning of miracles had begun.

The radio crackled to life in the cockpit of the B-47. Tom wrote a message on his clipboard as the plane climbed up to eighteen thousand feet. Suddenly it began to lurch and vibrate violently. Tom knew that the airplane was out of control and automatically reached for the ejection seat release in case he needed it. He never got a chance to pull the release. Without warning the airplane exploded. It was 6:07 A.M. and they were directly over the heart of Little Rock.

Tom's only thought was escape. The canopy blew off but before he could fire the seat ejection release he was instantaneously immersed in tons of burning fuel that poured into the cockpit. Tom knew he was going to die.

There were more explosions as the fuel tanks under the cockpit ignited. The fuselage broke in two immediately behind him. Tom screamed at the top of his lungs. He prayed. Not that he would live, but that he would die quickly. Strapped in the wreckage, he was burning alive as he hurtled towards the earth below.

Tom's helmet was ripped off by the force of the explosions. His whole head was engulfed in flames. His hands were a mass of burning flesh. The fire-resistant suit melted where it stretched tightly across his knees and shoulders.

Tom passed out from the pain. When he opened his eyes moments later his head was bent grotesquely forward and the only thing his eyes could focus on was his safety belt.

All his training warned him against loosening that belt. To loosen the belt would disengage the automatic ejection seat, his only hope of escape. Yet in that fleeting moment of consciousness, going against all training, he reached forward with a burning hand and released the safety belt. Again, he lapsed into unconsciousness.

When he opened his eyes a second time he was swinging from his parachute—free from the wreckage which was plummeting towards the city below. He assumed his ejection seat had fired anyway, or that he had released his parachute manually.

What actually had happened was that the fire which burned Tom so badly also burned away the canvas parachute pack. When Tom loosened his safety belt it separated him from his seat and allowed the parachute to unravel inside the cockpit. The wind, whistling through the falling wreckage, grabbed the parachute silk and literally sucked him out of the fuselage, allowing him to float free of the falling plane.

The pain was gone. As he dangled from the cords of his parachute he watched the wreckage plummet into the heart of the city below. Fires were breaking out in a dozen different places as the burning fuel splashed onto the innocent roofs.

Suddenly he realized the parachute was not descending at a normal rate. In fact, the ground was rushing up toward him at incredible speed. He tore his gaze away from the earth and looked upwards. The same fire that had burned off the canvas pack had also burned away one-fourth of the chute itself. He wasn't floating, but hurtling towards the housetops below. He began to pray again.

Others were praying also.

At 6:07 A.M. most of the people in the city were just getting up. Like many others, Mrs. O.B. Holeman heard the ear-shattering explosion and raced into her front yard. What she saw horrified her. Three and a half miles above the city was a tremendous fireball. Seven minutes later, out of that fireball, appeared a rapidly falling parachute. She began to pray for that lone, dangling survivor.

Her husband tried to calm her, but she became almost hysterical beseeching the Lord to save that helpless man. As she prayed, Tom Smoak's streaming parachute slipped him away from the heart of the city—directly towards the Holeman's backyard.

Mrs. Holeman, a nurse, said, "I was standing in my front yard and saw him coming down at a tremendous rate of speed, going over my rooftop, and into my back yard." She screamed as he disappeared, realizing that he would smash into her concrete driveway.

Even though Tom had led his class in basic training in parachute jumping, he knew that this time the end had come. One boot had been burned off. The horribly burned flesh was exposed. He breathed a final prayer of commitment as he saw the concrete driveway rush up to meet him.

The summer before the Holemans had debated cutting down two identical trees that spanned their driveway. They decided to let them stand. That morning, when Tom Smoak hurtled out of the heavens, his streaming parachute snagged the tops of both trees. They were the exact height of the combined length of his parachute silk, cords, and his body. As he flashed by them they grabbed his chute, bent inward just enough to let him recline softly on the driveway, and then gently straightened up, pulling him into an upright position.

When the Holemans and their neighbors rushed into the back yard, instead of a broken body they found a badly burned but very much alive Tom Smoak, standing on his good foot—and giving orders how to unfasten the parachute harness.

Two persons died on the ground that morning, and of the four crewmen aboard the plane Tom Smoak was the only survivor.

Tom spent the next two years going through twenty operations for plastic surgery. The doctors marveled that no fire had touched his lungs, eyes, or throat.

Because Tom Smoak believes that God saves to serve, today [written in 1968] he is back in the air again. This time he flies for the Lord as a member of the flying team for Wycliffe Bible Translators. He knows that a day committed to God is never wasted. And occasionally as he pilots missionaries and Bible translators into the steaming jungles of South America, Tom remembers that morning of miracles and he likes to paraphrase a verse that explains for him the whole experience of that day: "For he shall give his angels charge over thee, to keep thee in all thy ways. They shall bear thee up in their hands, lest thou dash thy foot against" (Psalm 91:11–12). —JAMIE BUCKINGHAM

Thin Ice

THE TEMPERATURE HAD HOVERED between freezing and zero for almost a week. When I got home from work that Friday in February, I glanced at the frozen Rocky River, just a few feet from our door—and it looked inviting.

"What about having some friends over for skating tonight?" I asked my wife, Sylva. Whenever the ice was good, we liked to floodlight the area behind our house and play skating music on the hi-fi. Afterward skaters would come upstairs for cookies and coffee before a roaring fire in our living room. But this time Sylva said no. She is a registered nurse and she had been working at the hospital since 7:00 A.M., so she was very tired.

The sun was still shining and I figured there would be a good half hour before dark for me to skate. Down the stairs I went and put on my skates on the dock under our house. The ice tested very strong, the temperature was twenty-two degrees, and there was no wind—a great combination. It was exhilarating. At a smooth clip I traveled across the lagoon in back of our house and suddenly felt so invigorated that I decided to skate on—to the river, up the west channel, and around the island on which the Cleveland Yachting Club is located. The club was closed for February; it looked like a ghost town of dry-docked boats.

"Great skating!" I shouted happily to a woman skating with some children, the only people around. I shot ahead, under the little bridge that connected the island to the far bank, on and on until I headed once more into the river, clipping along, now in the middle, a hundred feet from shore, when . . .

Oh, oh—a patch of soft ice. Slush. I thought I could coast through it, but I slowed down. I stroked with my right foot; the ice gave way under it. I tried to stroke with the other, but *it* broke through. I was in trouble. Bad trouble.

Immediately I knew why. It was because of the big bridge high above me. For days the city had been spreading salt on it to melt the snow on the roadbed. The salt had filtered down to the river, softening the wide path of ice I had skated into. Now I found myself sinking through the ice, then suddenly plunging up to my neck in freezing water.

I did not panic. I did not thrash about. I hollered. I pounded away at the mushy ice in an attempt to reach ice firm enough to support me. I knew I had to do something fast, for I had read somewhere that a person can survive only three minutes in freezing water. I was aware, too, of an unusual fact about myself—that I am incapable of floating. I'm so thin, more bones than flesh, that I have what is called negative buoyancy—when I'm not moving my arms or legs in water, I sink to the bottom.

I tried to work myself toward firmer ice by breaking off small pieces along the edge. But it was taking too much time. This way I'd freeze to death before I'd ever get out. I could hear no one answering my cries; the bridge above me was humming with rush-hour traffic, yet I knew, because of the railing and the angle, that no one in a passing car could see me. I simply had to think of another way to get myself out of the water.

Then it came to me. I swim regularly, every week, and it was not unusual for me to swim the length of the "Y" pool underwater. I looked at the shore a hundred feet away and realized that if I could swim that distance under the ice, I could break through at the shore. It was a gamble, but I saw no hope any other way. I took one last look around to see if anyone was in sight. No one. "And if I don't make it," I said to myself, "no one except God will ever know what happened."

There in the water, about to dive under the ice, thinking of God, I felt ashamed before Him. "I'm sorry," I prayed to Him. "I'm sorry I've been so careless with Your precious gift of life. I want to live, God. I want desperately to live, but I'll accept Your will."

In those brief moments I didn't ask God to save my life. It had been a long time since I had asked Him for anything at all. Sylva and I had married in 1953 and, of course, we wanted children. We did everything we could, including a lot of praying, but no children came. After praying for ten years I had come to the conclusion that God wasn't listening to me.

But He was listening now. I wasn't asking Him for help or for my life, yet now He was present; I could feel His closeness as I prepared myself for the plunge under the ice.

Don't do it! came the feeling.

I was mystified. I had set my mind on the plan.

Don't do it! came the feeling again.

My mind told me one thing, but His presence told me another. I had to decide now, this second.

I gave myself over to that inner command. But then I had no hope.

It was a matter of minutes, maybe two, when I saw the police car on the yachting club island and nearby, across the stretch of obviously treacherous ice, I saw a policeman standing in the dusk, looking at me. "Throw me a rope!" I yelled. He disappeared. At first I had had a surge of optimism, but now that he was gone from me, I despaired. "Hurry," I said to myself frantically. "Hurry!" Could he know how little time I had left?

I heard voices. "We're going to throw you a rope."

Throw it now.' I thought to myself. I could feel the paralysis setting in. It came fast. At first I couldn't move my legs. My arms stiffened. There was no part of me that I could move. No longer now was I thinking about ropes. I was thinking about . . . boyhood vacations on Mackinac Island . . . Sylva and me on a flying honeymoon . . . sailing on a moonlit night . . .

My hands . . . I saw my hands slip away from the surface of the ice. Yet I was experiencing a peace that was serene and actually pleasant. I felt my head go under the water. I felt icy water entering my mouth. I was sinking, but now I could move neither arms nor legs. I was rigid.

And then, suddenly, mysteriously, the power was there. I *could* move my arms. I pushed them down in the water. My head came up. I breathed again. And there in front of me was an orange life preserver. The last thing I remember was reaching for it.

My next awareness was opening my eyes and seeing the doctor peering into my face. He said, "There's someone here I'm sure you want to see." It was Sylva.

"How did I get here?" I asked, bewildered. Her answer was a litany of many miracles.

A bus was crossing the bridge at the precise moment I fell through the ice. The driver, sitting high up, saw me and radioed his dispatcher, who called the police. A girl happened to be walking along our river-front road on her way to a baby-siting job. She heard my cries for help and rushed to our neighbor's house. The neighbor stepped outside, saw me in the river, and then she also called the police.

A policeman came, then went to his car to radio for extra help, while I held on to the orange life preserver that had been thrown to me. My rescuers were able to walk about halfway out on the ice before it started to crack, and a rope was thrown, which they say I grabbed, but let slip through my hands when they started to pull on it.

By then a crowd had gathered on the island. Three times my head went under the water, each time the crowd gasping, shouting that I was gone, and three times my head came back up, spouting water. Finally a dinghy was found and one of the policemen rushed it to the spot where I was appearing and disappearing. I was submerged, completely out of sight before he could get to me, but he reached his arm down over the dinghy into the water and, miraculously, connected with the collar of my jacket. The dinghy nearly capsized as he tried to drag me into it, but he hung on to me as I dangled from its side, and we were pulled to safety. Oxygen in the ambulance kept me alive during the rush to the hospital.

Later I figured that I was in the freezing water a minimum of twelve minutes. I was unconscious for three hours. The doctor in the emergency room at the hospital said he never saw a person alive with a pH blood factor as low as mine—six. When I was in the icy water I was not aware of the pain, but I was shivering from cold when I came to, calling for blankets. I spent one night in the intensive-care unit of the hospital and, to the doctors' amazement, the patient who was in critical condition on arrival was permitted to return home the next day. Two months later my heart was back to normal, and eight months later the nerves in my arms and legs had regenerated.

It took about a week for me to believe fully that I wasn't just dreaming and was really living. Since then, life for me has taken on a new meaning. I am more appreciative of being alive. I feel very grateful to God for sparing my life and to the five people who had a major part in my rescue. Since then, too, a lot of questions have been answered for me.

Where did the message come from that stopped me from my rash plan to swim under the ice?

When my body was paralyzed, where did the power come from that let my arms move again?

When I was unconscious under the water, why didn't the current sweep me downstream?

I know the answers to those questions now, for I've learned that God is always listening. He hears our prayers. When it is within His plan to answer them, He can work miracles. He did for me.

—WILLIAM G. BENKELMAN

Someone's Kidding!

WHEN I WAS OUT OF THE ARMY and uncertain about my direction in life, I got a job at Superior Marking Products in Chicago, a company that made ink, type, type trays, date stamps, toy printing presses—anything that had to do with printing. I operated a vacuum press and enjoyed it, and I enjoyed my fellow workers. Especially Joe.

Joe was a big, burly man with a deep faith. He'd been at Superior for almost thirty years and commanded a lot of respect. Whenever he talked, we listened. But I never listened more closely than during an afternoon coffee break when he told us about something that had happened to him years before, right there in our company warehouse.

Joe had been in the warehouse, working. He was alone. When the time came to leave, he turned out the lights and headed for the freight elevator. He could hear his own footsteps echo in the silence as he walked down the dark aisles. He was about to step into the freight elevator when he heard, "Joe, Joe."

Someone was calling his name. He turned and looked still, but he could see no one. "Who's there?" he called out.

No answer.

Someone's kidding me, Joe thought. He called out again, but still there was no answer. He shrugged and turned again to the elevator, but this time he stopped.

Before him were the open doors of the elevator shaft, but no elevator, only a long, long drop into nothingness. —KENNITH BISHOP

O God of the Impossible!

O God of the impossible!
Since all things are to Thee

But soil in which Omnipotence
　　Can work almightily,

Each trial may to us become
　　The means that will display
How o'er what seems impossible
　　Our God hath perfect sway!

The very storms that beat upon
　　Our little barque so frail,
But manifest Thy power to quell
　　All forces that assail.

The things that are to us too hard,
　　The foes that are too strong,
Are just the very ones that may
　　Awake a triumph song.

O God of the impossible,
　　When we no hope can see,
Grant us the faith that still believes
　　ALL possible to Thee!

　　　　　　　　　　—*J.H.S.*

Of old thou didst speak in a vision. —Psalm 89:19, RSV

CHAPTER FOUR

God Prepares Us in Dreams and Visions

In the Bible the lives of two Josephs, centuries apart, were drastically influenced by message-laden dreams that God allowed them to interpret. God still speaks to us through dreams and sometimes visions, though not every dream is a meaningful message. Many of the stories in this section tell of dreams that seemed significant only with hindsight, as they increased the dreamer's sensitivity to an upcoming event, preparing him for action, helping him walk with confidence through a difficult transition. The dreams and visions described here served to assure the writers of God's knowledge, care, and love.

It's More Than a Dream

I SUPPOSE NONE OF US KNOWS the meaning of dreams. But I know what prayers can do.

I was working the three-to-eleven shift at Miners Hospital in Spangler, Pennsylvania, when a patient I was feeding asked, "Why don't you have a little pin on like the other nurses?"

"I do," I said, reaching to show him the golden, wreath-shaped R.N. pin on my collar—one of my proudest possessions. It had been given to me when I graduated from nursing school in Altoona, and it stood for years of hard work and study. But now, when I looked down, the pin was gone.

I knew I had pinned it to my uniform just before I left the house. I looked everywhere for it. A colleague and I searched through all the linens and bedside equipment but found nothing. I even took a mop and dusted under the beds. At home I turned the place upside down. No pin. Of course, I could replace it, but a substitute would never mean as much. That night as I lay in bed, I prayed that the Lord would help me find it.

Soon I was asleep. In the deep of night I had a dream. I dreamed that I got out of bed, put on my duster and slippers, and ran downstairs and out the door to a puddle of water in front of the house. And in the puddle was my pin.

The next morning I awoke disappointed. "It was only a dream," I muttered to myself. "A worthless dream." But as my head cleared, I seemed to hear a voice saying, *No, it's more than a dream. Go. See.*

I put on my duster and slippers and walked out to the road in front of our house, and there found a puddle of water. I placed my hand into the brown water. In a moment I held in my hand an answered prayer.

—*MARY LaMAGNA ROCCO*

The Dream That Wouldn't Go Away

BACK WHEN I WAS A YOUNG LIVESTOCK RANCHER north of Roosevelt, Utah, the news one cold November morning reported that a California doctor and his wife were missing on a flight from Custer, South Dakota, to Salt Lake City. As a student pilot, I had just completed my first cross-country flight with an instructor, though I had only twenty solo hours.

Paying close attention to all radio reports on the search, I was very disturbed two days later by a newscast saying that Dr. Robert Dykes and his wife, Margery, both in their late twenties and parents of two young children, were not likely to be found until spring—and maybe not even then. They had been missing four days, and the temperature had been below zero every night. There seemed little chance for their survival without food and proper clothing.

That night before I retired I said a simple prayer for these two people I didn't know. "Dear God, if they're alive, send someone to them so they will be able to get back to their family."

After a while I drifted off to sleep. In a dream I saw a red plane on a snow-swept ridge and two people waving for help. I awoke with a start. *Was it the Dykeses? What color was their plane?* I didn't remember any of the news reports ever mentioning it.

I couldn't get back to sleep for some time. I kept reasoning that because I'd been thinking of the couple before falling asleep, it was natural for me to dream them. When I finally did go to sleep, the dream came again! A red plane on a ridge—but now farther away. I could still see two people waving, and could now see some snow-covered mountain peaks in the background.

I got out of bed and spread out the only air chart I owned. It covered a remote area in Utah—the High Uintas region, along the Wyoming-Utah border. The Dykeses' flight plan presumably had to pass over this range. I was familiar with the rugged terrain, for I had fished and hunted it as a boy. My eyes scanned the names on the chart—Burrow Peak, Painters Basin, Kings Peak, Gilbert Peak.

Again I went to bed. And again, incredibly, the dream returned! Now the plane was barely in sight. I could see a valley below. Then it came to me in a flash—Painters Basin and Gilbert Peak! I rose in a cold sweat. It was daylight.

Turning on the news, I found there had been no sign of the plane and the search had been called off. All that day, doing chores around the ranch, I could think of nothing but the Dykeses and my dream. I felt God had shown me where those people were and that they were alive. But who would believe me and what could I do about it? I knew I wasn't really qualified to search for them myself. I knew, too, that even trying to explain my dream to my flight instructor, a stern taskmaster named Joe Mower, would have me laughed out of the hangar.

I decided to go to our small rural airport anyway. When I arrived, a teenaged boy who was watching the place told me Joe had gone to town for the mail.

The force that had been nudging me all morning seemed to say, "Go!" I had the boy help me push an Aeronca plane out. When he asked where I was going, I said, "To look for the Dykeses." I gave the plane the throttle and was on my way.

Trimming out, I began a steady climb and headed for Uinta Canyon. I knew what I was doing was unwise, even dangerous, but the danger seemed a small thing compared to what I felt in my heart.

As I turned east near Painters Basin, I was beginning to lose faith in my dream; there was no sign of the missing plane. The high winds, downdrafts and rough air were giving me trouble in the small sixty-five-horsepower plane. Terribly disappointed as well as frightened, I was about to turn back when suddenly there it was! A red plane on Gilbert Peak, just as I had seen in my dream.

Coming closer, I could see two people waving. I was so happy I began to cry. "Thank You, God," I said over and over.

Opening the plane's window, I waved at the Dykeses and wigwagged my wings to let them know I saw them. Then I said a prayer to God to help me get back to the airport safely.

Thirty minutes later I was on the ground. When I taxied up and cut the motor, I gulped, for Joe Mower was there to greet me.

"You're grounded," he hollered. "You had no permission to take that plane up."

"Joe," I said quickly, "I know I did wrong, but listen, I found the Dykeses and they need help."

"You're crazy," Joe said, and he continued to yell at me. My finding the lost plane in an hour and a half when hundreds of planes had searched in vain for nearly a week was more than Joe could believe. Finally I turned away from Joe, went straight for a telephone and did what I should have done in the first place. I called the CAP (Civil Air Patrol) in Salt Lake City. When they answered, I asked if there had been any word on the Dykeses' plane. They said there was no chance of their being alive now and that the search had ended.

"Well, I've found them," I said. "And they're both alive."

Behind me, Joe stopped chewing me out, his eyes wide and his mouth open.

"I'll round up food and supplies," I continued to the CAP, "and the people here will get it to them as soon as possible." The CAP gave me the go-ahead.

Everyone at the airport went into action. Within one hour we were on our way. A local expert pilot, Hal Crumbo, would fly in the supplies. I would lead the way in another plane. I wasn't grounded for long!

Back in the air, we headed for the high peaks. Hal's plane was bigger and faster than the Aeronca I was in. He was flying out ahead and above me. When I got to Painters Basin, at eleven thousand feet, I met the severe downdrafts again. I could see Hal circling above me and knew he was in sight of the downed plane and ready to drop supplies. Since I couldn't go any higher, I turned around.

Back at the airport I joined a three-man ground rescue party, which would attempt to reach the couple on horseback.

Another rescue party had already left from the Wyoming side of the mountains. For the next twenty-four hours our party hiked through fierce winds and six-foot snowdrifts. At twelve thousand feet, on a ridge near Gilbert Peak, we stopped. In the distance, someone was yelling. Urging our freezing feet forward, we pressed on, tremendously excited. Suddenly, about a hundred yards in front of us, we saw the fuselage of a small red plane rammed into a snowbank. Nearby, two people flapped their arms wildly.

Charging ahead, we shouted with joy. At about the same time that we reached the Dykeses, the other rescue party was coming over the opposite ridge.

After much hugging and thanking, I learned what a miracle the Dykeses' survival was. They had had nothing to eat but a candy bar, and their clothing was scant—Mrs. Dykes had a fur coat, but her husband had only a topcoat. The altitude made starting a fire impossible and at night they huddled together in their downed plane, too afraid to go to sleep.

"We had all but given up, had even written notes as to who should look after the children," Mrs. Dykes said. Then turning to me, she said, "But when we saw your plane, it was the most wonderful thing . . . our prayers were answered, a dream come true."

"Yes," I said, smiling, suddenly feeling as Solomon in the Bible must have felt after he received a visit from the Lord one night in a dream (1 Kings 3:5–14).

My dream, like Solomon's, had occurred for a reason. In His own special way, God gave me that dream in order to help give life to two others. In the most mysterious of ways, He had shown me He is always there, always listening. He had heard my prayers and the Dykeses' prayers and had answered all of us in His own infallible way. —*George Hunt*

Three Months in His Presence

W HEN FRIENDS ASK how I first discovered that my hands have been given a ministry of healing, I'm sure they don't expect to hear the kind of story that I am about to set down. Apparently the fact that I am a suburban housewife who looks for bargains and has to watch her weight seems a poor beginning to a story of divine intervention.

It started the year my father entered the tuberculosis sanitarium in Tampa, Florida. We had long since given up hope. He was too old for an operation and we had seen the X rays. The last thing on earth that would have occurred to any of us—Mother or my sister or me—was to ask God to step in and change medical facts.

And yet my husband, Ed, and I were active church members. As a banker, Ed was head of fund-raising, our two children went to Sunday school and I belonged to all the usual groups. We were, in short, typical, civic-minded churchgoers. Which is why the tears, when they began, caused us so much embarrassment.

It was in October, driving home from a PTA meeting, that I suddenly began to cry. I was in charge of the Halloween carnival that year, and at the meeting there had been some criticism of the plans. When I was still crying at bedtime, Ed put his arms around me and said, "Honey, all the carnivals in the world aren't that important."

But it wasn't the carnival. Even as I cried I knew that those tears were for something far bigger. I cried myself to sleep and in the morning, as soon as I opened my eyes, the tears started again. I choked them back while I fixed breakfast. But as soon as Ed and the children left, I burst into tears again.

This incredible state of affairs lasted four days. I took to wearing dark glasses even in the house so that my family would not guess how constantly I was crying. I was sure I was having a nervous breakdown.

It was on the morning of the fourth day, after Ed and the children had left, that a curious change took place. I saw nothing. I heard nothing. Yet all at once there was power in the air around me. The atmosphere itself seemed to hum and crackle as though I stood in the center of a vast electrical storm. As I try to put it into words it sounds fantastic, but at the time there was no sense that something beyond the possible was taking place.

I had sunk into the high-backed chair in the living room when suddenly through the window I saw the eastern horizon. Trees and houses stood between me and it, but I seemed to see right beyond to the place where earth and sky came together. And there, where they met, was a ball of light.

The light was moving, traveling toward me with amazing speed. It appeared white, yet from it poured all the colors I had ever seen.

And then it was beside me. Although it seemed impossible that anything with such energy could hold still, it took a position at my right shoulder and there it stayed. And as I stared, I started to smile. I smiled because He was smiling at me. For I now saw that it was not light, but a face.

How can I put into words the most beautiful countenance I have ever seen? "He is perfect" was the first thought that came. His forehead was high, His eyes exceptionally large. But I could never fix the color of His eyes any more than I could the color of the sea.

More, much more, than individual features was the overwhelming impression of life—unhampered life, life so brimming over with power and freedom that all living things I had seen till then seemed lumps of clay by comparison.

Not for a moment did I hesitate to call this Life at my side Jesus. And two things about Him struck me most. The first was His humor. I was astonished to see Him often break into outright laughter. And the second was His utter lack of condemnation. That He knew me down to my very marrow—knew all the stupid, cruel, silly things I had ever done—I realized at once. But I also saw that none of those things, or anything I would ever do, could alter the absolute caring, the unconditional love, that I saw in those eyes.

I could not grasp it. It was too immense a fact. I felt that if I gazed at Him for a thousand years I could not realize it all.

I did not have a thousand years; I had three months. For as long as that, the face of Jesus stayed beside me, never fading, never withdrawing. Many times I tried to tell someone else what I saw but the words would never come. And meanwhile I carried on with my tasks—meals and shopping and the PTA with its carnival—but effortlessly, scarcely knowing I was doing them, so fixed were my thoughts on Him.

At the same time, I had never seemed so aware of other people. How this was possible when my mind was full of Him alone I don't know, but it was true. My husband, especially. Far from feeling that a third person had entered our marriage, I felt that Christ *was* the marriage, as though all along He had been the force drawing us together.

And the Bible! All at once I couldn't read enough of it. It was like tearing open a letter from someone who had known this Presence as a flesh-and-blood person, full of just the kind of specific details I longed to hear. Certain passages in particular had a strange effect on me. When the Bible described Jesus' healing someone, the actual print on the page seemed to burn. The hand that touched it tingled as if I had touched an electric current.

And then one afternoon before the children got home, I was sitting, just looking at Him, when all of a sudden, in a patch of sunlight on the wall, appeared the X ray of my father's chest. It was all scar tissue and cavities. Then as I watched, a white mist moved slowly up the wall. When it passed the diseased tissue, there appeared on my wall a picture of a healthy lung.

"Then Dad's well!" I said aloud, and at that the Person at my side burst into peal after peal of joyous laughter, which said that wholeness was always God's way.

I thought my heart would burst as I waited for the next Wednesday's X ray. I enjoyed the scene in my mind again and again, imagining the ring of the telephone and Mother's voice stammering with excitement, "Darling—the most amazing—the most glorious—"

But when Mother called, her voice was flat. "The most annoying thing, Virginia. They got the slides mixed up! Poor Dad's got to go back for X rays tomorrow. Why, they sent down pictures of someone who never even had TB . . . !"

But, of course, the next day's X rays showed no sign of disease either; Dad was healed and lived out his long life in thanksgiving to God.

And it was Dad's healing that convinced me I must try to describe the indescribable that had happened to me. I went to an elderly pastor whom I had known a long time. To my astonishment he understood me at once. He gave me some books that described fairly similar things.

Then he said the words I have wished unsaid so many, many times. "Don't be surprised, Virginia, if the vision fades after a time. They usually do, you know."

Fade! I thought, as I drove home with that joyous Presence beside me. *Oh, it can't, it mustn't!* For the first time in the whole unbelievable experience my attention veered from Him to myself. And in that instant the vision was diminished, it actually disappeared for a second or two, though right away the radiant face was beside me again.

But the damage was done. The seed of self-concern was sown. The bright Presence would sometimes be missing for an hour or more. The more worried I got, the more self-centered I grew. *What have I done? What will I do without Him?* When He did return there would be no accusation in His eyes, just a tremendous compassion, as though He realized how difficult it had become for me to see Him.

At last all that was left of this experience was the strange tingling in my hands as I read the Bible stories of healing. One day I was visiting a friend in the hospital. She was hemorrhaging and in pain. On an impulse I reached out and touched her. My hand began to burn just as it did during the Bible reading. My friend gave a little sigh of comfort and fell asleep. When the doctor examined her, he found that the hemorrhaging had stopped.

Over the next eight years there were dozens, scores of experiences of that kind, all as inexplicable as the first. And yet for me they were still years of emptiness and waiting. "I will always be with you," He had said when I last saw Him.

"But how will I know if I can't see You?" I called to Him, for He had seemed so far away.

"You will see Me," He said, and then He was gone.

But the years went by and the vision had not come back. And then one day, while speaking to a church group, I saw those love-lit eyes smiling once again into mine. I looked again. The eyes belonged to a lady in the second row. Suddenly the room was full of Him; He was in the eyes of everyone there. "You will see Me . . ."

I used to wonder what would have happened if the old pastor had never spoken of the vision's fading. Might I have had it forever? I think not. I think that the days when Jesus was real to my eyes were the days of the "childhood" of my faith, the joyous, effortless time of discovery. But I do not think He lets it stay that way.

He didn't for His first disciples; He doesn't for us today. He gives us a glimpse only. Perhaps He let me look so long because I am slow to learn. But, finally, He takes away all sensory clues. He is bigger than our eyes and ears can make Him, so He gives us instead the eyes of faith, and every human being in which to discover His face.   —*Virginia Lively*

My Sailor Boy

I was married at seventeen, and my children—one boy and four girls—were born close together. The doctor said if I had another baby, I would die. But before long I was expecting again. The doctor said the pregnancy must be terminated. I pondered and prayed. Reluctantly, I decided to comply, and wearied from this decision, I lay down to rest.

After a brief nap I awoke to see—as clearly as I've ever seen anyone—a sailor boy. He was smiling and his sailor cap rested jauntily on the back of his head. On his forehead were short, shiny curls. I don't know why, but as I looked at this apparition, it came to me that I must cancel the impending surgery. I went on to bear a son named Robert.

Years later, in World War II, we received word that our elder son, Jack, had been killed. One day as I sat crying, young Robert touched my arm and said, "Mama, look at me. You've still got *me*." With that intense statement from the heart of my little boy, my numbness began to recede.

Robert grew and then he, too, joined the service. He was stationed in Pearl Harbor and we didn't see him for a long time. Then we got a wire that he was coming home. The day before he was to arrive, I was in the kitchen mixing a cake when I heard the door open. I turned around, and standing there was the same sailor boy I'd seen years before. He was smiling and his sailor cap rested jauntily on the back of his head. On his forehead were short, shiny curls.

It took a moment for me to realize that this was my son Robert, surprising us by coming home a day early. It was Robert, the son I almost didn't have. —ADA ADAMS, AS TOLD TO PHYLLIS SJOBLOM

Jason's Dream

GOOD NIGHT, JASON." I leaned down and gently kissed my eight-year-old son's forehead as he snuggled under his comforter. He was wearing his favorite baseball pajamas. His hair, always a little too long, fanned out over the pillow. His eyes were already closed when I turned to leave. But as I was pulling the door shut, he called to me.

"Mom? I just had a dream."

I returned to Jason's bedside. "Honey, you haven't even been to sleep yet. How could you have had a dream?"

"I don't know, Mom. It just came to me right after I said my prayers." His brown eyes held a serious expression. "I was in school, at my desk," he said in a strange matter-of-fact tone.

All of a sudden, I fell over onto the floor. People were staring at me. I was dead."

I sat with Jason until he fell asleep. His "dream" was disturbing. It seemed more than just a child's imagination.

Several times in my life I'd had similar experiences. I remember suddenly knowing my grandmother would die. Though she appeared to be perfectly healthy, she left us three days later. And I remember being certain a seemingly happy couple was having deep marital difficulties. I don't know how I knew; I just knew. Outwardly, they were the picture of marital bliss. A year later they admitted they had been near divorce at the time.

I went to bed wondering what Jason's dream was all about. Was it some kind of warning?

By the following week, however, the incident had been pushed to the back of my mind. Our home in Merritt Island, Florida, was a busy place, and I had plenty of other things to think about. Jason's school activities and caring for Nicole, his lively three-year-old sister, for example. Then one night a week later, I sat up abruptly in bed, wide awake. It was after midnight, and Jack, my husband, was sleeping soundly. For a moment I thought it was he who had woken me. But before I could give it another thought, I was overwhelmed with the need to pray—to pray for Jason.

As I eased out of bed, I felt tears streaming down my face. I crept into his room and gathered him into my arms. I cradled his warm body against mine as I prayed. I rocked him as I had when he was a baby. Jason slept soundly through it all.

Then it was over. The need to pray ended as suddenly as it had begun.

The next night it happened again—the sudden need to pray for Jason. And again the night after that.

There was a time in my life when I would have felt silly praying the way I did. There was a time when I would have told no one. There was a time when I would have been afraid.

But now I knew it was time to pray, and so I prayed.

By the third morning, my midnight prayers were becoming as predictable as the other routines of my life. As usual, I spent the few minutes before the children woke sipping coffee and savoring the quiet.

Nicole was usually the first to rise. But this morning she was still snoozing even after Jason was up and dressed for school.

It was gloomy and overcast. As I looked out the window, I was seized by a sense of sadness. Even as I made Jason's breakfast, my heart grew heavier by the moment.

I walked Jason to the end of our driveway. Right on time and with a whoosh of air brakes, the school bus pulled to a stop across the street, its red lights flashing.

Jason and I both looked up and down the busy highway. I gave him a quick kiss and he was on his way.

He never made it to the bus. His left foot had barely touched the pavement when a speeding station wagon came from nowhere and slammed into Jason, hurling his body fifteen feet into the air. He came down hard, headfirst.

It all happened so fast. Now, there he was, lying in the middle of the highway.

I fell to my knees beside him. His eyes were rolled back. His tongue was swollen and protruding. In a matter of seconds his right leg had swelled, straining the fabric of his jeans. His left arm was bent at a grotesque angle. I leaned close to his face and realized he wasn't breathing.

"No," I whispered. Then I lifted my head and screamed, "No, no, Lord, You can't let him die!"

A crowd gathered. They were all staring, horror-struck.

"Somebody call an ambulance!" I was amazed at the sudden control in my voice. "And get my husband. He's working in the orange grove down the road."

I bent over Jason and prayed aloud, "Dear God, I know You've raised people from the dead. Please raise up my son!"

I don't know how many people were in the crowd of onlookers, yet in their midst I suddenly felt a distinct presence. I glanced up and found myself looking straight into the eyes of a bearded man standing a few feet away. He had reddish-brown hair and stood relaxed with both hands in his pockets. Though it was only a second or two, it seemed like an eternity before he spoke in a surprisingly soft voice: "I have oxygen in my car."

Moments later the man knelt beside me and gently placed the mask over Jason's face. Almost instantly Jason gasped and drew a long breath. Weeping with relief, I leaned over and whispered into his ear, "It's okay, son, just think about Jesus. You're going to be okay."

But when I turned to thank the mysterious stranger, he was gone. And although the road was jammed in both directions, no one saw him leave.

Jason was in the hospital for months. His thigh and arm were broken. He had a severe concussion. But amazingly, there was no permanent damage.

Now, ten years later, I still shudder when I think about what might have happened if I had not heeded those urges to pray, and pray hard. You see, I know that the bearded man who saved Jason's life wasn't just some passing motorist. He was part of something bigger. Something that involved Jason's dream. Something that required my waking three nights in a row to pray for Jason.

That mysterious man was part of a heaven-directed rescue, and he was there in answer to my prayers. —*SHARON CRISAFULLI*

Dream Child

THE WOMAN'S NAME WAS MRS. CHARLES SMITH. She was older than her years, and the long days of hard work on the farm had pulled at her face until there were no curves at all, only sweet, resigned lines. There was a peaceful look in her dark and strained eyes, the look of a woman who has not expected too much for a long time.

We were sitting in the farm house and she was telling me about her children.

She had borne three and lost all of them, she said, when they were babies. She never knew what it was that took them, maybe inadequate nourishment, perhaps the rigors of being born without a proper doctor. Whatever the cause, three of them had come here and been loved and then had died.

"Just as we felt they were doing pretty well."

Then one night, she said, she had a dream. She dreamed she would have another baby and she sobbed, "O Lord, don't send me another one, just to lose it!"

She said the voice in her dream told her not to fret, that this one would be a blessing . . .

Then Mrs. Smith looked across the bare room at a boy in his late teens, who sat looking out the window at some kittens and a puppy playing in the swept yard.

"You know, it was about that time that Ralph came to us." Her voice caressed him. "He can't hear," she said softly, "and he can't talk, but he's good. I don't know what we'd do without him."

Ralph turned then and smiled back at her, as if he had received a message. His eyes were blue and bright and intelligent. His work shirt was clean and stretched across strong, straight shoulders.

"He can read and write, and he works every day. He saves his money, and he bought us a little car. And we go to meetin' in it.

The boy flashed another smile and tried to speak. She whispered back at him, too low for ears to hear.

"He can read lips right well. My husband and I can talk to him without ever raising our voices. He understands us, and we understand him." She looked down, overcome by her own full heart.

"He came here from a cousin's home, when he was six, after his father died," she went on. "We raised him for our own. He was the child I dreamed about, the one who lived—he is the blessing."

—DORIS LOCKERMAN

The Repeated Dream

I'VE ALWAYS BEEN IMPRESSED by the way men and women in the Bible were guided by dreams—from the angels climbing Jacob's ladder to the dream warning Joseph to flee with his family to Egypt. I've always known such things were possible, but it was only in 1978 that I received such a dream myself.

A dear friend had a terminal illness and yearned to see her son again. The young man led a nomadic life. He didn't keep in touch very closely, and when he telephoned he rarely told her where he was.

Then one night I had a strange dream of huge stacks of *Esquire* magazines. I couldn't recall ever having read the magazine. I dismissed the dream as being of no significance, but it persisted. After I dreamed of a house built entirely out of *Esquire* magazines, my husband bought a copy. But I saw nothing helpful in it.

Then one day, a sudden thought hit me—the name of a hotel in Chicago that somehow I connected with the son. Did he live there? When I was visiting my friend, I contrived to sneak a peek at her address book. There, next to her son's name, among years of addresses, I saw the name of the hotel.

I wrote a letter to the son at that address, telling him of his mother's illness.

That was Monday. At eleven o'clock on Thursday night, my friend's son called collect from Chicago. He'd only been back at the hotel for a few days and he'd just received my letter. Shortly before his mother's death, he was reunited with her.

Dreams can be very real, and anytime I'm tempted to just brush one off, I remember the name of that hotel.

The Esquire, just like the magazine.

—DOROTHY NICHOLAS

Gloria's Promise

THE FIRST TIME I SAW GLORIA MARSHALL she was singing in the choir at Fairview Community Church, here in Costa Mesa, California.

My six-year-old son, Colin, pointed her out: "Mommy, there's my Sunday school teacher." She was a small-framed woman with wispy brown hair haloing her face. And when she sang her face purely glowed.

My husband, four children, and I were newcomers at the church, and ever since we'd joined, Colin had been raving about his teacher. I patted his hand, grateful he liked her, thankful my kids were able to have the kind of Christian experience that had been missing in my own childhood.

While my mother was a traditional Christian, my father was not. They were divorced, and I'd lived with my mother, brother, and sister in a little duplex in California. As the choir sang that Sunday morning, I recalled those days vividly, especially the year I was eight. That was when Mama got cancer. We had a picture of Jesus on our living room wall, and sometimes Mama would look at it and say that if she died Jesus would take her to heaven, where she would watch over us.

One night I awoke to find Mama bending over the double bed where all of us children were sleeping. I watched dreamlike as she kissed each of us. The next morning she was gone. She'd been taken to the hospital, where she died that same day. She was forty years old. I thought about what Mama had said, that she would go to heaven and watch over us. More than anything, I wanted assurance that it was true.

I went to live with my father. He didn't believe Mama was in heaven. He explained that her soul had gone to sleep. Period. With time and tutoring I came to believe as he did, that death was an ending, that there was no consciousness, just the mist of eternal slumber.

That's pretty much the idea I'd lived with all my life. Then a few years ago I found a deeper, personal relationship with Jesus Christ. Now I was trying to believe in God's beautiful promise of eternal life. But to be honest, it was difficult sometimes to put those deeply ingrained doubts behind me.

After the service at church that Sunday morning, I made a point to meet Colin's teacher. Gloria Marshall was a single parent with three children; she worked at a center for mentally handicapped children. As we talked, I had the compelling feeling that she was someone I should get to know better.

In the weeks to come, however, I saw her only occasionally at church functions. Then one December afternoon I plopped into a dining room chair to read the church newsletter. Inside was a note from

Gloria thanking the church for supporting her as she faced a recurrence of her cancer. *Cancer?* Why, I didn't even know she was sick!

As I sat there, Tiger, our old tabby, slinked over and purred against my leg. I rubbed the cat's ear, a sudden idea nibbling in my thoughts. In my work as a stress counselor I often used positive mental imagery to help clients find healing. Maybe Gloria would consider working with me, no charge.

She was more than willing, and we began therapy sessions in January, meeting weekly in my office and at home. Gloria and I experimented with various meditations and visualizations that would help her envision God's love and healing being released into her life. Inviting a healing image into the mind can have a powerful effect on the body, and Gloria and I kept searching for the one just right for her.

One day as we began our session, a unique, imaginative image popped into my head. "Close your eyes, Gloria," I told her. "Call up a picture of a winged horse." As she followed my direction, I said, "Imagine that he has been sent to you by God and he can fly you anywhere you choose to go. Now climb upon his back and let him take you to your own special healing place."

Maybe it was whimsical, but after a few minutes, when Gloria opened her eyes she was more relaxed than I'd ever seen her. "Oh, Nikki," she cried. "He took me to the most beautiful garden, where I walked and talked with Christ. There were flowers and springs of water."

The winged-horse meditation became her favorite. Again and again she would travel to the imaginative garden to meet the reality of Christ's presence. During her communion she often pictured Jesus giving her "living water" from the springs along the garden paths.

As spring came and went, a bond of closeness formed between us. Best of all, Gloria improved. An exam showed her inoperable tumor was actually shrinking. "Whatever you're doing, keep doing it," her doctor said. And we did.

Meanwhile, Colin's attachment to Gloria deepened too. She became his most beloved babysitter. One weekend Gloria kept Colin so that my husband and I could get away for some time together. When we returned, Colin was quieter than usual. That night I tucked him in bed, planting a kiss on his forehead.

"Mommy, what will happen to Gloria if she dies?" he asked.

"Gloria will live in heaven with Jesus," I answered, hoping he did not sense the uncertainty in my voice.

Colin closed his eyes, but the little frown of worry remained on his face.

Gloria had been progressing for six months when the change began. Gradually I noticed her energy waning. She grew thinner. Soon the doctor confirmed my fear: the tumor was growing again.

Before long Gloria was unable to go on with our sessions. At our last one she presented me with a ceramic figure she'd made herself, a pastel blue horse. A winged horse.

"I will not give up hope, but I have to face the possibility I may die," she told me. "Perhaps the healing garden in my meditation is really heaven." She said it with such peaceful simplicity that I thought my heart would break.

"No—" I protested.

Gloria knew I struggled with doubts about the hereafter, and she interrupted me, a twinkling light in her eyes. "When I die, I'm going to be your best guardian angel, Nikki. I'll still be around; you'll see."

Autumn arrived. I threw myself into a busy schedule. I called Gloria often. Her voice seemed weak, like a sound fading in my ear. But while the leaves turned loose and drifted away, Gloria held on.

It was during the Christmas Eve service at church that I discovered her condition had suddenly worsened. After church I hurried to her house. Gloria's bed was surrounded with people speaking in hushed tones. "She's in a coma," her mother told me.

I lifted Gloria's hand into mine. "It's Nikki," I said. "I'm here. I love you." Her eyelids flickered. For a moment she seemed on the verge of speaking, then she lapsed back into her comatose sleep. I squeezed her hand and left. Outside, Christmas tree lights flickered in windows along the street. I knew I would not see Gloria again.

At home I retreated into my office, feeling desolate. Oddly, the pain of losing Gloria kept mingling with memories of my mother. I remembered that my mother had died at the same age Gloria was now, of the very same disease.

Oh, Gloria . . . I picked up the ceramic winged horse from my desk, thinking of the garden she had visited in her meditations. If only there could be a place like that!

Gloria died early Christmas morning. During the late afternoon, we attended her memorial service at the church. Gloria had requested we sing the French carol "Angels We Have Heard on High." But even when we sang the chorus, "Gloria in excelsis Deo," setting Gloria's name to angelic music, I could find little peace.

Later I stood before my bedroom window. The night was cold and starry. I gazed into the darkness for a long while, then went to bed, exhausted.

In the wee hours of the morning I awoke from a deep sleep, strangely alert. I cannot begin to explain what happened next. I simply felt what I thought to be the cat sink onto the foot of the bed against my feet. Tiger knew good and well she was not allowed on the bed. I moved my foot to nudge her to the floor, but she was not there. Then I remembered . . . I had put Tiger outside for the night.

I peered through the shadows. There was nothing on my bed at all, but the weight remained! It pressed against my feet, unmistakably, gently.

Suddenly a peculiar warmth glowed in the room as if it were enveloped by an electric blanket. My friend Gloria was there. I knew it. The certainty of it seemed indisputable to me.

I do not know how long I lay there with the mysterious pressure on the foot of my bed, but I had the overwhelming feeling that any moment I might actually see her sitting there.

Gradually, though, the weight on the bed disappeared. As it did, my mind was seized by a mental picture, like a movie playing on a screen inside my head. I saw Gloria in white, walking through a garden of unspeakable beauty, a garden blooming with bright flowers and flowing with streams of silver water. I saw her reach out her hand to a shining figure who I knew was Christ.

The image faded. I drifted into tranquil sleep.

When the alarm buzzed some hours later, the room was harsh with sunlight. I climbed from the bed, trying to come to grips with the experience of the night before. In the cold light of day, my intellect wanted a rational explanation. How could such a thing have happened? Was it some imagined illusion? Or had Gloria actually reached across the gulf to give me the assurance I needed so desperately in my life?

Bewildered, I wandered into the hallway. There I bumped into Colin, hurrying from his bedroom. His face was lit with wonder, with that special look a child gets when he sees something wonderful for the very first time.

"Mommy," he said, "why was Gloria sitting on my bed last night smiling at me?"

I gazed into his small upturned face, transfixed. Precisely at that moment I remembered Gloria's words: "When I die, I am going to be your best guardian angel. I'll still be around; you'll see."

I took Colin in my arms. "Perhaps Gloria came to assure you she is fine," I said full of certainty.

Today, two years after Gloria died, I still marvel at the glimpse of another reality which God granted to Colin and me that Christmas. I don't know why it happened. I only know I found the assurance I had longed for all my life—that death is merely a portal into another dimension, a heavenly dimension, which like the garden in Gloria's meditation brims with beauty and life and the radiant presence of Christ.

—NIKKI McFAUL

The Dreamed-About Baby

THE HOT SUMMER DAYS OF 1979 seemed to crawl by. My husband and I were waiting for our county adoption agency to complete the long process of clearing us so we could adopt a baby. We'd already gone through months of being interviewed and investigated—and we were told we would have another long wait even after we were approved.

Early one July morning, before dawn, I was startled awake by a vivid dream about a baby. What a happy dream *that* was—surely we'd have our baby soon!

But August passed without any developments, and September came before we even received our letter of clearance. Still, though our "credentials" were established, nothing happened. September dragged into October, and then November plodded by.

At last, two weeks before Christmas, the telephone call came. A woman at the adoption agency told me that the mother of a baby girl had reviewed the records of people and had chosen us. She gave me various details about the baby's birth and made an appointment for my husband and me to see her.

I hung up the phone and got out my desk calendar to mark the date and time. Riffling through the pages, I saw a notation in my handwriting.

A prickle ran up my spine.

On the calendar page for July 20, I'd written "dreamed about baby."

That was the very day God had chosen for our adopted daughter to be born.

—KATY BROWN

The Warning

THE VOICE WOKE ME FROM A SOUND SLEEP. I was so startled that I sprang out of bed and stood there in the dark, looking around wildly as the words echoed inside my head: "George! George, wake up, wake up! Something's burning!"

Outside, the November night was calm and still in our little town of Oxford on the eastern shore of Maryland. Yet there, in my bedroom, I stood in shock. There was no mistaking that voice; it belonged to my wife, Johanna.

But Johanna had been dead for six years.

Immediately my thoughts flashed back to another night years earlier, just after Johanna and I were married, when she had wakened in the middle of the night crying out those exact words. I had leaped out of bed then too, and I recalled that I seemed to see a white mist—or smoke—eddying around the base of our old brass bed. But Johanna and I had searched the house, and could find nothing wrong. Later we agreed she had simply wakened from a nightmare and triggered my hyperactive imagination.

Now, in my bedroom, just for a moment, that same white mist seemed to be curling around the brass bed. But the bed wasn't there—it had been consigned to storage years ago.

The flashback quickly faded, leaving me puzzled but worried. I hurried downstairs, fearful of what I might find.

Until now I had thought nothing could go wrong in this charming community of small houses, surrounded by woods full of deer and visited each fall by thousands of Canada geese that winter in the area. It's a good place to live, especially for a recovering alcoholic like me. After Johanna died, my drinking had spiraled out of control—until I entered a twelve-step program and turned my problem over to God. I credited Him with my sobriety and figured He had rescued me for a purpose.

As I inspected the downstairs rooms I found nothing amiss. Behind the fire screen in the living room a few dying embers still remained. Nothing alarming. I waited a few minutes, wondering if I had imagined the whole thing.

Then something urged me to go over and place my hand on the wall beside the brick chimney. It was scorching hot! And through a narrow gap between the mantel and the wall I could see flames.

The house was on fire!

Suddenly I felt calm and clearheaded. I picked up the phone, dialed 911 and reported the fire to the dispatcher. Then I heard crackling inside the wall; the fire was spreading upward between the studs, toward the attic. Two houseguests were asleep upstairs.

As I rushed up the steps, the piercing wail of a siren sounded in the distance, summoning Oxford's volunteer fire company. Still I felt that sense of peace. I woke the others, and the three of us calmly walked out just as the fire fighters arrived.

When the fire fighters cut through the roof, a terrifying tongue of flame shot thirty feet into the midnight sky, but thanks to their quick response, the house was saved. The cause of the fire was a defective chimney, and we were lucky to have got out alive.

But a lot more than luck was involved in our escape. I believe that God, who loves us, sent me that warning in a way that would get my attention: I'm usually not aware of dreaming.

When God rescued me from bondage to alcohol, I believed He had a purpose for me. Whatever else He might have for me, I know He wanted me alert, physically and mentally, to receive the warning and deal with the crisis when it came.

And I plan to continue being a careful listener. I want to be just as ready the next time He calls.

—George Todd

Thank You, Billie

HOW MUCH OF A MARRIED COUPLE'S TIME TOGETHER is spent in quiet pleasures, such as eating breakfast in the morning sun or enjoying an evening walk! Even late at night, when my husband was asleep, I enjoyed reading and writing and thinking, knowing he was there.

But when Billie died, those simple pleasures died with him. I was too tense to sleep. Each moment that I was awake and each tick of the clock reminded me that he wasn't there. I'd fall asleep only as dawn was breaking, and be wakened moments later by my alarm.

On one such morning I drowsily stumbled into the kitchen, put on the tea kettle, then wandered back into the bedroom and lay down on the bed. Instantly I was fast asleep, the deep exhausted sleep that finally comes, but never when I wanted it to. I had a dream. Billie and I were in the kitchen preparing coffee and toast. I saw him taking bread out of the bag and putting it in the toaster. I could hear him asking me if the water was boiling yet. Suddenly he became stern, saying, "Darling, you have the kettle on the wrong burner." And he repeated himself. Then he yelled, *"Darling, you have it on the wrong burner!"*

I jumped to my feet. There was an overpowering smell of gas in the room. The stove! The pilot light that I hadn't repaired! I dashed to the kitchen, turned off the stove, threw open the windows.

"Oh, thank You, God!" I cried out. And then I added the words that changed my life, "Thank you, Billie." —GRAYCE SHAPIRO

At the Foot of the Cross

B ACK IN 1975 I WAS OFFERED A part in the film *Jesus of Nazareth*, which through the years has been shown at Easter time on NBC television. Our cast, directed by the renowned Franco Zeffirelli, included Anne Bancroft as Mary Magdalene and Olivia Hussey as Mary, mother of Jesus. I played the part of the centurion who was present at the crucifixion, the one whose servant had been healed by Jesus.

Much of the film was shot in Tunisia on the Mediterranean during January and February of 1976. A cold, damp wind continually knocked over floodlights and stung us with desert sand. I was uncomfortable in my thick leather uniform. My neck ached under a ponderous metal helmet, and I even began to pity those ancient Roman soldiers who were called centurions because they commanded a hundred men.

When it came time for my scene during the crucifixion, the weather was chill and gray. The camera was to be focused on me at the foot of the cross, and so it was not necessary for Robert Powell, the actor who portrayed Jesus, to be there. Instead, Zeffirelli put a chalk mark on a piece of scenery beside the cameraman. "I want you to look up at that mark," he told me, "as if you were looking at Jesus."

"Okay," I said, moving into position and looking up at the mark as instructed.

"Ready?"

I hesitated. Somehow I wasn't ready. I was uneasy.

"Do you think it would be possible for somebody to read from the Bible the words Jesus said as He hung on the cross?" I asked.

I knew the words well from the days of my childhood in an Italian-American family in Connecticut, and I'd read them in preparation for the film. Even so, I wanted to hear them now.

"I will do it myself," Zeffirelli said. He found a Bible, opened it to the Book of Luke, and signaled for the camera to start rolling.

As Zeffirelli began reading Christ's words aloud, I stared up at that chalk mark, thinking what might have gone through the centurion's mind.

That poor Man up there, I thought. *I met Him when He healed my servant, who is like a son to me. Jesus says He is the Son of God, an unfortunate claim during these perilous times. But I know He is innocent of any crime.*

"Father, forgive them; for they know not what they do." The voice was Zeffirelli's, but the words burned into me—the words of Jesus (Luke 23:34-46).

Forgive me, Father, for even being here, was the centurion's prayer that formed in my thoughts. *I am so ashamed, so ashamed.*

"Verily I say unto thee, today shalt thou be with me in paradise," said Jesus to the thief hanging next to Him.

If Jesus can forgive that criminal, then He will forgive me. I thought *I will lay down my sword and retire to my little farm outside of Rome.*

Then it happened.

As I stared upward, instead of the chalk mark, I suddenly saw the face of Jesus Christ, lifelike and clear. It was not the features of Robert Powell I was used to seeing, but the most beautiful, gentle visage I have ever known. Pain-seared, sweat-stained, with blood flowing down from thorns pressed deep, His face was still filled with compassion. He looked down at me through tragic, sorrowful eyes with an expression of love beyond description.

Then His cry rose against the desert wind. Not the voice of Zeffirelli, reading from the Bible, but the voice of Jesus Himself: "Father, into thy hands I commend my spirit."

In awe I watched Jesus' head slump to one side. I knew He was dead. A terrible grief welled within me, and completely oblivious of the camera, I started sobbing uncontrollably.

"Cut!" yelled Zeffirelli. Olivia Hussey and Anne Bancroft were crying too. I wiped my eyes and looked up again to where I had seen Jesus—He was gone.

Whether I saw a vision of Jesus that windswept day or whether it was only something in my mind, I do not know. It doesn't matter. For I do know that it was a profound spiritual experience and that I have not been quite the same person since. I believe that I take my faith more seriously. I like to think that I'm more forgiving than I used to be. As that centurion learned two thousand years ago, I too have found that you simply cannot come close to Jesus without being changed.

—*ERNEST BORGNINE*

In Mother's Arms

W HEN MY MOTHER DIED IN 1983 I didn't feel depressed. Mother had lived a long and fulfilled life. Now she was with the Lord, so I felt peaceful about that. Still, I missed her a lot and she was often in my thoughts.

Every now and then I'd dream of my father, or another deceased relative. But I never dreamed about my mother. Sometimes I wondered why. After all, I'd loved her dearly. She'd loved me. And, as far as I knew anyway, I wasn't harboring any deep-down resentments.

Years passed. Then my beloved eighteen-year-old dachshund, Heidi, died. As an unmarried woman living alone, I had no immediate family. Heidi had been my family. We'd spent a lot of time together, going for long walks, or visiting friends in the country on weekends. I'd even taken her with me on a number of my vacation trips.

The night after Heidi died I had a dream. In the dream I could see her. She was being held by someone. It was my mother.

—*ELEANOR SASS*

What's the Doctor's Name?

HERE IN SOUTH KOREA, WHERE I'M STATIONED with the U.S. military, I recently met Ms. Kyong Cha Lee, a woman who had suffered a terrible loss.

Ms. Lee's house, like many older homes in Korea, is heated by large charcoal briquettes placed under the floor. During a cold spell last spring this primitive heating system malfunctioned, spreading poisonous carbon monoxide fumes throughout the house, almost killing Ms. Lee.

She lay in the hospital in a coma for days, with her family at her bedside. When she finally awoke, they were too grieved to tell her the extent of her loss. But she astonished them when she said she already knew her two children had been killed in the tragedy. "The doctor told me when he came to look after me," she explained.

"What doctor?" they asked.

"The doctor who prayed by my side and promised that God would watch over me."

They assured her they had seen no such visitor and they had been with her constantly. The physician must have been a dream, they said.

When Ms. Lee was well enough to go home, she was making her way out of the hospital when she caught sight of a portrait in the lobby. "There," she said, "that's the doctor who came to my bedside. What is his name?" "Jesus Christ," came the answer.

And that's the story I heard from Ms. Lee at a retreat recently. She was there with a number of others who, like her, were new in the Christian faith.

—*SAM NIX*

Dream Warning

WHEN I ARRIVE AT THE SCENE, *the old frame house on Chicago's South Side is burning furiously. Smoke and embers dance crazily in the windy winter night. I give the order to unroll the hoses and then dash madly inside. I pull out three people and administer CPR to two of them before the ambulance arrives, rubber screeching on asphalt. When the blaze is finally under control someone from the Department comes up to me. "You did a great job, Captain Cushing," he says, "but two of those three people you pulled out didn't make it."*

"No," I cry. "They're all alive!"

"I'm sorry, Cushing."

Suddenly I awoke in a drenching sweat, my heart racing. My wife, Rosemary, was awake too, staring at me. "Honey, what's wrong?" she asked. "You were shouting."

"Nothing," I mumbled, focusing my eyes. The clock read 4:30 A.M. "Just a bad dream." I fell back on my pillow. I had to get some rest. The following day was Christmas Eve, and I was scheduled for duty.

I was assigned to a single firehouse that quartered Engine 91, a hose company. In Chicago, firemen work three successive twenty-four-hour shifts, living at the firehouse during that time. I'd have under my command three fire fighters and an engineer to monitor the equipment. I was a little nervous. Because of all the holiday leaves, my company had some unseasoned men. I hoped nothing major developed.

By the time I arrived at work the next morning I'd completely forgotten about the dream. In fact, I was happy to find out that my relief engineer had just been promoted, so he must not have been quite as unseasoned as I had feared. Still I was apprehensive. The holidays are a busy time for fire fighters. People get careless during all the excitement. *God,* I prayed, *watch over our city on this wonderful night.*

The shift passed uneventfully. Then, one minute before Christmas, an alarm came in. We manned the engine and roared out of the garage, our siren piercing the night. The blaze was only a half mile from the firehouse, on North Drake Avenue. We were a block away when I spotted smoke. Fire was raging through an old frame house. I called in a second alarm for more equipment and a chief.

We pulled to a stop and I ordered the engineer to hook up both lines and send water through immediately. The first priority was to get the water moving. Then I directed my two other fire fighters to grab lines from the hose beds. "Move!" I shouted.

I approached the house. The policeman who had called in the alarm was hammering on the locked front door. "There are people inside," he panted. Through a dingy pane of glass I could dimly see the outline of a body lying in the hallway. "Step back," I told the cop.

I battered my way in. I lifted the body into my arms. It was a woman. She'd probably been overcome by smoke while trying to escape. I wondered if there were kids. Peering through the smoky darkness I could see that the whole downstairs was afire. I was on my way out with the woman when I spotted the second body. It looked like a child's.

Outside I ordered a fire fighter to get the child. I directed another to go in with a line and start fighting the blaze. I put the woman down in a snow bank. Her eyes were fixed and dilated and I could get no carotid pulse. I'd be back to work on her, but first I went to help with the child, a boy of about seven or eight. We put him down next to the woman. He still had a heartbeat.

I started CPR on the woman. It was a cold, icy night, but perspiration streaked from under my helmet. It had taken us only a minute to reach the scene. A person isn't clinically dead until at least six minutes have passed without oxygen, so I figured we had a fair shot at saving this woman.

I tilted her head back, cleared the breathing passage and gave her five quick breaths followed by fifteen chest compressions. I repeated the steps. No response.

In the background the wail of sirens rose from the night. The fire fighter inside called out that the main fire was centered in the front room. I ordered him all the way in to fight it. An instant later I saw one of the hoses a few feet away, bulging from water pressure, snaking rapidly toward the house.

The chief's buggy arrived. The woman still wasn't responding and my efforts were getting frantic. I rubbed snow on her face. "Come on, lady. You can do it."

"What do you have?" the chief snapped as he knelt by my side.

"I've got two people out and one fire fighter inside on a line by himself. I need a couple of ambulances."

The chief nodded. Then he peered at the woman. "You'd better give up on her," he said. "She's gone."

"No," I said, pounding her chest. "She still has a chance!" Then, exhausted and frightened, I silently called out: *God, bring her back! I've done all I know how. Only You can help now.* A split second later I felt her heart pound against my hand. *Thank You, God.*

Sinking back on my heels, I stared up at the blazing structure. *Three* people. There were three people in my dream.

Someone else is in there!

I dashed back into the house. My men would have found any additional victims on the ground floor, so I headed through the smoke toward the stairs. I climbed them slowly, sweeping my flashlight ahead of me. Near the top, I spotted him—a boy lying on his back, unconscious.

He had no carotid pulse. His eyes were dilated. I scooped him up and blew into his mouth, giving him fast cardiac compressions with the fingers of my left hand. I carried him down the steps and outside. As I knelt to lay the boy next to his mother, I felt his heart turn over like a tiny motor. He was alive.

After the fire was out and we were putting away our equipment, the chief returned to the scene from the hospital. He took me aside.

"You did a great job, Captain. But I'm afraid the woman and the little boy aren't going to make it."

"Chief," I said "no one is going to die." I didn't explain about the dream. He wouldn't have believed me.

Christmas morning I called the hospital. All three were stable but suffering from smoke inhalation. I was put through to the woman. I told her I'd been at the scene and asked her what she remembered.

"Well," she said, her voice raspy from the smoke, "I was asleep on the couch when one of the boys started screaming that our Christmas tree was on fire. I tried to get everybody out. The last thing I remember is everything going red. Then it turned to a beautiful white. I heard chanting, like music in church. I was very, very peaceful. Suddenly I saw an older man looking into my face. That's when I woke up outside. They told me one of the older firemen rescued me."

"Ma'am, that was me," I said.

She began thanking me but I cut her short. I told her about the dream. "That dream was a warning, a message not to give up on you and to go back in and find the boy. I didn't save you. God did."

That's all I wanted to say. I wasn't the hero. I'd been told what to do on Christmas Eve when I was awakened by the most vivid dream of my life. In a sense, like all good fire fighters, I was just following orders. —*EDWARD CUSHING*

"For Thou Art With Me"

O N DECEMBER 9, 1991, I HAD an unusual dream. I stood alone in a small auditorium. From backstage came a familiar voice: a young man reciting something I couldn't quite make out. Then he said, clearly, "Yea, though I walk through the valley of the shadow of death . . ." I recognized it immediately: the 23rd Psalm! "I will fear no evil: for thou art with me—"

Suddenly the voice stopped and I woke up. It was 2:00 A.M.

I realized the voice in my dream was that of a former student, my sister's son, Samuel C. Washam. The auditorium was in the rural school where I had taught him. He had a good voice and had often stepped out from behind the stage curtains in plays I directed. I had taught him many recitations, but the 23rd Psalm was one of his favorites.

Since then, I had prayed many times for my nephew, who was now middle-aged, terminally ill and lonely. He was afraid, and seemed to have lost his way from God. I had asked the Lord to let Samuel C. know that broken people are dear to his heart. I fell back into a fitful sleep with that same prayer on my lips.

The phone woke me early. It was my sister telling me her son had died. I asked her, "When?"

"Two o'clock this morning," she answered quietly.

I thought of the last words Samuel C. had said in my dream, "For thou art with me." I knew he had found his way again. —*FAYE FIELD*

"Please Hurry—I'm Hurt!"

M Y SON DID NOT COME HOME that foggy night. Justin, almost eighteen, had gone out in his car with a friend on Friday evening, August 6, 1993. At first I hadn't worried. He was a good boy, a careful driver and always dependable. He knew he had to be up early Saturday morning for his summer job cleaning pools.

I went to bed thinking I'd hear Justin arrive home any minute. As always, I prayed for him, his twenty-year-old brother, Strider, and my older sister, Mary Beth, who lives with us.

I awoke Saturday morning with a start. Justin! I hadn't heard him come in. Heart pounding, I jumped out of bed and checked his room. Then I rushed into the kitchen, where Mary Beth was making coffee.

"Justin didn't come home!" I announced.

The percolator trembled in Mary Beth's hand. She loves her nephews dearly. "Where do you suppose he is?"

"I don't know. He always calls, even if he's delayed a short time."

"Maybe he stayed over at his friend's house," Mary Beth suggested.

I hurried to the phone on the desk in the kitchen. No, said his friend, Justin had dropped him off last night and headed home to White Bluff from Nashville. That was only about a twenty-minute drive.

I started calling everyone he knew, including his high-school football teammates. Fall practice was starting Monday and that was all Justin had talked about recently. As I dialed number after number, I kept glancing out the window, expecting his car to come up the drive. I longed to see his golden retriever, Hunter, bound up to him; to hear Justin explain: "Hi, Mom. I'm sorry; I forgot to call you ..."

I slumped back after speaking with the last of his friends. No one knew anything. The thoughts I'd been pushing away finally broke through. *He's lying dead somewhere. Someone's hijacked his car. He's been kidnapped.*

I dialed our pastor, Mack Hannah of Harpeth Heights Baptist Church, who said he'd get a prayer chain going immediately. Then I dialed the Dickson County Sheriff's Department. Two deputies came right out.

"He's a little more than six feet tall, brown hair, brown eyes, two hundred twenty-five pounds," I told them. "A big guy, plays football." How could I describe his smile that lighted up a room? His wonderful sense of humor?

"Car? A blue 1980 MGB convertible." They wouldn't be interested in knowing that the car was both a birthday and early graduation present, or how proud he was of it.

As the older deputy wrote down the information, he commented on the unusually heavy fog the night before. Then, as they turned to leave, he patted my shoulder. "We'll do our best to find him, ma'am."

Mary Beth brought me a cup of coffee. "Now don't give up, Rose," she urged. "We're going to find him."

I smiled wryly. That was Mary Beth. Always trying to be optimistic.

But not Strider. He was beside himself with worry. "I can't just sit here, Mom," he said. Instead of going to work, he drove off to look for his brother. Mary Beth went with him.

I sat at the desk staring at the phone. It rang—over and over. But it was our pastor reporting that the entire congregation was praying. Then concerned friends called, asking what they could do to help. I laid my head on my arms. I was divorced from Justin's father; my boys meant everything to me. "God," I prayed, "please don't take my baby. If you need someone, take me."

I felt a touch on my shoulder. It was Mary Beth; she was back from the search.

At my pleading look she shook her head, but tried to cheer me. "Rose," she said, "I just *know* Justin will be all right." She picked up A.J., our cat, who had been pacing around my chair, and cradled her in her arms. "God has his eye on Justin," she said. I gratefully squeezed her hand, but wished I could be as certain.

All the rest of the day the phone kept ringing. The sheriff's office reported that authorities in two counties were combing the area, checking every route Justin might have taken, and that the Tennessee Bureau of Investigation had been notified. Strider went out again to search. It seemed Justin had vanished from the earth.

Mary Beth and I sat up long past midnight praying and dozing fitfully. About 5:30 A.M. I woke up and opened my eyes to find her sitting bolt upright in a chair. "Rose," she said, "a verse—Matthew 7:7—has come to me. 'Ask, and it will be given you; seek, and you will find; knock, and it will be opened to you' [RSV]. That means we can't give up; we have to keep praying."

Finally, in utter exhaustion, we both went to bed to try to get some sleep. I awoke to sunlight flooding the room and went downstairs to resume my vigil. I sat looking at family pictures. There was Justin as a toddler holding a football. Next to that was a photo of Justin as a first grader who stroked my face and told me, "I have the prettiest mommy." I couldn't hold back the tears.

I heard a step on the stairs and looked up. Mary Beth stood there, a strange expression on her face.

"Rose, I know you're going to think I'm crazy," she said, "but I know—I know where Justin is."

I stared at her. What on earth was she talking about?

She sat down across from me. "Justin came to me in a dream," she said. "I could hear him calling to me. It was so plain and clear. He told me where he was. He said, 'I can't move and I need help. Come and get me. I'm between Highway 100 and the railroad tracks. Please hurry—I'm hurt." Her voice was quivering. "I told him we'd be right there."

Strider, who overheard us, rushed into the room. "I know just where that spot is! On Old Harding Road."

I looked at the two of them numbly. Both were clearly exhausted and willing to grasp at anything. "If it will make you feel better, Mary Beth," I said wearily, "you and Strider go look. I'll stay here by the phone."

After they left, the minutes ticked by. I could only stare at my son's picture in his football uniform, wondering if I'd ever see his number sixty-one on the field again.

The phone rang. I barely had the strength to pick up the receiver. "Rose..."

It was Mary Beth, almost shouting with excitement.

"Rose, *we found him!*"

I listened in stunned disbelief as Mary Beth continued breathlessly: "Justin was exactly where he told me he was in my dream—between Highway 100 and the railroad tracks! In the fog, his car went off the curve there and down that steep embankment into a ravine. It was impossible to see him from the highway. He was unconscious and paramedics took him to Baptist Hospital in Nashville."

I hurried to Justin's bedside. He had been wearing his seat belt, but the impact of the accident had thrown him out of the car. He was in a coma, badly scorched from lying unconscious in the sun all Saturday. The doctors said he would have lived only hours if he hadn't been found. Even so, they gave little hope for his recovery.

For five days I sat by Justin's bedside, praying as he remained in a coma. His friends and teammates came in to cheer him on, hold his hand, and pray for him.

And then on the sixth day he finally opened his eyes. I leaned close to hear his first precious words; and when they came I had to smile. "I'm...hungry," he said.

"What can I get you?"

"Two...big...fat chili dogs." I almost laughed out loud. I knew then that my son would recover.

After months of therapy, Justin was back in high school in January 1994. He remembers nothing about that terrible night, only that the fog had suddenly became so thick he couldn't see.

But all of us who prayed for Justin believe that God allowed that dream to come to Mary Beth, who so implicitly believed in the promise "Ask, and it will be given you."

And seek, and you will find.

—*ROSE LEAR*

The Hearse in the Snow

M Y MOTHER HAD BEEN HAUNTED by the same dream for five nights in a row. She described it to me as I took her to the hospital for an operation to relieve a slipped disk.

"It's snowing," she said. "In the distance I can see headlights approaching. When they come close, I recognize a hearse. It stops in front of me. A door opens and the driver motions me inside . . ."

Against her wishes, I told Mom's doctors and nurses about the dream so they would be sensitive to her fears about the operation.

Before dawn on the day of her surgery, snow began to fall. At 7:15 I went to her hospital room to be with her while she was being prepped. An orderly came in and I helped him get Mom on the gurney. We were waiting at the elevator when a nurse hurried up. "The surgery has been canceled," she said.

Finally I was able to reach our doctor to find out what was going on.

"Well, I woke up during the night and couldn't go back to sleep," he said. "Something was bothering me. I looked outside and saw the snow. And I thought about your mother's dream. I got up, called the hospital and ordered a second electrocardiogram. It caught a condition that didn't show up on the first EKG. The lab called the anesthesiologist and he canceled the procedure." The doctor hesitated and took a deep breath.

"If your mother had had the anesthesia, well . . ."

Later I found out what he did not say then. Under anesthesia, Mom would have been in grave danger of dying of heart failure.

—*JUNE DAVIS, R.N.*

A Giant beside Our House

I'M IN OUR YARD ON BIG FIR COURT, *gazing up at the mighty two-hundred-fifty-foot tree the street is named for. Rising from the corner of our property to the height of a twenty-story building, the great white fir dwarfs our home and everything in sight like some ancient giant. It gives the illusion of leaning ominously toward me, creaking and swaying ever so slightly in the rustling wind.*

Look! It's not leaning, it's falling! It's toppling toward our house, gaining momentum rushing to meet its shadow, until finally it crumples the roof and splinters through the living room and front bedroom with a sickening, thunderous roar. I let out a cry. Alison's room!

I awoke in a drenching sweat and sat straight up trying to blink away the terrifying vision. Another nightmare. I slipped out of bed and stole a peek into Alison's room. Our nine-year-old daughter was sleeping peacefully, as was eleven-year-old Heath across the hall. But I couldn't shake the irrational fear until I'd checked. This was not the first time I'd dreamed of such an accident. In another dream I'd seen a giant tree limb tearing loose and slamming down on Heath, leaving him crippled.

As a computer engineer, I deal with quantifiable information. I don't pay much attention to impractical things like dreams. But these nightmares were so vivid and frightening. I eased back into bed next to my wife, Nita, but not before looking out the window at the tree. There it stood, stately and still, its coarse bark ghostly pale in the faint moonlight.

A few nights later I had another dream, this one more puzzling than alarming:

I am in our yard and in front of me stands a white angel. The angel has a broken wing.

What did all these dreams mean?

Then one day I noticed a twenty-foot dead limb dangling from the fir. Out here in the Northwest we call a dangerous limb like that a widow maker. I remembered the dream about Heath. "Don't go near that tree," I warned him. That Saturday I enlisted a neighbor to help me rope it down; all week I'd worried about the precarious branch. Later I had some other dead limbs removed too.

Why am I so concerned about this tree? I wondered. *It's stood here for generations. It even survived the fierce Columbus Day storm of '62.*

My nightmares about the tree eventually subsided. Christmas season arrived and Nita and I rushed madly to get our shopping done. More than anything, Alison wanted a Cabbage Patch doll. We scoured the stores around Portland with no luck. Everywhere we went it was the same story. "Sorry, folks," said the clerk inevitably. "We sold out our Cabbage Patch dolls weeks ago."

Finally Nita settled on a handmade rag doll. It was thicker and heavier than the Cabbage Patch version, but there was something about it that caught our fancy. "Well," sighed Nita as we paid for it, "this will have to do."

"Alison will love it," I reassured her.

We arrived home to a surprise. Alison had impetuously decided to rearrange her room. She'd been talking about it for days, but Nita had implored her to wait until the holiday excitement died down. "Then I'll help you," she'd promised.

Instead Alison had recruited her brother for the task, getting Heath to help drag her heavy bed across the room. "I just wanted to get it done now, Mommy," she explained as Nita surveyed the scene with obvious displeasure. "It's important." Alison's toys and furniture spilled out into the hall. By bedtime, however, Alison had her room in order again and we could scarcely hide our admiration.

"See?" said Alison knowingly. "It's not such a big deal."

Outside I heard the wind whistle through the big fir.

A howling blizzard marked Christmas Eve. I drove home from work through swirling snow and pounding winds. I pulled into the driveway, turned up my collar, and hurried inside to get ready for church. Church was not one of my priorities even under the best circumstances, and on a night like this I didn't want to be anywhere but inside my house, Christmas Eve or not. But I'd promised.

At the service with Nita and the kids, I felt strangely detached as I hunched in the pew with my arms folded tightly, thinking about whether I even believed that God was a part of my life. I'd been raised in church but that was a long time ago. Now I certainly didn't feel any "tidings of comfort and joy." God may have created the world and all its wonders, but I didn't see where that had much to do with my life. If God was real, He was much too remote for me to have faith in.

We arrived home late, and the wind and snow stung our faces as we walked up the driveway. Heath and Alison rushed inside to turn on the Christmas tree lights. From our bay window the blue lights cast a peaceful glow across the snowy yard. I draped my arm around Nita and led her in.

Wrapping paper flew as the children tore into their presents, and Nita and I settled back on the couch to view the happy chaos. Nita had turned the tree into a work of art. The crowning touch was a glorious blond angel perched high at the top. "It looks like Alison," I said.

Alison was so delighted with her big new doll that she granted it the honor of accompanying her to bed. "Told you she'd love it," I reminded Nita as we climbed under the covers. The moaning wind lulled us to sleep.

Roar! The explosive sound jolted the house. I hadn't been asleep long, and my startled, half-awake mind tried to separate fantasy from reality. *The dream again,* I thought. But then I sat bolt upright, and suddenly I knew. This was no dream. This time my nightmare was real. The tree really had fallen on our house!

I leapt out of bed and raced across the hall to Alison's room. "Daddy, help!" she was calling frantically. "I'm stuck!"

I couldn't budge the door. It was jammed shut. "Oh, my God," I whispered. "Don't move, honey!" I shouted through the door. "We'll get you out." I grabbed a flashlight and told Nita to call 911. "I'll see if I can get to her from outside."

I was horrified to find the tree filling the front hall, branches whipping in the gale. I stumbled through the family room to a side door. Outside I nearly collided with the massive trunk. Propped up on its giant ball of roots, which had been torn from the earth, it looked prehistoric. I crawled underneath as the rough bark tore at my robe and ripped my flesh. The wind sliced through me. Above the din I heard the distant wail of sirens.

Groping my way to Alison's window I aimed the flashlight beam inside and wiped the icy snow from my eyes. All I could see were branches, tattered insulation, and hunks of ceiling strewn about the trunk. Somewhere buried beneath the tree was my daughter, crying faintly, "Daddy! Daddy!"

Someone was standing beside me. "Alison! This is Captain McCullough of the fire department," he called. "Your daddy's with me. Can you move at all?"

"I think I can move my arm," came a brave little voice.

"Good. Push you hand up as high as you can."

Tiny fingers wriggled up through the debris. I breathed a tentative sigh of relief. Firemen rushed to set up lights and heat lamps. They fastened a plastic tarp over the rescue area. Captain McCullough turned to me and said quietly, "This isn't going to be easy, Mr. Gullion."

As I huddled with Nita, and neighbors looked after Heath, a terrifying game of pick-up sticks slowly unfolded. The night air was filled with the roar of chain saws and the reek of fir pitch as rescuers cut away at the tree and cautiously removed branches as they went. A slight shift of any debris could spell disaster.

Bit by bit they chipped away at the wreckage until, after an hour, Alison's head and shoulders emerged. Her right leg appeared to be crushed under the tree. A fallen two-by-six rafter clamped down on her torso. We could see Alison's new doll squeezed between her chest and the rafter. Apparently she'd fallen asleep clutching it.

McCullough shook his head grimly and called a halt to the work.

"We can't risk it," he said. "Show me the crawl space." Moments later he played his flashlight on the area under Alison's room. Limbs a half foot in diameter pierced the floor and stabbed the ground beneath. Again McCullough shook his head. "We can't cut away the floor without disturbing the tree. *And that tree must not shift.*"

The subzero wind had intensified. Hours had passed and now there was the threat of Alison succumbing to hypothermia. Neighbors rushed in warm blankets and hot-water bottles. A paramedic put his wool ski cap on Alison's head. But I could see she was drifting, her big eyes fluttering. Once or twice her head rolled back. If we didn't get her leg out soon, the surgeons might have to amputate it to free her.

Only one chance was left: to lift the tree. A crane was out of the question. In this wind it would be too unstable. But McCullough had called a towing company that used giant air bags to gently right over-turned semitrailers. "It's a gamble," he warned me. "But we've run out of options."

Huge rubber bags were packed under the tree. A compressor roared to life. Slowly the bags filled with air and swelled against the giant fir. Despite the blizzard, I could see sweat bead up on McCullough's tensed brow. My hands trembled as Nita buried her head in my chest, afraid to look.

Suddenly I heard myself praying to the God whose very existence, just hours earlier, I'd doubted. You would have thought I'd be ashamed to ask His help now, but something told me I must. "Please, Lord," I begged, "spare her life. I believe You are there."

The shriek of the compressor was deafening. The bags bulged like great billows, but at first nothing gave.

Then there was movement! Inch by agonizing inch, the tree was lifted. A cry rose from the crowd as paramedics rushed to free Alison and whisk her to a waiting ambulance. Nita and I jumped in with her, and we roared off. Alison smiled weakly. "I'll be okay now, Daddy," she whispered, still grasping her new doll.

That overstuffed doll, it turned out, was possibly just enough of a cushion between the fallen two-by-six rafter and Alison's chest to have saved her life.

The doctors confirmed that she would recover. And Alison's leg was only broken, not crushed.

Christmas Day, Heath and I kicked through the rubble of our house. I'd been thinking about that desperate prayer I'd said, thinking about it a lot. In Alison's room I saw that the bulk of the fir had landed near the southeast wall—right where her bed had been before she'd impulsively moved it. On the trunk directly over where Alison lay when the tree came crashing through, I noticed a wide scar from a recently cut branch—one of those I'd felt such urgency to remove after my dream. That branch might have killed her.

Had God been trying to warn me all along about the tree? To protect us? Had I been blind to God's ways?

In the snow outside what used to be our living room I found the angel from our Christmas tree, the one that looked like Alison. Its wing was broken, just as the angel's wing in my dream had been. As I brushed it off and held it up. Heath came running. "Dad, Dad!" He grabbed the angel. "I've seen this before! In a dream! An angel with a broken wing just like this one!"

Dreams. Does God speak to us through them? The Bible says He does (Job 33:14–18), as well as in many other ways. This much I myself can say: Alison is safe and well. And God is, and always has been, watching over my family.

—RON GULLION

After the Storm

The storms may come
And limbs may break;
Yet others bend
Beneath the weight—
Of heavy rain
And windy breeze . . .
A storm can mark
The strongest trees.

Life sometimes deals
With us this way;
In unseen trials
We meet each day.
It's not how much our bodies break
Or how much they may bend;
It's our outlook in our own life
That helps our spirits mend.

—HILEN LETIRO

In thy light do we see light.
—Psalm 36:9, RSV

CHAPTER FIVE

God Shines His Light

"God is light," the Apostle John tells us (1 John 1:5). And James 1:17 refers to God as "the Father of lights" and the giver of good and perfect gifts. So it's no surprise to discover that God uses light and lights to communicate. Some of the lights described in this section drew people to safety, some represented love. In several stories mysteriously glowing crosses seem to represent the abiding presence of Christ.

The Light in the Barn

I SHOVED THE BARN DOOR OPEN and yanked at the light chain. Only then did I remember. The bulb had burned out. I waited a moment until my eyes adjusted to the darkness and then made my way to the lambs' pen. In my hand I held a nursing bottle for two wobbly little creatures waiting for their dinner.

"Hi, guys," I said.

Two tiny tails leaped to life and eight little hooves scrambled across the straw. One lamb latched voraciously onto the bottle's nipple while the other bleated forlornly till it was his turn.

These were "bummer" lambs, twin males, and I was trying to save their lives. Their mother had rejected them at birth, not because they were twins, but because she had been unable to supply their milk.

When the bottle was drained, both lambs huddled next to me while I rubbed their stiff, curly coats. They seemed so content that I was reluctant to leave, so I just sat there in the dark cold, whispering sweet words, willing them strength, loving them for the mother who wouldn't. And then, in my cracked and uneven voice, I found myself singing, softly, as mothers have done down through the ages, my words half made up, a lullaby.

As I was on my way out of the barn, my husband, Jack, met me halfway.

"What kind of bulb did you put in there?" he asked.

"I didn't. It's still burned out."

"Did you have a lantern?"

I said no.

He looked at me quizzically. "When I came outside a few minutes ago, there was a light coming from the barn. It was bright, like sunshine, streaming out of every crack. It turned off just before you came out."

—*MARJORIE L. SMITH*

The Cross in the Water

O NE COLD EARLY EVENING many years ago, my wife, Bartie, and I set out in our cabin cruiser for a picnic dinner on south San Francisco Bay. We waved to a college crew team heading out for a practice row, then proceeded down the channel toward the San Mateo Bridge. The choppy water soon turned into huge waves.

At the drawbridge, I signaled to the bridge tender to let us through. He shook his head, pointing to the whitecaps on the water ahead. We were about to take our pitching craft home, when in the distance near some mud flats, we saw a ruby-colored light glowing, shimmering in the shape of a cross. Bartie and I were mesmerized. We turned our craft in its direction. It was irresponsible of me—in shallow muddy water an engine might suck up mud that can destroy it—but I felt *compelled* to follow the cross. Now mud was coming from the exhaust pipe, and the temperature of our engine had risen into the danger zone, but the light drew me on.

Then we came up to it, only to find that the light was merely a buoy reflecting the red sunset. Bartie and I felt foolish; we had actually risked our boat to chase a mirage.

"Look, the water is full of coconuts," Bartie said. But they weren't coconuts at all; they were the men from the rowing crew, whose shell had crashed into the bridge and sunk. One by one we pulled them aboard. They had been in the water for over an hour. Facing death, gulping the icy salt water, they had come to a point of desperation and had prayed together for rescue.

And that was when the cross began to shine for me.

—*Eros M. Savage*

The Promise

WHEN THE DOCTOR TOLD DICK and me that we could never have a child, we didn't believe it. We went ahead and bought a house on a horseshoe-shaped street where cars didn't go too fast. We chose our yard for the big climbing trees out back, and the neighborhood so that our children wouldn't have to walk far for friends.

But the years passed and no child came. I took to haunting the baby carriages in front of grocery stores and begging my friends to go out so I could baby-sit. Three babies in particular, through the years, I loved in a special way. They were all girls and every one of them had blonde hair and deep green eyes. When I held one of them my heart would start to thump and I'd have to blink back tears.

I couldn't understand it: Neither in Dick's family nor in mine was there yellow hair or green eyes. Yet, each time I picked up one of those babies, I felt that she belonged to me.

And all this while, we prayed—not for a baby, just that His will be done. Yet whenever I pictured His will for us, there was always a baby right in the center of it. I even got the room ready. It wasn't until afterwards that I realized that I'd chosen green walls and yellow curtains.

One warm summer night, when we had waited seven years without a child, I woke up with a tremendous elation racing through me. I tried to get back to sleep but instead I grew wider awake every minute. At last, afraid that I would wake up Dick, I got up and went into the living room.

I switched on the lamp and sat down in our old brown armchair. On the table beside the chair was a book of Bible quotations. I picked it up but felt too exhilarated to read. It slipped to my lap, falling open. At the top of the page where the book had opened, in letters that looked ten feet tall, were the words: "For with God nothing shall be impossible" (Luke 1:37).

And then the whole living room filled with light. The lamp was on, it's true, but all of a sudden the room was *full* of light—the way sunlight sometimes shines on dust particles, causing one to see that the air all around is crowded and active instead of empty. In the same way I was suddenly aware that Christ occupied the whole room.

After a while the awareness passed, but not the certainty. I never doubted for a moment that Christ had shown me His all-powerful creativity to tell me that our prayers for a child had been answered.

In the morning I told Dick that we were going to have a baby. On the calendar in the kitchen I drew a big red circle around the night before. Then I phoned my mother and told her, and then I told my next-door neighbor. Soon there was scarcely anyone I hadn't told.

"Are you sure?" my mother asked me. "Have you been to the doctor?"

But to me that would have been lack of faith. I had a promise from God! What did I want with a doctor?

But yet as the days passed, doubt arose in my mind too. And at last I didn't need a doctor to be crushingly, utterly certain that no baby was coming to us.

If I had fallen from a mountaintop I couldn't have dropped so far and so hard. I stopped answering the telephone. When my next-door neighbor rapped on the kitchen door I flattened myself against the wall until I heard her footsteps going away. I couldn't see anyone. I couldn't talk about it.

Yet, even at the worst moment of my disappointment, I couldn't get away from what I had seen and felt that night. Something had happened. But what? And how could I have misread it so completely?

That October, more to take my mind off myself than anything else, Dick suggested that we make the rounds of adoption agencies again. We'd been doing this for several years but the waiting lists were so long that we'd never even gotten our names down. This time, however, one place in New York City was more encouraging. Yes, they would take our application. Yes, we would be hearing from them.

It was in April, the following spring, when a phone call came. "Mrs. Larsen," the caseworker's voice said, "your little girl is here."

Dick, rushed from his office and met me at the adoption agency. We scarcely dared to look at each other. Then the caseworker brought in a small bundle wrapped in a pink blanket. "Here she is," she said.

But I could have picked her out of a thousand babies! There was the little wisp of fair hair, and the green, green eyes. When Claudia was three weeks old, we brought her back to the green-and-yellow room that had waited for her for so long, back to the house that she had suddenly made a home. With her came a very brief sheet of facts: parents' blood types, length of pregnancy, weight at birth, first formula . . .

All during those busy first weeks I kept trying to put that sheet of paper away, but something wouldn't let me. Like a fly buzzing around my head, something about it wouldn't let me alone. I'd brush it away; a few days later it would be back. The paper. Look at the paper.

At last to quiet the buzzing once and for all, I picked it up from the kitchen table where it had lain and began to read. My eyes stopped at the space for the months and weeks before the date of birth. It was very precise, down to the number of days. Slowly I took down the calendar from the wall and, getting last year's calendar from a drawer, I began counting back.

I knew the answer before I ever got to the month with the triumphant red circle. But I finished the count. And with the last number my finger rested on the very day and night when our house had filled with the promise.

We were indeed to have a baby, that much I had grasped. That another was to bring her into the world, I had not guessed. Nor did I know what confusion and grief were the other part of the story, nor how in His love Christ was reaching out at that moment to the boy and girl who were the parents. I only know that in His mercy He reached out to us, too, and that the new little life so marvelously beginning was ours from the very moment of conception.

"Bone of my bones and flesh of my flesh" (Genesis 2:23) are lovely words, the loveliest—I used to think—that a mother could say. But I know more beautiful ones still, the words I say to my daughter: "Hope of my hope, longing of my heart, the promise of my Lord."

—FRAN LARSEN

To an Adopted Child

Not flesh of my flesh,
Nor bone of my bone,
But still miraculously my own.
Never forget
For a single minute
You didn't grow under my heart,
But in it.

—FLEUR CONKLING HEYLIGER

I'm Going to Crash

THINGS WEREN'T GOING as I had expected that blustery March night in 1972 over Arkansas.

I was flying a single-engine four-seat Cherokee 180 from Chicago for delivery to Houston and had planned to reach Shreveport, Louisiana, that night. But as I passed over Fort Smith, Arkansas, I recomputed my ground speed and found that I was pushing into a head wind of much greater velocity than had been forecast. That meant I would not have enough fuel to reach Shreveport.

It was 8:00 P.M. A light rain beat against my windshield like scatter shot and a heavy overcast blocked out any moonlight. Even at my assigned altitude of seven thousand feet, I couldn't see a thing; it was pitch black outside my cockpit windows. Instrument weather.

No problem, though. Over my radio I requested clearance to land at nearby Texarkana, Arkansas.

Texarkana approach control came on clear: "Okay, Cherokee seven-nine-four-eight-n, descend and maintain two thousand feet; you are cleared for an instrument approach to the airport."

I settled back. I enjoyed these flights. Ever since I got out of the Navy in 1971, flying had been my main goal in life. And I was doing all right with it. I figured I could take care of myself.

I finished my landing check list and, by instrument check, found my position to be about thirty miles north-northwest of the Texarkana airport. I knew that a thick forest of pine trees and rolling hills were beneath me.

Suddenly my engine coughed, quit... started... and quit again! What was wrong? Frantically I checked instruments. There was plenty of fuel. I pushed controls, checked again. Nothing. A cold fear seized me.

Now only wind noise filled the cockpit as my 2450-pound plane began its inexorable drop to earth. I sat helpless at the dead controls as my ship hurtled into the total blackness. Terror shot through me as I thought of smashing into the thick pines that would tear my ship to shreds.

I began a series of emergency measures. I radioed a Mayday distress call to the air controller, advising him of my situation. Then I set the Cherokee into a glide speed of eighty miles an hour, extended-ten degree flaps, and noted that we were dropping 1100 feet per minute. That meant less than two minutes before we would crash. I still could not see anything outside the windows.

I then did the only other thing I could do. "O Lord Jesus," I prayed, "into Your hands I come."

Suddenly, unbelievably, a complete peace filled the cabin. Fear left me. In its place I felt a strange presence. Words seemed to fill my mind—words of calm and reassurance. *Everything is going to be all right. Look off your left wing.*

Then, through a clear spot in the murky skies, I saw a light from a house porch. Instinctively I swung the plane toward it.

Again the Voice in my mind. *Now look below to your right.*

When I looked, I saw the headlights of two cars coming toward me. *Head directly for those two cars; everything is going to be all right.*

The deep indescribable feeling of peace and beauty intensified.

I kept heading toward the headlights; they were the only thing I could see outside the cockpit. The plane shuddered from wind gusts as we silently sped downward. I switched on my landing lights and continued on.

Whoosh! I passed about thirty feet over the first car and was immediately engulfed by tall dark trees racing close by on both sides. I sensed I was lined up with the highway, but I seemed to be flying into a tunnel.

The Voice kept assuring me. *Everything will be all right.*

Now the second car was facing me head-on and I felt sure we'd collide. I tried to turn the plane, but my hands and legs would not respond.

Keep heading for that car, continued the soft, soothing Voice. *Everything is going to be all right.*

My air speed had dropped drastically; the red stall light was frantically indicating that there wasn't enough air flow over my wings to maintain a safe glide.

Then I felt an impulse to do the strangest thing. Despite my critically low air speed, I was suddenly prompted to pull back on the controls, raising the plane's nose into a high attitude so that the lighter tail section would hit the oncoming car first. Ordinarily such a maneuver would lead to a total stall and crash. I waited for the impact.

There was none. Instead, the highway pavement appeared in my landing lights, rising steeply. I was heading uphill! But because of my high nose attitude, the plane set down on the concrete in a perfect three-point landing. I rolled to the top of the hill and began using my brakes. There at the side of the highway was a roadside café, its neon sign saying "Penney's Cafe" glowing. I kept using the brakes, rolled into the cafe's parking lot and stopped.

Suddenly the immensity of the incredible thing that had happened overwhelmed me. All I could do was sit there thanking God.

Light flooded the parking lot as the café door opened and a man walked toward me. "How did you get *here?*" he asked in astonishment.

"A miracle of God," I said in a choked voice.

I asked the man to check down the road: I was worried about the people I might have run off the highway. After ten minutes he came back. He had found no one and did not recall seeing any cars earlier.

Were those lights real, I wondered, or had the Lord put them there just for me? All I know is that if I had not lifted my plane's nose to avoid the second car, I certainly would have slammed into the inclined highway. My lights did not shine far enough for me to react to landing uphill. The impact probably would have caused the plane to explode, since I had about fifteen gallons of fuel left in the wing tanks.

There was not a scratch on the plane. The air traffic controllers in Texarkana were amazed to find me alive. What had caused the engine to quit? A clogged fuel line.

I learned that the road I had landed on was U.S. Highway 71. So that night after I checked into a motel, just out of curiosity I picked up the Bible in my room and turned to the 71st Psalm. It began, "In thee, O Lord, do I put my trust. Let me never be put to confusion. . . ."

I put the book down and looked out the window. The dark mist was falling and the sky was still black. But I knew that above that overcast the stars were still shining, though I couldn't see them. And now I knew, more certainly than ever before, that the Lord of Heaven was there as well. —JACK ARMSTRONG

Everything Will Be All Right

WHEN THE DOCTOR TOLD US Jim had cancer, we could hardly grasp the words. This was something that just didn't happen to young marrieds, certainly not to *us!* It couldn't happen to a strong, healthy young man just beginning a productive life—not to a father of three small children.

But in some numbing, inexplicable way it had, and as Jim and I began to take it in, we did what I suppose most people do at such times—we turned to God in panic. Up till then we'd made feeble attempts to attend church, never really settling on one denomination, but trying first one and then another. Now in real earnest we began to explore spiritually—studying, praying, reading the Bible together.

One night I lay in bed beside my sleeping husband, unable to stop my thoughts. The house was dark and still, the children peacefully asleep. Through a crack under the window shade the stars were visibly twinkling in the sky. And I lay there cold with fear. My sweet, gentle, handsome young husband was going to die. "O God, help us, help him, help me to help him. Give us a miracle, Lord," I prayed.

And there, in the upper left corner of the room, the miracle began. It was a ball of light, whirling, coming closer, brighter and brighter, showering sparks around the room like a Fourth of July sparkler, moving, but with a powerful stillness like God's universe.

Blinking, I sat up in bed and still the light was there. Then I heard the words, tremendous and gentle as the light that seemed now to fill the house.

"Everything will be all right."

Five words, but somehow I knew that God Himself had spoken them.

Often in the following two years those words were all I had to hang onto. For in spite of repeated surgery and radiation treatments, Jim—to the outward eye anyway—was growing worse, the pain ever harder to bear, the once tall, strong body thin and wasted.

Then came that special night. For three days past, with every waking breath Jim had begged me to help in withstanding the pain. Now at last he was sleeping peacefully. But, exhausted as I was, somehow I couldn't go to bed.

The children were afraid but very perceptive. They did everything quietly and with an understanding obedience that said, "We know what's happening and will not add to the upset." After kissing their daddy and me goodnight, they had gone quickly to sleep without the usual rituals of the bedtime story and trips to the bathroom.

Some months before, we had moved Jim's bed to the living room. As I sat beside him there, watching him breathing regularly, his pleading voice quieted, I felt a wonderful sense of peace. Once again, as I had so many times in the last two years, I seemed to hear those words, "Everything will be all right."

Still I did not go to my own bed in the next room but sat beside him, silently reading the Bible and praying. I wanted so much to ask God to erase all of this, to let it be a bad dream. But it wasn't a dream. It was stubbornly, horribly real.

Finally, after two hours of praying, then sobbing, then reading, then hoping, then daring not to hope, I relinquished my hold on this person I loved more than anything else in the world. I said the prayer that I now believe gave my husband relief from his suffering: "O God, take him if You must, but don't let him suffer anymore." Then I kissed him, went into my room, and fell asleep immediately.

For several months preceding that night Jim had awakened me at three o'clock each morning to talk and pray with him. So it was habit, I suppose, that called me from sleep that night at 3:00 A.M. as usual. But it was what happened before I awoke that is so hard to put into words. For many years I didn't even try. Maybe I was selfish, wanting to hold onto it for myself, receiving comfort from it. Maybe I was afraid people would think me insane or self-deluding. But I have never been more certain of anything than of this event.

Suddenly I was wide awake instantly, as if my body were tensed for the unexpected. I lay there listening for any sound from the living room. I did not get up immediately but waited to absorb a Presence that once again seemed to fill the room. I looked around, expecting another bright light, for I felt the same exhilaration I had that other time. But there was no light, no voice. I lay there waiting and all at once I was remembering the dream I had just had. I closed my eyes and experienced the dream over again.

My husband's mother, who had passed away almost eight years before, and a good friend of the family, Aunt Charlotte, who had died some years before that, were standing in our living room. Together they looked down at the bed where my husband lay. They talked and laughed, joyously greeting their loved one. Although I couldn't hear their words, I understood they were telling Jim that they had come to take him home with them.

At first he seemed to be resisting; then just as easily and nonchalantly he nodded. By his acceptance he seemed to say that he knew he could no longer take care of his family, that he could leave them in God's hands. There was no more pain reflected on Jim's face. He got up, looked at the worn, painlined face of the body that was no longer his, took an arm of each woman, and together they left the house.

I rose from my bed and tiptoed to the door of the living room. Jim's body lay on the bed, strangely quiet.

There, in the silence of death, in a small house like thousands of other small houses in the world, I felt no sadness, no immediate grief, only humility and a sense of the reality of God. For He had visited me with His love and a promise, and had come again to show me the fulfillment—everything was all right, now and forever.

—RUTH WHITTET

Pisgah

By every ebb of the river-side
My heart to God hath daily cried;
By every shining shingle-bar
I found the pathway of a star;
By every dizzy mountain height
He touches me for cleaner sight,
As Moses' face hath shined to see
His intimate divinity.
Through desert sand I stumbling pass
To death's cool plot of friendly grass,
Knowing each painful step I trod
Hath brought me daily home to God.
—WILLARD WATTLES

The Orange Pickup

I HAD TO STAY LATE that evening at the bloodmobile, where I am a registered nurse working with the American Red Cross. By the time I trudged out to my car, it was dark, and fog was rolling in. I had an hour's drive home to our small town nestled near the base of the Oregon coastal range.

The traffic was light, which was good, because the fog was getting heavier. I could barely see the white line at the edge of the freeway and the streetlamps that lit it. Then I turned off onto our country road. Ten more miles to drive on a narrow, twisting road with deep ditches and a stream alongside.

"Help me, Lord," I prayed. Recently in church we had been discussing the use of mental imaging while praying. Now I visualized Jesus sitting next to me in the passenger seat. I poured out my fears to Him.

Hugging the steering wheel, I stared at the eerie whiteness. Suddenly ahead of me I saw the red taillights of another car. Slowly I drew closer. The red taillights were on an orange pickup being hauled by a tow truck. I was relieved. Undoubtedly the pickup was being taken to the garage in Forest Grove. If I followed it, I could make it home.

We came to Main Street—but we passed the repair shop. The tow truck drove on. It kept going. To my amazement, it turned into the dead-end road where we lived. With a sigh of relief I turned into our driveway, then quickly got out to thank the driver of the tow truck that had led me home.

There was no driver. There was no tow truck. It had not turned around to exit from the dead end. I stood staring into the silent fog at the end of our road.   —MARY PETTIT HOLMES

Why Were Our Landing Lights On?

O N A COLD JANUARY NIGHT I was captain of United Airlines flight 840 bound for San Francisco. We had taken off from Denver and had climbed to about twenty-nine thousand feet when a flight attendant knocked at the cockpit door. A passenger, she said, had just reported seeing a light flashing an SOS in the mountains beneath us. I no sooner got a fix on our position—sixty-two miles west of Denver on the J-60 airway—when the intercom chimed and another flight attendant told us of a second passenger who had seen the SOS signal.

Enough said. We called Air Traffic Control, advised them of the reports, and gave the estimated location. A commuter flight scheduled over that area was alerted to watch for the distress signal. The sheriff's office was apprised of the situation.

Not until we landed did we learn the whole story. Two people in a four-wheel-drive vehicle had ignored the "road closed due to snow" signs posted by the forest service and were trapped by an avalanche.

For two days and nights, they fought fatigue and frostbite. In desperation, they removed a headlight from the vehicle and rigged it to the battery so that they could send out SOS signals. Then they waited. But all the planes flying overhead were too high for them to see at night—until we came along. And the only reason they were able to spot our jetliner was because our landing lights were on.

Our landing lights? To this day I do not know why those lights were on. Or do I? —G. H. BEAULAURIER

Shelter!

ALL DAY LONG I HAD DREADED the thirty-mile drive. As a transplanted Californian, I wasn't used to the gray, unpredictable Aprils in Kansas. April 27 had been raw and drizzly, and at four o'clock, when I left to take the children to their cousin Stacey's birthday party, it was raining in earnest.

"Be extra careful," my husband, Bill, cautioned as Jennie, five, and Maria, three and a half, wrestled with their coats. I bundled our three-month-old baby, Will, into a satin sleeper. Bill wasn't coming with us because he needed time to study for upcoming medical-school exams.

The birthday party was worth the drive. My girls were impressed with Stacey's Holly Hobbie cake, and they were delighted to "help" play with Stacey's new doll. But when it was time to start for home, the sky was black and the rain torrential; the radio announced that fifty-mile-an-hour winds were buffeting the area. The dirt roads I'd come on would be nearly impassable, so Bill's father mapped out a route that would keep me on paved ones. I scooted the kids into our rattly '67 Plymouth.

I crept down the highway. I couldn't use my bright lights—the solid sheet of rain reflected them back in my face. With my dims, I could see only a few feet ahead. Somewhere I missed a turn and found myself on a gravel road. I turned at the next intersection, thinking I could backtrack to the highway

I crept along mile after mile. The highway never appeared. I crossed a bridge—and the bottom seemed to fall out of the road. The car dropped, then bumped, and the wheels spun. I found myself on a dirt access road which curved along farm fields next to the riverbank. I shifted into low gear hoping for enough traction to pull myself out, but the car slipped sideways into a slough of mud. And stuck.

Wanting to save the battery, I switched off the lights and sat in the darkness, trying to calm my panic. The road I'd glimpsed in front of me was little more than a path, and it was highly unlikely anyone would be traveling on it before morning. Worse, the river might overflow if the rain continued. We would be swept away.

Lord, I prayed, *help me get the children out of here.*

The instant I looked up I spotted what appeared to be a yard light.

"There's a house just up the road," I told the girls. "We'll walk up there and call Daddy. I'll have to carry Will, so you both must hold tight to my coat pockets. The road will be filled with puddles, so whatever happens, don't let go."

The rain subsided to a drizzle just as we got out of the car. I was thankful for that, but the road was slick and uneven and we kept losing our footing. Worse, we'd only walked a few yards when, to my bewilderment, I realized the yard light I'd seen from the car had disappeared. I couldn't see anything at all.

The girls were afraid, and so was I! To reassure us, we sang "Jesus Loves Me" over and over again. But then Jennie stopped singing.

"If Jesus loves us, why isn't He down here with us?" she asked.

"Honey, it isn't Jesus' fault that Mommy got lost and stuck," I told her. "But Jesus really is with us, and He's showing me the way to go."

"But why isn't Jesus *walking* with us?" Jennie persisted.

All I could think of to say was, "He doesn't want to get His feet muddy."

Jennie and Maria giggled, but my fear was only relieved for a moment. Will was heavy—thirteen pounds—and my arms felt ready to drop off. The girls were dragging on my coat pockets, and I knew we couldn't go much farther.

A huge bolt of lightning split the sky, then hung suspended for several seconds, revealing a two-story white farmhouse. If the lightning had flashed twenty seconds later, we might have missed it completely.

We slogged our way onto the front porch, and I knocked on the door, first firmly, then more and more frantically. But the house was dark inside and no one answered. In desperation I tried the knob. Locked.

I sat the girls down on the steps and put Will in Jennie's arms.

"I'm going to the back door," I said. "The people who live here must be in bed, but I'm sure they'll wake up and let us in."

The back door was locked too. I beat on it until my hands hurt. I yelled until I was hoarse. No one came.

The rain started again, an incredible downpour, and the wind whipped it into a stinging frenzy. My children waited unprotected in the chilling gale.

Break into someone's home? *Never.* But I *had* to get into that house.

"Mommy!" Jennie screamed from the front porch. I could hear Maria crying.

I took a deep breath, doubled my fist and smashed it through the pane of glass alongside the back door. I reached in, pulled back the bolt, and flung the door open. Then I ran back around to the front, swept up the children and rushed them through the back door.

We held on to each other breathlessly, then looked around. An old floor lamp shone with just enough dim light for me to see the outlines of a stove . . . a refrigerator . . .

And . . . a telephone! Help was only a phone call away! I hurried to it. The line was dead.

I put back the receiver and sank wearily against the wall. Will started to whimper. I flipped a light switch. Nothing. I tried another, then another. Nothing. Yet for some reason the single bulb of that dilapidated floor lamp gave forth a pale but steady light. Without it, we'd have been in total darkness.

The house didn't have much furniture, but there was a worn sofa covered in houndstooth-check nylon. I used the cushions to make a bed on the floor for the girls. When I pulled off their muddy slacks, I saw that Maria had walked right out of her little T-strap shoes somewhere on the muddy road and had continued barefoot. But she and Jennie had obeyed my instructions to hold on: my coat pockets were nearly ripped off.

"Mommy, are we safe now?" Jennie asked tiredly.

"Of course we are, darling," I said. Thank goodness she and her sister were too tired to detect the quiver of uneasiness in my voice. I was feeling anything but safe.

We had found shelter, but was that enough? True, there was a roof over our heads, and walls between us and the stormy blast. But my heart still beat anxiously. I had broken into the home of people I didn't know, damaged their property and used their possessions without permission. The walls around us kept out the wind and the rain, but my heart still beat uneasily. I was cold and feeling like the intruder I was.

A lightning flash illuminated the room, and my eyes fell on a small wooden plaque on a built-in hutch. I picked up the plaque and carried it to the kitchen lamp, where I read these words written in white:

THE LORD IS MY SHEPHERD.

A sense of peace enfolded me like two loving arms. This was a house where God-fearing people lived. And God was here. Now.

I lay down with my arms around the children, watching the play of lightning and listening to the wind, rain, and thunder. I was still worried about Bill and his parents. What would they think had happened to us? But I felt calm and secure for the first time in hours.

It must have been about 1:30 in the morning when I heard the click of a key in the front lock. I jumped up and hurried to the door and came face-to-face with a young man who looked as surprised as I was.

I poured out my story of why I was there, explaining that I'd never have broken in if I hadn't been desperate. "And," I ended breathlessly, "I knew, whoever you were, you'd be nice."

"Lady," he said, "I'm the owner of this house, and I hoped, whoever *you* were, that you'd be nice too."

The young man lived with his parents in town but was fixing up the house to live in after his upcoming marriage. He worked the late shift at a nearby plant, and on his way home had felt a strong urge to come by the house to see if the storm had done any damage.

He helped me carry the children to his car and took us to his parents' home, where I called my family. They had been frantically driving all over the countryside looking for us.

The next day, we returned to pay him for the damages and give him a plant as a small token of our thanks. He towed our car out with a tractor, and he even found little Maria's shoes in the mud. By that time his electricity, which had been knocked out by the storm, had been restored. He had no idea what yard light we could have seen, or why the dim kitchen light had continued to glow.

But he did know why the plaque was there. "Well, sure," he said matter-of-factly. "I put it there."

The *Lord is my shepherd.*

The young man's home was not just a shelter for us; it was a sanctuary.

—*CHRISTINE BRANDENBERGER*

The Light and the Cross

I N AN AIRLINER I FOUND MYSELF sitting next to a young woman who told me that she was a registered nurse. When she learned that I was a writer, she said, "I'll tell you a story, a true one. Maybe you can use it."

I smiled a little. "Maybe I can."

"Last week," she said, "I was on night duty. The patient in Room 78 was very frightened. Surgery was scheduled for the next morning and I knew the doctors did not give this woman much of a chance.

"I tried to cheer her and suggested that she pray for strength. She said she did not believe that prayers were answered, but I urged her to pray anyway.

"During the night I went into her darkened room with my flashlight to see if she was all right. Then, rather suddenly, I was called away.

"In the morning a most extraordinary change had come over her. She no longer seemed frightened. 'I'm going to be all right,' she told me. 'I know, because I prayed, and my prayers were answered. I asked for a sign, and I was given one.'

"A sign?

"'I saw a light,' she said in a whisper. 'And in the center of the light, a cross. It was on the wall at the foot of my bed. I'm going to be all right.'

"The attendants came then, and wheeled her away. When she was gone, I looked in the blankets at the foot of her bed and found what I was looking for—my flashlight. A week or so earlier I had dropped it, had cracked the glass, and had mended it with a tiny cross of adhesive tape. Obviously, when I came in during the night, I had left it by mistake. Half-buried in the blankets, it must have projected a circle of light, just as the patient said . . . with a cross in the center."

"And did the patient recover?"

"Of course she did! She thought her prayers were answered."

The nurse's voice died away. For a moment there was nothing but the drone of the engines.

"And what do you think?" I asked her.

The nurse smiled and shook her head. "I don't think," she said. "I know!"

—ARTHUR GORDON

Seeing the Light

IN THE LATE 1970S A CHAIN OF DEATHS—my mother's, a younger brother's, a close aunt's—left me utterly grief-stricken and despairing. If only I had used my time with Mama more wisely during her last days! Did she and Richard and Aunt Julia ever know how much I really loved them? Was there anything they had wanted to tell me before they died, but I never gave them a chance?

Despite my professional background in rehabilitation counseling, I was haunted by painful feelings and questions. I decided to enroll in a graduate workshop on "Counseling for Death, Dying and Bereavement" at Hofstra University in Hempstead, New York. And it was in that class, on a frosty January morning in 1981, that I came to terms with a mysterious event in my life.

The professor began talking, in a matter-of-fact voice, about something she called "near-death experiences." Such experiences, she stressed, were so well documented that there was even a worldwide group devoted to them called the International Association for Near-Death Studies, Inc.

My thoughts whirled. Could this professor be talking about the same sort of experience I'd had twenty-one years before? An experience so real, yet so bizarre, that I'd never told a soul about it? A rush of long-held-back memories flooded my mind. It seemed like yesterday.

It was spring, 1960. I'd learned to live with a severe hearing impairment that had affected me since childhood, and I'd even earned a master's degree in special education, majoring in rehabilitation counseling. But I was very ill. The news from my doctor was devastating: acute uremic poisoning with complications. He said I had three to six months to live.

At first I didn't have the courage to reveal this prognosis to my husband, Bernie. When I told my mother, she urged that I be treated at a special clinic in Texas run by a doctor she trusted. She offered to help take care of my children, three and six, while I was away. So I traveled to Dr. Herbert Shelton's clinic in San Antonio, Texas. Mama and Dad took the children, and since money was tight, Bernie stayed home to work.

The clinic, in an isolated area far from the downtown and residential areas of San Antonio, was surrounded by the scrubby Texas brushland and mile upon mile of open sky. I fully expected to die there. After about three months of following a strict vegetarian diet and drinking nothing but pure water and juices, I seemed to be getting worse. I was very weak. The thought of dying frightened me, but I was so ill that I almost began to welcome death to be free from pain.

And then, on a clear September day, the most extraordinary thing happened. I left my body on the bed and was hovering up by the ceiling of my room. And then—I was outside the building. I had no more pain and was no longer aware of my body. Below me and around me was a panoramic view of the vast Texas landscape and the horizon. I seemed to be at one with the universe. I had no sense of time or space.

Next I became aware of sounds that I hadn't been able to hear without my hearing aid since I was a little girl. And what I heard was the most beautiful music—an ethereal blend of sounds, so natural as to surround me, envelop me. In addition to the music, I heard some words—the same phrase chanted over and over again. I didn't know the language, yet it was strangely familiar.

I floated and seemed to be beyond the horizon, and then in the distance appeared the graceful profile of a being with shoulder-length hair. It was a blazing silhouette from the waist up and glowing with its own most beautiful brilliant-white light. Like the music, this light seemed to surround me, envelop me, shine right through me. Although it was white, it seemed to possess all the colors of the rainbow, like the light that radiates from a perfectly cut diamond.

I was filled with a sense of wholeness and peace unlike anything I'd ever known. "The Light" I experienced was love, pure and unconditional—the "something more" that I'd yearned for since I was a child.

Now, with crystal clarity, came these words: *"Baruch Atah Adonai . . . Baruch Atah Adonai."* They were woven like a golden thread through the beautiful music that surrounded me. *". . . Baruch Atah Adonai."* I had no idea what the words meant.

Then I was back in my room again, in my bed. I felt weak and racked with pain. My chest felt crushed. I couldn't breathe. And there was something terribly wrong with my left side. Dr. Shelton and some attendants crowded around my bed.

Later on I learned I had suffered an angina attack, but I would be all right. My left side was palsied, but months of intensive physical therapy enabled me to regain the use of my arm and leg; gradually my overall health improved. Three months later, in December 1960, I was able to go home.

Though I am Jewish, I wasn't brought up in a religious home. Nevertheless I sensed that I had undergone a deeply spiritual experience. Something too meaningful to risk being ridiculed or diminished in any way. So I told no one, not even Bernie, about "The Light." I felt protective. The experience was too deeply personal to be shared at that time.

Then, twenty-one years later, while sitting in a college classroom with the nurturing support of about twelve of my peers, I felt a powerful sense of affirmation; I began to see a connection between the deaths that had led me to attend this class and my own near-death experience. It was an awakening.

I completed the course and plunged into advanced studies on death, dying, and bereavement. Meanwhile, I solved the puzzle of those words I'd heard. They had sounded vaguely familiar, like Hebrew, so I made an appointment with the rabbi of our local synagogue.

I met with him several days later in his paneled office and told him about my experience and the words. I was sharing what happened for the first time—and I felt as if it had just occurred. "Rabbi," I said, "it was many years ago that I heard those words. What do they mean?"

He looked at me intently. *"Baruch Atah Adonai,"* repeated the rabbi softly, stroking his chin, "means 'Blessed art Thou O Lord.' " I gasped and repeated, *"Baruch Atah Adonai*—Blessed art Thou, O Lord." How appropriate!

Blessed art Thou, O Lord. So many nights as I drifted off to sleep, dog-tired from studying, I felt my strength and well-being restored as I recalled the magnificent "Light," the beautiful music, the reverent words.

Over the next year, I found myself increasingly drawn toward the study and practice of hospice care and counseling to help terminally ill patients and their loved ones. At the heart of hospice philosophy is understanding death as a natural part of life; an experience not to be shied away from or denied, but met with confidence and hope. The idea is to improve the quality of the life remaining to the patient and not to prolong the dying process.

Recalling Mama's, Richard's, and Aunt Julia's drawn-out battles with cancer, I understood the hospice belief that, while pain control is always necessary, in some cases a course of radical surgery or the use of heroic measures or extended therapy with drugs, chemicals, and radiation, may not be the best use of the time the dying patient has left.

Healing can occur on many levels, and it may not always mean a physical cure. The dying person is often in need of deep emotional and spiritual healing as well. And so is the family. "You can't learn everything about hospice work from books," explained a dear friend who is a clinical-oncology nurse specialist. "You need to be able to listen at a different level, intuitively, so you can respond to the unspoken needs of dying patients and their families and friends."

Listen at a different level. That was one thing I knew I could do after nearly half a century of living with a severe hearing loss. Many times

I'd, watched a person say one thing with his lips, while his eyes and face and body communicated an altogether different message.

On Christmas day, 1981, I was nearing the end of a double shift as a volunteer in the hospice unit of one of our local hospitals. One of the patients was a middle-aged man dying of cancer; he had been hospitalized for a period of time and had become comatose.

The medical community generally agrees that, even when comatose, the patient is aware—however dimly and mysteriously—of the presence of others, aware not only of their presence, but also aware of what they are saying and doing. I explained this to the man's wife and two grown daughters as they stood in painful silence outside his room.

"He knows you're here," I said. "He knows it's Christmas day. Come into the room. Say his name. Talk to him. Share your love for him. He *will* hear you." I asked his wife, her face drawn with exhaustion and grief, to stroke her husband's cheek. "Kiss his forehead," I whispered.

Death was imminent, and the man's extremities were cold and turning blue. I asked one of the daughters to take her father's hand into her own. "Hold it tightly with both of your hands," I said.

I asked the other daughter to cradle her father's feet. "Cup them in your hands and massage them gently," I said. "Stroke his toes, his ankle . . . There, give him some of your warmth and life . . ."

Then I stepped aside, over to the window. I joined the family in my mind and spirit, praying that healing would take place where it was needed, in whatever form that might be.

I saw the man's toes start to move just the tiniest bit. And then a bit more. His color began improving.

"Look!" exclaimed the daughter at his side. "He's beginning to move!"

Then the man's eyes opened wide. He was not disoriented in any way, as might be expected considering his critical condition. Clear and bright, his eyes shone with joy, reflecting love. He was aware of all that was going on around him.

Before leaving the room to allow the family time alone, I encouraged them to share their deepest feelings with him. "Now is your chance to complete any unfinished business you may have with one another. Now is the time to talk about love—to say words you always wanted to say but never had time to—or to ask forgiveness."

As I left, I realized that my own pain about Mama, Richard, and Aunt Julia had been eased by helping this family.

And when I returned some three-quarters of an hour later, I saw something that took my breath away. For present in that patient's room were not only the patient and his family—but *"The Light" was there too!* Filling the room with a glorious radiance, shining in our eyes, *"The Light" was with us!*

My hospice work has taught me that in this life, along with the joy, are pain, sorrow, suffering, death. But through it all, God cares. He is light—*"The* Light." And when God's Light breaks through our darkness, it is with a power strong enough to redeem even the most hopeless-seeming situation—even death itself. To me death is not hopeless. It is not the end.

Baruch Atah Adonai! —VIRGINIA SENDOR

When the Cross Shone

IN LATE WINTER 1970, Bud and Jane Surber helped erect a large cross on a hill near their home as part of a 4-H Club project. "We got it up and lit just in time for Easter," Jane Surber recalls. For a while its huge beams were illuminated by eight-foot-long fluorescent tubes, but in time it fell into disrepair, the electrical wiring failed, and the lights on the cross went out.

Nearly twenty years passed. In October 1989 the Surbers' son-in-law died and they wanted to make the cross shine again as a memorial to him. So Bud Surber climbed the hill to see if he could fix it. A skilled electrician, he worked on the cross for several days, but he was unable to get the lights back in working order. The cross remained dark.

But when winter arrived, something strange happened. One night the lights on the cross went on again, seemingly of their own accord. No one knew why. Truckers who passed the cross on U.S. 285 near Salida, Colorado, found it shining on the hill. Families hurrying to worship services could see it from their car windows.

That night the Surbers felt especially warmed by the cross's glow, for of all nights, that night was best. That night was Christmas Eve. —RON SLAUGHTER

A Friend Was in Danger

AFTER WORLD WAR II, I MADE a close friend in Alicia, an American living in London, who had been a very brave Red Cross worker in the Pacific. On a volunteer job in the tropics, she had picked up one of those grim diseases which are slow in developing. She had married, with outstanding happiness, before she found that the germ was insidiously eating away her strength.

Then she put up a heroic fight to keep her marriage and her home going. When the doctors said that most other people would have been dead, she set out to regain her health, by courage—and by faith. She stayed up most of the time, dragging about gamely, but every now and then she would have a spell which would keep her in bed for weeks, in pain and fever and attrition.

Oddly enough, wherever I might be, and even though we might not write to each other for weeks, I always seemed to feel it in my bones when she was having one of her attacks. Then I would send her a cheerful letter by special delivery, or a light, irrelevant telegram.

One November day I was down in Italy when I sensed—out of nowhere, like an odor—that she was very ill indeed. I sent off a non-chalant telegram about missing her in Rome and hoping to see her at Christmas time. Then, though I had no answer, I wrote every two or three days for several weeks. I carried the sensation of her need with me like a drop of cologne on my handkerchief, so that I was poignantly aware of her wherever I went.

I do not happen to be a Catholic, but I love to go into the old Roman churches with their rich residue of the countless prayers that have gone up like incense, and the contact with the innumerable people who have said them in sorrow and hope and gratitude. During those weeks, I often lit a candle and put a few lire in the box for the poor, and also for Alicia.

In Italian towns there are little shrines on many street corners: majolica plaques built into the masonry above the cobblestones, with a lamp flickering; or painted and lighted figures of the Madonna and Child. And whenever I saw these—hundreds of them, as I returned northward through Italy and up into Switzerland—I would pause and think a prayer for Alicia.

In Switzerland, my bedroom window looked out into an Alpine snow scene, with white-frosted fir trees and the spire of a small Gothic church. Above the church door, in a niche curtained with hanging snow, was a miniature shrine, with a stone-carved Madonna, simple and touching as a country doll. A little lamp was kept burning underneath.

Whenever I went to the window, there was the shrine; and there, for me, was Alicia. One night I could not sleep. I got out of bed and crept shivering to the window. In the snowy stillness, with not even a star in the hushed dark, the tiny lamp was burning steadily. I put all my heart into the thought of it then, for I sensed somehow that Alicia had reached her crisis.

And as it turned out—she had. A few days later, I had a note from her husband, telling me that she had been very ill for weeks and was just starting to recover from the worst attack of all.

When I got back to London before the holidays, I found her pale and bony, but nevertheless up on her feet and struggling to make a vivid Christmas for her Charlie—who adored her, as well he might.

"I was really very critically ill this time," she told me, while we sat on a sofa before the fire. "Charlie says I was delirious. He says I kept babling about a little shrine. And one night, when my fever was very high, and I was in desperate pain—I can't recall anything else out of the blur of misery, but one thing stays with me distinctly. I can remember seeing a dark scene, and a tiny lamp burning, and—clear as if it was right before my eyes—a Madonna and Child in a little shrine."

—MARGARET MACKAY

When the Lights Came On

IN 1971, AS A NEWLY LICENSED PILOT, I was flying with my flight instructor from Vero Beach, Florida, to Longview, Texas. That night, we hit bad weather over Mobile, Alabama, and air-traffic controllers suggested we fly north toward Jackson, Mississippi, to avoid an approaching storm.

As we rose above the clouds, I noticed the instrument panel lights flicker. A minute later, radios and instruments started going dead; then all our lights went out. Our situation was desperate, and as we flew an emergency triangle, we prayed to God for His protection. We decided to drop below the clouds and try to see the ground. Soon we spotted the distant lights of Jackson and headed for the airport's rotating beacon.

We circled the control tower twice, then got a green light to land. Without any electrical power, we had to lower the landing gear manually. At that moment, all the strobe landing lights came on and slowly, safely we touched ground.

Then the landing lights went off. *That's odd.* I thought, *at least they could have waited until we taxied to the ramp.* It was even odder when a man from the tower asked us, "Who gave you permission to land?"

And then, little by little, we learned that no one in the tower had seen us circling overhead. The green light had been flashed by a traffic controller who was explaining to his visiting pastor what he would do in case a plane ever attempted to land without radio communication. The emergency landing lights were part of the same demonstration.

But the whole story can never be explained—just accepted with gratitude, as I strive to serve the Lord each new day.

—*Franklin Graham*

The Loner

T HE SHADOWS IN THE CANYON were already deepening to purple by the time my friend David and I left the biting cold of the mountain river to climb back up the ridge to the mesa above, where we'd stashed our heavy hiking gear. Wearing only tee shirts and jeans, we had earlier descended a gentler slope to one side, drawn by the sight of that idyllic valley so far below. Now, looking up from the dusky canyon floor toward the looming cliff face, still rimmed at the top in gold from the rays of the setting sun, we decided to avoid the easier path and to climb straight up into the light.

The challenge suited me. I was proud of my strong, lean body—proud of my "toughness," my independence.

As we started the climb, I glanced toward David, whom I had met just a couple of weeks before. I had to admire his own lean strength as he nimbly scaled that rocky wall. I felt I could like him very much if I would choose to do so, but I'd fought against the idea—was still fighting it. Any kind of closeness to another human being seemed to me to be a dangerous thing. To invite a person to come near meant also to invite emotional pain, and *that* I could do without. I'd watched my parents suffer through a divorce when I'd been a child, and I hadn't liked what the stress did to them, or to me. I'd decided to keep everyone at a distance, surround myself by an invisible wall. I would shut out all emotion and become totally self-sufficient.

I'd succeeded in that goal. After growing up and leaving home, I'd held several different jobs, one of them as manager of a restaurant. That, too, had been a challenge, but I'd liked being in charge of a business. Just as I liked being in charge of my own life and destiny, climbing up this cliff.

As the way grew steeper, edging toward vertical, I constantly tested the stability of the rocks before trusting them with my weight. Several times I found a rock to be loose and I searched for a different handhold or foothold before moving higher. Soon I had ascended almost two hundred feet. I glanced again toward David, seeing that he was off to one side and a little higher than I. We had only thirty or so more feet to go before reaching the top.

And then it happened. I hooked my fingers around the edge of a shelf of rock above me that I'd thought was secure, only to have it suddenly give way. With a feeling of disbelief, as though everything had gone into slow motion, I lost my balance and dropped into space, followed by a huge chunk of ledge. I heard David scream, "My God, O my God!"

God was Someone else I'd shut out of my life. All my growing years I had attended a strict religious school where the teachers described God as an angry, vengeful Being who would send me to hell for my sins. I didn't like that God, and I'd decided I wanted no part of Him. I'd go it alone, assuming responsibility for my own actions, instead of cowering in fear before some cruel, mythical judge.

And so, even in my present extremity, falling toward death, I did not call on God. But David continued to cry out, not in prayer, but in an agonized, involuntary repetition of the name.

Now occurred in sequence several events so incredible that I find them hard to believe to this day. I had fallen with my face toward the cliff, but now *my body flipped around in midair,* like a cat's, so that I was facing outward. Consequently, when my feet twice touched slight protrusions in the cliff's surface. I was tilted backward, toward the cliff face, instead of being catapulted farther into space. Then my feet landed on a small ledge, barely wide enough for one person, and the *only ledge on that whole cliff between me and the ground.* A few inches to either side, and I would have fallen past it. Sliding *between* two large cacti, I came to a halt with my legs hanging over the ledge. In one more second, I should have been crushed by the falling shelf of rock, which was several cubic feet in size. Instead, just before it would have hit me, it *veered inexplicably to the right,* grazing my shoulder and arm as it roared past.

I hung there in a daze, clutching at my narrow perch with my left hand while watching that boulder fall away toward the canyon floor one hundred fifty feet below. David came scrambling back down the cliff, frantically calling out to me. As he drew near, I heard him breathe, "Thank God, you're alive!" And then his voice changed as he groaned, "Susan—your leg..."

As yet, I felt no pain. Consequently, it was with amazement that I viewed my shattered left leg. Through the tattered remnants of my jeans, I saw three holes in the flesh of my lower leg from which broken bones protruded. My foot hung twisted around at an odd angle, like the leg of a discarded doll. I turned my head away, only to see that the inside of my right arm had been sliced completely open, elbow to wrist, exposing ripped ligaments and tendons, and a rubbery length of artery—scratched but not severed—pulsing deep inside the gaping wound.

I looked back toward David and saw that he had turned dead-white. He asked me if I thought my spine was damaged. I took mental inventory of my body, trying to determine if I had internal injuries, but I just couldn't tell. At last David said, "I don't dare try to get you off this cliff alone. I'm going to have to leave you and go for help."

I knew he was right. But the initial shock that had numbed me was beginning to wear off. I was suddenly hit by pain so devastating it froze my breath.

"Hurry—just hurry," I gasped.

He scrambled away at an angle up the ridge, heading toward the mesa and the trail that would take him out of these rugged Sangre de Cristo mountains (a Spanish name meaning "Blood of Christ") toward the jeep road, far away, where we'd left our four-wheel-drive pickup truck. I knew that the nearest hospital had to be in Española, New Mexico, about twenty miles away. I also knew it would take hours for a rescue crew to hike in with a litter. The light faded fast, taking with it the last heat from the sun. I began to shiver in my thin shirt, for September nights in the high country get very cold. In the distance I heard the rumbling thunder of an approaching storm.

As the minutes passed, the pain grew in intensity until I felt consumed by it. The storm arrived, bringing darkness and an icy rain. The surface of the ledge became slick with water and mud, so that I had to concentrate all my strength in my left arm, trying to hold on.

My mind whirled with giddiness. It would be so easy to let go and slip into that void. To die, and end the pain.

I'd recently read a book called *Life After Life* in which people who had been declared clinically dead returned to life with stories about having met a sentient light filled with love. I didn't know if such a Being existed. But if it did, it couldn't be that hateful personage called "God."

I wanted to pray to that light, but I didn't know what to call it. Finally, I did call it God, for want of a better name. I prayed for help to arrive, and for the strength to hold on until then. I said I was frightened, I said I didn't want to be alone.

And He came.

I saw no light. I heard no voice. All I can tell you is that suddenly, beside me on that ledge, there was a Presence. A Presence filled with warmth and love. I could feel strength pouring into me from that Presence, joining with, and energizing, my own fading will.

The thoughts in my mind were in my own voice, but they said, *Hold on. You can make it. You are not alone. Help will come.*

The comfort I felt in this Presence is indescribable. Whenever I would begin to fade out, something would snap me awake once more and I would discover just enough willpower left in me to pull away from the edge.

But I wanted more. I wanted the touch of a human hand. All these years, I had kept people away. Now, suspended in air on this cold cliff, crying out in pain with almost every breath, I longed desperately for someone to hold me, to talk to me, to distract me from the prison of agony my body had become.

Time flowed into a meaningless blur. And then, between my cries, I heard someone, faint and far away, calling my name. Peering down into the darkness, I saw a tiny light bobbing along the canyon floor.

I called to that light, and the light answered. I saw it veer toward me and proceed, slowly but surely, up the cliff. A face came into view over the side of the ledge, eerily white in the flashlight's glow.

It was a child. A boy about twelve or thirteen years old. I thought for a moment that I was hallucinating. But the boy scrambled up beside me on the slippery ledge. He carefully set the flashlight down in a depression in the rocks. And then he took a folded blanket from his shoulder and draped it over me, shielding me from the rain.

"Who are you?" I whispered.

"I'm Michael," he replied.

He was real. The touch of his small, dirt-roughened hands told me that. He explained that David, frantically looking for a phone, had shown up at the door of Michael's house, outside the canyon. But Mr. Browne, Michael's father, had no phone and was too ill to help with any kind of rescue effort. After hastily telling the Brownes about the accident, David had rushed away, heading once more down the mountain in his search for help.

"I thought you might be cold," Michael said, "so I came to find you." He said he'd ridden his dirt bike until the brush got too thick. Then he'd hiked on into the canyon, and at last he'd heard my cries.

He asked what he could do for me, and I suggested that he elevate my injured arm. Surprisingly, my wounds had clotted soon after the accident, so I was no longer bleeding profusely; but elevating the arm seemed to help ease the pain. However, as we shifted on the ledge, I once more slipped toward the edge. Michael quickly grabbed my shoulders and held on, stopping my fall. After he had maneuvered me back to relative safety, he continued to hang on to me, while assuring me that the rescuers would arrive soon. He made me talk in order to keep me awake. Each time I started to slide forward on the slick surface of the ledge, Michael tightened his hold, dragging me back again. He was so determined to save me that I am convinced, had I actually gone over the edge, he would not have released his hold, but would have fallen with me to his own death.

As my mind wandered, I got to thinking that Michael might be a guardian angel. But he chattered on, like any normal boy, telling me about his friends in the Española Junior High and asking me questions just to make sure I was still with him.

I had totally lost track of time. I know now that Michael held me on that ledge for over two hours before more lights appeared in the canyon—David, with a doctor and two paramedics.

The ordeal they went through for the next several hours getting me off the cliff is another story. All I can say is that there were many acts of heroism from them all as they climbed the slippery rocks, splinting my leg and arm, strapping me into a litter, lowering me on ropes to the canyon floor. Michael acted as messenger, relaying instructions from one rescuer to another. All this in cold, wet darkness.

As groggy as I was, I still realized their terrible danger, and my prayer changed: *Please, God, don't let one of them die on that cliff in helping me.*

Because of a head injury I hadn't even known about, the doctor was not able to give me pain-killers. My screams, every time I was accidentally jostled, had to be unnerving for the men, but they didn't give up. Even though they were cold and exhausted, they carried me as carefully as they could over the rough canyon floor and up the slopes to the pickup truck, then drove me over rocky jeep trails to the road where the ambulance waited. Because of the seriousness of my injuries, the doctors in Española couldn't treat me, but sent me on to St. Vincent's Hospital in Santa Fe. At last, twelve hours after my fall, I went into surgery, where the doctors pieced my torn and broken body back together.

I awoke to find myself immobilized in heavy casts. Me, Ms. Independence, totally helpless and having to rely on others for everything—bedpans, baths, food, therapy. Dozens of flower arrangements and over a hundred cards arrived, soon filling my room. Friends and acquaintances flocked to see me, saying eagerly, "You've always been such a loner, Susan, holding us off. But at last we're going to get to do something for you!"

The God I met on that ledge was neither angry nor condemning. The God I met there was love. Love, flowing from an unseen Presence to give me strength; love, coming from David and the rescue team as they struggled to get me off the cliff; love from doctors, nurses, and old friends; and love from Michael, a child who sustained me during that lonely, painful night.

When that rock fell, so did the wall I'd built around myself to shut out that love. I will never be the same.   —*Susan Peoples*

When I Saw Heaven in Mother's Eyes

THERE'S SOMETHING ABOUT A HOSPITAL in the dead of night that is different from anything else—muted sighs and stirrings, the light from the nurses' station at the end of the floor.

I sat by Mother's bed, watching. There wasn't much else I could do. Jean Hudson, the night nurse, was in and out, checking Mother's pulse and blood pressure.

In fact, as the minutes crawled past, I grew more and more sensitive to the impulse that had made me leave my husband and our three children asleep and drive to the hospital at midnight. We'd known for six weeks that Mother was dying. Ever since surgery had revealed inoperable cancer, I'd spent part of each day at her side. This night I *had to be with her.*

It was true, the last few days she'd been failing rapidly, in much pain, drifting in and out of a coma. Several times the doctor had been on the verge of telling her that further treatment was useless—but we all hesitated. All her life Mother had been such an active person, teaching at the high school, running the farm, doing office work for dad's pulpwood business, raising five children, and cheerfully taking on jobs at church. To be able to fight now, however vainly, we felt was important to her.

She still had not moved or opened her eyes since I arrived. I repeated again the prayer I had said so often in that room. It was that Mother not have to go with drugs numbing that close harmony of mind to mind and heart to heart we had always had in our family. As I had done daily the past six weeks, I prayed that Mother—who had served God so faithfully these seventy years—be allowed to come to Him in dignity and acceptance and peace.

"Julia!" Mother stirred on the bed. "Are you there, Julia?"

I assured her that I was, and she asked me to come closer. She wanted to apologize, she said, for having been so difficult (which of course she hadn't).

Her eyes opened; they looked straight into mine. "The doctor told me. And, Julia, it's all right. I've left it up to God. I'm in God's hands now, and it is so wonderful."

As she was saying this, she seemed bathed in light. As I stared at her, the mysterious radiance enveloped me as well; I felt as if I were drowning in the love and joy on her face.

I realized that she was smiling and I smiled back—but I could not express this awareness enough through smiles; it seemed that my body must burst with the fullness of that instant.

The instant stretched into minutes and the minutes into almost an hour as we looked at each other, exposed and filled with the living presence of God. I felt that Mother was seeing a world beyond the physical one, and that I was *almost* there with her.

I said to her, "Do you mean, Mother, that you see God?" and she answered, "Yes, Julia, face to face, and it is so important that everyone know. Tell Murray, Carol, Miriam, George," naming my brothers and sisters. "It's so wonderful!"

She seemed so alert, so like her former self that in frustration I almost shouted at her. "What's so wonderful? Tell me!"

"Millions and millions of people," she began slowly. "So many millions ... and all on different levels. There's light ... light everywhere ... so much light!"

Her eyes seemed so full of love and they never left mine. Her voice remained strong as she continued. "Things get between us and God. Tell them all not to let things separate them from God. I've been so concerned with my own little problems and desires. Tell them, Julia— the glory of the Lord—it is wonderful!"

They were the last words that Mother spoke. Her eyes closed, but the smile did not fade.

—*Julia Tinkey*

The Light from Somewhere

THE RAIN CRASHED like clouds of bullets on the cobbled streets of Oslo. Yet steadily more people joined the ranks, until they were eight-deep on each side of the road. And they were smiling.

"What's taking place?" I asked a man.

"It's Haakon's birthday," he said. "He'll ride through Oslo at two o'clock."

It was only noon, yet there they stood, surely everyone of Oslo's four hundred thousand, in the heavy deluge.

It was 1952 and I was making a color film of Norway. The procession obviously would provide some fine shots. But in the rain there was barely enough light to see, let alone for color photography.

And yet I sensed a strange glow all around me. A soft light seemed to fill the streets. I searched everywhere but could not find its source. Puzzled, I took out my light meter and measured the light; it registered nil. Still I knew there was a light, coming from somewhere.

Then, quite foolishly for a professional photographer who should know better, I reached for my cameras and started.

At last, at long wet last, the procession came out—one ordinary, everyday *open* car, one motorcycle cop at each side, a sound-car behind. That was all!

In the back seat of the open car an elderly man sat alone. As He approached, an immense sound arose from the people. It started as a mighty cheer, then seemed to stumble: four hundred thousand lumps in four hundred thousand throats. One got into mine, too, as I looked at that kindly figure, erect and smiling, with the rain beating him mercilessly.

I ground my camera and then dashed ahead in my car. I reached the big hospital ahead of the procession and there, to my horror, on the pavement in the pouring rain, in beds, wheelchairs, stretchers, I found the sick, the lame, the halt—umbrellas held over them, carefully covered up with hospital rubber sheeting, nurses and doctors standing behind them—all smiling radiantly.

I cried out, impulsively, "Oh, dear people, you mustn't wait out here! There's nothing to see. There's only one car with one man in it."

They all looked at me compassionately, their bright smiles never leaving their rain-spattered faces. Then one man spoke:

"Thank you," he said in English, "but, you see, that one man is Haakon, today is his eightieth birthday. And it is not only that we want to see *him,* we want *him* to see *us.* Each of us wants Haakon to know that today we wish him well."

As I listened to him other things I'd heard came back to me . . . The tailor, fitting my new coat, who had chatted of the Oslo Rotary Club where the King drops in informally. "Haakon is the head both of our government and our Norwegian Lutheran Church. He likes to know about all of our problems..." The bus driver who talked about the German invasion and Haakon's refusal to replace the Norwegian cabinet with Nazi-picked men. Escaping the German purge, Haakon removed his government to England where he kept up the fight. I remembered, too, that Norwegians never say "The day the war ended," but "The day Haakon came home..."

Just then the car with Haakon in it drove past. Up went the most robust cheer I ever heard—from wheelchairs, beds, and stretchers. He waved to them and was gone. The cheer quieted into a collective, tender sigh.

When, at 6:30 that evening in the pouring rain, Haakon spoke from the balcony of the Town Hall, I was there with my cameras. And as the crowds still danced in the streets at eleven o'clock, I was still, idiotically, filming in the dark.

Next day I stacked up all the film I'd used and wasted. Weeks later, when they came back to me, processed, I tossed them aside without troubling to examine them. I knew they would be blank.

But one day, tidying up my workshop before throwing the whole pack out, I half-heartedly put one roll of "Haakon's Birthday" on the projector. I gasped! It had all come out—in color!

Stunned, I reran the film, again and again. Everything I had photographed was there: the rain, the people, Haakon. Despite the dark day, the scenes were vividly clear and colorful. Suddenly, I discovered where the precious light originated. It was in the people's eyes as they looked fondly at their leader—the man whose own devout goodness and dedication had aroused in them a deep devotion. Studying their faces on the screen, I realized that on a dark day in Oslo I had filmed King Haakon's birthday procession by the light of pure love!

—DICKY ROTH

The Blue Flash

WE HAD BEEN CAUGHT by a blizzard, and I was in a caravan going down a winding, snow-packed mountain highway near Lake Tahoe, Nevada. My wife and three children were in someone else's car. Because of a malfunction, our van's lights, radio, wipers, heater and windows no longer worked. Snow whirled through an open window. My body ached from the cold. Then the windshield became a white wall. I tried to lean out and sweep off the blinding snow with my arm. It was no use.

Straining to see, I pulled onto the shoulder of the highway. The van lurched as a front wheel thudded off what felt like a boulder. I hit the brakes. When I jumped out, I found myself looking down into a white abyss: I'd almost driven over the edge!

"Jesus," I cried as I got back into the van, "I need Your help."

Another driver stopped and got out of his car to direct me. I put the van in reverse. Just then a stunning blue-white light shot through the windshield and struck the steering wheel. I pressed my back into the seat as the flash raced through the steering column. In that instant, radio, lights, windows, wipers, heater—everything started working at once!

"Did you *see* that?" the other driver said.

At the bottom of the mountain our family was reunited. People have told me the strange flash might have been snow lightning. For me it was an answer to prayer. —CHARLES KAELIN, JR.

A Narrow Window

A narrow window may let in the light,
A tiny star dispel the gloom of night,
A little deed a mighty wrong set right.

A rose, abloom, may make a desert fair;
A single cloud may darken all the air;
A spark may kindle ruin and despair.

A smile and there may be an end to strife;
A look of love, and hate may sheathe the knife;
A word—ah, it may be a word of life!
—FLORENCE EARLE COATES

Whether you turn to the right or to the left, your ears will hear a voice behind you, saying, "This is the way: walk in it."
—Isaiah 30:21, NIV

CHAPTER SIX

God Sends a Message

As you've seen throughout this two-book set, God can be very creative in getting his message across. Sometimes He allows one person to hear something that no one else perceives. Sometimes the messages come in the form of an inner nudge that causes someone to change direction, to stop or keep moving when common sense and circumstances tell her to do just the opposite. And after the fact she realizes that obedience to that internal message has put her in the right place at the right time, to help someone else or to protect herself.

A Father's Care

IN 1992 MY SISTER JOY WAS FIGHTING her final battle against cancer. I wanted Joy to go into a hospice here in Tucson, where we both lived, but she didn't want to leave her home. I couldn't be with her constantly. *God, who will watch over her?*

Joy and I had come from a medical family. Mom was a nurse. Dad was a small-town GP in Glenview, Illinois, twenty miles north of Chicago. His concern for his patients was legendary; he often made house calls without being summoned. Sometimes Joy and I had felt overlooked, longing for the attention he seemed to reserve for his patients. But no matter how busy he'd been all week, Dad stood on the basement stairs every Sunday morning, polishing his shoes for church.

I called Dr. Marilyn Croghan, Joy's radiologist, hoping she could convince Joy to move into a hospice. "Your father called also," she said. "He wants Joy to come live with him when we've done all we can medically . . ." Her beeper went off, and the doctor was abruptly called away before I could correct her.

Three days later Joy died at home. I called Dr. Croghan to thank her for all she'd done. Then I mentioned the phone call. "It had to be someone else," I said.

"He *distinctly* said he was Joy's father," Dr. Croghan insisted. "He talked about her case and understood all the medical details—as if he were a doctor too."

And then I knew God had provided the reassurance I needed. Dad died in 1967, but he still watched over his children.

—STEPHEN G. GLADISH

The Cross That Wasn't There

FOR MANY YEARS I OPERATED a Christian bookstore beside our home north of Toronto, and on our lawn a large neon sign called to travelers on the busy highway that passes our house. We were accustomed to strangers dropping in.

But one July evening a man drove in and called my husband over to his car. He thrust the car keys into my husband's hands, saying, "Here, take these. I'm not fit to be on the road." He confessed that he'd had several drinks.

After talking for an hour, the man said, "I need help." My husband called up an organization that helps alcoholics, and two men from a nearby chapter came by. Later, having returned from work, I made a pot of coffee, and we sat around the kitchen table, talking.

He'd been on business at the beach thirty miles to our north. He was headed home, sixty-five miles to the south of us. "I could have killed someone," he repeated over and over. I thanked God that he had reached our house safely.

In the course of conversation I asked the man if he was familiar with this area.

"No," he said.

"Do you travel this way much?"

"No."

I was perplexed. "Why did you stop at our house?"

"The sign," he said. "I saw the sign on your lawn."

The sign? How could he have seen the sign? I had given it away when I closed the bookstore . . . nearly three years before. It was gone. There was nothing left of the yellow neon cross that once stood on our lawn.

Or was there?

—LOIS TAYLOR

Strange Day at Lake Munkamba

1968. KASAI PROVINCE, ZAIRE, AFRICA. As one of the missionaries who had been allowed to return to his former station in what was once the Belgian Congo, I'd been "itinerating" for several weeks—that is, visiting among the tribal missions in a radius of about a hundred miles of my station in Moma. One evening, after preaching and showing Cecil B. DeMille's 1927 classic film, *King of Kings*. I found that I was only about thirty miles from our house on Lake Munkamba.

Almost on impulse I decided to spend the night there. It was late, after eleven, and I was very tired. But I was also tired of sleeping in my house-truck. Besides, I wanted to see the house again.

This was no ordinary house. I don't mean architecturally, though that too, given the local standards. It was extraordinary because it was *ours*—the only home in Africa that was our very own. We had built it years before as a hideaway for little family vacations, and now, with Virginia and our two sons far away in America, I longed even more to go there. The house represented home and love and a security that often seemed elusive in those days of internal African strife. I needed to be reminded of these qualities once more.

As I drove toward the lake, I wondered in what condition I'd find our hideaway this time. During the tribal fighting of the early 1960s, it had been looted frequently. Doors and windows and most of the furnishings—as well as the much-coveted tin roof—had been carried away. Our roof now covered the local chief's hut, but he had explained his taking it. "When I saw those looters taking everything from your house," he had said, "I knew you would want me instead of them to have that tin roof!" Logic against which I could offer no rebuke.

At last I arrived. The house was still there. I fumbled my way in the darkness through the bare living room to a cot in one of the bedrooms and fell upon it. Exhausted, I was soon asleep.

I awakened early the next morning, looked about a little, and said my prayers. I thanked God for another day of life and asked Him to watch over me. Outside, through the morning mist, I saw a lone native fisherman on the shore nearby. There seemed to be no one else about. All was quiet. African quiet.

Time to get going. I told myself, and took my five-gallon jerry can to the spring and filled it with drinking water. Back at the house, I picked up my hat, and was about to leave when I caught sight of the fisherman again. It made me wish I had time to join him for a quick catch. *Well, someday,* I thought. *I'd just better check to see if that outboard motor I left last summer is still here.* With so much looting, there was no telling what might have become of a prize like an outboard motor.

I put down the jerry can and went to a small storeroom in the back of the house. It was windowless and gloomy inside, but I could see that the motor was still there. *That's a relief.* I thought, reaching down and patting it as if to say, "Good boy! Stay there, because you and I have some fishing to catch up on as soon as I can get a day off!"

At just that moment I became aware of something else in a corner of the room. It was black and coiled into a circle, as though very carefully placed there. *I don't remember having a rope like that.* I said to myself. I went over to have a closer look. I went *too* close.

Oh! Oh, dear Lord!

Zoom!

I felt a spray of liquid; it was as though a red-hot nail had been driven through my right eye!

Instantly I knew that what I had taken for a coiled rope was a spitting cobra, one of the most poisonous snakes in the world!

I screamed out loud and started running, running away, but I no sooner got to the door than I stumbled over the jerry can of water. Quickly I threw myself down on all fours and frantically splashed cold water into my face, trying to put out the fire that was spreading through my head.

A figure loomed over me. "*Muambi!** What is the matter?" It was the fisherman from the lake.

He looked at me, looked at the room, and ran away. *He knows what has happened.* I told myself. *He knows there's nothing he can do. He's probably gone to tell the chief that I am here and dying.* Every native African knows that the spitting cobra first blinds and paralyzes its victim with a deadly venom before attacking again.

The pain was excruciating. Where was the snake now? I went on splashing water on my face even though I knew my flailing might cause it to strike again.

Was I beginning to feel a numbing sensation creeping over me? It seemed that way, but I wasn't sure.

Minutes went by, maybe five, maybe ten. Three people entered the room. Strangers. A man and two women, white.

The man rushed to me. "What's happened?" he asked, and I stuttered out the word, "Cobra."

He ran outside and came back with a large stick. "There it is!" he yelled, as he lifted the stick and again and again brought it down on the snake's head, killing the creature—a seven-foot-long female carrying seven eggs!

One of the women came to me, checked my pulse, and tried to look into my blinded eye. "I'm a nurse," she said. Then she looked up at the other two people helplessly. "I don't know what to do, but I feel I *must* do something!" Then, as almost an afterthought, she opened her handbag and started searching for something. "A sample of an eye medication came to me in the mail the other day. I don't know anything about it," she said, addressing me, "but it's all we have. Shall I try it on you?"

I understood what she was really saying: The poor man is going to die anyway—or go blind; why not take the gamble?

*"Preacher" or "Missionary" in the Tshiluba language.

I nodded and she put a few drops of the unknown prescription in my eye.

"It's just possible that the water you threw on your face helped," the nurse said. Now we waited to give the medication time to do its work, if it was going to.

A half hour passed. Just as the pain seemed to be easing, we heard footsteps. Another white man appeared, a stranger to the others. I was mystified. Where were all these people coming from? In those days in that part of Africa, no unidentified white man traveled alone.

Who was he? A French doctor, he said, on his way to a diamond mine fifty miles away. He'd heard of the beautiful Lake Munkamba and he'd detoured several miles off his route, parked his car a half mile away, and walked down to the shore of the lake.

The nurse explained to him what had happened to me. "Do you know how to treat venom in the eye?" she asked.

"Yes," he answered. He told us of an effective new antibiotic. In fact, he had used it successfully on a man at the diamond mine just the month before. Unfortunately, he didn't have any with him.

"Do you know anything about this?" the nurse asked, handing him the medication she had put in my eye.

He looked at it carefully. "That's it! That's it! That's the very one I was telling you about!"

The French doctor stayed for a while. Then, after giving instructions for applying the drops every thirty minutes and telling me to stay in bed for the next twenty-four hours, he left us, as quickly and mysteriously as he had arrived. None of us had even learned his name!

Now, however, I learned who my other saviors were: a Scottish missionary and his wife who were vacationing nearby and a nurse visiting them from an English mission. The kindly Scotsman took me to his house and put me to bed.

The next morning my eyesight was fully restored, my energy had returned, and my eye was not even red! Today I see as well from one eye as from the other.

But for the rest of that long day, and throughout the longer dark hours of the night, I lay reliving everything that had happened. It was easy enough to keep my body quiet, as the doctor had directed, but stilling the flow of emotion was impossible.

I prayed, of course, thanking God for His unfailing mercy and grace. I thanked Him for all of those who had had a part in my recovery and what I earnestly believed would be the restoration of my sight. I whistled hymns through my teeth and was relieved to feel no facial paralysis.

In the assurance of God's presence, I also slept. But during waking hours I played a game of "what if." What if:

... I hadn't gone for water before checking the storeroom?

... the fisherman had been on another part of the lake?

... the missionaries and their guest hadn't been visiting?

... the guest hadn't been a nurse?

... there had been no sample of a new antibiotic in her purse?

... the doctor had not appeared?

And so on and so on. This "what if" game went endlessly on.

And yet, I knew it wasn't a game at all. I knew that all of us at Lake Munkamba that morning had been participants with God in yet another of His unfathomable deeds. Had I been the object of an extraordinary series of coincidences? No, absolutely Not. For in God's world, there are no coincidences.

—WILLIAM F. PRUITT

Seeing Beyond

See the blossom on the bare branch;
See the harvest in the tiny seed;
See the wholeness in the illness;
See God's order in the confusion;
See life in the midst of death—
See the substance of things unseen.

—MILDRED N. HOYER

The Shared Dream

IN THAT MYSTERIOUS CHAPTER 2 of the Book of Daniel. God saves Daniel's life by revealing to him the content of King Nebuchadnezzar's dream. I'd long been awed by this story, for it spoke of a dimension of the Spirit that was strange to me.

Then one stormy night my wife, Elizabeth, and I sat in front of a fire with our friends Len LeSourd and his wife, Catherine Marshall. After an hour of prayer we took a break. Catherine made cocoa and our talk turned to the subject of dreams.

"I've had a recurring dream," said Catherine, leaning back in her easy chair. "Every now and then I see myself in a—"

"Field," I said, interrupting. The room fell silent. Wind blew a puff of smoke down the chimney.

"How did you know that?" Catherine asked softly.

What could I say? ... Only that as she had begun to describe her dream, I suddenly felt I knew its contents. I went on, "You are standing in a flat field. There is a stream running through the short, cropped grass ..."

I knew from Catherine's expression that I was accurate. "The peculiar thing about the scene," I concluded, "is that the creek banks don't slant the way banks usually do. They're straight up and down, yet they're not made by machinery."

And Catherine whispered that this was indeed the content of her dream.

All of us were quiet for a while. I think each of us must have had the same thought. Here we were, people of the twentieth century, experiencing a mystery from the days of Daniel. —*John Sherrill*

The Invisible Finger

*M*IDNIGHT. The warm September air surrounds me, and I am lying in bed, trying vainly to sleep. My wife, Sharon, is out of town, speaking at a women's retreat. I am all alone in this ancient ten-room house, my only company a squeaky fan in the far corner of the room. I am exhausted, but I can't seem to relax and fall asleep. I try reading my Bible, but after a few passages I don't have the concentration. I lay it open on the bedside table and snap off the lamp.

One o'clock. I stare at the ceiling and see specters of fear. Unpaid bills. Imminent conflicts. Regrets. Waves and waves of worry. Loneliness.

Two o'clock. Suddenly, there is a sound in the darkness, just inches from my head. It's the crinkle of paper. I stop breathing. It's my Bible! The pages are turning themselves, as if an invisible finger is nudging the pages. A chill goes through me. Another page turns. Then another. At last the pages are still.

I flip on the lamp and look around the empty room. Then I glance at my open Bible, wondering what my mysterious visitor has selected for me to read. A passage is underlined with a ballpoint pen that I recognize as Sharon's: "It is senseless of you to work so hard from early morning until late at night, fearing you will starve to death; for God wants his loved ones to get their proper rest" (Psalm 127:2, TLB).

Two-fifteen. I flip off the lamp, lie back and pray:

Lord, thank You for my bedroom fan, a kind of Holy Ghost, Whose gentle fingers of wind reached across my room and picked a passage of truth to remind me to let You run the world.   —DANIEL SCHANTZ

Without Knowing Why

SHIRLEY'S STORY:
The orange juice was already poured, the oatmeal nearly cooked, and I was stirring the scrambled eggs, when the crazy thought popped into my mind.

Take the kids to breakfast at McDonald's.

At first I ignored it. I'd been warned by other young widows that your mind plays tricks on you, living alone. I hadn't really been alone since my husband's death in April 1984, six months earlier—but the children were only six and four.

Go to McDonald's.

The thought came more urgently, and for a second I wondered if I was cracking up. But surely the time for that would have been those two-and-a-half years of watching my tall, blond, athletic young husband die inch by inch of a brain tumor.

If grief hadn't been able to destroy my sanity, I thought, mainly to keep my mind off this silly McDonald's notion, money worries might have. Jim had been a stockbroker here in Tulsa, Oklahoma, operating on commission, which stopped when he could no longer work.

I'd found a job selling Visa and MasterCard services to Tulsa businesses. It kept me out in the car a lot, and I'd cried a lot, there in the car. If I'd been going to fall apart, that would surely have been the time, with everything seemingly against us. Even the washing machine broke down, with no money to repair it, so that in the evening after working and cooking and caring for Jim and mowing the lawn, I'd have to drive out to the Laundromat.

Without faith in God, I thought as I gave the eggs a final turn, I really might have gone crazy. I'd carried a Bible in the car; when I felt panic rise I'd pull over and read and pray until I could go on.

The oatmeal was ready too. In the living room the kids were watching the Saturday morning cartoons. "Marie! Jason!" I called. "Wash your hands and come to the table."

And still something inside my head, quite independent of my own thoughts, was insisting that we were to leave this good hot meal right where it was, get in the car, and drive a mile away to a fast food outlet. I'd never in my life eaten breakfast at McDonald's! Where could such a notion be coming from?

Where indeed...? From the bathroom I heard Marie and Jason splashing water on the floor. I stood there at the stove, spatula in hand, thinking back to a chill December day almost two years before. Wondering if the nudging in my head now was in any way like the nudging that had come to me then...

For a week I had been giving Jim and the children cold cereal because the stove, like the washing machine, had broken down, and Jim could no longer trust himself to try electrical repairs. We were three months behind on the house payments, and as for Christmas—Santa just wasn't going to find our chimney.

All that winter morning I had called on potential clients without success. As always when our situation threatened to overwhelm me, I'd pulled the car to the side of the road. And there God spoke to me as clearly as though He'd used audible words: *Will you trust Me, Shirley? For Jim, for the children, now and forever?*

I wanted to—oh, how I wanted to! But where could I get that kind of faith? Certainly I couldn't work it up on my own. "Father," I whispered, "give me that trust."

At once a kind of peace seemed to enter the car. And into that peace dropped the names of three local restaurants. I called on all of them that afternoon and signed on three new accounts.

From then on, these "impressions" came often, sometimes about work, sometimes about Jim's medication or about one of the children, until I learned to recognize them by a quality of loving urgency very unlike my ordinary thinking process.

This idea in my head now—if it had been anything except "Go to McDonald's," I would have said this was one of those times. But that was too ridiculous!

Wasn't it?

Marie and Jason scrambled into their chairs, still in pajamas on this one morning of the week when we could loaf around the house. Well, we could go to the drive-through window...

"Get your bathrobes on," I told them. "We're going to bring breakfast home from McDonald's."

"Yay!" shouted four-year-old Jason. "Can we get French fries?"

But Marie, two years older, looked from the waiting food to me, her face as bewildered as I felt.

Not the drive-through. Go inside to eat.

"On second thought," I called as the kids headed for their rooms, "let's put our clothes on and eat there."

"Boy," I heard Marie tell her brother, "does Mommy ever change her mind."

Twenty minutes later I was steering through Tulsa's Saturday traffic, as baffled as ever as to why we were doing this, when Marie burst into tears. "McDonald's makes me think of Daddy," she sobbed.

Jason was too young to remember the days when Jim could still drive and used to take the two of them out. But he wasn't too young to understand sorrow. "Don't cry, Marie," he said.

"Why don't we pray about it?" I interrupted. So we did, and then Marie said, "God's going to give us a new daddy."

"And someone who loves God," added Jason.

I said nothing. Not out loud. But inwardly I was crying, *No!* No one could replace Jim. Not ever. It wasn't that I was mourning, exactly, I'd done that during the years of seizures and pain. Death had come as such a release for Jim that I'd had to release him too. It was just that I wasn't ready to open again to that kind of total involvement.

Before he died, Jim had asked me to remarry. "You're young, Shirley. You have your whole life ahead of you. Promise me you'll find someone else—when I'm gone."

But I don't want "someone else"! I protested inwardly as I pulled into the crowded McDonald's lot.

As I'd feared, on a Saturday morning there were long lines at the counter. Thinking ruefully of the eggs congealing in the skillet at home, I inched forward while the kids raced around the playground outside. At last I carried our trays to a window table.

That's where we were sitting when they came in, a stocky curly-haired man with a round, pleasant face—probably in his early forties—and three children, ages maybe twelve to five. I recognized the father at once: Terry Law, director of a singing group I'd seen on Oral Roberts's TV program. Certainly no one I knew personally. And yet . . . the unmistakable "impression" came as I watched the four of them get into line at the counter:

This is the reason you are here.

These four people! This particular group, of all the parents and children jamming the restaurant at this moment?

I went on eating, but the food stuck in my throat. Two years' experience in trusting God was insisting, *Introduce yourself.* When I looked up they were setting their trays down at the very next table.

Lord, I objected silently, *he doesn't know me! I can't just say. "Hello, I'm Shirley."*

Then I remembered that a girl I'd known when I was growing up back in Portland, Oregon, had joined Terry Law's music group, Living Sound, several years ago. I could ask Mr. Law about Paula.

He seemed sort of startled to have me speak to him. Paula had married a young man from Living Sound, he said, and together they were pastoring a church in Alaska. He was still looking at me oddly. Probably wondering why I was butting in on the one day he had with his family. More details about his work were coming back to me. Living Sound traveled all over the world, especially behind the Iron Curtain, where young people turned out by the thousands to hear contemporary music with a Christian message. He must hate to have strangers break into his precious time at home.

Just being polite, no doubt, he asked some questions too. When I'd come to Tulsa from Portland, what the kids' names were, what my husband did.

"Jim died last spring," I said. "I'm a widow." Mr. Law set down his coffee container so hard it slopped over. He mopped it up quickly, said he was sorry about Jim, and wrote down my phone number to give to a lawyer he thought could be helpful. Then with an apology he turned back to the youngsters who were clamoring for his attention.

What in the world, I wondered as Marie and Jason and I went out to our car, had flustered him so? And what, for that matter, I thought as I cleared away the cold remains of our uneaten breakfast back at home, had this whole strange episode of dashing out to McDonald's been all about?

I wasn't really expecting God to tell me. I'd learned to trust Him these past two years, not to understand Him. The trusting is everything: it's peace and joy and security long before the answers come. We see only a step at a time, so He can't usually tell us why.

Except that, in this case, He did . . .

T ERRY'S STORY:
  The conversation with Don Moen occurred on a Monday. Don was music director of our organization, Living Sound, and as usual he and I were aboard an airplane. This particular September day in 1984 we were returning from Arizona to our base in Tulsa, Oklahoma.

Our "base"—that's how I thought of Tulsa now: the place we traveled from. Not "home," not since my wife, Jan, died, even though our three beautiful kids were there, and my mother, who'd come down from Canada to care for Misty and Scot and Rebecca.

Across the aisle of the airplane, Don was watching me. "It's two years this month, Terry," he said, as though reading my thoughts.

Two years since my world had changed in as long as it takes for a car to leave the road and crash into a ditch. I'd been far away in England when it happened. No one ever knew what caused the accident. Perhaps the afternoon sun was directly in Jan's eyes on that east-west Oklahoma road.

I only knew that my life seemed to have ended along with hers. I plunged into a bottomless despair, unable to pray or work or believe that I would ever do these things again.

It was in this mood that I went to see my friend and mentor Oral Roberts. Three months before I lost Jan, Oral had lost a son. "How do you keep going?" I asked him.

"I do it," he said, "by praising God."

Praise? When everything in me wanted to cry and curse? "I didn't say feel it," Oral said. "It is simply a fact that God is very great. Tell Him so."

As Oral predicted, praise was the road back into life. Hollow and mechanical at first, it soon became genuine. Praise for Jan. For the thirteen years we'd had together. For her faith. For knowing for sure that she was right now with Jesus.

Week by week the praise grew stronger—and so did my ability to do the things which at first had seemed impossible: to make plans, to travel, to minister to others around the world. Only the loneliness did not change. Praise helped me to live with the emptiness; it did not fill it.

Friends asked, of course, if I would consider marrying again. I knew I should, for the kids' sake. Eleven, nine, and four—how much they needed a mother!

I knew I should consider it for my mom's sake too. No one could have stepped in more selflessly than she had. But she'd raised her family. In justice she should be taking it easy now.

And yet . . . to consider marrying was just what I could not do. Every time I took my loneliness to God, He seemed to tell me: *two years.* It was always the same. I was not even to let the subject enter my head before that time. And that's what I'd told these friends.

Don was leaning across the narrow airplane aisle. "Two years," he repeated. "Remember what you said?"

"That I couldn't think about marrying for two years," I said. "And I haven't."

"Well, two years are up," Don persisted. "You'd better start thinking."

I leaned my head back in the seat, turning over my not-very-hopeful position. To me my three children were the greatest in the world, but what woman would want to take on marriage and motherhood all at once?

Where, for that matter, would I even meet an unmarried woman my own age? There were plenty of single girls in Living Sound, but they were kids in their twenties. I was forty-one. I'd want someone I could talk to. Someone who could understand the trauma that Misty and Scot and Rebecca had gone through.

I kept waiting for Don to pick up a magazine or something, but from the other side of the aisle he was regarding me expectantly.

"She'd have to be a widow," I heard myself say. "Someone who had as good a marriage as Jan and I had, and knows what it is to lose the most important person in your life. Anyhow," I finished, embarrassed at this outburst, "I don't know any widows."

"God does," Don said. "Let's pray about it."

"I will," I promised him, trying to close off a subject I wasn't ready for.

But Don had bowed his head. "Father, You know Terry's need, and his children's need. We believe You have a plan already at work..."

I glanced self-consciously at the other passengers. "Father," I joined in, keeping my voice as low as I could, "there's a widow somewhere who—"

"There's a widow in *Tulsa*," Don corrected.

"All right. In Tulsa. I ask that in Your own time—"

"Quickly."

"Okay. I ask that You quickly reveal..."

We prayed for several minutes, there on opposite sides of the aisle, I in generalities, Don in specifics. At the close, he stuck out his hand. With another nervous glance around, I reached across and gripped it.

"Thank You, Father," he pronounced, "that it's done."

Just like that. Prayer, in Don's view, didn't have to be long and eloquent. Just concrete and totally trusting.

At the office in Tulsa a number of crises were waiting for us. Living Sound had teams on the road both in the United States and

Europe, including several Iron Curtain countries, and the week was hectic.

Crises or no, however, Saturdays belonged to the family. This was the morning, when I was home, that I took the kids out to breakfast. And the outing always started with a debate.

"Grandy's," I suggested as we piled into the car, naming the place that made the pancakes I liked.

"Denny's," thirteen-year-old Misty voted.

"McDonald's," said six-year-old Rebecca.

"You just like the slide," Scot scoffed with the sophistication of just-turned-eleven. "I say Denny's."

"Denny's wins!" cried Misty.

"Now wait a minute, you two," I said. "Rebecca hasn't gotten to choose for weeks. Let's let her decide today."

And that was how, a few minutes later, the four of us were standing in the line at the McDonald's counter and I was gazing across the room at one of the most beautiful women I'd ever seen. Not a brunette beauty like Jan. This girl had hair the color of sunlight. In fact, where she sat at the window with two little tow-headed kids, the sun streaming through her long blond curls seemed to light up the room.

Maybe it was because I hadn't thought about marriage at all for two years, but I felt a stab of envy for her husband. I was thinking that it would be great just to sit near someone that pretty when, as we left the counter with our trays, the table next to her opened up.

I was trying to decide how to strike up a conversation when to my surprise she did it for me: "Aren't you Terry Law?" A friend of hers, it turned out, had sung for a while with Living Sound. We talked about her friend and then about anything I could think of. I found out that her kids were named Marie and Jason. Their mother's voice was as nice to listen to as her face was to look at.

I peeled the lid from my coffee container as I thought of more questions. Like, "What does your husband do?"

When the girl with golden hair said, "I'm a widow," I took a swallow that scalded my throat all the way down.

What else I said to her I can't remember, except that I managed to get her phone number with some excuse about a lawyer. All I could hear was Don Moen's prayer on the airplane only five days earlier.

All I could think was, *O Lord my God. You are very great.*

—*Shirley and Terry Law, as told to Elizabeth Sherrill*

EDITOR'S NOTE: *Shirley and Terry were married in January 1985, five months after the "chance" meeting at McDonald's. A sixth child, Laurie Ann Law, was born in March 1986, "but she's not 'ours' any more than all the rest."*

I Heard His Cries

I'M A SOUND SLEEPER. Only thirst or a headache ever wakes me up. A car speeding past, a dog barking, a passing thunderstorm—I can sleep through almost anything. But for no apparent reason I woke up with a start one cool fall night.

At first I thought it was time to get up. No, my clock showed 1:00 A.M. I listened. All was still, yet I felt as though I had awaked for some reason. I sat on the side of the bed, bolt upright. Several minutes passed. The bedroom windows were closed and the curtains drawn. No noise from the outside. There was total silence.

Then I heard, distinctly, a man's voice: "Help me, help me. Oh, please, help me!"

The voice sounded like it was in the room with me. "Help me, help me! Oh, please, help me!"

Immediately I called the police emergency number. "Someone needs help," I said, "out near my street." I told the dispatcher where I lived and, satisfied that I had done all I could, I went back to bed.

Even before I fell asleep, the police dispatcher called me back. She sounded incredulous. "How did you know someone was there?" she asked.

"I heard his cries," I said.

"But how could you?" she asked. She knew my condominium was set well back from the street. My windows were closed and I hadn't heard the police drive by. "The man you heard," she explained, "was trapped in a car at the bottom of a ravine nearly two blocks away."

"I heard him," I said. Somehow I heard him.

—*VIRGINIA ANN VAN SETERS*

Unscheduled Appointment

MY FLIGHT HOME from a brief trip to New York had been a pleasant one—up until the last half-hour. Then, for no reason at all, apprehension began to gather in me like the dark clouds of the turbulence we'd just passed through over Texas.

But the turbulence hadn't unnerved me. After fifteen years of being a nurse, it takes a lot to rattle me. That's what was so strange about my unease. When the pilot announced, "We passed through the turbulence easily with only a small time loss," my hand shook so that I spilled my coffee. One thought flashed through my mind like a danger signal: *We'll be late landing in Phoenix.*

Why worry? I asked myself. I wasn't trying to make plane connections. I was just going home. My husband and children would be in no hurry. It had long been a practice in our family to make meeting planes a family-fun occasion. The children enjoyed watching the other planes land before the special plane was met. Then we would always have Cokes together in the airport before going home. So, there was no *reason* to be upset over being a few minutes late, I chided myself. That thought was followed by the warning, *Hurry!*

I looked about me. Who had spoken? Or had I only *felt* someone had spoken? In spite of my protesting logic I folded my blanket and returned it to the rack above the seat. Then I straightened myself and collected all my belongings as if we were on the ground, ready to disembark.

I felt no calmer once my things were collected. In fact, I felt more upset. I glanced at my watch. How ridiculous! Fifteen more minutes. I asked the stewardess for a glass of water and fumbled in my purse for an air-sickness pill. But, as I fingered the white capsule, again I felt it. *No. The pill will relax you. And you will need to hurry!*

But why would I need to hurry? I'd just phoned my family before getting on the plane. They were all well and safe—unless they had had an accident on the way to the airport. No, I was sure that my family was all right. But I didn't take the pill.

For the next fifteen minutes I sat, belongings in hand, waiting to land. Soon below us Phoenix was a glistening canopy of lights in the black night.

"When will we land?" the man behind me asked the stewardess. "Are we very late?"

"Any minute now," she answered, checking her watch. "We'll be about four minutes late." Her words sent a chill through me. *You should be down there now!* But what possible difference could four minutes make?

Yet, I felt it again. *Hurry up. Get out your baggage stubs.* The words were felt more than actually heard, so definite this time that I obeyed without question. The plane landed safely and taxied to the terminal.

When the "fasten your seat belts" sign flashed off, I jumped out of my seat and scrambled down the ramp. I was glad to see my family well and safe. But still that didn't relieve my feeling of anxiety. A stronger force was now guiding my very footsteps. I barely kissed the family, scooped up my four-year-old into my arms, and kept walking. My husband glanced at me questioningly when I headed away from the restaurant, the scene of our usual gab-fest.

"I *need* to get my baggage," I called over the children's heads. They followed me reluctantly toward the baggage depot. There I could see my two blue suitcases, but something else caught my eye!

Three feet in front of my bags was a small cluster of people around a wheelchair. *Hurry up! Go to him! You're late!* I ran to the group and pushed my way through. A man in his sixties lay slumped in the chair. His skin was ashen. "He's got a chronic lung condition, but he's never been this bad before," said the man's wife, her voice shaking.

"I'm a nurse," I said. I examined the man. He wasn't breathing. There was no pulse. I put my ear to his chest; I thought I heard a very faint heartbeat.

"Dear God, help me," I said under my breath, then aloud:

"You! Call an ambulance," I pointed to a young man in the tiny gathering. To another I said, "Call the Fire Rescue Squad."

"Louis," I turned to my husband, "help me get him to the floor."

Once the ill man was flat on the floor, I began mouth-to-mouth resuscitation, alternately blowing, resting, not daring to stop. By the time another nurse, also a passenger, arrived on the scene, an occasional beat of the man's heart could be felt in the pulse at his wrist.

The additional nurse and I were able to massage the heart externally. We continued mouth-to-mouth resuscitation until the Fire Rescue Squad came with an oxygen unit. Then a passing doctor arrived to help us. By now, the ill man's pulse was becoming more and more frequent.

When the ambulance arrived ten minutes later, his color had changed from ashen to life-pink.

My children, who had stayed off to the side, out of the way, joined my husband and me as we watched the ambulance drive off.

"I've got your suitcases, Mom," my son said.

"Thanks," I murmured, and then I said another heartfelt "thanks" to that voice I'd felt—to the One who knew that four minutes made the difference between life and death.

A phone call to the hospital the next day reassured me that the man would fully recover. I've recovered too—recovered my faith that over the years had become so casual I no longer expected the type of guidance that came to me on the airplane.

Yet, I know now that God can speak to us in many ways. He can even nudge us to hurry when He has a job for us.

—*Jeanne Murray Hill, R.N.*

The Angel of Opportunity

O
N A FRIDAY EVENING in November, as was my habit, I stopped by the delicatessen after work. All day I had looked forward to an end-of-week treat—fish and chips, perhaps, or a stodgy pork pie. But the evening was soaking wet with a penetrating Pacific Northwest chill.

I joined the throng of umbrellas clustered around the deli window. Standing next to me was a hunched-over figure in a thin, frayed jacket. From the peak of the cap pulled low over his forehead dripped a steady stream of rain. Every few seconds he gave a shudder, as though his bones were rattling from the cold. He looked at the food with the hypnotic stare of a most hungry man. *Poor fellow,* I thought. I wondered whether I should buy him something to eat. I checked my watch. My bus was due momentarily; another was not due for over an hour. No, I couldn't take the time to buck the crowd, either for myself or for him. I elbowed my way out and started to walk briskly to the corner.

But as is so often the case when the push of our soul leans against the hardness of our heart, I hesitated and looked back. He was looking directly at me . . . pathetic, pleading. I spun on my heel and walked on. But only for a few paces. Again I was gripped by that overwhelming desire to look back. I knew suddenly that whether or not I missed the bus, I needed to get that man something to eat.

But he was gone. Vanished. I walked up and down the street with an urgent obsession, but I could not find him. *Was he an angel of opportunity in disguise?* I wondered miserably as I rode my bus home. If so, I had missed the opportunity.

A few years ago I had a conversation with a man who had met Mother Teresa. Touched by her messages, he asked her, "May I come with you back to India? I want to learn more of all your teachings."

"If you want to learn my teachings," she replied, "you do not have to come with me. Take the money you would spend on the air fare and give it to the poor. There! You have *all* my teachings." —*Fay Angus*

Deep in God's Wilderness

T HERE IS A SACREDNESS in nature. Perhaps you feel it too. Nature has molded me and taught me, and it is deep in the heart of the woods that I feel happiest, and closest to a spiritual presence, closest to God.

The story I'm going to tell you is about a time when I experienced that mystical presence. It came in an unusual way, and it taught me the importance of being still, of listening.

At the time I didn't know what to do with my life, how I would make my living. I had a degree in art from the University of Maryland, and yet, with all of that education, I didn't want a regular nine-to-five job. Like many young people out of school, I wondered, *What now?*

I had no job offers and no idea of what to do with my degree. I'd grown up in the Chesapeake Bay community of Severna Park, Maryland, in the fifties and sixties. Now, in the early seventies it was time to fill some purpose, time to earn my way.

Growing up had been the same for me as for most kids in our area. Scouting, public school, supportive parents, and Sunday church had helped in the making of me. The only difference, I suppose, was that I seemed much closer to nature. Dad always said, "Doug knows what's under every rock between here and town," and that seemed fine with my folks. No one ever disapproved of my backyard menagerie or yelled at me when a frog was seen hopping across my room. They listened faithfully to the nature "lectures" I gave to Cub Scouts and to classes.

For a time after finishing school I dabbled with paints and did landscapes and abstracts at my grandmother's farm in New Hampshire. But that was a tough way to make a living. I grew restless. I wanted to see the rest of the country, and one spring day I stuck out my thumb and headed down the road.

I traveled through New York, then southwest across the Appalachian Mountains down to Memphis and the banks of the Mississippi. I took a factory job, briefly, then headed on through Arkansas and Oklahoma and across the top of Texas. And everywhere I went the same question traveled with me: *What will I do with my life?*

It followed me across the Rio Grande and into the Indian town of Gallup, New Mexico, where I hopped a freight for California and watched landscapes to the rhythm of the wheels.

Clickety-clack, clickety-clack through the mesas, where Navajo women herded sheep. *Clickety-clack, clickety-clack* through Arizona's desert painted by sunset. *Clickety-clack, clickety-clack* into the cold of the night. *Clickety-clack, clickety-clack—what will I do? What will I do?*

After a number of weeks along the Pacific Coast I made my way north, up to British Columbia and the edge of the Rockies, where one morning I was hitchhiking along the New Denver Road. I hadn't seen a sign of civilization for miles. I was wondering if a car would ever come along. Finally a young couple stopped to give me a lift, and after an exchange of introductions and a few miles of getting acquainted they invited me to camp with them.

"What do you do?" they wanted to know.

"Well, that's a question," I told them. "I studied art in school, and now I'm traveling around the country to see what I can see."

There was that question again. People everywhere wanted to know *what do you do?*

We stayed by the stream that followed the road. We fished and shared our food. I showed them how to find stinging nettles and to steam them like spinach. But we didn't talk much. They were quiet, and that wound me down. I began to listen, carefully. To sounds around me. To feelings inside of me.

The peaks of the mountains loomed overhead, and I felt an urge to climb to the top. To stand at the top and to look out and to feel that mixture of elation and humility. To be one with nature.

I told my friends that I'd be back by nightfall, packed a lunch, my sketch pad and pen, and waded across the stream toward the slope. A dipper bird fished upstream from me, and on the other bank a couple of large toads sprang out of my path. There was no trail. I had to bush-whack my way up the mountain, through brush and forests. All morning I climbed up, and up, and up.

It was hard work, and in the heat of the climb I peeled off my sweater. It was spring in the Rockies, early June, and young leaves were just beginning to open on the lower side of the mountain.

Despite the upward struggle, the fallen trees and thickets, the tricky footings, I felt exhilarated by the challenge and by the anticipation of reaching the peak. There would be something special there. A view. A feeling. Something, I felt.

Breaking a wad of spruce gum from a tree trunk, I chewed it on the trek up. I scrambled higher, higher, through the spruces, until, finally, I reached a high rocky ridge.

Oh my! I'll never make that peak, I realized. It was far in the distance, magnificent, covered in snow. I could never reach the top and return to camp by nightfall. *I'll have to turn back,* I thought, disappointed.

I sat on a ledge and ate my lunch, and thought to myself that few people had ever reached this perch or looked out at this majestic wilderness. Maybe none. I felt that I could see forever, over miles and miles and miles of God's creation. And in the quietness of that spot, I opened myself to the beauty around me.

I listened. And I sketched the panorama of peaks; then I started back. And that is when it happened.

I was going down, down, back into the timber, pushing my way quietly into a thick growth of spruce trees, when I was startled by a sudden *whir-r-r-r* of wings.

I'd flushed a bird, a large one. But instead of flying off, it landed on a branch hardly ten feet away!

It looked like a partridge, with red wattles on each side of its beak. Its feathers were mottled brown, except for its tail, which was chestnut-tipped.

I later identified it in a guidebook as a bird rarely seen because of its wilderness habitat. It was a spruce grouse.

"How strange," I muttered to myself. I felt almost in awe of this bird. But what struck me as particularly eerie was this—the bird almost seemed to be *talking* to me!

Ko-o-o-ok, ko-o-o-ok, ko-o-o-ok. It stared at me and made that soft sound. Very quietly.

I waited, spellbound, for it to fly from the branch. But it didn't. It stayed and kept looking at me and uttering, *Ko-o-o-ok, ko-o-o-ok, ko-o-o-ok.*

I watched for several minutes. Then I eased out my sketch-book and started to sketch him. And he remained.

I'd never known a bird to act like that. It was as if he wanted to be near me. Quickly I drew a rough sketch, hoping that he'd stay. He just perched there curiously bobbing his head, watching me sketch, and uttering, *Ko-o-o-ok, ko-o-o-ok, ko-o-o-ok.*

I made another sketch, and another with a few more details. I felt myself caught up in the excitement of drawing this strange and beautiful bird. Excited by the discovery. Excited? Thrilled!

I felt a thrill. *This is it! This is it!* My mind seemed to explode with the discovery, with the relief of knowing.

"Here I am high in the Canadian Rockies drawing pictures of rugged wilderness landscapes and unusual wildlife, combining my love of the outdoors with my years of training in art school. I'm a *wildlife artist!*" This seemed like the fulfillment of a lifelong dream. "A wildlife artist!" I could hardly contain myself.

"Here I am on my own, drawing this bird. Nobody hired me. No museum sent me. I came here on my own, and I can develop a career on my own—combining nature and art. It is possible! I'm doing it now, and I can do it for the rest of my life."

And that's what I've done. I wrote and illustrated a book entitled *Roots,* an underground botany and forager's guide. I've taught people how to weave fibers from wild plants, how to make baskets from bark, how to make silk from cocoons. I've lectured at the Museum of Natural History and I've taught at the Smithsonian Institution.

The spruce grouse, the bird that started me on my way flew out of my memory until a year or two ago, when an Indian friend brought him back to mind.

"I'll bet I know a bird you've never seen," he challenged me.

"Which one?" I asked.

"The spruce grouse. A bird that lives in the far north," he said.

"I did see a spruce grouse once," I told him, "in the Canadian Rockies. He made a strange little sound like this: *ko-o-o-ok, ko-o-o-ok, ko-o-o-ok.*"

"Do you know what the Indians say about him?"

"No," I replied. "What?"

"We call him the messenger bird. He often brings an important message."

I stood speechless, thinking back to that grouse staring down at me, repeating over and over his message. A message that had shaped my life.

And now, in nature, I try to listen more closely, with my whole spirit. And it is in nature that I feel most aware of the spiritual messages that I need to hear. Listen carefully. You might hear them, too

—DOUG ELLIOTT

"Mom, Mom!"

WHEN THE GIRLS WERE YOUNG I could hear them calling for me at night, "Mom, Mom!" if they were sick or troubled, and I would go rushing down the hall to their bedsides. But this time when I heard the cry "Mom, Mom!" both daughters were grown, and Kathryn was a married woman, traveling halfway around the world with her husband, Peter. Still, it was unmistakable—she was calling me.

Picking up a Bible from the nightstand, I went into the family room to pray. I had a feeling of great urgency; Kathy needed help. "Dear God, show me what to do," I prayed. Then I turned to the 91st Psalm, repeating it over and over again, before I was able to feel at peace.

A few weeks later we got a letter postmarked from Singapore. "I'm grateful to be able to write this," Kathy began. "I can now tell you I was quite ill in Borneo with some sort of flu. We were there, doing our usual exploring one afternoon, when I suddenly became very sick and feverish.

"Back in our room, Peter became worried. As I rambled incoherently, he searched for someone who knew of a good doctor. Finally he found a local doctor who came to our scruffy, rented room. Seeing our predicament, this good man invited us to his house, where he and his housekeeper nursed me back to health—thank God."

What touched me most came at the end of the letter. "Remember when I was a girl, and I would call out, 'Mom,' and you would come rushing down the hall? That night in Borneo, in my fever, I called ...

"And then I could hear you rushing down the hall."

—CAROL L. MACKAY

He Passed the Test

TEN-YEAR-OLD BILLY FOY WAS BUSY with his homework in the family's mobile home outside of Albany, Indiana. His mother was at work and his father was out in the barn working on a tractor. Suddenly Duke, the mutt at Billy's side, began barking and jumping at the window.

"Calm down, Duke," Billy said. He looked to see if someone was outside or if a cat or a squirrel was racing up a tree. Nothing. But Duke went on running from the window to the door. "Okay, okay," Billy said as he got up and let the dog out. There was something about the way Duke raced straight to the barn, barking all the way, that made Billy follow him.

In the barn Billy was shocked at what he found. A seven hundred-pound steel bracket had fallen off the tractor and pinned his father to the floor.

Billy started to run back to the phone to call for help. "No," his father gasped, fighting for words, "get a jack."

Billy had worked with his father and knew how to operate the equipment. He used a hydraulic jack to raise the heavy bracket. Then with a floor jack he lifted the bracket enough for his father to roll out. "Thank God you came," Mr. Foy said to his son. "I was about to black out."

While recovering in the hospital, Billy Foy's father was told about what Duke had done. Mr. Foy had not wanted another dog and so Duke had been with them "on trial." He'd only been there three days.

He's been there ever since. —PATRICIA WALWORTH WOOD

The Strip Miner

I WAS BARELY OUT OF MY TEENS when our weekly paper in Greenville, Kentucky, began running stories about the great new shovel Peabody Coal was putting together at their mine in the low hills just outside of town. Whenever I could, I'd ask for time off from my stockroom job and drive out to watch.

I could hardly believe the size of the machine that was taking shape out there. Her crawlers went up first, so big they dwarfed the buses that brought the welders out to work on her. Her housing went up next, and then came the boom carrying the stick and bucket that would strip away the hills from the miles-long, six-foot-thick seam of coal that lay beneath the surface. That bucket was the size of the living room in the new home my bride, Dorothy, and I had. No wonder the crews that would operate No. 3850 were already calling their shovel "Big Hog."

Then came the day in March 1962 when I joined a small crowd of men to watch the huge yellow-and-green shovel fire up for the first time.

"You could stand the Statue of Liberty under that boom," said a voice behind me, "and still have ninety feet to spare."

I turned and saw a neighbor who worked at another mine.

"Someday," I told him, "I'm going to run that shovel."

"Not me," the miner said with a laugh. There was an approving murmur from other men standing around. The problem, it seemed, was responsibility. The mine and the TVA power plant that made electricity from her coal would employ four hundred men. To keep them busy Big Hog had to operate twenty-four hours a day every day of the year. If that shovel stopped working, everybody stopped working. "I'll take a little less money and sleep nights, Bill," the miner said and turned to walk away.

But responsibility was something my daddy had raised me to live with. It was my job as a boy to chop kindling and milk the cow morning and night. Once, I didn't get my work done. That day my father came in from the underground mine where he worked and took me aside and told me that when I had a job to do I was expected to do it. Always. No questions. We depended on each other, my father said, and that was a good and a God-given thing. So men depending on one another didn't stop me and Dorothy from praying that someday I'd be up there in that glassed-in operator's cab.

At last when I was twenty-nine years old and three of our four children had already been born, a position on the shovel did open up. Midnight, April 14, 1969, I stepped onto the company bus with the rest of the hoot-owl shift. It was a mile trip now, across the plain Big Hog had been making out of the Kentucky hills, to the place where the shovel was sitting on the seam of coal she was uncovering. The bus stopped beside Big Hog, and we got out and stood in the floodlights and noise beside the crawlers.

"Well, Carver," shouted the shift operator, "there she is—Big Hog."

He nodded us toward the elevator, and moments later we were standing in the housing just outside the operations cab, a hundred feet above the pit floor. Big Hog's generators whined and her winches screamed, but to me the noise sounded great. We stepped into the cab and shut the door, and at last you could hear! The cab was spotless, just as I thought it would be, a bright yellow and green, with a lot of glass above and around us. The first thing that struck me was the great speed. The operator turned his housing back and forth on its rollers like a man running a whirl ride at an amusement park.

I was introduced around, and the men seemed glad to have me aboard, as if they sensed I was part of the breed that would like it up there. My job was the lowest on the four-man crew—mostly it was cleaning and moving things, but it was a way to get ahead.

I spent the first three years learning the ways of Big Hog, moving slowly up the ranks. One of my chores as oiler was to scramble up the boom to its highest point. Not everybody would like riding point. Those days, they didn't stop the shovel while you climbed the boom's ladderlike steps. The boom danced up and down, swiveling left and right at a dizzying speed. If Big Hog hung her bucket into hard rock while you were up on point, she shuddered and bucked, and you'd better grab onto something if you didn't want to fall two hundred fifty feet.

I tried to ride point just at dawn so I could see the sun come up. What a place for my own kind of quiet time, sitting on the very highest part of the shovel with nothing above me but just heaven. Peabody prided itself on putting the land back the way it was, minus the coal. They saved the topsoil we dug and then spread it on the worked-over land and replanted it. Wildlife was already coming back. I'd wait up there on point, watching as the deer came down to drink at the new lake. Muskrats and coons and possums and foxes and a raft of geese were out too. That was my time for thinking what an amazing thing it was for God to give us this place to manage.

The company encouraged operators to train crewmen on the controls, because on-the-job was the only way anyone could learn. One night after I'd been on Big Hog a little over three years I came in for coffee and stood behind the operator. Then came the question I'd been waiting for.

"Want to see what she feels like, Bill?"

Did I! The operator showed me what I already knew: which lever moved the housing, which moved the boom, which lowered or raised the stick and bucket. He showed me the emergency kill button that would shut the shovel down dead. "Hope you never have to use *that*," he said.

The operator stood up and I took his place, and then I barely touched the lever that moves the stick toward the highwall. I was astonished. It was not at all like the work I had done on a bulldozer. Big Hog's living-room-sized bucket moved with no more effort than it takes to throw a light switch.

"Different from a dozer, isn't it?" the operator said.

Different, yes, but not easy. Your bucket was half a football field away from you. You had to time yourself just right or you'd scramble thousands of dollars worth of cables. Each move had to be precise. You just eased that bucket up, shearing off the dirt and rock.

Years went by and I liked my work more as each day passed, especially when I was up on point, knowing Dorothy was home praying for us. Dorothy kept a CB radio scanner by our bedside, tuned to the company channel which off and on through the night would crackle with talk between the shovel and the office. When the radio woke her up she would pray for us.

Which is the only way I can explain what happened the morning of the accident.

I'd finally made it to the top. Our operator had been letting me take longer and longer turns at the controls, and when he retired, after I'd been working on Big Hog for eight years, I was next in line for the job. Everything went smoothly at first. But then came the night of March 4, 1980.

Fifteen minutes before quitting time it was still dark outside. Three of us were in the cab; our oiler was off somewhere. How can I understand what happened then? Something was *wrong* with Big Hog. I heard inside my head the idea, *The bucket's going to break in two.*

I whirled around.

"Get down!" I shouted. I hit the kill button.

Big Hog stopped. The men backed away from me, puzzled because nothing seemed wrong out there in the night.

At that instant there was a sharp report, like shot going off at the highwall. I watched dumbfounded as the bottom of the bucket fell off. Tons of dirt and rock hit the pit floor. Dust flew up in the floodlights. The stick snapped its cables. Exploding sounds cracked all around as the arm-sized cables broke and lashed our cab and wrapped around the boom.

Rivets popped like machine guns going off. "This is it!" someone whispered. Through the dust cloud I saw the great boom buckle, crumble, fall almost in slow motion to the floor of the pit. Rocks. Smoke. Screaming metal.

And then silence.

I looked around the cab, covered with shattered glass. The two men with me in the cab were shaking but safe. Where was the oiler? "Richard!" I shouted. We pulled and yanked and pried at the wedged door until at last it gave . . . and there stood Richard in the ruined housing just outside the cab.

Stunned, safe.

I got home hours after the ambulances came racing into the pit. Now I was sitting at our kitchen table with Dorothy, neither of us talking much. It wasn't until I tried to tell her about the strange warning that I knew how strung out I was.

The warning had given me only a few seconds, but without it I wouldn't have hit the kill button *ahead* of time. We'd still have been under power and those cables would have just kept on hitting us. As it was, no one was hurt.

No one, that is, but Big Hog.

There in our kitchen my mind went back to the shovel lying in her own wreckage on the floor of the pit. Suddenly my lip began to tremble. I looked at Dorothy and we both knew I was going to cry. I put my head down on the kitchen table, not ashamed to weep, and Dorothy didn't stop me.

At first I didn't want to go out to the mine to see Big Hog stretched out. But then Peabody announced that they had made a decision. They'd rebuild No. 3850 if it took every welder in the United States. Sure enough, three months after the accident I climbed into the operator's chair again and looked through the floodlights toward the highwall. I touched the starter. Big Hog fired up smooth as could be, and once more we began making coal.

One thing about any mine: sooner or later the seam itself runs out. We worked for four more years but then reports began to filter through that the coal was pinching off. We knew our jobs would be finished soon, and one day the superintendent himself came in.

"Boys," he said, "it's been a good mine, but we're about through."

And so we were. I'll never forget the day, fifteen years after I first went to work on the shovel, when I got into the elevator for the last time, climbed onto the company bus, and rode away.

And Big Hog? It was impractical to walk her to another mine, too expensive to cut her up and move her elsewhere. So they took our shovel to the middle of the pit and there they made her dig her own grave. When she couldn't go any deeper they brought in a drag line to finish the job.

For weeks I refused to go out to watch or even to think much about Big Hog. What was over was over.

But then I got to thinking. Soon 3850 would be gone. Maybe I could do something to keep her *memory* alive. Which is why I'm putting this down now, so my grandchildren will know what kind of work we did at the mine.

I don't think I'll end with the account of the burial, though. Instead I'll talk about the morning when I was back up in the cab for the first time after the accident. The shift was coming to a close that morning, and it was the hour I used to have by myself up on point. I couldn't go up there much anymore. But that morning from my operator's chair in the cab I spotted a deer on the highwall, and I recalled all those dawns when I used to watch the wild animals break cover.

. For a quarter century here at our mine, human beings and wild creatures and hard black coal had come together, and it all took place around Big Hog. You can't watch that without something happening to you. That's what I want to say to my grandchildren. I want to tell them how it is that a man and a coal shovel can have something between them that goes ... well ... beyond just having a job to do.

—BILL CARVER

Lookout on Loneliness

ON A LOFTY PEAK, above the four-thousand-foot level in the rugged Cascade Mountain range in Washington state, I learned a lesson about loneliness. I was a fire lookout who lived in a small twelve-by-twelve cabin atop a forty-foot tower known as Haystack Lookout, which was poised on the edge of a cliff.

One day during a hot, dry spell, I was outside on the catwalk scanning my territory for smoke. The air was so still that the calls of elk, screaming on distant peaks, sounded high-pitched and clear like bird calls. Suddenly a feeling of deep depression swept over me and I could not shake it off. It was an overpowering sense of complete aloneness. I was miles from the nearest human being—and I broke into sobs.

A slight breeze came over the northeast ridge; a leaf fluttered up and past me. Then, from nowhere, a tiny bit of downy fluff rose on the air currents and slowly floated toward me. I held my breath as I watched the bit of fluff settle on the tip of my tear-moistened nose.

At that moment I heard a transmission on my tower radio. I turned quickly, listening for my call letters. The message was not for me. I caught sight of my reflection in the windowpane. My face and nose were red from weeping and the bit of fluff bobbed merrily, still clinging to the tip of my nose. I grinned at my reflection. It grinned back. The absurdity of the moment touched me and I laughed aloud. It was as though the Almighty had tapped me gently on the nose, saying, "See, young lady, you are not alone."

The breeze grew stronger, bringing storm clouds up from the Pacific Ocean. Thunder sent me scampering to check the antenna and close the windows. I was braced and ready when the storm hit. Lightning filled the cabin with eerie blue light. Thunder crashed, amplified by the tin roof above me. My hair stood on end as I swung my Osborn fire-finder to sight the cloud-to-earth lightning strikes and record them.

When the storm departed, leaving behind it a gentle rain that bathed the hills and valleys, I sank onto my bunk, emotionally exhausted. I looked for the bit of fluff and discovered that it was gone.

Gone, but it had left a message for me—God is kind. He had knocked some sense into my head in a most gentle manner—not with a clap of thunder or bolt of lightning, but with a reminder as delicate as my mood.

It was an experience I'll never forget. And whenever friends ask if I was ever lonely up there on Haystack Lookout, I smile brightly and answer, "Only once. Then Someone reminded me that we are never really alone." —DOROTHY C. GRASSMAN

"Pray for Helen"

P RAY FOR HELEN. The words came to mind during my morning devotions. "Helen who?" I asked myself.

I had three friends named Helen but, to the best of my knowledge, none needed special prayers. Still, I asked God to be with "Helen"— whatever her need. Later I checked with the three Helens I knew. I was right. They had no special need for prayer.

For seven mornings I heard the same request, and for seven mornings I prayed for the mysterious Helen. On the eighth day the order stopped. *Has Helen solved her problem?* I wondered.

I'd forgotten the Helen incident by the time a letter with a Florida postmark arrived. My mother had forwarded it from our home in Arkansas to Los Angeles, where I was living. "I'm writing this for our mutual friend, Helen Chambers . . ." the letter began. "Helen told me that you played together as children. She has always valued your friendship." I smiled. Yes, I recalled Helen Chambers.

Then I read on: "Now she is desperately ill with pneumonia. Even though you haven't communicated in a long time, she wants you to pray for her." The letter had been mailed on the same day that I'd received the first mysterious order to pray.

Quickly I dialed the telephone number given at the bottom of the page. Helen sounded excited to hear from me. "Oh, yes," she said, "I'm much better. I'm so thankful you received my message."

"Yes, Helen," I replied. "I received the message." —EDITH M. DEAN

She Called My Name

M Y WIFE, ELIZABETH, and I were driving home to Racine on a cool, starless night when the motor of our ancient Chevy died and we glided to a halt on a two-lane highway. I got out of the car and saw that there was a slight downward incline ahead of us. "Good," I said, "we can try to jump start the engine."

I asked Elizabeth to get behind the steering wheel. "Press the clutch to the floor," I said. "I'll push with my shoulder against the door. As soon as the car picks up speed, let your foot off the clutch."

Elizabeth wrapped her fingers firmly around the steering wheel. After I got the car rolling, I stepped to the rear to push it from behind. Just then I heard Elizabeth call my name: "Jake!"

I moved quickly to the side of the car and *bam!* A car, speeding so fast that I didn't hear it approach, smashed into the Chevy's rear, hurling me off the road and into unconsciousness.

I woke up in the hospital with a broken shoulder, and other breaks and bruises. Fortunately the three young men in the other car survived, but it took months before my injuries (and Elizabeth's badly sprained ankles) healed. During one bedside visit, Elizabeth told me that both cars had been totaled.

"If I hadn't moved when you called out my name, I would have been totaled too," I said. "What good timing."

Elizabeth was puzzled. "I didn't say anything," she said. "I was so frightened, my lips were clamped shut." —*Jake Erdmann*

The First to Know

M Y HUSBAND, OLLIE, had retired from teaching and we were making plans to spend time in Florida, to travel, to relish our time together. Then a devastating illness struck and Ollie was left weak and gaunt, hardly able to speak. Weeks passed and it became clear that Ollie was near death. We held tight to our faith.

Someone was always in Ollie's hospital room—either I was there or our grown children, Bruce and Karen; sometimes our pastor. One day, in his faltering speech, Ollie told our son, "Go home, Bruce . . . you should be with Gwen."

Bruce lived many miles away and his wife was about to have a baby. We felt an extra sadness, knowing Ollie would never see his first grandchild.

"I don't want to leave you, Dad," Bruce protested.

"You belong . . . with Gwen."

Reluctantly, Bruce left. "When the baby comes," he said to Ollie, "you'll be the first to know."

A few days later, around two in the afternoon, Ollie awoke from a nap. He turned and looked at me. I leaned close to hear his halting words. "The baby . . . is coming now . . . it's . . . a boy." For an instant the old sparkle was in his eyes as he smiled at what he saw. Then he dozed again.

I had sent Karen home to rest, but soon she was back. "Bruce called," she told me. "Gwen went into labor around two o'clock."

That night, peacefully, Ollie died. A few hours later, his first grandchild was born. A healthy baby boy.

Ollie had been the first to know.

—M. J. GARDNER

The Yellow Rose

NOVEMBER 3 WAS MY BIRTHDAY. As I drove down the mountainside to Holy Apostles Episcopal Church in Hilo that Sunday morning, I couldn't help but miss Mother. It had been six months since her death, and this would be the first birthday I had to celebrate without her, without the cake she always baked, or the table she always decorated with yellow roses. Our family had lived in Hawaii for fifty years, but Texas-born Mother was always "The Yellow Rose of Texas," her house filled with that mainland flower.

At church I slipped into the pew. "I miss Mother so," I sort of prayed, kneeling with my head in my hands. I couldn't bring myself to look at the flower-filled urns on their tall koa-wood stands. The brilliant orchids and anthuriums could only clash with my gray mood inside.

The first hymn brought me unwillingly to my feet. That was when I saw it, not on the stands where flowers were always placed, but right on the altar: a tiny bud vase.

And in the vase a single yellow rose.

It was the best birthday gift I could have received, this reminder that those we love are never far away.

At the service's close, I hurried to the Flower Guild chairman to find out who had left this bud on the altar, a place I had never seen flowers before. But she was as puzzled as I and told me that the vase didn't even belong to the church. And though we queried every guild member, and anyone else who might have brought flowers, no one could explain how the rose came to be there.

To this day I don't know how—only Who.

—CHARLOTTE DOTY

Answers

Answers to prayers
Come in various ways,
Sometimes in minutes,
Sometimes in days.
And some take years

To fully unfold
The harvest of love
And blessings they hold.

Answers to prayers
Come in various forms,
Sometimes in sunlight,
Sometimes through storms.
Some blossom early
And some blossom late
But each one will flower—
Have faith and wait!
　　　　　—*HELEN INWOOD*

He gives power to the faint,
and to him who has no might he increases strength.
—Isaiah 40:29, RSV

CHAPTER SEVEN

God Gives Help and Strength

You probably know the Bible story of young David, against great odds, killing the giant Goliath. God helped and strengthened David, but not by momentarily matching David's girth to Goliath's. God's help came in the unlikely form of small pebbles, a steady hand, and perfect aim. Though David acknowledged being a sharp shooter, he gave God the credit for the hit, saying, "The battle is the Lord's" (1 Samuel 17:47). ¶ Like David's battle, our daily struggles have a spiritual dimension. God provides help and strength to meet the challenges at hand, whether they be physical or emotional.

The Everlasting Arms

W HEN THE DOCTOR TOLD ME that my precious six-week-old son, Paul, was blind, I went into shock. I tried to pray, but for some reason I couldn't.

Hours passed and I still could not form words into prayer. Meanwhile, news of our baby's disability spread among our family, friends and church congregation. An army of prayer warriors carried their concern for Paul, my husband and me to the Lord.

Two days later, while I was bathing Paul, something almost mystical happened. Ever so quietly and gently I was reminded of the Bible verse "and underneath are the everlasting arms" (Deuteronomy 33:27). I had the distinct feeling of being buoyed up, supported. And my depression began to lift.

Paul is an adult now. Though legally blind, he went to college and is employed; he can read with special magnifying glasses.

I discovered on that day long ago that even when you yourself cannot pray, the prayers of others can intercede for you. That barrage of prayers didn't change Paul's problem, but it changed me. Ever since, in good times and in bad, I've been sustained by the knowledge of His everlasting arms. —*FRIEDA E. NOWLAND*

A Calendar for Courage

T HE GATEKEEPER AT OUR MISSION compound limped into the kitchen doorway, bowed crookedly, and announced, "*Hsieh si-mu,* pastor's wife, here is his excellency, the colonel."

I held my breath. The colonel commanded the troops currently protecting this city of Shenkiu in Central China. It was January 1941; the invading Japanese were only a few miles to the east.

The colonel entered briskly and made his announcement: "The enemy is advancing into Honan Province. We have orders not to defend this city. You should find refuge in one of the villages outside."

I crossed my hands over the sleeves of my wadded *e-shang* and bowed politely, thanking him for his gracious concern for a "miserable" woman. As the colonel left the room, the icy January blast swept through the doorway. My baby cried. Suddenly the enormity of our danger overwhelmed me.

Our Margaret Anne was scarcely two months old, Johnny just over a year. Yesterday my husband, urgently needing medical care, had been taken by rickshaw to the hospital 115 miles away. I looked at the little Daily Scripture calendar on the wall: January 15. Not until early February would he be back. How would I manage without him? How would I make the myriad decisions that now crowded upon me?

You see, I had not yet experienced the full wonder of God's power to guide us when all other guides fail.

Nor did I guess that as His instrument He would use anything as prosaic as a calendar on a kitchen wall.

By mid-afternoon the army garrison in our little city was empty. The departure of the soldiers created panic. Families packed their goods and fled.

The elders of the church called on me before they left. "Come with us," they pleaded. "We will care for you while Pastor Hillis is away."

I looked at the concern in their eyes and I thought of the country homes to which they were headed. My husband and I loved these village homes because we loved the people in them. But they held death for Western babies, as too many little graves in our mission compounds showed.

How could I explain to these friends—without offending—that I could not take my children into their homes? Unheated, mud-floored huts, they crowded three and four generations together amid vermin and filth. Just a few weeks ago the six-month-old son of the nearest American family had died of dreaded dysentery. No, my babies were chained to this kitchen where I could boil dishes, milk and water.

But these were not things I could say to Chinese friends. I bowed, I thanked them, I spoke of waiting for my husband's return, of watching the mission property—and I went to bed that night shaking with terror. When Johnny woke up whimpering in the cold, I took him into bed with me and lay awake a long time, listening to the wind rattle the waxed paper windowpanes and praying that my little boy would live to see his daddy again.

Next morning I was in the kitchen early to start the water boiling for Margaret Anne's bottle. Automatically I reached up to the wall calendar and tore off yesterday's date. The Scripture verse for the new day gleamed like sunlight. "What time I am afraid, I will trust in thee" (Psalm 56:3).

Well, I was certainly afraid. I fulfilled that part of it. Now, indeed, was the time to trust God. Somehow the verse sustained me all through the tense day.

The city was being evacuated rapidly. Other church members came to invite me to their family huts. But the Scripture held me. I was *not* to panic, but to *trust*.

By mid-morning the next day the city was nearly deserted. Then the gatekeeper came to me, eyes blurred with fear. He must leave, he said, and begged me to find refuge with him in his village beyond the city.

Should I? What could I do without our gatekeeper? The deserted city would be an open invitation to bandits and looters. But the risk to my babies outside was certain; here I still faced only fears. I declined the gatekeeper's offer, and watched him as he sorrowfully took leave.

It was noon before I remembered to pull the page off the little daily calendar on the wall. The tenth verse of the ninth Psalm read, "And they that know thy name will put their trust in thee: for thou, Lord, hast not forsaken them that seek thee."

As I bowed my head over my noonday meal, my heart poured out its gratitude to God for these particular words at this moment.

My main concern now was food. All the shops in the town were boarded shut. Meat and produce no longer came in daily from farms. I still had the goats for the babies' milk, but the man who milked them had left for his village. Tomorrow I would have to try to milk them myself. I wondered if I could ever make the balky little beasts hold still.

I slept uneasily that night, wondering how I would feed my children, and sure of very little except that we should stay in the city and, somehow, trust God. The sound of distant gunfire woke me.

Before facing the goats, I fixed myself a bowl of rice gruel. Then I tore the old page from the calendar and read the new day's message. "I will nourish you, and your little ones," said the God of promise (Genesis 50:21).

The timeliness of these daily verses was becoming almost uncanny. With some curiosity I examined the back of the calendar pad. It had been put together in England the year before, but God in His all-knowing had provided the very words I needed, a year later, here on the other side of the world.

I was still eating the gruel when a woman stepped into the kitchen. She was carrying a pail of steaming goats' milk. "May I stay and help you?" she asked. "See, I have milked your goats."

Mrs. Lee had been our neighbor for years, but that morning I stared at her as though she had dropped from heaven. She had no family living, she explained, and wished to show her gratitude to the mission.

Late in the day a loud rapping at the gate set our hearts pounding. Braver, Mrs. Lee was the one who went to open it. Her face beaming, she returned leading our caller.

"*Gee-tze! Gee-dan!*" she cried triumphantly. "Chicken! Eggs!"

A frail, black-robed country woman came in with a live chicken and a basket of eggs. "Peace, peace," she gave the customary Christian greeting as she bobbed to us shyly. Noise of the cannons had not kept her away when she remembered that the missionaries would be hungry.

The calendar promise had come true! God *would* see to it that our little ones were nourished! That night my heart was full of hope. To the sound of shells bursting in the sky I prayed that somehow God would spare this city and these gentle people whom we loved.

Next morning I rushed down to the little square of paper hanging on its nail and tore off the page. "When I cry unto thee, then shall mine enemies turn back: this I know; for God is for me," the Scripture declared (Psalm 56:9).

But this time it was too much to believe! Surely it couldn't be right to take literally a verse chosen just by chance for an English calendar?

As the gunfire drew closer, Mrs. Lee and I began to prepare the house for invasion. Any papers that might possibly be construed to have military or political significance must be hidden or destroyed. We searched my husband's desk and the church buildings. By nightfall the gunfire sounded from both sides of the city. We went to bed dressed, prepared at any moment to meet the Japanese invaders.

I awoke abruptly in the early dawn and strained my ears for the crunch of military boots on gravel. But only a deep stillness surrounded me. There were no tramping feet, no shrieking shells or pounding guns, only the waking murmur of little Johnny in his crib.

Misgivings warred with excitement as I woke Mrs. Lee and we went to the gatehouse, each carrying a child. She was the first to stick out a cautious head. "There is no one in the street," she told me. "Shall we go out?"

And then, we stepped through the gate and watched as the streets began to fill, not with Japanese soldiers, but with towns-people returning from their country hiding places. Had the Chinese won?

As if in answer to our question, we met the colonel. "Pastor's wife!" he greeted me with relief. "I have been concerned about you!"

Then he told us that the Japanese had withdrawn. No, they had not been defeated, nor could anyone arrive at a reasonable conjecture concerning their retreat. The enemy had simply turned back.

I stepped into my kitchen, eyes fixed on a little block of paper pinned to the wall. Oh, you could say it was just a calendar. You could say strangers had chosen those verses without any thought of China, or of the war that would be raging when those dates fell due. But to me it was more than a calendar, and no stranger had picked those lines. To me it was the handwriting of God.   —MARGARET HILLIS

When I Am Sore Beset

When I am sore beset. I seek some quiet place,
Some lonely room or barren windswept hill,
And there in silence wait apart until
I see again the smile upon God's face,
Until His presence floods me like the dawn,
And I can hear His whispered, "Peace be still,"
And know again the strength to do His will.
I turn to take my load and find it gone.
                                    —ANTOINETTE GOETSCHIUS

Farewell on the Mountainside

SNOW HAD FALLEN ALL NIGHT and the mountain was a fairyland of whiteness. I was twenty-one years old and expecting my first baby in the spring. All my life until the past ten months had been spent in a fairly good-sized town, and the deep, narrow valley between the tall mountain and ridge where I was living with my husband and his mother was a constant source of interest and new experiences. The mountain folks I had come to know and the many customs of the "old folks" that they still cherished had formed a new world for me.

During the previous summer I had insisted that we attend the little white Methodist church about two miles down the valley, and even though the circuit-rider preacher only came once a month, I had helped organize a Sunday school for the in-between time.

This particular morning was Monday and "washday" by an infallible rule of the mountain community. Snow or no snow, we washed, and I hummed a gay little tune as I helped my mother-in-law fill the zinc tubs on the glowing kitchen range and sorted the clothes for washing. My thoughts were of the coming baby, and the warm, steamy kitchen, accentuated by the white coldness seen through the windows, gave me a feeling of security and snugness. In thinking of my own happiness, I talked with my mother-in-law about the pity we felt for a young couple, who, we had been told, had lost their three-week-old baby during the night just the day before. We were still speculating as to what might have caused such a death when a knock at the back door gave us both a start.

Opening the door we were even more startled to see standing there the very same father of the dead child we had just been discussing. His name was John and he seemed hesitant to come into the kitchen but stood twirling his cap in his hands and staring at his feet. All of a sudden he took a deep breath and blurted out, "Betty, we was aimin' to bury our baby today, and now this snow an' all, and the preacher can't get acrost the ridge, and from the way hit's snowin' can't reckon when he could get here." Then as we started to sympathize, he said, "My Maude . . . she's right smart tore up, and ain't able to git outta bed this mornin', but she says we just can't put our baby away 'lessen we have a service over her, and you're the only one I knowed round here I thought could do it."

It was a moment before my stunned brain could take it in that he was talking to and about me. I couldn't believe he was asking me to do the service. I started to stammer that I couldn't possibly preach a funeral, and besides we couldn't get the car out of the shed even to go two miles down the valley. I might have saved my breath, for he stood there with such grief and stubborn determination in his eyes that I felt like I was butting my head against a brick wall for all the progress I was making.

Then he said quietly, "How'd you feel if it was your young 'un?" That did it. I had no answer for that, so I dumbly wiped my still wet hands on my apron and began to untie it. I don't remember another word spoken as I pulled on high rubber boots and coat and muffler. All I could do was pray frantically over and over, "Dear God, help me, give me words to help. Help me to say what will comfort them, Lord. . . ."

Leaving word about where I was going for my husband who was feeding cattle. I set out with John for the long cold walk to the church. Slipping, sliding, often wading drifts, with no conversation between us, the silent white flakes of snow pounding in our faces, we reached the church at last and went in. My heart came up into my throat. In spite of the snow, the little chapel was filled with mountain folks, and the little homemade coffin rested under a wreath of crepe-paper flowers in front of the rough altar.

Such a small, crude little chapel, with its oil lamps hanging on the walls, yet in that moment it seemed to me as vast and awesome as St. Patrick's Cathedral, which I once visited. I thought I'd never reach the front and as I stumbled down the aisle, my frantic brain could only repeat the same prayer: "Dear God, help me, help me. Let me say the words that will help them feel Your presence."

When I turned to face the silent congregation, I had to grip the pine pulpit tightly to keep from just going down. It hit me, too, that there was not even a Bible in front of me and I had not thought to bring mine!

As I realized that, I thought, *Well, this is it. I cannot go any further.* And then my eyes fell on that pitiful little box. Then and there God worked a miracle for me, just as surely as if He had reached out and touched my mind and lips. From somewhere unknown, the words came, disjointed as to correctness of quotation I am sure, but essentially those I had heard from early childhood on similar occasions. "I am the resurrection and the life . . ." "Casting all your care upon him for he careth for you." "Suffer the children to come unto me . . . for of such is the kingdom of heaven." On and on the words came, as if a scroll were being unwound before my eyes. Last of all came a prayer—and that was mine, for as I felt my own unborn child stir within me, my petition for a grieving mother in a log cabin on that lonely mountainside found the right words for the final commitment of "earth to earth" at the tiny graveside.

I am now a grandmother, and through the years I have faced many trials and crosses where I have felt like giving up before I started. But always the memory of "my miracle" comes to me and I go on, for surely the loving God who could give an ignorant twenty-one-year-old girl a funeral service can guide a more mature woman through any difficulty. Always, too, in such a crisis I seem to see John's face and hear the simple words he spoke as I turned from that grave toward home.

"Thank you—I knowed you could do it."　　　　—BETTY BANNER

Send Someone . . . Anyone!

ON THAT SUNNY AUGUST AFTERNOON several years ago, there was no indication that anything could mar the beauty and peace of the day. It was a Friday, and I could hear the hum of my husband's tractor as he mowed the grass in the field next to our backyard.

Our house stands on a hill above the highway about a mile from the little town of Marble Hill, Missouri. Mr. Stephens, a farmer, is our nearest neighbor and he lives a quarter of a mile down the road.

I don't know what it was that caused me to turn suddenly and look at my husband on the tractor. As I did so, I watched in horror and disbelief as the tractor hit something hard in the grass, then turned over, pinning my husband beneath.

In a panic I began running toward the tractor knowing that I had to get Howard out from under before it burst into flames.

Jack, our ten-year-old son, was already by his father's side. Together we pulled and pried, but all our efforts seemed only to hurt Howard, who was lying on his back with the steering wheel pressing against his chest. One of his legs was caught under the back end of the heavy machine, a Farmall Cut, which weighed three thousand pounds.

Our cries for help rang out across the empty field. We could hear the cars go by on the highway, but they couldn't possibly hear us.

Howard was struggling to breathe—if the weight of the tractor wasn't lifted off his chest, he might die! Frantically we searched for something to prop up the tractor. There was nothing.

O God. I thought in despair, *send someone . . . anyone!*

I didn't stop to think how hopelessly ridiculous it would be for a woman alone to try to lift a tractor. I only knew that Howard would die if it wasn't done. With one shoulder leaning against the radiator, I took hold and lifted with all my might . . . and the tractor moved. I was holding it up, thank God! Howard was breathing easier. He was saved, at least for the moment.

"You try and pull Daddy out," I said to Jack. "I'll hold the tractor."

Jack was pulling as hard as he could, but Howard wasn't moving.

"I can't." Howard was straining to breathe and talk at the same time. "A rock . . . under my back . . . I'm hurt." His leg was still pinned under the tractor. It was obvious that we couldn't get him out without help.

"Run," I said to Jack. "Phone Mr. Stephens and ask him to bring help."

I watched Jack race across the yard and into the house and prayed that our neighbor was at home.

Then, for a while, it was as if time had been suspended. I didn't seem to be aware of the weight of the tractor and I wasn't even bothered by the heat. Meanwhile, Howard was struggling to speak. "I . . . can't . . . take . . . it . . . much . . . longer."

In many private conversations Howard and I had agreed that death was not something to fear. We had surrendered our lives to God many years before. Miraculously, we felt, He had brought Howard back after a head wound nearly killed him on Saipan during World War II. And now, once again, Howard was in God's hands. With a sudden calmness I knew that if Howard was to live, God would use me to hold up the tractor till help came.

Finally I saw them running toward us—Jack and Mr. Stephens and his son, Jerry, and Henry Thiele, another neighbor. Together they lifted the tractor. The doctor arrived, and then the ambulance. Howard's leg had to be stitched up, and the doctor said X rays would be necessary. "But I don't think he's seriously hurt."

Then Mr. Stephens took my right arm firmly and said, "Now I'll take *you* to the doctor."

"Me, what in the world for?" I could feel no pain anywhere. But then I looked and saw that the skin and flesh of my left arm and shoulder was hanging in shreds. I could hardly believe what I saw. At the clinic the doctor explained that the heat from the radiator had actually cooked the flesh on my arm and shoulder to the bone.

In a few days Howard came home in a wheelchair to nurse a crushed vertebra in his back. My left arm was helpless until the burnt muscles slowly healed. For months we were quite a pair, both semi-invalids with a house and two children to care for.

Every time we think back to that August Friday, we marvel at the way things worked out. When Jack telephoned our neighbor for help, Mr. Stephens just *happened* to walk into his kitchen in time to take the call. His son Jerry, who no longer lives at home, just *happened* to be there visiting that day.

And all the while God was lifting that tractor for almost one hour. I wasn't. On my own I couldn't. We still have the tractor, and I have since tried lifting the front end. I can't budge it.

—*Mildred Shell, as told to Jorunn O. Ricketts*

Crossings

I came to the swift, raging river,
    And the roar held the echo of fear;
"Oh, Lord, give me wings to fly over,
    If You are, as You promised, quite near."

But He said, "Trust the grace I am giving,
    All-pervasive, sufficient for you.

Take My hand—we will face this together;
But My plan is—not over, but through."
—LEE WEBBER

The Washing Machine

IN 1968 MY HUSBAND, BILLY, was about to go to Vietnam, leaving me in Nashville with a three-year-old, a second child on the way—and an erratic old washing machine. Every morning the machine would merely complete its wash cycle and then stop dead, its tub full of soapy undrained water. Billy had a way of fixing the machine: taking the top off, jiggling a wire. But what would we do when Billy went away? In the meantime I prayed for Billy's safe return to us, and I didn't think about the washing machine until the day after he left.

That morning I reluctantly filled the machine with dirty clothes and then said, "Lord, what am I going to do with a three-year-old, a new baby and a busted washer? Please, God, help me through this."

An hour later I returned to the machine and—to my amazement—the clothes had gone through a complete wash and rinse, and were now ready for the dryer! For days after that the washer continued to work perfectly. Soon I forgot the problem altogether.

In January 1969 Billy came safely home. He brought a duffel bag of dirty clothes. That very day I threw them into the machine and quickly returned to the living room to be with Billy as he got to know our new son.

An hour later I went back to the washing machine. Can you guess what I found?

Soapy undrained water!

I could only laugh and feel more blessed than ever. Billy was home and the washer was back to its old dirty tricks!   —ANNETTE SIMS

"Man in the Water!"

I RARELY WENT INTO DOWNTOWN CHICAGO, but early one morning in May 1978, while my husband was at work and my two children in school, I decided to go into the city to look up an old newspaper article for a friend. It was about nine o'clock, brisk and chilly, when I headed across the Michigan Avenue Bridge toward the *Sun Times* Building.

Then something very strange happened. From somewhere inside my head I heard a distinct inner voice crying: "Man in the water! Man in the water!" I leaned over the railing, feeling a bit foolish, and peered into the greenish-brown murk of the Chicago River. There was no one. Nothing but bits of floating garbage and an unappealing film of pollution.

Thank God no one's actually in there, I thought with relief. *I guess I was just daydreaming.* The call I heard sounded like an appeal for help—and I was not the heroic type. I hadn't even gone swimming in years. As a homemaker in suburban Evanston, Illinois, the only exercise I got was taking care of the house and my family. Yet, ever since I had become an active Christian two and a half years ago, I had been concerned about how to relate the parable of the Good Samaritan to my own life. How do we help others, including strangers, in difficult and even dangerous situations? As I continued across the bridge my relief was mixed with dismay at the realization that a man in the water was not something I really felt equal to. *There are policemen, firemen, emergency squads for that kind of thing,* I thought. *I'm just an average person.*

At ten o'clock, my research at the *Sun Times* finished, I walked back over the bridge, the inner call I had heard just an hour earlier forgotten, my mind on other things. Then like a piercing alarm jolting me to attention, I heard almost the same words, but this time unmistakably real and urgent: "Man overboard! Man overboard!" Ahead of me on the bridge, a man was shouting and gesturing wildly, trying to get the attention of two dockmen below.

I ran over to him. "What happened?" I asked.

"He jumped! I saw him—just a few seconds ago."

This time, when I looked over the railing, I saw a frightening and pathetic sight. Thirty feet below, in the river, was a man fully clothed. He was only about ten feet from the dock but he made no effort to save himself. He just lay passively in the water, either unconscious, drugged, or simply willing to die. I felt paralyzed. A feeling of unreality came over me, as if it weren't really happening—as if I were watching footage on the five o'clock news.

At last the two dockmen realized what was happening and flung a life ring into the water. But it did no good. The rope tangled, and in any case the man was unable to get it.

Now, as I watched in horror, the man slowly began to sink under water. Just as he was almost out of sight one of the dockmen dived in and grasped him by the hair. He pulled him up to the surface but then he seemed to be in trouble himself, gasping and spitting as he called for help. "Someone up there, help me!" he screamed. "I can't hold him up myself!"

The other dockman was frantically attempting to untangle another rope to throw in from the dock. On the bridge a fascinated audience of about one hundred passersby watched—but no one moved.

The thought came to me—*Could—should it be me?* But what of the risks? Images of my husband, Ed, and my two children, Douglas, twelve, and Julie, nine, flashed through my mind. Didn't I have a greater responsibility to them?

But the man needed help. I was fairly trembling with the force of my inner uncertainty. I don't know how long I continued to stand there with the others, my hands gripping the railing as though to keep me from bursting apart. Then, suddenly, I was running down the stairs that led to the dock. *Surely*, I thought, *someone else will have gone in to help. I'll just stand by to pull them out.*

Though I was running, stripping off my sweater and kicking off my shoes as I cleared the dock, it wasn't until I was actually lowering myself into the water, slowly and gingerly, that I realized I was the only help the dockman would be getting.

The water had a brackish taste and an unhealthy odor. I was afraid of the cold and I recoiled from all the filth floating on the surface. The icy water seemed to squeeze me like a fist, forcing out the air from my lungs.

The most sensible thing seemed to be to go for the life ring. Immediately, as I started to swim, the risk of what I was doing overwhelmed me—what if I were never to see my husband or children again? I had heard of drowning men panicking, pulling down their would-be rescuers with them. Or what if my muscles cramped in the cold water?

But then, instantly, the comforting words of prayers I had known since childhood came to my lips: "Lord God, Lamb of God, Son of the Father, have mercy upon us," I prayed aloud. Every word gave me new courage.

"Good! Good girl!" the dockman in the water shouted to me. "The rope!" he said. "We need the rope!" I looked back to see that his assistant on the dock had finally unraveled the rope and thrown it into the water. But not far enough. I swam over to it, grabbed it and, towing the rope behind me, headed toward the two men.

The weight of my sodden clothes was making every move an effort. I could only imagine the terrible struggle of the dockman as he carried not only his own weight, but that of a semi-conscious man.

"Lord have mercy, Christ have mercy, Lord have mercy," I repeated with every stroke, praying I would reach the two men before the dockman's strength gave out.

"Put it under his arms," he said to me as I approached. "Loop it under and swim back with your end."

Treading water, my hands shaking with cold, I somehow managed to carry out his instructions.

"Is it all right?" I asked him through chattering teeth. "Are you going to be okay?"

"Yeah. Just get back there as fast as you can!"

I headed back, praying constantly. Ahead of me I could see that a fire-rescue squad and an ambulance had finally arrived. *Thank God.* Now I knew that we'd all be pulled out.

Reaching the dock, I handed my end of the rope to a waiting fireman and then clung to one of the dock's support posts, exhausted. Another fireman reached down, grabbed me by the beltloops of my jeans and pulled me onto the dock. Wrapping a blanket around my shivering shoulders and patting me on the back, he said, "Thanks for doing my job."

I didn't understand what he meant at first. "What?" I said, "Whose job?"

But he just asked, "Are you all right?" I nodded that I was, and, too spent to move, watched as the rescue squad pulled in the drowning man while the dockman held him afloat. In seconds, he was hoisted onto the dock and attended to by the ambulance crews.

When the dockman was pulled out, he just smiled wearily at me. I knew exactly how he felt: too tired for words and a little embarrassed at all the thanks and pats on the back we were getting from the crowd of reporters and photographers who had gathered on the dock.

"Why did you go in?" one of them asked me.

"No one else did."

"But what made you do it?" another asked, apparently unsatisfied with my answer.

"God gave me the strength," I said, a little surprised at my own words.

They wanted to ask more questions, but the firemen were hurrying us into the ambulance. "How do you feel about being a heroine?" I heard as the door closed. *But it wasn't me,* I thought to myself.

On the way to the hospital the dockman and I introduced ourselves—his name was Bob Bergstrom—but we didn't do much talking—our teeth were still chattering. I had time to think about the reporter's questions. Me—a heroine? Although every muscle ached with the effort I had just made, and my whole body trembled with cold under my wet clothes, I felt that I had really done nothing. I was not a brave, strong person, but an ordinary woman with the usual fears and hesitations. I was able to overcome my weakness and jump into the water to help, only because of God's guidance and protection. The mysterious forewarning on the bridge that had been my preparation, the sudden decision to act and the strengthening prayers that attended me in the river—all had come from God.

It was just as St. Paul had written: "I can do all things through Christ which strengtheneth me" (Philippians 4:13). This was what I wanted to say to the reporters. Never had these words, which I loved so much, taken on such literal meaning. I felt a new peace and humility.

"He's going to survive," one of the attendants said to us as he treated the rescued man. "He's got a broken arm and leg and he's suffering from exposure. But he's going to be all right."

I could see that the man was now conscious, but so chilled he could hardly speak. I silently thanked God for saving his life. Later I learned that he was only twenty-eight years old.

I wrote him a letter, saying that God has a purpose for him in life, but received no answer. Yet I often remember his face, so sad and despondent, and pray that someday he will meet Jesus and feel the saving power of God that can transform weakness and fear into strength.

—Marilyn Beis

St. Patrick's Armor

I bind unto myself today
The power of God to hold and lead,
His eye to watch, His might to stay,
His ear to hearken to my need,
The wisdom of my God to teach,
His hand to guide, His shield to ward;
The word of God to give me speech,
His heavenly host to be my guard.
—from St. Patrick's Breastplate

Turn on the Lights!

A s a teacher here in chicago, in a big-city school, I am aware of the concern these days about crime and violence, especially in our larger urban areas. Every night on television I see reports of robberies and shootings. But I am not afraid, because of something that happened to me a number of years ago.

One fall when my husband, Len, was in his third year of seminary, he was serving an internship as preacher in a small midwestern town. Our parsonage was a sun-bleached house next to the white frame church with its tall steeple and wooden sign announcing services. Even though we were city folks, we fit right in, and our parsonage door swung open and shut often.

One evening a woman I'll call Mrs. Mack came to discuss a personal problem. She was a gym teacher in the local high school where I taught math. Her husband was the principal of the elementary school. She wasn't a church member but I hoped our tiny congregation might get a new addition or two.

As I washed dishes I heard Mrs. Mack sobbing and stepped to the living room door to see if I might be needed. Len waved me in.

"He really loves me," cried Mrs. Mack. "It's just that he has this horrible compulsion. The other night, after being away for the weekend, he drove up, brakes screeching, and stomped into the house. He proceeded to terrorize our son and daughter, breaking their toys and yelling, 'You probably love these more than me!'"

I asked if her husband drank. "Oh, no," she said. "He usually acts like this after he comes home from a town about a hundred and fifty miles from here. There is a woman who calls our house every so often, and I see calls to that town on our phone bill. I think he has a problem with her."

She dabbed her eyes with a tissue. Then, looking up, she pleaded, "Reverend, would you drive up there with me? I'm afraid he's in trouble. I have her address."

I could tell this was more than Len had bargained for "Well," he demurred, "I'll think about it and let you know tomorrow."

We discussed it that evening. Finally Len said, "I feel I should try to help them. Let me see if Larry will come with us." Larry was the minister of a Methodist church in a town north of us. The next day when I arrived home from school, I found a note: "Honey, decided to go. Larry is with us. Don't worry. Should be home after midnight."

A chill went through me. *Trust in God,* I told myself. After all, God was with them.

I managed to get through the evening, first teaching my two piano students, then taking our dog, Charlie, for a walk, and working on some church papers. At ten o'clock I turned out the lights and started for bed.

At that moment I was startled by gravel hitting the house like shotgun pellets as a car roared into our driveway. I put on my robe, went downstairs and tiptoed in the darkness toward the front window.

Suddenly fists pounded on the door and a man's voice roared: "I know you're in there, Mrs. Arnell. I'm Mr. Mack and I've got a gun!"

I froze. In the dim light I could see a man on the porch, his face contorted with rage, holding a gun.

"You listen to me," he barked. "See that car in your driveway? That's my wife's car. I know she drove away with your husband this afternoon, and when they get back I'm going to kill him. Your husband is a womanizer!"

My blood ran cold. "But, Mr. Mack . . ."

He ran down the front steps and crouched behind the evergreens. "I'm going to wait here," he yelled, "and when they pull up, *zingo!*"

I shrank back. What should I do? I started toward the phone to call the police when the front door seemed to explode with pounding.

"Don't you call the police," he raved, "because I'll shoot anyone who comes near—and I'll kill you too before they get me!"

Our phone rang. I grabbed it on the first ring.

It was my husband. "Are you all right, honey?"

"Listen," I whispered, "Mr. Mack is waiting in the shrubbery right outside our front door. He has a gun—" My voice broke. "I think he plans on killing all of us."

Len tried to calm me. "We'll be careful. We found out he has a woman here who claims they're going to get married. We'll be home in about three hours. Meanwhile, I think Mr. Mack is bluffing, but keep the door locked and stay quiet. I love you."

I hung up the phone with a trembling hand. It was nearing midnight.

Pounding thundered on the front door again. "Don't you try anything; I'm still here."

I sank down in a rocker and prayed. "O Lord Jesus, please help me. Please help that poor demented soul out there." In the darkness I cried. I knelt. Then, exhausted, I slumped back into the rocker again.

Suddenly a thought came: *Turn on the lights! Every light in the house. Then go down, unlock the door, explain to Mr. Mack that Len had called and that he is with Mrs. Mack along with another minister, so he doesn't have to worry anymore. And,* the thought commanded, *invite him in.*

"O God, no!" I cried. "I can't do that. He's got a gun. If I admit Len is with his wife he might kill me."

Do it.

With hands shaking, I snapped on every light in the house. Then I opened the front door and said, "Mr. Mack? Mr. Mack?"

The bushes rustled. "Why are all the lights on? Have you called the police?"

"No, Mr. Mack. Pastor Arnell just called. And you are right. Mrs. Mack is with him, along with another minister. They're on their way home right now." I pressed on, trying to keep my voice from quavering. "Put your gun away. You won't need it now. Come inside where it's more comfortable. I'll make some coffee."

Mr. Mack slowly rose from the bushes and came up the front steps. He slid the gun inside his coat as he walked through the front door. Hands pressing his temples, he moaned, "Oh, my head, my head. It hurts so."

"Let me get you some aspirin."

The phone rang. It was a neighbor asking if anything was wrong. Mr. Mack had followed me to the phone; he locked one arm around my neck and, breathing heavily, tried to listen to the party at the other end.

"Oh, the lights," I said. "Yes, Mrs. Johnson, I know it's strange at this hour but we have guests. They'll be leaving soon."

He released me and slumped down on the living room couch, holding his head. I brought him the aspirin, and started making coffee. As it perked I sat with him and talked about his family and our wonderful Lord Jesus, who would help him through his troubles. He seemed to calm a bit. I got the coffee and served it, knowing I had to hold his attention for at least two more hours.

As the mantel clock ticked, I prayed aloud for Mr. Mack, his family and all of us. I got our Bible and read to him. The more I talked to him the more assurance I seemed to feel. It was as if God was right in the room with us, giving me a sense of peace.

Mr. Mack nodded a bit and I encouraged him to rest.

"No! No!" he shouted, jerking himself upright and feeling under his coat for the gun. I continued talking to him, soothing him, reading from the Bible. Another hour went by, then two. I fought sleep, hoarse from talking and praying. Something seemed to be happening to him, for the rage had subsided. At 4:30 A.M. a car pulled up in the driveway. Mr. Mack jumped to his feet as his wife rushed in through the front door. I was amazed to see her throw her arms around him; the two stood there hugging and crying. I collapsed in a chair, thanking Jesus for being with us.

Mrs. Mack knew her husband needed psychiatric help and persuaded him to enter a hospital. After extensive medical treatment and spiritual counseling, he eventually recovered and returned to his family.

To this day I am awed at the way the Holy Spirit directed me that night, giving me the courage to turn on the lights and invite a distraught, armed man into my home. It was a lesson I will never forget. So today when I see those television reports of crime and violence, I am thankful that I do not have to be afraid. Instead I rely on God for His sure protection.

—*Lucille Lind Arnell*

Appointment in Escambia Bay

F ROM THE START I had a peculiar feeling about the trip.

"It's an emergency," the caller had said. Down at Escambia Bay, a railroad bridge was damaged; its swing-trestle wouldn't open. They wanted a repair crew from the company I owned, and they wanted it there by six the next morning.

I remember sitting alone in the office after I put the phone down. It was after working hours and all my men had gone home. If I accepted the job, I'd need a barge with a crane and the only one available was twenty-seven miles away at Chico Bayou. That would mean driving there immediately; what's more, I'd have to spend the night on the water tugging the rig back. *Doggone it,* I thought, *I'm not going to do it.*

Yet now, here I was, somewhere in Escambia Bay off the Pensacola coastline. *Little Mac,* my tough thirty-foot work-boat, was chugging away with all its diesel cylinders, its nose locked into the barge ahead with steel cables. It was hard, slow going. The barge was seventy feet long and thirty feet wide. The crane itself weighed forty tons; it rose above us fifty feet in the air.

I flashed a light at my watch. Eight o'clock. I shook my head and nervously chewed my lip. I didn't like the spot we were in. It was dark, we were off course, and a fog was thickening around us.

The fog. Another reason for not making this trip. During the past weeks the fog had been giving us a lot of trouble, unusually thick stuff, settling in early at night. It would have been wiser to wait until daytime to get the barge, when the sun had burned the fog away. But no, I'd picked up the phone and called Bill Kenney, who lived closer to the office than any of my other men. He was young, strong, and like me, a salvage man and a diver.

Bill's willingness to work a double shift had seemed to settle it: I would make the night trip to bring the barge back.

But *still* I'd hesitated. I put in a call to Janet, and our home phone just rang and rang. Janet, our three girls and I are exceptionally close. I never like the idea of being away from them at night, especially *all* night.

Yet here I was out on *Little Mac,* doing the very thing that common sense said I shouldn't be doing. I worried about whether Janet had received the message from the friend I'd phoned.

Nine o'clock.

The fog swirled around us like clammy gray velvet. We were running on compass; no use trying to spot the channel markers. I reduced the speed to two knots. "Better go up to the bow and keep a lookout," I shouted to Bill over the noise of the engine. "Somebody might be anchored in this muck." We were running slow enough to avoid a collision, but I was uneasy.

Zoom! An airplane. The scream of jet engines reverberated around us in the thick air. We couldn't see the plane, but it seemed to be flying close to us, too close.

Zoom! There was another one. Obviously we must be near one of the Pensacola airport approaches. I looked up at the crane that disappeared into the fog above us, and the thought ran through my head, *What if one of those planes clipped that boom?* All of a sudden I began to have an eerie feeling, the odd sensation of being some kind of target, a helpless tool in a plot I didn't understand, a passenger on a voyage I hadn't wanted to take to a place I didn't want to be. I tried to shrug it off. What was it all about, anyway?

Suddenly, out of the sky behind us, with a high-pitched whine, came another plane. I could see it. Its lights blurred through the fog, a 727 jet, and it was angling down. "He's going to hit!" I screamed. Bill rushed up to me and the two of us watched helplessly as the huge plane plunged through the fog and slammed into the bay. There was a terrible sound of rending metal. Fountains of water exploded into the sky as the lights on the jet went out. Then eerie silence.

Holding my breath, I waited for an explosion; none came. I could see that the plane hadn't disintegrated; the fuselage remained intact. Quickly I ran to our spotlight and started playing it on the 727's cabin. It was settling lower as water poured in, but no one seemed to be coming out. Were they all dead?

Bill had run into the wheelhouse and was calling "Mayday, Mayday!" into our radio. I grabbed the wheel and turned *Little Mac* hard to port, moving toward the sinking plane. If there were any survivors, our big old flat barge would have plenty of room for them. "Get all the life preservers you can find!" I shouted to Bill. He collected armfuls, flinging them on deck. Then he began cleating lines to the barge and throwing the free ends into the water. The deck of the barge was only four feet above the waterline. Survivors might be able to grab hold of those lines and pull themselves aboard.

I steered the rig around the hulk of the plane, approaching it nose to nose, inching along toward the forward exit. *Careful now,* I said to myself, *don't go too far or you'll crush that plane like an eggshell.* By this time, dazed-looking people were plunging from the open doorway into the water. "Jump," one of the crew members was shouting, "you *must* jump!"

As we came closer, more and more bobbing heads appeared in the murky water. Some of the passengers could swim; others couldn't. Some had life preservers; some didn't. Some clutched seat cushions; others clung to the plane's fuselage. The water seemed to be getting rougher, and a strong current was sweeping past the plane, carrying people out into the darkness. I wondered if anyone had heard our radio call and if help was on the way.

I lost all track of time. It was like a nightmare fishing trip in which Bill and I fished for survivors. We beamed the spotlight in the direction of their cries, then urged them to climb the lines that dangled from our barge. Jet fuel had gushed out of the plane, people were soaked with it. Some of our lines were getting too slippery to handle. I knew that the tiniest spark could ignite an inferno.

By now, since the water was only thirteen feet deep, the 727 had sunk as far as it was going to go. Most of the fuselage was under water. I ran the barge over one of the submerged wings and managed to tuck

Little Mac's flying bridge under the plane's tail assembly that rose like a silvery channel marker high out of the water. Bill was on the barge, working like a madman. At first he thought of jumping in to grab some of the people who were floundering in the sea beneath him, but he changed his mind. Instead he clamped his legs around a cleat, then leaned over the side to lift the terrified survivors in his strong arms. People straggled aboard wherever and however they could, gasping, retching, thanking God, then turning around to help somebody else. Among them I suddenly spotted a neighbor of mine, a physician who was an experienced CB operator. "Joe!" I yelled. "Get on that radio." He did, and he stayed on it, calling for help.

More time went by. There was a lot of shouting and yelling, especially from the injured trying to get our attention, but there was no panic. "Hang on! We'll get to you," the people already on board shouted. "Swim this way! We'll throw you a rope." Someone put a plank from the barge to the plane's fuselage. A few of the weak and injured were slid up onto the plane's exposed back until they could be carried across the plank. The first man I saw come across was Bill. He had two people on his back. And when at last we had fished out everybody we could find, Bill dived into the water and down into the cabin of the 727 to make sure that nobody was left inside.

Other boats finally found their way to us in the fog, bringing help to a wet and shivering collection of survivors. The main rescue work was done, though. There had been fifty-eight people aboard the plane. Three of them were drowned. I am still haunted by our failure to save them.

And yet . . .

I am also haunted by other feelings. Not a day goes by that I don't think about why I was in that particular place in the world at that particular time. I think of the barge with its ample space, its powerful spotlight, its lifelines, even the large wooden plank lying on its deck, waiting to be used. I think of my choice of Bill Kenney, and his youth, his strength, his courage. I think of my reluctance to go on that all-night voyage, and how I couldn't seem not to go. And then I think of my own personal trust in God, and how I am absolutely certain that He is aware of every move of my life.

That's when I know why I went out that foggy night into Escambia Bay, and why Somebody wanted me there. —GLENN MCDONALD

He Giveth More Grace

He giveth more grace when the burdens grow greater,
    He sendeth more strength when the labors increase;
To added affliction He addeth His mercy,
    To multiplied trials, His multiplied peace.

When we have exhausted our store of endurance,
    When our strength has failed ere the day is half done,
When we reach the end of our hoarded resources,
    Our Father's full giving is only begun.

His love has no limit, his grace has no measure
    His power has no boundaries known unto men;
For our of his infinite riches in Jesus
    He giveth and giveth and giveth again.
                 —*Annie Johnson Flint*

Mama, Come Quick

AFTER MY GRANDFATHER DIED, my uncle Bill was the only one left living in the old family home with my grandmother. She was ninety-three and he was sixty-five, but they depended on each other like siblings. He'd get the Nashville newspaper every morning and bring her breakfast and keep her up-to-date on the rest of the family.

One morning, though, after twenty-three years of the same routine, he got up at seven o'clock, swung both feet over the side of his bed, and suddenly collapsed to the floor with a stroke. Conscious but unable to move, he yelled to my grandmother in her bedroom, "Mama, Mama!"

"Why are you hollering so early in the morning?" she called back, roused from her sleep.

"Mama," he said, "come quick."

Grandmother knew then that something was terribly wrong. Quickly she called to the One who had never failed to hear her every prayer, then got out of bed. She hurried to my uncle's room, where he lay paralyzed. Knowing help was needed, she telephoned their next-door neighbor and went downstairs to let the neighbor in. Together they went to Bill's room; medical help was summoned and soon arrived.

What was so unusual about this? Wouldn't any mother have done the same? Yes, perhaps. But you see, Grandmother had been permanently injured in a car accident and since then had fallen, breaking her hip twice. She had been in a wheelchair for nine years. During that time she had not taken one step by herself.　　　　—JOAN B. PARIS

The Premonition

What is it, Lord? What's this weird feeling that something unpleasant is waiting for me down the road?

AS USUAL, I WAS TALKING to my Friend as I drove through the muggy August night at 3:00 A.M., hauling forty-eight thousand pounds of steel in my eighteen-wheel rig.

I knew nothing mechanical was wrong. As careful truckers do, I'd done a thorough job of checking everything before leaving on this round trip run between Fort Worth and Bryan, Texas. The only thing I'd found to worry me was a creepy spider skittering across the dashboard. I'm six feet two and fifty-two years old, but I'm a baby about spiders. Using my leather driving gloves, I'd brushed it out of the cab.

But now this strange sixth sense was telling me that I ought to be extra careful, extra wide-awake. I'd never had it before, and I kept trying to turn it over to the Lord:

Lord God, You're my Father, and I know You want what's best for all Your children. So now I ask You to ride this run with me—sit real close, keep me alert, help me get rid of this crazy feeling that's bugging me. I give You the honor and the glory . . .

A lot of truckers are big on CB radio talk for passing the time. I'd rather talk to the Lord. I had grown up in a family where talking to Him and singing His praises were as natural as breathing. So on these long, dark, lonesome runs I make for Central Freight Lines, it is second nature for me to ask Him to keep me company. Each night I always pray and sing the old familiar hymns. Doing that helps me feel ready for any surprises that might come my way. But this night I couldn't seem to relax.

By 6:45 A.M. I'd picked up my return load of forty-three thousand pounds of bleach and was on my way back to Fort Worth. I planned to make my usual breakfast stop at the Dixie Cafe. But when I got there and parked—do you know that sneaky uneasiness wouldn't let me go in? *Don't stop now,* came the urging. *Keep on moving down the road.*

I sat still a few seconds, trying to resist it, thinking about juice and eggs and coffee. Then my hand reached for the ignition switch.

With something like a groan, I began to ease the rig out of the parking lot. *J. V.,* I told myself, *you can handle a truck just fine, but this fool thing going on in your head is something else.* And then: *Please, Lord, I'm counting on You to stay here in this cab with me.*

Out on Highway 6, I concentrated on the road. Only two lanes wide, it didn't give a tractor trailer much room for maneuvering. Unconsciously, I began to sing again: "Jesus loves me, this I know, For the Bible tells me so . . ." I hadn't sung *that* since I was a little kid.

About thirty miles from Waco, I glanced in my side-view mirror and saw a trucker coming up fast on my tail. He was in an empty truck or he wouldn't have been able to highball it like that. Since I was hauling a slow, heavy load, I pulled over to let the empty truck overtake me. As the driver whizzed by, he raised his hand in the traditional signal that says, "Thanks, good buddy." Soon he was three hundred yards down the road.

And then it happened. Sitting high in my cab, thirteen feet off the ground, I had a bird's-eye view of the trucker's nightmare unfolding in front of me. In a flash, something had made that big rig go out of control. It reeled across the wrong side of Highway 6 and careened along the shoulder. Then, in a flight incline about seventy-five yards off the highway, it flipped over, jackknifed, and turned bottom-side up. I heard a monstrous *vroom,* as if a giant match had been struck. Fire and black smoke mushroomed from the cab area.

I'd already stopped my rig a safe distance away. Now I raced down the highway, my knees pumping like pistons. *O Lord, have mercy,* I prayed as I charged toward the fiery cab.

When I came around the truck and saw the driver, I thought he was a goner. His bleeding head and shoulders were wedged in the broken window behind the steel supporting braces of the big side mirror. The braces were bent so they formed prison bars, and the bottom of the mirror was embedded deep in the ground.

O Lord, have mercy! Give me the power to yank that stuff loose! Just then, the man moaned and I knew he was alive. I took a deep breath, grabbed the mess of steel braces and half-buried mirror, and jerked it with all my strength. Unbelievably, the whole thing broke free!

Please, God, don't let him be stuck in that flaming cab.

"You're gonna have to try and help me, buddy," I pleaded. The trucker's arms were pinned to his side, but he began to move.

"That's it! Keep wiggling!" I pulled and eased him out of the cab window frame onto the ground.

O God, let us get away from this truck before its gas tanks explode.

I helped the man up, and he began stumbling up the incline on his own. But he was in shock—covered with blood, dirt, and shattered glass—and he collapsed on the grass almost immediately. We *had* to get farther away.

It was then I looked up, because something very unusual was going on. The wind was out of the south, more than just a breeze. Fire and smoke should have been billowing in our direction. In fact, the wind should have blown fire and smoke directly on me as I was dragging the driver out of his burning cab. But it hadn't. Instead, I could see the smoke swirling straight up, arching over the truck—over us—and coming down in the middle of the highway like a rainbow. How long could it last?

Frantically I helped the man get up again. Just as we reached a safe distance about fifty yards away, the gas tanks blew, incinerating the tractor trailer as if it were just a wad of dry paper. And at that same instant, the smoke and fire began blowing the way they should have all along—igniting the area we had left only seconds before.

Thank You, Almighty Lord!

Suddenly people began appearing out of nowhere, beating out the grass fire and then gathering around us—another truck driver, motorists who'd stopped. In the distance I could hear an ambulance siren.

Someone showed up with a first aid kit. Other people started picking glass out of the man's shredded shirt and cleaning him up. The ambulance arrived. So did the Highway Patrol and a local fire department. My job was done.

As I was walking toward my truck, a bystander caught up with me. "Hey, you saved that man's life! No one else had the guts to go near that truck—scared it would blow any second."

I shook my head. "I don't want the credit," I told him. "I just try to stay close in touch with the Lord. So when I need help, He's there to give it. *He* gave me the push and the strength and a couple of miracles this morning, and He gets the glory."

I thought for a minute and then I started to chuckle. "You think I've got guts? Why, man, you're looking at a guy who's scared of a little spider!"

—*J. V. Calvert*

Overboard!

I REMEMBER HOW BADLY our kids wanted to go fishing with us that November morning. The two boys tried to talk us into letting them skip school, and even the little girl was for it. But of course we said no.

My wife and I always went fishing Mondays. I'd shut down my filling station and we'd haul our outboard to Lake Chickamauga, north of Chattanooga. This particular Monday was gray and raw. But that meant good fishing, and we'd have the lake to ourselves.

Sure enough, when we reached the beach there wasn't another car or boat in sight. We pushed the boat into the water, I got the motor going, and we were off, without so much as a frown over the fact that Vivian couldn't swim a stroke and wasn't wearing a life jacket. Funny how you figure some things just won't happen to you.

Vivian had brought a coat for me to put on, but I couldn't take time before starting. Seems like I couldn't wait to get to a spot I knew where I could just smell those big black bass waiting for us. Out on the water, though, it was a lot colder. We were moving along pretty good, maybe eighteen miles per hour, and the wind was fresh.

"You'll catch cold!" Vivian hollered over the noise the outboard was making.

Well, I reached for the coat, and I guess I gave the tiller a twist, because that boat gave a terrific lurch. I was holding on so I didn't fall. But Vivian was thrown from the seat into the water.

I choked the motor down, never taking my eyes off the spot where she went under. Then I dived. I swam straight down, looking for her through the brown water. I saw her, got my arm around her and started kicking for the surface. We broke water just when I thought my lungs would burst.

Vivian was wonderful. She didn't fight me or grab me the way some people will, just lay back on my arm and I saw she was praying. I looked around for the boat. I couldn't hold her up much longer with our heavy clothes full of water.

I couldn't see the boat. I turned around the other way, figuring the dive had mixed me up. I made a compete circle in the water. There was no boat. Then I saw it. It was two hundred yards from us and moving away fast. In my hurry to get in the water I hadn't shut down the motor all the way. The boat was gone and so were we.

I saw Vivian had seen it now, too, but she just whispered, "God's going to take care of us, Bennie."

Well, I knew *I* couldn't take care of us much longer, that was sure. The shore looked a million miles away. There wasn't a sign of anyone else on the beach, and even if someone came right now, by the time they could put a boat in the water and get out to us, it was going to be too late.

It was the weight of our clothes, plus the ice-cold water, that made it so bad. I knew we had to get Vivian's coat off. I got my arms under her shoulders and she wiggled and tugged at the heavy, clinging thing, and we both swallowed a lot of water. But at last she broke free of it.

But getting my boots off was a different thing. I had on the high-laced shoes I wore at the filling station and they got heavy as iron and dragged me down. I tried to get one hand down to undo the laces, but we both got ducked. Vivian had had all the water she could take.

She wasn't scared, though, not even now. "God's going to help us," she said, over and over.

Well, Vivian seemed so sure I began to figure how maybe God could do it. Perhaps He could send a seaplane and set it down on the water beside us. But the only thing in that gray winter sky were a few birds.

I was too tired to hold my head out of the water all the time. I sank down below the surface where I didn't have to kick too hard in those iron boots, holding Vivian up above me. Every little while I climbed up and got a swallow of air. Each time it seemed like I wouldn't make it.

Then I knew I was dying, because I could see my whole past life. And it wasn't much to look at. Not until two years ago, anyway. I saw the years I'd spent stock car racing, the money I'd wasted, the heavy drinking, the close calls racing a car after a few drinks.

And I saw Vivian, the way she'd been all those years. She'd never given up on me, she'd just kept on praying for me. No matter how late or how drunk I'd come home, she'd have dinner hot and waiting. And no cross words either, just:

"God loves you, Bennie. He's waiting for you."

Then one night, two years ago, I'd come home at 2:00 A.M. when the bars closed, and there was Vivian just sitting and waiting like she always was. And suddenly I knew she was right about God because no one could be as good as Vivian on his own. I got down on my knees then and there and gave my life to Him . . .

I swam up to the air and breathed for a while, remembering these things and the wonderful family life we'd had ever since. I hauled one of my boots up as far as I could and clawed at the laces again, but they were hard as steel. I sank back below the water. I didn't think I'd make it to the top again. My arms ached with holding Vivian above me.

Well, it was God's life now and it was all right for Him to take it any-time. I just didn't like to think about the kids, coming home from school, and us not there. I was too tired, too tired to keep struggling. I thought I could sleep—except that Vivian was pulling at me, tugging my arm. She was shouting:

"The boat! The boat!"

Now I saw something moving on the lake. I couldn't make out what it was at first, but it looked like it was coming nearer.

"It's the boat!" Vivian said.

It couldn't be. But it was, our own empty boat, somehow turned around and headed straight for us. I knew it couldn't happen. But I was seeing it. And even then I didn't dare hope I could grab it. I didn't have any swim left. That boat would have to come to the very square foot of water where we were for it to do us any good. If it was even three feet away it was going to pass us by.

I watched it come, moving straight as if a sure hand was on the tiller. And suddenly I knew—sure as I'd ever known anything—that that boat was coming right to us.

I just lifted up my hand and my fingers closed over the side of it. It was the last strength I had. I couldn't do any more for a long while than just hold on. Vivian had more strength than I had by then. She climbed aboard and shut the motor down, and for a long time I just hung on. Then, when I was rested a bit, I climbed in too.

Well, we sat there, water streaming off us, and we just shouted for joy. Then we sang for joy. Then we prayed for joy and just magnified God in every way we knew. Vivian saw I was rubbing my arms and she said:

"Bennie, it wasn't God alone. You held me up until He could come."

But I shook my head. "You've held me up too, Viv. I was thinking in the water how you prayed for me all those years when I couldn't. Well, I was just swimming for you, when you couldn't."

And I guess that's about all we can do for each other, just hold one another up, until God provides the help we need.   —BENNIE SHIPP

"Someone Help Me!"

I AM A FARMER'S WIFE. I work often under the open sky, and if I should seek an uninterrupted conversation with the Almighty, I easily could have it for we have no neighbors for miles.

But for a long time I had ceased to pray for God's help because it seemed useless. It was our third straight summer of drought. An early hailstorm had cut down our seedlings in April. Now—with my husband away on a stock-buying trip, with two small children to care for, livestock to feed, and parched crops to be handwatered from the brook—now, on top of everything the house well had run dry. If there was a God in that vast, cloudless sky why couldn't He show some compassion with a little rain?

But there was work to be done. The battle against drought had to go on. I climbed into our three-quarter ton truck, which drags our "watering tank" on a flat wagon behind, and headed for the fields. It was a clumsy, oval, galvanized water tank, but it held a great deal of liquid. There was a three-foot opening on top, through which we filled it by pailfuls from the brook, and through which we could bail out water onto our thirsty crops. The tank was held in place on the flat wagon by several wooden blocks.

On this particular day, our little daughters, Carol and Susie, were with me. They liked to stand on the wagon while they laughingly held onto the swaying, sloshing water tank.

Because of my preoccupied brooding that day, I did not at first hear their cries. Suddenly their screams were loud in my ears. I looked around but couldn't see anything. I stopped the truck and leaped out.

There, standing on the wagon were Carol and Susie, their faces wild with terror. Then I saw. One of the wooden blocks had slipped and Carol's small bare foot was caught under the tank. Another block midway under the tank was at a weird angle and I could tell that in minutes it, too, would slip and the full weight of the tank would crush her foot.

"Are you hurt?" I cried.

"I don't think so, Mommie. But I can't get loose."

"Don't move!" I commanded.

The wooden block had inched out a little more. I knew there could be no assistance near.

Then I was beside my child, my hand sliding under the small space below the tank till I felt her bare foot against my skin. "Get ready to jump," I panted. I put my shoulder against the heavy tank. It felt cold and damp—damp like the rain I had once believed in praying for ...

Heave! I threw myself against the dead weight of almost a ton of water. It didn't budge. Heave! O *God, help me! Someone help me!* Every ounce of strength was needed. Heave . . . something gave, pain ripped through my back, the tank lurched away as the wagon tipped up, and I was knocked spinning to the ground.

At first I thought I was sitting in a pool of blood but it was water sloshing from the tank. The wagon and tank lay crazily on their side. In a daze I saw that Carol's foot was unharmed except for a wide red bruise.

But the children were looking at me strangely, for I did not realize at first that I had been shouting.

I was suddenly looking at the sky, full face. My cheeks and dress were wet. "You hear!" I was shouting over and over, "There is a God! There is a God and He hears us . . ."

When my husband learned what had happened he could not believe that a lone woman had the strength to lift that huge steel tank full of water—and he was right. It took extra strength, and in the moment of my greatest need God gave me His strength.

A year has gone by. Spring already is behind us. The rain that began with such frequency in late April is still with us and the barrenness of the past summers is only a harsh memory. At times there is a pain in my side that was not there before, and now and then it makes a dull bid for attention. But when it does I smile to myself. It is a quiet reminder that no task is insurmountable, no loneliness unshared, and no sky empty—of God.   —MARY VIRAG

Recital for One

M Y HUSBAND AND I HAD BEEN FARMING just a few years up to the summer our sons were two and four years old. We were trying hard to get established, so my husband still worked full time off the farm. My days were full—driving a tractor to do field work, tending livestock, trying to be a good homemaker and mother. But at one point there came a welcome lull in my labors. A good chance to get away.

I loaded the boys in our ten-year-old car and drove all the way across Wyoming to visit my parents for a few days. We arrived exhausted, and so my bedtime prayers were a quick "Thank You for a safe trip" and the usual "Please, dear Lord, be with me tomorrow."

The next afternoon, Grandma was pleased to have her only grandsons all to herself in the kitchen. And for me, here was a rare opportunity: time to indulge my love of piano playing.

I had brought a pile of long-neglected sheet music with me: my favorites and some I knew my father would enjoy. Shortly after I began to play, Father came in and sat in a living-room chair near the piano. He listened a minute, then pointed to a book on the music rack and said, "Play something out of that."

My father was a longtime fan of the Lawrence Welk television show, and the book he indicated was a collection of ragtime songs arranged by Tiny Little, who played piano on the show in its early days. Ragtime was my favorite kind of music and I'd had the book for several years. I had tried diligently to learn the songs, but with little formal training and even less natural ability, I hadn't been very successful.

I played the one song in the book that, with a lot of effort, I had mastered, and then I started to set the book aside. I knew the other songs were beyond my skill.

"Oh, play another one," said Father.

I looked through the book. Perhaps there was one other song I might be able to bluff my way through. I tried it and found I could play it almost perfectly, surely the best I'd ever done. Surprised and encouraged, I tried one more song...and then another, until I'd played— passably—the whole ragtime book.

My father enjoyed my ragtime recital, enjoyed it in a quiet way. I could tell he was feeling tired, but I didn't realize at the time that he wasn't feeling well. There was no way for me to know the shock that lay ahead. My father died of heart failure the next morning.

I was where I needed to be for the next week, and when I returned home after Father's funeral I was tired and sad. But I had to resume the farm chores, and maybe that was just as well, for the work took my mind off my sorrow.

Finally, a few weeks later, I found time for a few minutes of recreational piano playing. I dug out the ragtime book, thinking, *Now that I know all these songs. I'll just play straight through this book.* I first played the one song I'd always been able to play. Then I went on to the other familiar one. I didn't play it very well. And how about the rest of the songs, the ones I'd sailed through that last afternoon with Father? Well, those songs were once again as far beyond me as they'd always been, my fingers utterly incapable of playing the notes my eyes were reading.

You might think this sudden return to incompetence would have saddened me. But it didn't. Instead, I felt consoled, even happy. Clearly

God had given me a momentary gift, the chance to play gladdening songs for my father in his final hours. I closed the ragtime book and put it back in the piano bench, knowing more than ever that God is loving and kind.
                                                    —*Phyllis M. Letellier*

The Lame and the Halt

U P. UP. UP. UP. Inch by inch, stiff and headachy, I toiled up the stairs to my bedroom to get ready for my swimming lesson. The boys had been late leaving for school and now I was late, too. Snow fell implacably outside the window. *This is ridiculous,* I told myself, and plopped down on the top step. *Lord,* I pleaded, *when is this pain going to end? Please, can't You send me some relief?*

For five months I'd been tormented by rheumatoid arthritis—that fiendish disease that strikes at any age, from childhood on up, and sets your joints on fire—and my doctor had prescribed swimming therapy. In the water I could move quite freely, but once out of the pool I had to resume my creaking walk. I felt conspicuous and discouraged. And sorry for myself.

Now, sitting on the stairs, I wanted to give up. *What's the use?* I argued. *By the time I get there, swimming will be half over anyway.* Suddenly, a single thought shot through all my despair: *Get going!*

It was so startling that I actually pulled myself up, got into some clothes and shuffled down to the car. But before I pulled out of the driveway, which was already covered with a film of slick snow, I hesitated again. "What's the good of this?" I asked aloud.

Just go! the inner voice commanded. I went.

As I slowed to turn the corner, my eyes flicked to the left, aware of an odd movement in what looked like a large trash bag, torn open and flapping in the wind. I rolled my window down to look closer. The object moved again. Then I heard a moan, a cry for help.

"Coming," I shouted.

I opened the car door and forced my body to bend, forced it to get out and go to the dark, bundled shape in the snowdrift at the side of the street.

"Oh, thank God you're here," a small voice cried feebly.

The "bundle" was a tiny old woman who had lost her footing and fallen into the snowdrift. Her glasses, unbroken, lay a few feet away.

"I can't move," she said, her teeth chattering. "Help me."

How could I tell her that I couldn't help her up? That I couldn't even bend down to comfort her?

"I prayed," she said in a stronger voice. "I prayed you'd come along, and now here you are."

Me? For one wild moment, I wanted to laugh. How could a woman crippled with arthritis be an answer to a prayer? But there was no one else on the deserted street. It had to be me.

"O Father, be with us," I said quickly. And in one swift, effortless motion I bent down and scooped her up. In the next instant she was on her feet, picking up her glasses, smiling at me.

"Nothing broken, not even hurting," she said triumphantly, and then suddenly, we were laughing.

I drove her to her home, then went back to mine, exulting. I'd missed my swimming session, but God had given me therapy of a different kind. He had actually used me—arthritis and all—as His messenger in answering the need of another person.

Being strong for someone else had strengthened my own spirit. Now I knew I could cope.   —BARBARA WERNECKE DURKIN

Flight of Faith

Regardless of weather their trip is begun;
No alibis cause a delay.
The small feathered flyers take off, rain or sun,
Heading north,
Trusting Him, day by day.

The heavenly power that makes them persist—
That guides fragile creatures like these—
Gives wings to my faith when I need an assist
And I soar
When I'm down on my knees.
                    —MARGARET RORKE

Out of the Storm

I DIDN'T EXPECT THE STORM to break until later that day. When the sky cracked open and the rains began, I was still driving on the main road with my granddaughter, MaryBeth. The wind howled, swirling bits of sagebrush around my little car, and I peered anxiously out of the windshield. My farm in Arnegard was still twelve miles away! Then I remembered the shortcut around some grazing land.

It was a gravel road, deeply rutted by tractor marks, as is common in these rural parts of North Dakota. Something warned me not to risk it, but darkness was coming on and I was anxious to get home. I came to the fork and turned off the paved road.

"How did your practice go, MaryBeth?" I asked brightly. I knew my ten-year-old granddaughter was deathly afraid of storms. She had come to spend the Easter holiday with me and, to pass the time, had joined the church choir. Tomorrow, Easter Sunday, they would be singing the beautiful "Hallelujah Chorus" from Handel's *Messiah*.

"It was fine, Grandma," MaryBeth said in a small voice, keeping her eyes on the road.

I zigzagged along, grumbling each time I swerved to miss the giant cuts of the tractors. Then suddenly, as I rounded a curve, a blur of lights exploded in front of me. Horrified, I pulled hard on the wheel. A big car *swooshed* by, crowding us into a deep rut. The steering wheel jerked out of my hands and the car flipped over. We rolled over one more time into the roadside ditch. Then an eerie stillness filled the car except for the furious drumming of the rain...

Dazed, I tried to move myself. The crash had pushed me under the steering wheel and into the leg space in front of the driver's seat. I heard a weak whimper from the back seat. "Are you hurt, child?" I called.

There was a brief silence. Then a faint voice said, "I think I'm okay, Grandma."

I remembered stories I had heard of cars bursting into flames with the occupants trapped inside. "Come to me if you can," I called frantically. I knew I was too hurt to move to her. My legs were twisted and there was a strange heaviness in my chest.

The car had landed on its roof and MaryBeth had to crawl along it, pushing aside the seat cushions that had come loose and blocked her way. In a few moments I saw her frightened face peering at me from between the spokes of the steering wheel.

"Lord, forgive me for bringing this upon her," I groaned to myself. But there was no time to chide myself for choosing the shortcut. I had to think of a way to get help. Should I send my frightened granddaughter out in the rain where lightning flashes cracked across the sky? There was little chance of another car coming by and seeing us because we were hidden from the road. Dismally, I recalled that my husband wouldn't return from a business trip until tomorrow. The rest of my family wouldn't come by until it was time for tomorrow's church service. There was only one solution. MaryBeth would have to go out in the storm that terrified her and look for help.

My eyes searched the car for an opening. Just before the crash, MaryBeth had partially cranked down her steamed-up window to see out, and it was still open. "Crawl through the window, child," I told her feebly.

Soon she managed to wiggle out into the rain. "I'm scared, Grandma," she wailed through the wind and thunder crashes.

"Don't be frightened," I called. "Look for a light or a house." There was silence. Then at last she said, "I think I see some lights!"

"Go to them," I urged, and prayed for God to be with her as she splashed off through the fields.

I tried to free myself, but it was useless. The pain in my legs and chest was becoming unbearable, and I had to rest my head against the steering wheel for support. "Dear God, please protect and guide MaryBeth," I prayed over and over again. "Send Your guardian angel to be with her!"

The rain continued to pour on the crushed car as I waited and prayed. It seemed like hours and hours. What had happened to MaryBeth? Had she found someone? Was she lost in the storm?

Faith had always been strong in my family. We came to the farm lands three generations ago from Norway, and had always lived by the land and our faith. "My faith looks up to Thee, Thou Lamb of Calvary," I repeated to myself over and over.

I don't know how long I lay in the car, praying. But suddenly through the steady movement of the rain and wind I began to detect a new motion. What was it—a rubbing? Craning my neck painfully, I was able to see cows nudging my wrecked car!

"Hiyah, hiyah! Get home, you critters," I heard someone shouting. *It's a farmer,* I thought joyfully. I began to call for help.

"What's that?" came a startled reply from out in the storm. Soon a rain-soaked farmer was peering through the opened window of my car. I tried to smile at him. "Are you hurt?" he cried, vainly trying to pull open the jammed door.

"Somewhat," I answered weakly. "But I can't move and had to send a little girl for help. She's out there somewhere..." I looked helplessly into the fields.

"Don't worry," the man said. "We found her in my field. My cattle strayed in the storm and I found her right in the middle of my cows. She was so frightened and exhausted that she wasn't able to make any sense, so I brought her back to my house. Then I came on horseback to round up the cattle, and found you." He shook his head. "It's amazing. I wouldn't have seen a darn thing in this storm if it weren't for these here cows!"

Suddenly I knew how the Lord had answered my prayers. *He had sent the cows!* They were our guardian angels—a herd of cows!

The farmer took off his horse's saddle blanket and covered me with it, promising to go for help. Soon I was taken to Arnegard Hospital. MaryBeth, already there, rushed to my side.

"You'll be all right now, Grandma," she said happily.

I nodded, thinking about God's special answer to my prayers. My old body would mend. MaryBeth was safe. She would still be able to sing that wonderful song of praise at the Easter service.

"Yes, child," I said to her, "the 'Hallelujah Chorus' will surely be sung in church tomorrow!" —*EMMA STENEHJEM*

Easter Morning

The stone wasn't rolled
 away from the tomb
So that Jesus could leave.
 He was already gone.

It was rolled away
 so that doubters like me
Could look in and cry,
 "I believe! I believe!"
—*LEROY THOMAS*

"O death, where is thy victory?
O death, where is thy sting?"
. . . Thanks be to God, who gives us the victory through our Lord
Jesus Christ. —1 Corinthians 15:55–58

CHAPTER EIGHT

God Removes the Sting of Death

In this section two kinds of stories show God's presence in the world and His power in and through life *and* death. Some illustrate the many ways by which God comforts His children saddened by the death of a loved one— a voice, a song, a rose, even a rainstorm. In other stories, people hovering on the brink of death briefly glimpse a world beyond this earth, before they are "sent back" to live out their mortal days—with new awareness of their Lord and the purpose He has for their lives.

"You Should See What I'm Seeing"

SPRINGTIME IN WASHINGTON, cherry blossom time. When that wonderful sea of pink blossoms foams along our Capitol's avenues, I always wish everyone in the world could see it. And one year I did invite my parents to come down from Cape May, New Jersey, and visit me at cherry blossom time, but word came back that health problems made such a trip impossible.

Then, on the very day when I had hoped they could be with me, I had a telephone call at the office, telling me that my mother had just died.

I sat there stunned with disbelief and shock. Finally I organized my office work after a fashion, told my coworkers that I would be gone for a week, and walked down the stairs of the U.S. Naval Oceanographic Office. As I reached the street, I was trembling, overwhelmed by the terrible sense of grief and loss. Somehow I made my way to my car and put my keys in the ignition. And as I did I heard Mother's voice say quite clearly and distinctly, "Oh, Audre, if you think the cherry blossoms are beautiful, you should see what I'm seeing!"

Then I cried, but in joy as well as sorrow.   —*Audre L. Tribbe*

Uncle Wilson's Last Words

IN SEPTEMBER 1983 UNCLE WILSON, my mother's only brother, underwent surgery for an intestinal tumor. The doctors, discovering a tumor too large and complex to remove, gave him from four to six months to live. Uncle Wilson was brought home to spend his remaining days. With no wife to see to his needs, his care fell to my mother, her two sisters and us nieces and nephews.

We all worked hard to make Uncle Wilson comfortable, but he was bedridden, helpless and in great pain. Day after day we tended to his needs, tried to soothe his fears. And every night before bed I knelt and asked God to heal this good, kind man.

In July 1984, ten hard months having passed, Uncle Wilson took a turn for the worse. I was called and told to come at once. I stood by his bed, waiting for the rescue squad ambulance to come, and even in his pain Uncle Wilson tried to communicate his love and thanks by kissing my hand.

By now I was no longer praying for his healing, but simply asking that God take my uncle to be with Him. And then, early in the morning of his third day in the hospital, my sister and I were with him when Uncle Wilson suddenly opened his eyes, and in a loud and clear voice he cried, "My God! My God! My God!" My sister and I were wonderstruck.

Uncle Wilson died soon after, but my family was sustained by his words. My uncle, you see, had been deaf and mute since birth. These words were the first he had ever spoken. —MARGARET MURRAY

The Music Box

MY HOBBY IS COLLECTING MUSIC BOXES—nothing expensive or rare or old, just music boxes I like and enjoy listening to. For years my mother's favorite was a figurine of an old woman sitting in a rocking chair and holding a few balloons.

Every time my mother came to visit me, she would go into the den and look at the music box and smile thoughtfully. Then she'd say, "If Pa goes first, that's me—sitting on a rocking chair in Lincoln Park, selling balloons." We would laugh. Then she would push the button and listen to the song it played—"Try to Remember" from *The Fantasticks*.

In 1970, Mother, then approaching eighty, suffered a mild stroke that put her in the hospital for a week. After that, she never became completely well again. Gradually her weakness increased. My father, who had been retired for several years, now became Mother's constant attendant. My sister and I took turns going over there one day a week to shop, clean house and prepare casseroles and stews that my father could warm up for their meals.

Often my mother would ask me, "How's the old lady with the balloons?"

"Fine," I'd say. "She asks about you all the time." And we'd laugh.

In October 1974, my phone rang very early one morning. It was my father. He said, "Honey, you'd better get over here. It's Ma."

"What happened?" I asked, fearing the worst.

"She fell getting out of bed," he said. "I don't have the strength to lift her."

"I'll be right there," I said. I called my sister, told her the bad news and said I'd pick her up on the way.

We found Mother sitting on the floor in her room, resting against her bed. Her face was sad and helpless, with tears of humiliation in her eyes. We got her back in bed.

"I'm sorry this happened," she whispered. "Thanks for coming. I'll make it up to you."

Those were her last words to us.

I called the doctor. An ambulance was there in minutes, but on the way to the hospital Mother lost consciousness. She was put into intensive care. While out in the waiting room the doctor told us, "It's very bad. There's been a lot of brain damage. She may not come out of this."

It was the beginning of a long ordeal for all of us. Mother went into a coma. Ten days later she was transferred to a private room where we could stay with her all day. Dad left the room frequently for a cigarette, his pain a constant frown on his face.

I was there every day, all day. Mother remained in a coma but I talked to her anyway hoping she could somehow hear me. "We're all praying for you, Ma," I told her, "everybody—even the old lady with the balloons."

Early in the morning on November 19, with our house still in darkness, the phone rang. I braced myself. "Hello?"

"Mrs. Miller, this is the head nurse at the hospital. I'm sorry to have to tell you that your mother died ten minutes ago."

Even though I had been expecting them, her words were like a blow. "Thank you," I managed to say somehow. "I'll take care of everything." As I hung up, I glanced at the clock. It was 5:10 A.M. My mother had died at 5:00, after being in a coma for forty-nine days.

Somehow we all got through the next few days. Then came the strain of adjusting to the loss, of waiting for the sorrow to fade. Time passed, but the sorrow did not disappear. When death takes a loved one, even though you trust in the promise of everlasting life, something in you longs for reassurance, for proof of that promise. It's only human, I guess.

The months went by. One season slipped into another. One day, my husband, Lenny, came home from work with a bad cold. I suggested that he spend a couple of days in bed, but he said he had too much work to do at the office and couldn't spare the time. A few days later, the cold was so bad that he had no choice. I nursed him all day, and then, so he could sleep undisturbed, I spent the night on the sofa in the den.

It had been a hard day for me, because it was the day before the first anniversary of Mother's death. I kept thinking about her, missing her, wishing she were only a telephone call away. It would have been so helpful just to talk to her, ask her advice about Lenny, feel the warmth and reassurance she always gave.

Tired and worried about Lenny, I tossed fitfully on the sofa for a while. I kept thinking about all the uncertainties of life, and I felt lost and lonely somehow. I missed our familiar bed and Lenny's comforting presence. Finally I drifted off into a restless sleep.

Hours later I woke with a start; something strange, something unfamiliar had wakened me. For a moment I didn't know what it was. Then I heard the music. The soft sounds of a familiar song drifted through my mind. But where was it coming from? There was darkness all around me. Had I been dreaming it? No, the music was still playing. In the darkness I could still hear its eerie tinkling.

I sat up. I stared into the gloom. There, on the desk, was the silhouette of the old lady with the balloons, and the song I heard coming from the music box was my mother's favorite, "Try to Remember."

"But it can't be playing," I said to myself. "Nobody's touched it. And the last time I played that box I distinctly remember letting it run down!"

And then I remembered what day it was. November 19. I glanced at the desk clock. It was 5:00 A.M. Ma had died exactly one year ago to the day, to the hour, to the minute! I began to cry. I whispered to the dark: "If that's you, Ma, I hope you're safe and happy. You know that we still love you and miss you and, yes, we still remember."

I lay down again, weeping, listening to the music until it stopped, and I fell asleep, reassured at last.

I awoke again around 7:30 and smelled bacon. I got up and went to the kitchen. There was Lenny, shaved, fully dressed, at the stove frying bacon and eggs. "You were so sound asleep that I decided to fix breakfast myself," he said. "I'm going to work."

I stared at him, astonished. "Are you well enough for that?"

"Yes," he said. "During the night the cold just seemed to melt out of me. I feel great."

I felt as if I were going to cry again. "I'll do that," I said. I took the spatula away from Lenny and turned my back to him, close to tears.

Lenny went to the table and sat down to his cup of coffee. He said, "Tell me something. Did I hear you playing Ma's music box during the night or did I dream it?"

I fought the tears. I couldn't talk about it yet.

"No," I said. "I didn't play it."

And in my heart I thanked the Lord for using a little mechanical music box to let us know that our mother was safe with Him, that she still loved us, still missed us, and, yes, still remembered.

—*Shirley Miller*

The Legacy of Mary Elizabeth

SARAH BIRD WAS NEARLY EIGHTY-SIX, but her eyes were bright and her mind alert. When I visited her in the Home for the Aged here in St. Cloud, Florida, she reminisced about days gone by, as if talking about them would bring closer the friends and loved ones now gone or separated by distance. Here is one story she told me that has lived in my mind ever since . . .

Sarah Bird was born on a farm about three miles south of Baldwinsville, New York. She married the boy next door and the young couple moved with proper ceremony into a home given them by her parents. "Come joy or sorrow, we know that God is head of this home," her husband declared.

At first there was mostly sorrow. Their first baby, a boy, died before he was two. Then little Mary Elizabeth was born and brought much joy. She was a strong and healthy child until she developed heart trouble after a siege of pneumonia at the age of five. For the last few years of her life, Mary Elizabeth lay in her little brass bed in her own brightly furnished room at the head of the stairs.

The child spent much time reading. Once, when a picture of four little orphaned sisters appeared in the local paper, Mary Elizabeth asked a special favor of her father. "Would you please go to the orphanage and buy them for me? I have eight dollars. Please, Daddy. That one little girl has the same name as me—Mary Elizabeth."

But the father had to say no, explaining that with the cooking for the two hired men, the care of her blind grandmother and all the other work, it would be too much for her mother. Time passed.

When she was nine, life slowly ebbed away. Somehow Mary Elizabeth knew what was happening. But she showed no fear. Instead, she had one final request. Would her father please buy a baby girl at the orphanage because her mommy would be so lonesome when she left? The baby was to have blue eyes like the sky outside her window.

With heavy heart, her father gave her his solemn promise.

Mary Elizabeth died on Maundy Thursday, and on Easter Sunday was laid to rest in the little cemetery nearby. Weeks later, her father at last told his wife of his promise.

"It would be too much to care for an infant," Mrs. Bird said, still grief-stricken. "I'm busy from dawn until far into the evening."

"But I gave Mary Elizabeth my word," her husband said. "We could hire someone to help you."

They visited the orphanage, made an application for adoption and went home to wait for their baby. Two months later the call came; the baby was ready to be taken home. It was a beautiful infant, just six weeks old, but it had brown eyes! The man remembered his promise that it be a blue-eyed baby. Was there one?

The orphanage director admitted there was another child, a blue-eyed girl, eighteen months old. "She is rather sickly, and screams whenever a man comes near her," she added.

The child was named Adelaide. The director would bring her down for Mrs. Bird to see, but perhaps her husband wouldn't mind stepping to the back of the room?

He did so. But Adelaide saw him right away. Her thin arms stretched out to him, and when he held her, she smiled. They took her home that very day.

After a month, Adelaide looked like a different child. Sunshine and good country food put weight on the frail little body and in six months she was healthy and happy. On several occasions the orphanage director visited the farm to see how little Adelaide was getting along. During one of these calls, she asked Mrs. Bird if she would grant her a favor.

"There is a very unusual nine-year-old girl at the orphanage who has never been on a farm," she told Mrs. Bird. "Could you possibly take her for a weekend visit? Her name is Mary Elizabeth."

Remembering her own Mary Elizabeth, Mrs. Bird agreed to take the girl but only for the weekend. On Friday evening the little girl arrived, looking very forlorn, very lost and very subdued in her somber orphanage clothes. Even though she was staying only two days, the couple decided to pretty her up. On Saturday they took her shopping and bought her an entire new outfit: pretty black lace stockings to replace her heavy ribbed ones, and slippers with bows, a new blue coat with a hat to match and a dress trimmed with yards of lace. The child stood in front of the mirror at the farmhouse, her hands lovingly caressing the lace, her eyes alive with joy.

Over the weekend, Mary Elizabeth joined the household routine. She insisted on helping with the dusting, making the beds and playing with little Adelaide. Then Monday morning came and the lady from the orphanage arrived to take her back to the home.

Mary Elizabeth stood at the door with the box of new clothing under her arm. She smiled at Mrs. Bird, thanked her and asked wistfully, "I didn't make good here either, did I?"

"We told you it was only for a weekend visit," the lady from the orphanage explained.

Mary Elizabeth didn't answer. As she turned to go, Mrs. Bird could see the tears trickling down her face.

"It stabbed my heart," Sarah Bird said. "We couldn't let her go." Within a few weeks the adoption papers were in order, and Mary Elizabeth joined the family. In fact, she moved right into the room at the head of the stairs that had always been kept just as Mrs. Bird's own little Mary Elizabeth had left it—twin dolls sitting up in the corner, her favorite toys neatly arranged on the shelves alongside her book of Bible stories and scrapbooks.

One rainy Saturday afternoon when Mrs. Bird was mixing molasses cookies in the kitchen, the little girl asked if she could look at the scrapbooks. She promised to put them back just as she found them, for she knew that the room was very special to her new mother.

The second batch of cookie dough was rolled out on the board ready to be cut when the child ran down the stairs shouting:

"Mother, Mother, your Mary Elizabeth has my picture in her scrapbook!"

Mrs. Bird tried to convince the youngster that it couldn't be. Her own little girl had passed away nearly four years before and had no way of knowing her. But the child insisted:

"Yes, she did. She wanted me. She picked me out!"

Mrs. Bird wiped her floured hands on her long apron and went to the foot of the stairs. The child brought down the old scrapbook and, there, pasted on one of the last pages, was the newspaper clipping with pictures of four little orphaned sisters. Circled in crayon was the oldest one—Mary Elizabeth.

I'll never forget Sarah Bird's radiant face as she finished her story: "I was convinced then that my own little girl had indeed sent me both the blue-eyed baby Adelaide and the second Mary Elizabeth. They were like gifts from heaven." —*Theresa Budinger*

Missing

When the anxious hearts say "Where?"
He doth answer "In My care."

"Is it life or is it death?"
"Wait," He whispers. "Child, have faith!"

"Were they frightened at the last?"
"No, the sting of death is past."

"Did a thought of 'Home-Love' rise?"
"I looked down through Mother-eyes."

"Saviour, tell us, where are they?"
"In My keeping, night and day."

"Tell us, tell us, how it stands."
"None shall pluck them from My Hands."
—*Author Unknown*

Return from Tomorrow

W HEN I WAS SENT to the Base hospital at Camp Barkeley, Texas, early in December 1943, I had no idea I was seriously ill. I'd just completed basic training, and my only thought was to get on the train to Richmond, Virginia, to enter medical school as part of the army's doctor-training program. It was an unheard-of break for a private, and I wasn't going to let a chest cold cheat me out of it.

But days passed and I didn't get better. It was December 19 before I was moved to the recuperation wing, where a Jeep was to pick me up at 4:00 A.M. the following morning to drive me to the railroad station.

A few more hours and I'd make it! Then about 9:00 P.M. I began to run a fever. I went to the ward boy and begged some aspirin.

Despite the aspirin, my head throbbed, and I'd cough into the pillow to smother the sounds. At 3:00 A.M. I decided to get up and dress.

The next half-hour is a blur for me. I remember being too weak to finish dressing. I remember a nurse coming to the room, and then a doctor, and then a bell-clanging ambulance ride to the X-ray building. Could I stand, the captain was asking, long enough to get one picture? I struggled unsteadily to my feet.

The whir of the machine is the last thing I remember.

When I opened my eyes, I was lying in a little room I had never seen before. A tiny light burned in a nearby lamp. For a while I lay there, trying to recall where I was. All of a sudden I sat bolt upright. The train! I'd miss the train!

Now, I know that what I am about to describe will sound incredible. I do not understand it any more than I ask you to; all that I can do is relate the events of that night as they occurred. I sprang out of bed and looked around the room for my uniform. Not on the bedrail: I stopped, staring. Someone was lying in the bed I had just left.

I stepped closer in the dim light, then drew back. He was dead. The slack jaw, the gray skin were awful. Then I saw the ring. On his left hand was the Phi Gamma Delta fraternity ring I had worn for two years.

I ran into the hall, eager to escape the mystery of that room. Richmond, that was the all-important thing—getting to Richmond. I started down the hall for the outside door.

"Look out!" I shouted to an orderly bearing down on me. He seemed not to hear, and a second later he had passed the very spot where I stood as though I had not been there.

It was too strange to think about. I reached the door, went through, and found myself in the darkness outside, speeding toward Richmond. Running? Flying? I only know that the dark earth was slipping past while other thoughts occupied my mind, terrifying and unaccountable ones. The orderly had not seen me. What if the people at medical school could not see me either?

In utter confusion I stopped by a telephone pole in a town by a large river and put my hand against the guy wire. At least the wire *seemed* to be there, but my hand could not make contact with it. One thing was clear: in some unimaginable way I had lost my firmness of flesh, the hand that could grip that wire, the body that other people saw.

I was beginning to know too that the body on that bed was mine, unaccountably separated from me, and that my job was to get back and rejoin it as fast as I could.

Finding the base and the hospital again was no problem. Indeed, I seemed to be back there almost as soon as I thought of it. But where was the little room I had left? So began what must have been one of the strangest searches ever to take place: the search for myself. As I ran from one ward to the next, past room after room of sleeping soldiers, all about my age, I realized how unfamiliar we are with our own faces. Several times I stopped by a sleeping figure that was exactly as I imagined myself. But the fraternity ring, the Phi Gam ring, was lacking, and I would speed on.

At last I entered a little room with a single dim light. A sheet had been drawn over the figure on the bed, but the arms lay along the blanket. On the left hand was the ring.

I tried to draw back the sheet, but I could not seize it. And now that I had found myself, how could one join two people who were so completely separate? And there, standing before this problem, I thought suddenly: *This is death. This is what we human beings call "death," this splitting up of one's self.* It was the first time I had connected death with what had happened to me.

In that most despairing moment, the little room began to fill with light. I say "light," but there is no word in our language to describe brilliance that intense. I must try to find words, however, because incomprehensible as the experience was to my intellect, it has affected every moment of my life since then.

The light which entered that room was Christ. I knew because a thought was put deep within me: *You are in the presence of the Son of God.* I have called Him "light," but I could also have said "love," for that room was flooded, pierced, illuminated, by total compassion. It was a presence so comforting, so joyous and all-satisfying, that I wanted to lose myself forever in the wonder of it.

But something else was present in that room. With the presence of Christ (simultaneously, though I must tell it one by one), there also had entered every single episode of my entire life. There they were, every event and thought and conversation, as palpable as a series of pictures. There was no first or last, each one was contemporary, each one asked a single question, *What did you do with your time on earth?*

I looked anxiously among the scenes before me: school, home, scouting, and the cross-country track team—a fairly typical boyhood, yet in the light of that presence it seemed a trivial and irrelevant existence.

I searched my mind for good deeds.

Did you tell anyone about Me? came the question.

I didn't have time to do much. I answered. *I was planning to, then this happened. I'm too young to die.'*

No one, the thought was inexpressibly gentle, *is too young to die.*

And now a new wave of light spread through the room, already so incredibly bright, and suddenly we were in another world. Or rather, I suddenly perceived all around us a very different world occupying the same space. I followed Christ through ordinary streets and countrysides, and everywhere I saw this other existence strangely superimposed on our familiar world.

It was thronged with people. People with the unhappiest faces I ever have seen. Each grief seemed different. I saw businessmen walking the corridors of the places where they had worked, trying vainly to get someone to listen to them. I saw a mother following a sixty-year-old man, her son I guessed, cautioning him, instructing him. He did not seem to be listening.

Suddenly I was remembering myself, that very night, caring about nothing but getting to Richmond. Was it the same for these people; had their hearts and minds been all concerned with earthly things, and now, having lost earth, were they still fixed hopelessly here? I wondered if this was hell: to care most when you are most powerless.

I was permitted to look at two more worlds that night—I cannot say "spirit worlds" for they were too real, too solid. Both were introduced the same way: a new quality of light, a new openness of vision, and suddenly it was apparent what had been there all along. The second world, like the first, occupied this very surface of the earth, but it was a vastly different realm. Here was no absorption with earthly things, but—for want of a better word—with truth.

I saw sculptors and philosophers here, composers and inventors. There were universities and great libraries and scientific laboratories that surpass the wildest inventions of science fiction.

Of the final world I had only a glimpse. Now we no longer seemed to be on earth, but immensely far away, out of all relation to it. And there, still at a great distance, I saw a city—but a city, if such a thing is conceivable, constructed out of light. At that time I had not read the Book of Revelation, nor, incidentally, anything on the subject of life after death. But here was a city in which the walls, houses, streets seemed to give off light, while moving among them were beings as blindingly bright as the One who stood beside me. This was only a moment's vision, for the next instant the walls of the little room closed around me, the dazzling light faded, and a strange sleep stole over me . . .

To this day, I cannot fully fathom why I was chosen to return to life. All I know is that when I woke up in the hospital bed in that little room, in the familiar world where I'd spent all my life, it was not a homecoming. The cry in my heart that moment has been the cry of my life since: Christ, show me Yourself again.

It was weeks before I was well enough to leave the hospital, and all that time one thought obsessed me: to get a look at my chart. At last I was left unattended; there it was in terse medical shorthand: Pvt. George Ritchie, died December 20, 1943, double lobar pneumonia.

Later I talked to the doctor who had signed the report. He told me there was no doubt in his mind that I was dead when he examined me, but nine minutes later the soldier who had been assigned to prepare me for the morgue came running to him to ask him to give me a shot of adrenalin. The doctor gave me a hypo of adrenalin directly into the heart muscle, all the while disbelieving what his own eyes were seeing. My return to life, he told me, without brain damage or other lasting effect, was the most baffling circumstance of his career.

Today I feel that I know why I had the chance to return to this life. It was to become a physician so that I could learn about man and then serve God. And every time I have been able to serve our God by helping some brokenhearted adult, treating some injured child, or counseling some teenager, then deep within I have felt that He was there beside me again. —Dr. George C. Ritchie, Jr.

Danny's Dad

STAY AWAY FROM THE POOL, Danny," I told my three-year-old as he headed for the backyard to ride his Big Wheel.

"Yes, Mom," he said obediently.

Listening to the sound of his plastic tricycle, I returned to the kitchen, sighing. It was not easy being a widow, and raising two children on my own was often a strain.

I busied myself about the house until something made me stop dead still. I cocked my ear. No sounds of Danny's tricycle.

I rushed to the kitchen window and looked out at the swimming pool. Danny's Big Wheel was bobbing in the water, and there, floating face down, was Danny.

Desperately I pulled Danny out of the water and tried to administer CPR, but his body was cold and his face was gray. Then the sirens, the paramedics, the helicopter whisking Danny off to the hospital, where he lay in a coma. Finally, after my long, prayerful vigil, Danny opened his eyes. Soon he was well again, back home playing as usual. But somehow he seemed changed.

One day he blurted out, "Mom, I want to see a picture of my daddy." I had not realized I had never shown him a picture of his father, who had died before Danny was born. The first photograph I brought out showed my husband and his baseball team.

Danny looked at it for a few moments. Then he pointed to one of the coaches.

"That's my daddy," he said.

"How do you know?" I asked.

"He talked to me in the hospital before I woke up. He said, 'You must go home now. Mommy needs you.'"

I looked at the man he'd pointed to; it was the father he had never seen. —CATHY SLACK, AS TOLD TO SKIP WESTPHAL

The Awakening

DURING THE EARLY MORNING HOURS of a warm night in June 1987, I was asleep in our home when something caused me to awaken. At first I thought I was dreaming. But no, I was sure I was awake, and still I heard it. Music. Beautiful, melodic strumming. I got up to check if someone had left a radio or TV on, but that wasn't it. I looked in on our four children to see if any of them was up playing a record. But all were sound asleep—except for our two-year-old, Jeriel, who was staring out the window.

"Jeriel, what are you doing?"

He turned toward me, his blue eyes wide. "Mommy, I hear songs."

I crouched down by his curly blond head and looked out the window, but I saw nothing, just the leaves on the tree. I picked him up. "Sweetheart, I hear it too. But let's try to go back to sleep." As I carried him back to bed and plumped up his Donald Duck pillow, my heart pounded. What *was* it?

Back in our bedroom I woke my husband, Michael. "Do you hear the music?" I asked. Groggily he shook his head and was soon snoring again.

The beautiful strumming became louder. Then it stopped, and a lively high-pitched voice began to sing, coming from the direction of our fenced-in, above-ground swimming pool. I clearly heard the words:

> *"In all things give Him praise,*
> *In all your days give Him your praise.*
> *He alone is worthy of your praise.*
> *Though you be racked with pain.*
> *Still proclaim He is Lord*
> *And give Him praise . . ."*

Next morning, as bright sunshine filled the house, and Mike went off to his job as an electronics engineer at the Highland Park Chrysler plant, I wondered if it had been a dream. Then as I poured cornflakes, Jeriel asked, "Mommy, who was that singing last night?"

I caught my breath, my mind whirling. Jeriel was soon rolling his little car across the breakfast table, but I continued to wonder. The message had sounded like what I'd always thought the singing of angels would be, and I've always believed in angels, God's messengers. But if it was indeed the music of angels, what could it mean? Jeriel and I were the only ones, apparently, who had heard anything. I just didn't know what to make of the strange experience.

Two months later, on Wednesday, August 19, 1987, Jeriel was so wound up that he didn't want to nap. Always a climber, he was up on the sofa back, then on my kitchen counters. Finally he crawled next to me on my bed, laid his head on my chest, and then looked up. "Game, Mommy." It was a little amusement we enjoyed. I pointed to his eye and said, "Eye, eye," then to his nose, "nose, nose," and on to his mouth, teeth, and cheeks. I brushed my fingers through his soft blond curls and he laughed. Then, as always, I ended by saying, "Mommy loves you, Jeriel; Jesus loves you." He kissed me and said, "Jerielly loves you, and Jesus loves you too."

He relaxed and, looking at the picture over my bed, whispered, "Mommy, that's Jesus." I was thrilled. I had been trying to teach him that for months.

At supper Jeriel was the clown as usual. He had learned a new giggle, and all of us had fun in our attempts to mimic him. Afterward, the children asked to go swimming. I wasn't feeling well, so Mike said he would watch them while I rested on the sofa. Soon I dozed off.

Suddenly I was wakened. "Mommy, Jeriel fell in the pool!" It was six-year-old Athena, her eyes wide in terror.

I leapt up and raced out the back door. There on the pool's wooden deck Jeriel lay wet and motionless. Mike was bending over him, frantically giving him CPR. "Call the police!" Mike yelled.

In minutes, Mike and our landlord, who lives nearby, were putting Jeriel into our van to rush him to the Saline Hospital. Before leaving, Mike brokenly explained that while he was in the basement getting some toys, he hadn't noticed that Jeriel had slipped out of the house and climbed the pool fence.

Athena, five-year-old Gabriel, and three-year-old Josiah were crying. "Jerielly is dead!" screamed Athena. "I don't want my baby brother to be dead!"

"We don't know that," I soothed. Then I sat them down. "Look, Jeriel is in the hands of God. We must trust Him. Now let's pray for Jeriel to be strong. We are a family, and must stay together in Jesus, no matter what."

I put our children in the care of neighbors and rushed to the hospital. There Mike and I waited, gripping each other's hands.

When the doctor appeared, her face was grave. "We finally got a faint heartbeat," she said. "But"—she touched my shoulder—"you must remember, there may be some brain damage."

"I don't care," I cried. "I just want my baby back alive."

Finally they let us see Jeriel. He was lying in the trauma room with machines beeping. I brushed wet curls from his closed eyes. How small and helpless he looked. Soon a helicopter came to whisk him to Mott Hospital in Ann Arbor, which the doctor said was the best pediatric center in the area.

Mike went home for Jeriel's Donald Duck pillow and his favorite shirt and pants, for Jeriel to wear when he came home. Then we waited at Mott Hospital. I felt as if I were in a bad dream, and I kept asking God, "Please, wake me up."

Finally, the doctor came out. "Your son is in a deep coma. His brain has been without oxygen long enough to suffer damage. To what extent we don't know."

Mike and I turned and held each other, and prayed. Friends and relatives came to sit with us and pray. I sensed God's sweet Holy Spirit surrounding us all.

Two days later the doctor came in with Jeriel's test results. "It's not promising," he said. "Your son is ninety percent brain dead. He might live on or die in a few days or weeks. We can't tell."

I began sobbing. My friend Glenda put her arm around me. "Michelle, you have to give Jeriel to Jesus."

I stared at her. *No,* I thought, *God has turned things around before for me. He can heal Jeriel too.* Later that day as I held Jeriel's hand and talked to him, he drew my hand up to his heart. My spirits soared. He could hear me!

But every report was worse than the one before. On Sunday night, after Jeriel had been in a coma for four days, the doctor offered no hope. "It could be," he said, "that the time may soon come when we should turn off his life-support system." He looked up at us gravely. "We could keep him going, or do you want us just to let him go? We will need to know your decision soon."

Mike felt it would be best to let Jeriel go but I could not think of it.

Rachel, one of the many friends who had comforted us, stayed with me in the waiting room that night. I took off my shoes, lay down on a chair that converted into a bed, and finally went to sleep. But then I dreamed that I rose from my bed and walked into Jeriel's room. His body was attached to all sorts of needles and tubes. I leaned over and whispered in his ear, "Jeriel, my little sweetheart, I have always tried to teach you to obey Mommy and Daddy. Well, now there is another who is calling you. I told you that above all others we are to obey our Heavenly Father. And if He is calling you, you must go to Him."

I picked up my child, and to my surprise, all the needles and tubes fell from him. I cradled his limp body in my arms. As I stood crying, I heard someone call my name. I looked up. It was Jesus! His eyes were full of compassion.

"O Father, heal him, please, whether it be by his living or going home with You," I begged. But I already knew the answer. "Father," I continued, "when Jeriel was born, we dedicated him to You. He is Yours. I have always prayed that Your will be done."

He smiled. "Daughter, I love you and will give you strength and comfort."

I held Jeriel close, kissed him, and laid him at Jesus' feet. I stepped back and the Lord picked him up. Instantly Jeriel awoke. He looked up at the Lord, grinned, and said, "Hi, Jesus!"

The Lord held Jeriel out to me, and once more we played our little game. I touched his ear, his eye, his nose, mouth, and cheeks, and finished as always by saying, "Mommy loves you; Jesus loves you." He kissed me and said, "Jerielly loves you, and Jesus loves you too."

Then Jesus, with Jeriel in His arms, began to walk out of the room. The Lord motioned me to come. We walked along the darkened hospital corridor, took the elevator down to the lobby, and went past the reception desk to the double glass doors of the hospital entrance. Outside, instead of the courtyard, there was a hill covered with deep green grass, and the sky was pure and clear.

I stood inside the door, watching in awe as Jesus set Jeriel down. He took off in a run for the hill, stopped, picked a flower, and counted the petals, his voice crystal clear: "One, two, three, nine!" (He still hadn't learned to count.) "See," Jesus said to me, "he is alive. All who are in My care are alive and growing here."

Then He and Jeriel walked over the hill together. Once, Jeriel looked back, smiled, and called, "Mommy, I love you and will always be at your side." Then they were gone and I went back to sleep on my makeshift bed in the waiting room.

In the morning when I awoke, Rachel asked me a startling question: "Did you know you were walking in your sleep last night?" She went on to tell me I had left the room, walked down the corridor, and taken the elevator.

"I couldn't have," I insisted.

"No," she said, "you did some walking all right." Rachel pointed to my feet. "Okay, then explain why your shoes are on. You took them off when you went to bed. Now each is on the wrong foot."

I looked down. She was right.

Then the night nurse stuck her head into the room and said to me, "I hope I didn't disturb you last night—when you were in Jeriel's room, praying."

I was stunned. I had thought it all a dream. And yet . . .

Had it been only two months since I'd wondered if I'd had another dream—the music of the angels? But that music had been real. I had heard it. Jeriel had heard it. Why? Now, looking back, I knew. God was preparing us. But last night? It must have been the hand of God as well.

I got up and went into Jeriel's room, now half expecting to find his bed empty. But he was there, still connected to the tubes and the hissing machine. Yet something was different. As I looked down at him, somehow Jeriel was not the same. Then I knew: Jeriel was gone; only his body lived on.

From that moment on I was at ease. I did not have to insist on keeping his life-support system running; I could let go.

But Mike and I didn't have to make that decision. In forty-eight hours Jeriel's heart stopped beating. And for the first time since the accident, he was smiling.

—MICHELLE YATES

Peace

My soul, there is a country
   Far beyond the stars,
Where stands a wingèd sentry
   All skillful in the wars:
There above noise and danger,
   Sweet Peace sits crown'd with smiles,
And One born in a manger
   Commands the beauteous files.
He is thy gracious Friend,
   And—O my soul, awake!—
Did in pure love descend
   To die here for thy sake.

> If thou canst get but thither,
>   There grows the flower of Peace,
> The Rose that cannot wither,
>   Thy fortress, and thy ease.
> Leave then thy foolish ranges;
>   For none can thee secure
> But One who never changes—
>   Thy God, thy life, thy cure.
>
>   —*HENRY VAUGHAN*

The Phone Call

OUTSIDE THE BEDROOM WINDOW on this Sunday morning in July, the birds were just awaking. The air had the freshness that seems to exist only in those moments before the sun rises.

Inside, two people lay side by side. For forty years they had shared their lives and been attuned to each other, but never as intensely as now. For fourteen months, since the surgery that revealed the presence of cancer in his body, their marriage had taken on another dimension. The possibility that their time together on earth was drawing to a close made every moment precious.

She'd found herself studying his face when he wasn't aware of her presence. She wanted to memorize every feature: the eyes revealing the kindness inside the man, the large nose that the family lovingly teased him about, the mouth that smiled so easily or was so often pursed for whistling.

He'd been spending more hours lying on the couch or out in his hammock under a tree. Often he'd been lost in thought with a faraway look in his eyes. She longed to know what he was thinking, but to ask would be an intrusion on the thoughts which seemed to be one of the last things he could control as his body weakened.

She was in a deep sleep. He was beginning to stir. His first movements brought her quickly from her slumber, and she was immediately wide awake.

"Do you need some help?" she asked.

"No, I think I can take care of it," he replied as he reached for the urinal beside the bed. Lately, he'd not had the strength to walk down the hall to the bathroom when he awoke during the night.

After several minutes of fumbling, he admitted he would need her help after all.

"This is so ridiculous!" he said as they settled back into their warm bed. How difficult it was for him—indeed, for anyone—to have to depend on another for even the most basic needs.

"It's not at all ridiculous," she reassured him.

They were drifting off to sleep again. His arms were around her when suddenly he raised his head off the pillow and looked intently toward the east window of the bedroom.

"What is that bright light?" he asked, his voice intense.

She looked at him and then toward the window. "It's just the sun coming up."

"No, it's—"

He struggled to speak. His eyes showed that he'd seen something he wanted to tell her about, but he could not bring out the words. At that moment he drifted into unconsciousness.

Was this the moment she had been fearing? Quickly making sure he was carefully covered up, she slipped out of bed, reached for her robe, and climbed the stairs to the bedroom where their youngest son and his wife were sleeping. The doctor was telephoned, then their youngest daughter and her husband, who lived a short distance away.

The doctor confirmed what they had sensed already, that he had only hours to live.

The hours passed. The members of the family took turns sitting at the side of his bed. Even though he was in a coma, they felt that he would sense their presence and their love. It was she who was there beside him when the telephone in the hall rang. It rang again. Everyone else seemed to be in a different part of the house. Though the family had protected her from calls that morning, she knew she must answer this one. She picked up the phone just as the others were rounding the corner to answer for her.

"Hello?" she said.

On the other end a small, weak voice said, "Don't be afraid—the Lord's blessings are with you."

Her mind raced as she searched her memory trying to identify the strange voice. She was unable to respond because there was something so odd about the call. The look on her face was one of confusion as she held out the phone to her son-in-law.

"Hello?" he spoke into the receiver. Then he turned to her. "There's no one there now. Who was it, Mother?"

"I don't know, dear. It was a voice that sounded weak, far away, strange."

As the phone was replaced on its cradle, her daughter-in-law was the first to ask. "Did you see it, Mother? Did you see the phone? Did you see the phone glowing?"

And surely, they had all witnessed the strange phenomenon. There they were, a wife and mother of forty years surrounded by members of her family; a statistician with a master's degree, a statistician with a bachelor's degree, a plant pathologist with a doctoral degree, and a businessman, all standing in the dim hallway by the golden wall-phone. The very moment she had handed the phone to her son-in-law, the glowing had ceased and the caller was gone.

The glowing phone with the strange message did not change the course of the morning. When the moment of death came a few hours later, she was sitting, once again, at his side. She was watching the slow pulsing artery in his neck when the pulsing simply stopped. She remained near when the doctor pronounced death, and then she went downstairs to the basement. To watch her husband leave home for the last time was more than she could bear.

It has been seven years since that morning in July. I share this story with you today as an encouragement. You see, the man who died was my father. And my mother, who had so dreaded his death and was frightened by what life would be like without him, walked gallantly through the difficult days when her family returned to their own homes and their own lives. The two-story family home which she'd been sure would never offer her comfort without her husband became a place of solace and refuge after all. She never experienced any fear of staying alone. Mother immediately took over the upkeep of the yard, the house, the car, the finances, all duties which Daddy had performed and in which she had taken little interest. She not only handled these things, but accomplished them with skill and with a rewarding sense of fulfillment as well.

I believe that Mother was changed and strengthened by the mysterious voice on the glowing telephone.

And we, her children, have observed with amazement and humble thanksgiving how faithful the Lord is to His children when they are in need. We will not know until we meet the Lord face to face what wonderful bright light my father was seeing just before he lost consciousness. Nor will we know who was on the other end of the glowing phone. Yet the words "Don't be afraid—the Lord's blessings are with you" continue to have their impact. Is it not possible that the Lord, who understands every desire of our hearts, had compassion on my mother and allowed my father a final phone call? —*LINDA A. FUESZ*

I Saw Erica Running

O UR DAUGHTER, ERICA, came into this world blind. Later, grave medical problems followed. Erica was almost four when it became clear she was dying. As Jack and I kept vigil at her hospital bedside, our prayers for her healing gradually became prayers for wisdom and acceptance.

Then Jack looked at me searchingly. "Linda," he said, "we should do more than pray to God about Erica. We need to talk to Erica about God."

I knew he was right. Erica was afraid, afraid of dying. Despite her pain, I sensed she was holding on to us because we were the surest love she knew.

Cupping her tiny hands, we told her that God's love was so much greater than ours, and that she had to try to let go—of this hospital room, this bed, even us.

"Where you are going is a safe place, more beautiful and full of love than anything you've ever known . . ."

In my mind I saw Erica running, skipping over emerald grass through fields of rainbow-colored flowers. Her golden hair blazed in the sunlight. Her voice was laughter, and her eyes were like the sky, cloudless and blue. She was no longer blind.

A nurse came by to record Erica's vital signs. Though it was clear Erica's physical condition remained the same, I sensed a change, something deep in her spirit.

I was about to tell Jack when he said, "You know, just before the nurse came in I had the strongest image. I saw Erica, so vividly, skipping and running across a field of beautiful flowers. She was laughing. And her eyes were clear and blue as the sky." —*LINDA HANICK*

The Gentle Rain

F OR ROBERT AND ME, rain was always heaven-sent. During our courtship there was not much money for entertainment; however, we always enjoyed walking together—particularly in the rain. The rain poured continually on our wedding day. For the next twenty-one years of our marriage Robert often told of stopping for gas in my little town of Watkinsville, Georgia, on the way to our wedding. Since Robert was from south Georgia, no one knew him. The owner of the gas station laughed and told Robert about some poor nut who was getting married in this downpour. Some poor nut indeed!

For our wedding, Robert had had an inscription engraved inside my ring, but I didn't know how it read until I removed the ring as he checked us into our honeymoon suite. There I saw the words, *Because You Walked With Me in the Rain*.

Through the years of child rearing, losing parents through death, moving, and worrying about jobs—no matter the problem—our faith in God remained steadfast, and we always took comfort in His word, just like it says, "My words shall fall upon you like the gentle rain" (Deuteronomy 32:2, TLB).

Then one night Robert died suddenly from a heart attack. Soon family and friends gathered around me, but after they left, I didn't want to go to bed. I felt so alone. I wandered outside and stood on the front porch. The night was quiet, the sky was clear. And then, for only a few remarkable seconds, there came the familiar, comforting, reassuring sound—of raindrops splattering on the sidewalk before me.

—SARA SNIPES

The Far Side of Midnight

FROM THE TIME I WAS A CHILD my parents taught me to believe in God and to know Him. But as I grew up I learned that knowing God and being a professional Christian do not always keep difficulties or heartbreak away. Indeed, there was one time in my life when I felt that God had deserted me altogether.

It happened during World War II, when I was only twenty. Allen was twenty-one. He was in the artillery, the Timberwolf division. He was a Christian, too, and we pledged our lives together and our love to God.

When Allen went overseas with his division, a part of him stayed with me. We were to be married when he returned. We prayed for an early end to the war.

But then there was the Battle of the Bulge. Allen did not come through it.

Words cannot express the agony I felt. From the beginning, from the first time we met, our lives had been so intertwined I had felt that there could be no life for me if his ceased. I could not see how a loving God could permit such sorrow to come to me.

The night I learned of Allen's death was one of heavy, gloomy rain. Unable to talk to anyone, I put on my slicker and hat, and went out to walk in the downpour, trying to escape the unbearable loss, the despair. But they stayed with me.

I don't know how long I walked, or where I went, but finally I found myself on the bridge over the river that flowed through our town, an old-fashioned drawbridge with a bridge-tender who stayed in a little house on the main span, raising the center section when boats came by. I knew he was there, but I was sure that he would not be able to see me in the darkness and the rain.

I leaned over the railing and gazed down into the churning water below, just barely visible by the lights of the town. I had always lived for God, trying to do His will, and now He had betrayed me. If I could just slip over the side into the dark water, oh, the blissful oblivion, the release from pain. The agony of drowning would be over in moments—nothing compared to the torment now tearing me apart. *Oh, Allen,* I thought, *Allen, Allen . . .*

I heard no sound, but suddenly I felt a hand on my arm. "Come in out of the rain," the bridge-tender said quietly. Numbly I let him lead me to his tiny house on the bridge. He sat me down on one of the two chairs, and poured a cup of coffee from his Thermos. Pain possessed me, consumed me. I felt as if I *were* pain.

"It's a nasty night to be out," he remarked. He had removed his slicker, and I did not recognize him as one of the regular men. He was a little man, with an ageless face, and his eyes—the bluest, deepest-set I had ever seen—were compassionate and kind. I had never seen him before, but I felt his spirit touching mine.

I began to cry, and he sat there, across the little table from me, saying nothing. Oddly, his silence didn't seem strange to me; he did not seem like a stranger.

A boat's whistle hooted three times down the river. The man set in motion the huge mechanism that raised the bridge. The boat passed through, and the bridge settled back into place.

My sobbing had quieted, and I found myself telling him about Allen, spilling out my soul as if I'd known him all my life. When I finished, I felt drained, exhausted, but the unbearable knife-edge sharpness was gone.

His eyes stayed on my face as he said quietly, "I can understand your grief." Then he took both my hands in his. "Father," he murmured, "come to Your child."

He bowed his head in silent prayer for several minutes. Then he raised it. "Come now. I'll walk with you to the end of the bridge. The Lord will see you through this. Remember that."

I walked home. I still grieved, but the awful despair was alleviated. I knew somehow that God had not forsaken me. I felt I was no longer alone.

Several days later, I walked down to the river to tell the bridge-tender that I was slowly learning to live with my loss, and to thank him. But he wasn't there.

I described him to the man on duty.

"I don't know who you're talking about, miss, and I know all the tenders," he told me.

"But the night it rained so hard . . ." I persisted.

"I'm sorry. I don't know who was on duty that night."

I never found out who that man was, and I know I never will.

But I do know Who sent him to me.   —IRENE J. KUTZ

Her Playing Days Were Over

MUSIC WAS LIKE A SECOND LANGUAGE to my mother. She learned to play the piano by ear, without lessons. She had perfect pitch, and her musicianship was so good she could transpose musical scores in her head. As a young woman she played the pipe organ for silent movies, craning her neck as she watched the films to interpret the antics of Buster Keaton or the fervor of Lillian Gish.

When I was a boy in Canton, Ohio, Mother often performed with our hometown symphony. Whenever famous violinists, cellists, oboists, or sopranos came to town on concert tours, my mother, Ruth, was the requested accompanist. And every Sunday for many decades she was a church organist.

My mother and father seemed to have an intuitive musical understanding between them. Mother told me how a song would run through her head as she worked in the kitchen while Dad, puttering in the basement, would hum the same tune—in the same key.

In her final years Mom lived in a nursing home. There was a piano in the activities room, but she never went near it. Severe arthritis had gnarled her fingers. Her playing days were over.

So it came as a surprise one evening when Mother asked to be taken to the activities room. The nurses wheeled her in. "Over to the piano," she whispered. They obeyed. Then my ninety-two-year-old mother put her hands to the keys for the first time in years, and she played. Beautifully.

That night, with the strains of Brahms and Chopin still echoing in the nursing home, Mother died in her sleep. —*PHILIP K. MARCH*

"She Couldn't Have Said a Word!"

THE HOSPITAL CHAPLAIN SAT by the dying woman's bed in the hospice ward. He knew little about her, except that the end was near. She had fought bravely, but her last operation the doctors said there was little that could be done. Now she was unconscious, and although he could not speak with her, he tried to find the right words of prayer.

Her bed was cranked up and she was half sitting, in order to make it easier for her to breathe through a tube in her throat. Her breaths came harshly and slowly, but their rhythm was even. In the warm room, the chaplain felt tired and closed his eyes for a minute.

Suddenly he was startled awake by a loud cry from the bed. The woman was sitting bolt upright. "My God!" she cried out.

The chaplain rose quickly to summon a nurse. But just then the woman sank back against the pillows, her eyes closed, a look of radiance on her face.

A nurse rushed in. "Did you call out?" she asked the chaplain as she took the woman's pulse. Quickly the nurse summed up the situation. "I'm afraid she's gone."

"No, I didn't speak," the chaplain said in wonderment, still thinking of the woman's ecstatic expression. "She did. She cried out, 'My God!'"

The nurse turned to him, puzzled. "But she couldn't have. Didn't you know? She had cancer of the larynx. Her voice box was destroyed weeks ago. She couldn't have said a word." —*JEANNE M. DAMS*

The Sign

I WAS ON A HUNTING TRIP that gray September afternoon when the word came that Frank was dead. Frank, our twenty-year-old son, the baby of our family. I was stunned. I wanted to scream that it couldn't be true.

But it was true. Frank had been killed instantly when the small plane he was flying had gone into a spin and crashed.

All the time during that long trip home, through my tears, I relived in my mind Frank's short life. So much had been crowded into it.

One day when he was thirteen, I found him lying in the street unconscious from multiple injuries from a motor-scooter accident. He spent weeks in the hospital recovering from a skull fracture. During that time Frank had developed a deep personal relationship with God.

As Frank recovered at home, we'd catch him studying the sports pages longingly. He'd been a star baseball and football player in school, but now his damaged body seemed to rule that out. When he was finally able to limp about, he craved exercise and I built a set of out-door high bars for him.

After the funeral, our two older sons returned to their homes and my wife, Polly, and I were alone in our grief. I tried to go back to my work as a petroleum geologist but it was useless. I'd sit in my office, turning a pencil over and over in my hand asking, *Why? . . . why?*

I couldn't seem to do anything any more except think about Frank. "O God," I cried, "please give us some sign . . . some acknowledgment that he is safe with You."

But Polly and I sank deeper into our depression. One Sunday, how-ever, we took a drive. When we returned home and I reached to turn off the ignition, Polly stiffened and clutched my arm. "Bill, look!" she gasped. She pointed to the earth below the high bars.

I could not believe what I saw. There glowing in the late afternoon sun stood two blood-red lilies in a place where nothing had ever grown before. They grew straight and sturdy from the earth in the same spots Frank had placed his feet to exercise.

Polly and I marveled how they got there. The area had been mowed only a day earlier. We had once placed a swing on the high bar for our grandchildren and the trampled earth was like iron. But there they stood.

The lilies flourished for two weeks. Then they were gone.

But we didn't need them any more to assure us that Frank was safe with Him.

—*WILLIAM SCHMITZ*

God's Footprint

I took a day to search for God,
And found Him not. But as I trod
   By rocky ledge, through woods untamed,
   Just where one scarlet lily flamed,
I saw His footprint in the sod.

—*BLISS CARMAN FROM VESTIGIA*

The Lifted Curtain

Certain I am that God from time to time chooses to reveal Himself to us. Sometimes He comes to us in moments of stark drama, sometimes so softly, so unobtrusively, that only our souls seem to have seen Him . . .

FOR MANY YEARS MY WIFE and I waged a life-and-death battle for our two sons, both of whom had muscular dystrophy. Only when the long, long struggle was over did was realize that God had revealed Himself to us. Yet we would have missed His visit had it not been for a good friend, Edwin Ferree—and for our church.

Ed and Henrietta Ferree, and my family belong to St. Paul's in Darien, Connecticut, and when I say "belong," I mean just that. It is part of us and we are part of it, part of the Body of Christ on earth, and, as the Bible says, "we bear one another's burdens." This is not just a pretty phrase; it is something that became a living daily reality as we watched the day-by-day, year-by-year deterioration of our two growing boys.

My son Ken was three years old when doctors diagnosed his slowness in walking as muscular dystrophy, Duchennetype. Prognosis was for progressive deterioration of his muscles until, sometime in his teens, those muscles necessary to life itself would be affected.

A few weeks after we received this verdict, Ken's younger brother, Billy, was born, suffering from the same condition.

Several years later, Jan and I, knowing we would have Ken and Billy so short a time, determined to enjoy every day together to the utmost. And there was much to enjoy as the boys walked and talked and explored their world. But with this disease every gain is temporary. Ken, being older, was the first to move into a wheelchair. Some days I would come home to find Jan shut in an upstairs bedroom, tears streaming down her face, while downstairs the therapist painfully straightened bent legs and uncurled clenched fingers.

The strain on Jan as they grew older was enormous: toiletting the two large boys, dressing them, feeding them. As Ken's circulation slowed he had to be turned in bed throughout the night. One morning I came downstairs to find Jan, head down, asleep at the dining room table; she'd been catching naps between trips to the downstairs room where the boys slept.

At last in June, 1968, when Ken was fourteen, Billy, eleven, we entered them both in New Britain Memorial, a hospital specializing in long-term and terminal cases. We could probably have managed Billy at home for another year, but it seemed to us that hospitalization would be traumatic enough without separating the boys as well. Billy, with his mop of straight black hair and huge hazel eyes, had never had the muscle control of lips and tongue to speak clearly. Only Ken seemed to have no trouble understanding him. They would talk by the hour, Ken's blond head bent close to Billy's dark one, the older boy interpreting the younger one's thoughts for the rest of us. We knew they must stay together.

To Jan and me the move to the hospital was defeat, the moment we'd been dreading for so many years. But for Ken and Billy, surprisingly, it turned out to be an exhilarating change. Here, instead of being the ones who forever needed help, they discovered that they had help to give.

In the young people's wing at New Britain everyone who possibly could attended the regular public high school in town, in wheelchairs, even on stretchers, their life-support machinery going with them via the ramps and wide doorways the townspeople had provided. Ken soon found himself helping kids all over the ward with their schoolwork.

Billy, who could still maneuver his own wheelchair, found delight in push-wheeling other young patients into the rec room or to the bedsides of friends.

Having turned our precious sons over to the care of others, and finding that their world did not collapse, Jan and I began to wonder whether in other ways we were relying too much on ourselves alone. It was at this point in our lives that we began the great experiment at St. Paul's, turning ourselves, our family, every detail of living over to the Lordship of Jesus.

It was the beginning of a whole new way of perceiving reality. Not us and our problems in a box over here, others in their separate boxes over there, but all of us at St. Paul's sharing our heartaches, our defeats and victories, together. And one of the parishioners whom we drew especially close to was Edwin Ferree. When Jan and I didn't understand some spiritual concept, when something was too hard for us, we could use Ed's understanding, Ed's strength. It was that real and simple.

Nearly four years after the boys entered New Britain, Billy caught pneumonia. The doctors saved him, but he could no longer breathe without machinery. He was moved to the Intensive Care Unit on the floor below, where his older brother could be wheeled to visit him each day.

For four months, while Ed Ferree and the others at St. Paul's supported us in prayer, Jan and I made the hundred-thirty-mile round trip to New Britain almost every evening. Our invariable routine was to visit Billy first, then go up and be with Ken.

On August 30, 1972, however, for no reason we could have explained, we went first to Ken. He was full of the visit he'd had with Billy. "They let me stay twice as long as usual because Billy's feeling so good. He wasn't even stuttering much."

Down in Intensive Care we found Billy just as Ken had said, hazel eyes shining as he watched television through the tubes and wires linking him to his life-support system. The TV was tuned to the Munich Olympics: With obvious delight he was watching the Russian gymnast, Olga Korbut. Like many handicapped youngsters Billy was fascinated by physical perfection. Olga was his heroine.

Her flawless routine ended, he turned to us. "I'm going to do all those things!" he said, pronouncing each word distinctly. "Just like she did."

It wasn't a question or a wish, it was a statement of fact.

"Billy!" cried Jan, leaning over him. "What's the matter?" His color, so ruddy a moment ago had turned a sickly blue.

In an instant a nurse was at the bedside, then the doctor. But in spite of all they could do, Billy slipped gradually into deep coma.

Through the long evening I kept thinking about the tenderness of God. If Ken had died first as in the normal course of the disease he would, being three years older, stammering Billy would have been left without his link to his world. And so in spite of all medical probability the Lord was taking the younger boy first.

Peggy, the night-duty nurse came on. The clock crept to midnight . . . 1:00 A.M. . . . 2:00 A.M. And at that moment Billy's eyelids fluttered open. His hazel eyes found Jan.

"Thank you, Mom."

Then me: "Thank you, Dad."

Then they opened wider still, looking not at us, but beyond, at something we could not see. "Oh!" he cried out. Then with a joyous shout: "God!"

His eyelids closed; he was again in deep, unreachable coma. Peggy and I bent over the bed; Jan closed her eyes, praying. After about twenty minutes something like a warm breeze blew past me in the still air. The same instant Jan opened her eyes.

"Billy's gone," she said.

"I know."

At three o'clock we went upstairs and woke Ken. He made us tell over and over again about the look on Billy's face as the curtain between earth and Heaven drew aside. When the day nurse came on Ken asked her, "Can I be the one to tell the kids about Billy? I want to tell them he wasn't afraid and I'm not going to be, either."

Before leaving the hospital we telephoned Ed Ferree who had given us so much support. How glorious to tell him that we *knew* Billy was with Jesus.

I kept wondering if Billy were already swinging from the high bars in some heavenly arena. Back flips, somersaults, handstands...just like Olga.

And then a year and a half later, we were driving home from New Britain one final time. Nineteen months had passed since Billy's death. Time for Ken to graduate from New Britain High, to cast his vote by absentee ballot, to handle his lonesomeness by befriending new youngsters entering Memorial, especially those with speech defects: "I can understand him, nurse. You see, he talks a lot like my little brother did."

That afternoon, March 23, 1974, Ken had died. Only—this time—Jan and I had not been there. We had arrived at the hospital around 3:30 on a perfectly routine visit, to be told that Ken had passed away very unexpectedly an hour before.

Why? I wondered, all the long drive home. Why couldn't we have got there one little hour sooner? I turned off the parkway at our home exit. I'd been so sure that the Lord would give us some new reassurance, some fresh glimpse of His Presence, when Ken had to leave us, too.

I pulled into our driveway. What were we going to tell the people at church, this time? I'd phone Ed Ferree; he'd help us think of what to say. Inside the house I dialed the number as slowly as I could. This would be as big a shock to Ed as to us.

"Ed Ferree speaking." There was his voice on the line.

"We're just back from New Brit . . ."

"Ken's with Jesus," said Ed.

It was a moment before I could find my voice. "Yes, Ed. But how could you . . . ?"

It happened at 2:30, said Ed. He hadn't been thinking about Ken especially, in fact he was down in his study digging some papers out of a drawer, when all of a sudden it was as though a movie were unrolling on a screen in front of his eyes. There before him was Ken, tall and straight, striding like a long-distance hiker up a grassy hillside, his blond hair glowing like gold in the bright air.

Then, as Ed watched, Ken came to a swift-flowing stream and stopped, apparently uncertain how to get across. At that moment Ed saw coming down the hill a shining figure that he knew to be Jesus. The radiant Being came to the edge of the stream and stretched His hand across to Ken. Ken reached out, clasped it, stepped easily across. The next moment both had turned and were climbing the hill together, hand in hand.

"That's what you called to tell me, wasn't it?" said Ed. "Ken is with Jesus."

The unfinished feeling disappeared. God had lifted the curtain once again. For a moment I had simply forgotten that Jan and I no longer had to depend on our own sight alone, that we had many eyes and hearts with which to know Him.

"Yes, Ed," I said. "That's what I called to say."   —*Edward K. Leaton*

God Fashioned a House

Weep if we may—bend low as ye pray!
What does it mean?

Listen! God fashioned a house. He said:
    "Build it with care."
Then softly laid the soul . . .
    To dwell in there.

And always he watched it—guarded it so,
    Both day and night:
The wee soul grew as your lilies do,
    Splendid and white.

It grew, I say, as your lilies grow,
    Tender and tall;
Till God smiled, "Now the house is too low
    For the child, and small."

And gently the shut the shutters one night,
    And closed the door;

"More room and more light to walk upright
On a Father's floor."
—AUTHOR UNKNOWN

I'll Meet Them Again

My FATHER, WHO DIED at eighty-five after a distinguished career as a physician and minister, had struggled against a very real fear of death. But after his funeral, my stepmother dreamed that he came to her and said, "Don't ever worry about dying. There's nothing to it!" The dream was so vivid that she woke up, astounded. And I believe that he did come to reassure her, because that is precisely the phrase I had heard him use a thousand times to dismiss something as unimportant.

Years before, when news reached me that my mother had died, I was alone in my office, numb with grief. There was a Bible on my desk, and I put my hand on it, staring blindly out the window. As I did so, I felt a pair of hands touch my head, gently, lovingly, unmistakably. Was it an illusion? A hallucination? I don't think so. I think my mother was permitted to reach across the gulf of death to touch and reassure me.

Once when I was preaching at a big church convocation in Georgia, I had the most startling experience of all. At the end, the presiding bishop asked all the ministers in the audience to come forward and sing a hymn.

Watching them come down the aisles, I suddenly saw my father among them. I saw him as plainly as when he was alive. He seemed about forty, vital and handsome, singing with the others. When he smiled at me and put up his hand in an old familiar gesture, for several unforgettable seconds it was as if my father and I were alone in that big auditorium. Then he was gone. But he was *there,* and I know that someday, somewhere I'll meet him again.

—NORMAN VINCENT PEALE

So Long, Son . . .

SOMEWHERE IN THIS UNIVERSE is a timeless, undeniable force. It's stronger than granite, steel, majestic mountains towering into the sky—or nuclear fission.

Sooner or later—in strange and different manifestations—that force touches every human. Sure, some pass it off as a phenomenon that somehow cannot be reduced to an exact scientific formula. To others it is the hand of the Almighty—a reminder that regardless of the grandeur of man and his accomplishments—God is still "running the show" here on earth.

Now, I want to tell you of such an experience. I have remembered it across the years and it will ring in my memory for as long as I live.

It's about my dad—God bless him!

Let me explain a little about my dad. He was one of the most brilliant and warm persons I have ever known. A lecturer, newspaper man, magazine writer, and raconteur—he was at home in any society. He was the well-rounded man I always wanted to be.

Of course, he had his failings, too. One was a disinclination towards business and finance. As a result, he went through several small fortunes and sometimes things were tough at home. That's why I went on my own at fifteen. But I never blamed dad.

All this is prelude to the point I want to make. But, if in telling it—one human, faltering on the precipice of lost faith or shaken belief—takes heart, my telling the story will have been worthwhile.

For out of it, I learned firsthand about that timeless force in this world. Now, whenever the adulation of the crowd dins in my ears . . . whenever temporary wealth and fame assault my senses and balance—it helps me remember that force—transcendent above the world itself.

It makes me remember how the hand of God is at work constantly and I am humble in His presence.

It was in 1923. I was stationed on board a Navy destroyer—in charge of radio communications. I had knocked around a lot since I left home. The years and life had not been too kind but the Navy had been a sanctuary, the only security I had known for a long time. One day, tired, I fell asleep in my bunk and I dreamed.

My dad—I had not seen him for years—suddenly walked into the room. He offered his hand, saying, "So long, son." I answered, "So long, Dad." I said some kind of prayer. It wasn't eloquent, but it came from the heart.

I never saw him again. When I woke up, my buddies told me that at the exact time while I was asleep, the wires from shore hummed the news of my dad's death.

Don't tell me about science and its exact explanation of everything. Some things are bigger. God is the difference. He gets around.

—ARTHUR GODFREY

The Rose That Wouldn't Die

IN FEBRUARY 1978, I MET a boyhood hero of mine. One of the first movies I can remember seeing was *Hell's Angels,* a picture about fighter pilots in World War I, and it starred Ben Lyon. I remember reading that Ben Lyon did his own flying and even shot some of the combat photography aloft. For a long time, I was Ben Lyon on-the-attack, bent low over my bicycle as I raced around the neighborhood.

Movie stars had a great aura about them in those days. They were our American royalty. For many years, Ben Lyon was the king, before Gable, before Bogart or Spencer Tracy, and he remained a king for me even after he and his lovely wife, Bebe Daniels, moved to England, where they remained stars for another thirty years.

That February, I had the joy and the privilege of spending an afternoon with Ben Lyon at his home in Beverly Hills, where we talked about many things. When we talked about his marriage to Bebe, Ben told me a haunting story. Listening to it, I knew that it was more than a fragment of a great love story. It was also a statement of faith.

Bebe, Ben said, always loved roses. When they were first married and living in California, part of their garden was set aside for what Bebe regarded as her rose chapel. Every morning before leaving for the studio, she would spend several minutes alone among her roses. "Arranging my day," she would explain. But Ben knew these were her moments of prayer and meditation.

In 1933, Bebe and Ben were invited to make some personal appearances in England. They expected to be there just a few months. Instead, they stayed for thirty-eight years. In World War II they chose not to return to the safety of America. They did radio programs for British soldiers overseas, appeared in canteens, toured the combat zones in plays.

When America entered the war in 1941, Ben joined the U.S. Air Force and was assigned to intelligence work. Bebe kept on entertaining the troops. As American servicemen began moving through England, their house in London virtually became a canteen for them. Bebe somehow saw to it that the house was always full of roses. American Beauty roses. Her favorite. After the war they had a television series, made more movies and appeared in more plays. They were busy, happy and very popular with the British people.

Then in 1963, Bebe suffered a stroke that put her in the hospital for several weeks. Eight years later, in 1971, she had another, this a bad one.

Doctors told Ben there was not much hope, but this did not stop his prayers. Every morning, he and the children went to Mass and prayed for Bebe. For hours every day they stood at her bedside and prayed. Clergymen of all faiths told them that the whole of England was praying for Bebe.

There seemed to be some improvement, and at last they were able to bring Bebe home, with nurses around the clock. On the evening of March 15, Ben was with Bebe in her room when she awoke from a nap. A phone call came from a close friend of hers, and Ben heard Bebe say: "My dear, I've just been for a walk in the most beautiful rose garden."

She had not, of course. She had been sleeping, perhaps dreaming. By dawn, Bebe was gone.

Thousands of messages of sympathy came from all over the world. A few days later, at the funeral services, the church was a mountain of flowers. There was one wreath from the taxi drivers of London. There was another from the Royal Family.

Ben knew what farewell gesture Bebe would want from him. He had a florist prepare a sheath of forty American Beauty roses—one rose for each year of their marriage. The roses were in the sanctuary during the Mass of the Angels.

The day was cloudy, misty, with a cold wind. As the choir sang "Abide With Me," and reached the words, "Through cloud and sunshine, Lord, abide with me," the sun came out and filled the church with the colors of the stained glass windows.

All the flowers were sent ahead to the cemetery and were in place when the cortege arrived. They would, Ben knew, be given to children's hospitals later. After the brief service, he impulsively broke off one of the forty roses in the sheath, and took it home. He put the rose in a slender vase, added some water, and placed it on his desk. He did not need the rose to remind him of Bebe. But he felt it was a way to keep her with him a little longer.

Ben expected the rose to live a few days, then fade, so he was pleasantly surprised when the flower was still in bloom after a week. He added fresh water. The rose was still in bloom a month later. Three months later. Six months. One day he noticed that the stem had become petrified, and yet the rose lived on. None of the experts he consulted could explain it.

A year after Bebe died, Ben decided to move back to California. Before leaving London, he took the rose and the slender vase to his son

Richard's house, told his daughter-in-law about the rose, and said: "Angela, please do me a favor. Keep this rose in a safe place, on the mantlepiece or somewhere. Just let me know when it dies."

Last September, over seven years after Bebe's death, Ben went back to London to visit his children and grandchildren. In Richard's house, he saw the slender vase on the mantlepiece, the rose still whole on the petrified stem, still perfect.

"I no longer need an explanation for it," Ben told me. "I believe that the rose is God's way of letting us know that Bebe is herself alive, living with Him, waiting for us in that rose garden He showed her as she went to Him. Believing this has made my own faith more meaningful."

Soon after that, our time together ended. It was, I'm sure, one of the last interviews that Ben Lyon granted. A month later, he died of a heart attack while on a Pacific cruise. For me, his memory will always live on—like that rose.

—GLENN KITTLER

A Glimpse of Heaven's Glory

I DON'T KNOW WHY TRAGEDY struck our family that bright October morning. Nor why I, of all people, should have been allowed that glimpse of glory. I only know that a presence greater than human was part of the experience from the beginning.

The strangeness started the evening before, when I allowed six-year-old Travis to play outside past his bedtime. I'd never done this before. Travis's two younger brothers were already asleep in bed, and he should have been too; he had to go to school in the morning, after all. But Tara, the little girl who lived across the street, was playing outdoors late too. Though Tara was a year older, there seemed to be a special bond between her and Travis. I heard their happy shouts as they played hide-and-seek under the enormous stars—just as I used to here in our little mountain town of Challis, Idaho.

And then, later, when I'd called him in at last and he was in his pajamas, he'd suddenly grown so serious. . . .

"Mommy?" Travis had finished his prayers as I sat on the edge of his bed. He took his hands and placed them tenderly on my cheeks. Such a solemn little face beneath the freckles!

"What, Babe?" I smiled.

"I . . . just love you, Mommy," he said, searching my eyes. "I just want you to know that I love you."

The words remained with me as I got ready for bed. Not that it was unusual for Travis to show affection. His outgoing nature had become even more so after he accepted Jesus as his Savior, at age five. Little children who know Jesus seem to bubble over with love for the whole world. It was the intensity—almost the urgency—with which he'd said the words that was unlike him.

As I lay in bed that night, the sense that something out of the ordinary was about to happen stayed with me. Our house is small, and since my mother came to stay with us I've shared a bedroom with the children. I could hear their soft, restful breaths as they slept. That wasn't what kept me awake. Nor was it the empty space beside me— my husband was now married to another. Yes, our family had certainly had its moments of pain, but our faith had brought us this far.

I thought back to that time, four years before, when I'd realized my need for the Savior and invited Him to take over my struggle. How magnificently He had! So much help had been lavished upon us going through the divorce, the changed lifestyle, the financial difficulties. From our pastor and church friends I'd gained strength and hope. But it was the conversion of little freckle-faced Travis that brought me the day-by-day lessons.

"Why are you worried, Mommy?" Travis had said so many times, a hint of impatience in his wide brown eyes. "You have Jesus. We'll get the money for that bill." And we always did.

Two in the morning. "I love you, Mommy" still pealed in my ears like some distant, gentle bell. I remembered that as my closeness to Jesus increased, my spirit would sometimes hear messages from Him.

I am preparing Travis for something, I'd heard this silent voice tell me, many times. And this did seem to be the case. Hadn't there been that night a couple of months ago . . . ? I'd awaked before daylight and noticed Travis sitting on his bed . . . just sitting, in the purple predawn.

"What's the matter, Babe?" I had asked him.

"Don't you see them?" He sounded disappointed.

"See what?"

"These two angels."

I breathed in sharply; I saw only the familiar room. The boy was wide awake, perfectly calm. I asked him if he was afraid.

"No, Mommy," he'd said. I waited by his bed a little while. Then he said, "Okay, they're gone, you can go to bed now." That was all. But thinking back on that experience, I felt again that sense of the extraordinary pressing close upon us.

The morning of October 28 dawned bright and still. There was the usual bustle of getting breakfast, finding socks that matched, pencils with erasers and so on. Ten minutes before the time he usually left to walk to school Travis became suddenly agitated:

"Mommy, I've got to go now."

"Babe, it's early. You've got lots of time. Sit down."

"I've got to go now! I've just got to!" Travis cried.

"Why?" I asked in bewilderment. He mumbled something about his teacher, about not being late. It didn't make sense: He was never late. "Wait a few minutes," I insisted. "Finish your cocoa."

"Mommy, please!" To my amazement big tears were rolling down his cheeks.

"All right, all right, go ahead," I told him, shaking my head at the commotion. He dashed out the door, a hurrying little figure pulling on a tan jacket. Across the street, little Tara was coming down her walk. I saw the two children meet and set off toward Main Street together.

Five minutes later I was clearing away the breakfast dishes when it happened. A shudder of the floor beneath me, then a hideous screech of writhing wood. There had never been an earthquake in Challis, but I knew we were having an earthquake now. I ran from the house calling over my shoulder, "I've got to get to Travis!"

I was at the driveway when another tremor flung me against the car. I waited till the earth stopped heaving, then climbed into the driver's seat.

I'd gone two blocks when I saw a woman standing beside a pile of rubble on the sidewalk, the debris of a collapsed storefront. The look on her face was one of nightmare horror. Unrolling the window, I was surprised at the calmness of my voice as I asked, "Was someone . . . caught?"

"Two children," the white face said thinly. "One in a tan jacket . . ."

I drove swiftly on. Past people running toward the damaged building. Around the corner. To the school. Oh, I knew. I knew already. But maybe (please God!), maybe farther down the street there'd be two children standing bewildered at a curbside. There were not, of course. I drove back to the rubble heap.

Then a numb blur of events: police, firemen, people struggling with the debris. Identification. Arms around me. I was at the clinic. I was being driven home. I was in my living room again. My mother was there, and I was telling her and my two little boys what had happened. Mother was praying.

Suddenly, as I sat there in the living room, perhaps even in mid-sentence—I don't know how long it took—I was being lifted right out of the room, lifted above it all, high into the sky, and placed by a beautiful gate. A cluster of happy people stood within the gate. In utter amazement I began recognizing the youthful, robust faces: Dad, my favorite aunt, Grandpa...and in the center of them all, the radiant form of Jesus! As I watched, He stretched out His hands to welcome a child who was approaching, a smiling boy dressed in what seemed to be an unbleached muslin tunic over long trousers of the same homespun-looking fabric. Travis ran forward and grasped the hand of Jesus, looking up at Him with eager brown eyes. The cluster of people welcomed my son, and he seemed to recognize them, although some he had never met. As the joyful group turned to leave, Travis suddenly turned his shining face toward me.

"It's really neat here, Mommy."

"I know, Babe." My throat felt choked, and I don't know whether I spoke aloud or not.

"I really like it here."

"I know."

"Mommy...I don't want to go back."

"It's okay, Babe." And it was okay, in that transcendent moment. Nothing I could ever do, nothing that could ever happen here on earth, could make Travis as happy as I saw him right then. When I looked around me, I was back in my home.

That's where the long battle of grief was fought, of course: in the kitchen with its empty chair, in the bedroom where he'd said his good-night prayers, and the yard where he'd played hide-and-seek. Transcendent moments do not last—not for us on earth. Three years have passed since the day of the earthquake, passed among the daily routines of cleaning, cooking, chauffeuring, praying.

But neither do such moments fade. That scene at heaven's threshold is as vivid in each detail today as in the measureless instant when I was allowed to see. I have been granted another glimpse since then, this time of Tara among a group of joyfully playing children, all dressed in those tuniclike garments. (I did not see Travis this time, nor anyone else I recognized.)

Tara's mother understands no better than I the why of a child's death, the why of heaven's glory. I know only that both are real, and that—when we hear the answer at last—it will start with the words, "I love you."

—*Janet Fisher*

Summer Storm

IT WAS ONE OF THE LAST THINGS Mother wrote in the journal she left me: *When God calls, I will let you know when I have arrived on the other side. Either the day I leave or the day of the funeral, I'll ask Him to send a storm.*

It drizzled when she died, and on that sad day of her funeral there were blue skies and sunshine. I had never been so unhappy to see good weather in all my life.

The funeral home was filled with people who remembered Mother fondly. Afterward there was a motorcade through our small town, and the summer sun was brighter and hotter than ever. Not a cloud to be seen anywhere.

At the burial Dad asked one of the ministers to read Mother's note about the storm. Now everyone else knew about it too.

That afternoon we had a luncheon on the patio of our home. By 5:00 P.M. most of the guests had gone, and as I was clearing crumbs off a table I heard a rumble that sounded like an army marching through the heavens. Black clouds rolled into the sky. Lightning zapped between the clouds. I lifted my head and rain poured down my face.

The lights went out in the house. Lightning struck the front of Dad's store, the burglar alarm went off and the power went out. Our phone didn't stop ringing with people who had found hope in the storm. And in between answering, I kept thinking how appropriate it was for Mother, whose name, Thora, means "the thunderer."

—THORENIA WEST

A Written Sign

August 1, 1993

Dear Guideposts:

My mother died on July 1, 1993, after an extended illness. I had given up my job in another part of Michigan to move to her home in Frankfort to care for her. She and I had a wonderful seventy-nine days together. We discussed many things, and she spoke of one day giving me some sort of sign that she was with God and at peace.

Mother had spent her last two decades as a well-known journalist for the local county newspaper. This past month has been hectic as I wrote hundreds of thank-yous. Yet always in the back of my mind was the fact that I had not received the sign Mother had promised.

Yesterday, exactly one full month since she had died, I sat down exhausted. I spied the August Guideposts in a mountain of unanswered mail. I picked up the magazine and it fell open to "His Mysterious Ways." I read about a woman who had found hope in the thunderstorm that occurred on the day of her mother's funeral. She wrote: "I kept thinking how appropriate it was for Mother, whose name, Thora, means 'the thunderer.'" The article was signed Thorenia West.

My mother's name was Thora too, and so is mine! How appropriate that my journalist mother would choose the written word to tell me, "I am with my Lord, and all is well."

Sincerely,
Thora Wease

The Clearer Vision

When, with bowed head,
And silent-streaming tears,
With mingled hopes and fears,
To earth we yield our dead;
The Saints, with clearer sight,
Do cry in glad accord,—
*"A soul released from prison
Is risen, is risen,—
Is risen to the glory of the Lord."*
—JOHN OXENHAM

For he orders his angels to protect you wherever you go. They will steady you with their hands to keep you from stumbling against the rocks on the trail. —Psalm 91:11–12, TLB

CHAPTER NINE

God Orders His Angels

It's hard to explain some of God's mysterious ways without thinking in terms of God's angels, heaven-sent messengers who protect, comfort, lead, warn—inexplicably minister to us mortals, for God's good purpose. As you read these stories, the last in this volume, may you become more aware of the God who never sleeps or slumbers—who watches over you night and day, guarding, guiding, commanding His heavenly forces to expand His Kingdom and work for the good.

"Send Some of Your Angels"

IN THE LATE 1940S MY HUSBAND, Frank, and I were driving late at night on a deserted road in the mountains near Chattanooga when we had a flat tire. Because of the rocky road edge, Frank was unable to brace the car and change the tire. Out of the night a car appeared. Two of the biggest, roughest-looking bearded men I'd ever seen got out. With powerful hands they steadied the car, swiftly changed the tire, and drove off. They had not uttered a word.

In 1952, Frank was a naval officer stationed in Europe. We were driving with our family through thick fog in the Swiss Alps when a gap in the road, about six feet wide and four feet deep, confronted us. Night was coming on, so Frank walked the others down to the next village. Since all our belongings were in the car, I stayed behind. I waited. Nervously I tried to pray. The words of Psalm 91:11-12 came to mind: "For he shall give his angels charge over thee ... They shall bear thee up in their hands ..." And then I blurted out, "Lord, *send some of Your angels.* Please."

A truck suddenly appeared. Out of it piled six big, rough-looking bearded men. Without speaking, they picked up their truck and carried it across the washout. Then with strong, powerful hands they picked up *my* car—with me in it—carried it across the trench, and set it safely on the other side. They never said a word, and disappeared into the night.

I drove into the village of Brig, where I found my family. Nobody in the village could imagine who those men were. All I knew was that they had come, and they had borne me up "in their hands."

Who are these silent men? Will they have reason to help us—again?

—*MARY HATTAN BOGART*

"Someone Pulled Me Out"

WE WERE STANDING IN MY PARENTS' FRONT YARD saying good-bye when we heard her scream—it was our little daughter, two and a half. Rushing to the backyard, we found Helen standing in the center of the flagstone sidewalk, crying and dripping wet. It was apparent that she had fallen into my parents' small but deep fish pond. Thank God she was safe!

Then, as my wife rushed over to pick Helen up, it hit me. I couldn't see any wet footprints anywhere around the pond, yet our baby was standing a good twenty feet away from the water. The only water was the puddle where she stood dripping. And there was no way a toddler could have climbed out of the pool by herself—it was six or seven feet in diameter and about four feet deep.

As Helen grew up, we often puzzled over those strange circumstances. She herself had no memory of the event; she was, however, haunted by an intense fear of water.

Many years later, when Helen and her soldier husband were living in San Antonio, she began to work through that fear with the help of an army chaplain, Pastor Claude Ingram. After spiritual counseling and prayer sessions, he asked her to go back in memory and relive the frightening fish pond experience. She put herself in the scene again and began describing the pond and the fish in detail. She cried out as she relived the moment of falling into the water. Then suddenly Helen gasped. "Now I remember!" she said. "He grabbed me by the shoulders and lifted me out!"

"Who did?" asked Pastor Ingram.

"Someone in white," she answered. "Someone pulled me out, then left."
—*William T. Porter*

Call for Help

Two days before Christmas, while a sleet storm beat against the windows, I was alone in the house with my sick baby. By mid-afternoon her temperature had flared to 104 degrees, and my hand shook, holding the thermometer. The year before, despite all medical science could do, our little boy had died of pneumonia. Ellen had to have a doctor right away.

But how? I was without a car. My husband, a flood engineer in the Tacoma office, had put our car in the shop for new brake linings before he left for three days to measure the rising water of the Skagit River. And with no telephone (we'd moved into this new house only last week and ours wasn't yet installed), I'd have to run across the street to the one house besides ours here on this hilltop and ask to use theirs to call a doctor.

Bending over the baby's crib, which I'd pulled into the living room where it was warmer, I listened to her quick shallow breathing.

"Darling, Mommy's going to get help for you!" Snatching up raincoat and scarf, I hurried out the door.

Yesterday, a warm chinook wind had partially melted our recent snowfall. Today, freezing temperatures formed icicles along the dripping eaves and coated trees and telephone wires with ice.

Frozen ridges of snow crackled beneath my feet as I ran across to my neighbors', praying they were home. On their front porch I rang the doorbell once, and after a few seconds, again, long and hard. No one came. Then I recalled hearing their car go out early in the morning. If they were away for the entire holiday weekend, what was I going to do? Shivering, I looked down our long, unpaved hill leading to the nearest built-up area, twelve or more blocks away. If only some car would drive up here now! Anyone would be glad to call a doctor for me. Our hilly street ended in a cul-de-sac, so we had little traffic aside from an occasional delivery truck or the postman—who had already come earlier in the day. Of course, I could phone from one of the houses along the bus line, but I was afraid to leave Ellen while I went down there and back. Would I dare bundle her up and take her with me in this freezing weather?

As I started back across the street, with sleet stinging my cheeks and wind tearing at my scarf, I slipped and fell, wrenching my ankle— not badly, only enough to warn me that carrying the baby down our slippery hill would be dangerous. There had to be some way to reach a doctor! And suddenly I knew what I was going to do.

I turned and went back onto my neighbors' porch where I rang the bell again, just to be certain. My heart thumping, I tried the knob. *Would this be "breaking and entering"?*

The door didn't open; it was locked. But sometimes people leave a key beneath the mat. I lifted the mat. No key. So down the steps once more and around to the back porch. I was going to get to that telephone if I had to break a window! Luck, however, was with me. Beneath a flowerpot I found the key, unlocked the door and tiptoed into a strange kitchen, half-expecting someone to leap out at me crying, "What are you doing here?"

But the house was silent, and there on a little stand in the hall stood the blessed telephone! No directory to find a doctor's phone number, so I dialed the operator. A buzzing and crackling sounded and an indistinct voice said something.

"Operator?" I called. "This is an emergency. I am alone with a very sick baby. I must have a doctor."

The faraway voice answered, but I couldn't understand a single word. I gave my address and repeated my request, "Please send me a doctor!"

Then came an explosive noise and the line went dead. The wires, probably heavy with ice, had broken down. Did my call for help get through? Had someone heard? There was no way of knowing.

When I opened our door, Ellen was crying—the pitiful wail of a sick baby. After I'd sponged her hot little body, I sat in the rocking chair, coaxing her to take her bottle with a quarter tablet of aspirin dissolved in orange juice. I knew nothing else to do. If only Jim were here, he'd find a doctor. His office could reach him, send for him to come home. But how could I call the office without a phone? I thought of my mother and father and my younger sister and brother getting ready for Christmas in Portland.

"We're only across the Columbia River from you!" Dad always said. Now they seemed a thousand miles away.

Suddenly I heard the sound of a car engine laboring up our icy hill. Quickly I put Ellen back into her crib and ran bareheaded out the door. But the car had lost traction and stalled, and already the driver was backing down, too concerned with his steering and too far away to notice my signals.

I went slowly back into the house. My mind felt numb. I couldn't seem to think. I tried to get the latest weather report of the storm, but now the radio was dead. Down in the basement, I put more wood in the furnace. Then I brewed a fresh pot of coffee in the kitchen, thankful that neither the furnace nor the gas range were dependent upon electricity. The pungent odor of coffee reminded me I had eaten nothing all day, so I made oven-toast and sat with it and my coffee mug, staring at the little Christmas tree Jim had brought home before he left. "Fresh off the slopes of Mount Rainier," he'd told me. Its crisp branches were festooned with strings of electric lights, ready to be lit for Ellen's first Christmas. We'd hoped that watching her joy would help to soften the memory of our grief a year ago. Now she was too sick to notice the silver birds and shining balls.

When December's early dusk closed in, since the electricity was off I searched out candles and watched their flames flutter in the icy air seeping beneath the windowsill. From time to time I glanced across the street, hoping to see lights in my neighbors' windows. But they remained dark.

When Ellen awoke crying, I took her up and, huddling in the big morris chair, held her against my shoulder, bracing myself to endure the long hours ahead until Jim got home. What did the pioneer mothers do in the olden days when their children were sick and no doctor was nearer than a hundred miles away? Then I seemed to hear my grandmother's voice answering me: "Why, we prayed."

So with my cheek against my baby's silken head I *tried* to remember some prayer, but the words wouldn't come. I was so tired and discouraged, and God seemed far away. But I think *all of me* must have gone out in a silent cry for help, for as Ellen quieted and I leaned back in the chair, breathing the spicy fragrance of the Christmas tree and staring at the candles' flickering light, gradually fear and tenseness began to drain away. A feeling of peace and comfort closed about me.

I woke with a start, knowing someone had entered the room. Hadn't I locked the door? In the candlelight, a tall man stood looking down at me.

"I am the doctor," he said.

Afterward, I could never remember his face—only the kindness and compassion in his voice. When he examined the baby, she scarcely stirred beneath his gentle hands.

"No lung congestion. But her ears are infected. This medication will help. Keep her warm—let her sleep—she'll be much better by this time tomorrow. Stop worrying, Mother! Try to get some rest." Then he was gone.

For the rest of the night I dozed in the morris chair beside Ellen's crib. She slept straight through fourteen hours! By the time Jim got home on Christmas Eve, her temperature was normal. She was ready to smile at her daddy, and point at the unlighted Christmas tree, saying, "See? Pitty!"

Knowing she would be all right was our most precious Christmas gift.

Days later, after the ice storm was over and its damage repaired, Jim went to the telephone company to try to locate the doctor who had come at midnight. "I want to pay his bill," Jim said. But, of course, the company had no record of my call.

When I went across the street to apologize for my "breaking and entering," the neighbors offered their explanation: "The telephone wires were so mixed up," they said. "Maybe when you thought you were talking to an operator, you were really connected with a hospital that took your message."

Well, maybe . . .

We never found out about our midnight doctor—who he was or how he came. But I believe that after I'd done everything I knew to do for the baby, a Higher Power had heard my silent prayer and sent me help. And sometimes I think of that passage in the Bible, Hebrews 13:2: "Be not forgetful to entertain strangers: for thereby some have entertained angels unawares."

—DOROTHY ROOD STEWART

God Answers Prayer

I know not when He sends the word
That tells me fervent prayer is heard;
I know it cometh soon or late,
My part is but to pray and wait.
I know not if the blessing sought
Will come in just the guise I thought.
I leave all care with Him above,
Whose will is always one of love.
—AUTHOR UNKNOWN

The Fourth Man

IT HAD BEEN RECKLESS OF ME, taking a before-dawn stroll through the tangle of streets behind the Los Angeles bus terminal. But I was a young woman arriving in the great city for the first time. My job interview was five hours away, and I couldn't wait to explore!

Now I'd lost my way in a Skid Row neighborhood. Hearing a car pass, I turned and, in the flash of light, saw three men lurking behind me, trying to keep out of sight in the shadows. Trembling with fright, I did what I always do when in need of help. I bowed my head and asked God to rescue me.

But when I looked up, a fourth man was striding toward me in the dark! *Dear God, I'm surrounded.* I was so scared, it took me a few seconds to realize that even in the blackness I could *see* this man. He was dressed in an immaculate workshirt and denim pants, and carried a lunchbox. He was about thirty, well over six feet. His face was stern but beautiful (the only word for it).

I ran up to him. "I'm lost and some men are following me," I said in desperation. "I took a walk from the bus depot—I'm so scared."

"Come," he said. "I'll take you to safety."

He was strong and made me feel safe.

"I . . . I don't know what would have happened if you hadn't come along."

"I do." His voice was resonant, deep.

"I prayed for help just before you came."

A smile touched his mouth and eyes. We were nearing the depot. "You are safe now."

"Thank you—so much," I said fervently.

He nodded. "Good-bye, Euphie."

Going into the lobby, it hit me. *Euphie!* Had he really used my first name? I whirled, burst out onto the sidewalk. But he had vanished.

—*EUPHIE EALLONARDO*

The Mangy Angel

C OLD MARCH SHOWERS PELTED MY FACE as I stepped from the warmth of the church and threaded my way across the lot toward the parsonage.

Thursday evening's meeting of the women's missionary society had finally closed, and as the pastor's wife, I was the last to leave.

My husband had gone to a general conference in Detroit, and the children and I were alone. I half expected to find the parsonage cloaked with night, for the hour was late and the children should have been in bed hours ago.

Letting myself in quietly, I was surprised to find the kitchen light still burning. Ted, our oldest, his dark head bent over his books, was studying at the table. He looked up as I came in.

"H'lo, Mom. Wet out, isn't it?"

"It's a wild night, all right," I said wryly, peeling off my dripping coat and boots.

He went back to his homework.

As I turned to leave the kitchen I looked down. Then I gasped. Our huge mangy dog lay stretched out at Ted's side!

"Ted! What's Brownie doing in the house?" I demanded. "You know he's never stayed inside before!"

Ted glanced up from his book and shrugged. "Why, he just wanted in so I let him in. Then I decided I might as well bring my homework down here."

Brownie wanted in! That, in itself, was utterly incongruous. For that matter, so was everything else about that dog.

Black, brown and smelly—and of undetermined breed—he had wandered into the parsonage one day and simply decided to stay. He adopted our family and was fiercely protective of us in every way. In fact, he loved us so much, that he wanted to be where we were. Yet, once we'd let him into the house, he developed a peculiar claustrophobic streak. He would race in terror from window to door to window until we'd let him out. No amount of bribing or petting could persuade Brownie to remain indoors. Even the dreary *drip-drip* of rain from the eaves failed to lure him inside. He preferred the most inclement out-door weather to being enclosed.

Until now.

There he was, lying calmly beside Ted in the kitchen like a very ordinary house dog.

I remembered his previous fierce possessiveness of us. Our large, red-brick parsonage sprawled comfortably on a big grassy plot behind the church and opposite the public school. Children often cut across the church property and through our yard when hurrying to and from school. We didn't mind. In fact, they were our friends. Against our better judgment, we often had report cards thrust at us even before parents saw them.

That is, until the dog came. He growled threateningly at anyone who dared cross our yard. Yet Brownie always came when I called him off.

Still, with people dropping in at our parsonage at all hours of the day, I was afraid some day I wouldn't get him called off in time.

I tried desperately to find another home for him, but with no success. Once I even called the Humane Society.

"Sure, lady," they said. "We'll get him. But you gotta catch him and shut him up for us."

Shut Brownie up? Impossible! One might as well try to imprison a victim of claustrophobia in an elevator! Until a better solution presented itself, he would have to remain with us.

And that's how things stood that wild, stormy night I came home from church.

Shaking my head at Brownie's strange behavior, I went down to the basement to bolt the door that leads to the outside. I came back up directly and retired to the living room with the paper.

Ted already had gone up to bed, and I decided to turn in, too. The dog still lay on the kitchen floor, his shaggy head resting on his front paws.

Better put Brownie out first, I thought as I entered the kitchen to lock the back door. Rain still drummed steadily against the windows.

But when I tried to get the dog out of the door, he refused to budge. I wheedled. I coaxed. I pushed and pulled. He remained stationary.

Going to the refrigerator, I took out a chunk of meat and tried to bribe him to the door by dangling it in front of him. He still refused to move.

With a bewildered sigh I picked up his hind end, yanked him toward the door, and out of it. Like quicksilver, his front end slid back in!

I grabbed his front end, and the back was in. His four feet seemed like a baker's dozen. Stubborn, determined, yet somehow placid. Talk about Balaam's donkey—I knew exactly how Balaam felt!

Should I call Ted to help me? No, the hour was late and Ted needed his sleep. I decided to shut all the doors to the kitchen and leave the dog inside. Then I went wearily to bed.

The next morning the dog reverted to his true nature and frantically tore out of the house.

A puzzled frown ribbed my forehead as I went down to the basement to turn on the furnace. What had made Brownie behave so strangely? Why had he been determined to remain in the house this one particular night? I shook my head. There seemed to be no answer.

When I reached the bottom of the stairs, I felt a breath of cold, damp air. Then a queer, slimy feeling swept over me. The outside door was open! Was someone in the basement?

After the first wave of panic had drained from me, my reasoning returned.

Someone had gone out of the basement!

Limp with the reality of that fact, I looked around. The windows were as snug and tight on the inside as ever. Whoever had gone out of that door had been in when I had gone down to bolt it the night before! He apparently had heard my unsuccessful attempts to put the dog out and knew he had to come up through the kitchen and face the dog—or go out the door he had come in earlier.

That smelly, stray pooch had known this, and God had used him to keep us safe. Why didn't he growl or bark? I don't know. Maybe he knew he didn't have to.

I had always believed that God has definite work for His holy angels, and that as His child I could lay claim to the verse in Hebrews 1:14: "Are they [angels] not all ministering spirits, sent forth to minister for them who shall be heirs of salvation?"

But His "ministering spirit" had taken a peculiar form that wild, stormy night. Instead of glorious, dazzling wings, the Lord had given our guardian angel four stubborn, mangy feet!   —ESTHER L. VOGT

Now the Day Is Over

Now the day is over,
Night is drawing nigh,

Shadows of the evening
Steal across the sky.

Jesus give the weary
Calm and sweet repose,
With Thy tenderest blessing
May our eyelids close.

Grant to little children
Visions bright of Thee,
Guard the sailors tossing
On the deep blue sea.

Through the long night-watches
May Thy angels spread
Their white wings above me,
Watching round my bed.

When the morning wakens,
Then may I arise
Pure and fresh and sinless
In Thy holy eyes.
—*SABINE BARING-GOULD*

The Day We Saw the Angels

IT WAS NOT CHRISTMAS, it was not even wintertime, when the event occurred that for me threw sudden new light on the ancient angel tale. It was a glorious spring morning, and my wife, Marion, and I were walking through the newly budded birches and maples near Ballardvale, Massachusetts.

Now, I realize that this, like any account of personal experience, is only as valid as the good sense and honesty of the person relating it. What can I say about myself? That I am a scholar who shuns guesswork and admires scientific investigation? That I have an A.B. from Harvard, an M.A. from Columbia, a Ph.D. from Hartford Theological Seminary? That I have never been subject to hallucinations? All this is true, and yet I doubt that such credentials can influence the belief of another.

In the long run, each of us must sift what comes to us from others through his own life experience, his view of the universe. And so I will simply tell my story.

The little path on which Marion and I walked that morning was spongy to our steps and we held hands with the sheer delight of life. It was May, and because it was the examination reading period for students at Smith College where I was a professor, we were able to get away for a few days to visit Marion's parents.

We frequently took walks in the country, and we especially loved the spring after a hard New England winter, for it is then that the fields and the woods are radiant with new life. This day we were especially happy and peaceful; we chatted sporadically, with great gaps of satisfying silence between our sentences.

Then from behind us we heard the murmur of muted voices, and I said to Marion, "We have company in the woods this morning."

Marion nodded and turned to look. We saw nothing, but the voices were coming nearer—at a faster pace than we were walking, and we knew that the strangers would soon overtake us. Then we perceived that the sounds were not only behind us but above us, and we looked up.

How can I describe what we felt? Is it possible to tell of the surge of exaltation that ran through us? Is it possible to record this phenomenon in objective accuracy and yet be credible?

For about ten feet above us, and slightly to our left, was a floating group of glorious, beautiful creatures that glowed with spiritual beauty. We stopped and stared as they passed above us.

There were six of them, young beautiful women dressed in flowing white garments and engaged in earnest conversation. If they were aware of our existence they gave no indication of it. Their faces were perfectly clear to us, and one woman, slightly older than the rest, was especially beautiful. Her dark hair was pulled back in what today we would call a ponytail which appeared to be bound at the back of her head. She was talking intently to a younger spirit who looked up into her face.

Neither Marion nor I could understand their words, although their voices were clearly heard.

They seemed to float past us, and their graceful motion was as gentle and peaceful as the morning itself. As they passed, their conversation grew fainter until it faded out entirely, and we stood transfixed on the spot, still holding hands. Then we looked at each other, each wondering if the other also had seen.

There was a fallen birch tree beside the path. We sat down on it, and I said, "Marion, what did you see and hear? Tell me exactly."

She knew my intent—to see if I had been the victim of hallucination. And her reply was identical in every respect to what I'd seen and heard.

I have related this story with the same respect for truth as I would on the witness stand. But I know how incredible it sounds.

Perhaps I can claim no more for it than that it has had a deep effect on our own lives. For this experience of over thirty years ago greatly altered our thinking. Once both Marion and I were somewhat skeptical about the absolute accuracy of the details at the birth of Christ. The story, as recorded by St. Luke, tells of an angel appearing to "shepherds abiding in the field" and after the shepherds had been told of the birth, "suddenly there was with the angel a multitude of the heavenly host praising God, and saying, Glory to God in the highest" (Luke 2:8–14).

As a child I accepted this multitude as literal heavenly personages. Then I went through a period when I felt that they were merely symbols injected into a legend. Today, after the experience at Ballardvale, Marion and I are no longer skeptical. We believe that St. Luke records a genuine objective experience told in wonder by those who lived it.

Once, too, we puzzled over the Christian insistence that we have "bodies" other than our normal flesh and blood ones. We were like the doubter of whom St. Paul wrote: "But some man will say, How are the dead raised up? and with what body do they come?" (1 Corinthians 15:35).

In the thirty years since that bright May morning, his answer has rung for us with joyous conviction.

"There are also celestial bodies, and bodies terrestrial but the glory of the celestial is one, and the glory of the terrestrial is another.... So also is the resurrection of the dead...It is sown a natural body: it is raised a spiritual body. There is a natural body, and there is a spiritual body.... And as we have borne the image of the earthy, we shall also bear the image of the heavenly" (1 Corinthians 15:40–49).

All of us, I think, hear the angels for a little while, at Christmastime. But we reject the very possibility that what the shepherds saw two thousand years ago was part of the reality that presses close every day of our lives.

And yet there is no reason to shrink from this knowledge. Since Marion and I began to be aware of the Host of heaven all about us, our lives have been filled with a wonderful hope. Phillips Brooks, the great Episcopal bishop, expressed it beautifully:

"Hold fast to yourself the sympathy and companionship of the unseen worlds. No doubt it is best for us now that they should be unseen. It cultivates in us that higher perception that we call 'faith.' But who can say that the time will not come when, even to those who live here upon earth, the unseen worlds shall no longer be unseen?"

The experience at Ballardvale, added to the convictions of my Christian faith, gives me not only a feeling of assurance about the future, but a sense of adventure toward it too.   —*S. Ralph Harlow*

The Snakebite

WE HAD JUST FINISHED Sunday dinner when our twelve-year-old son, Mark, asked if he and his dog, Bo, could go out into the field beyond our house for a while. "Just be careful," my husband told him. It was the advice Bobby always gave our children whenever they went out alone, especially in the three years since we'd moved thirty miles out into the brushland of southwestern Florida. Several of our animals had been bitten by rattlesnakes.

As I cleared away the dinner dishes, I watched Mark and Bo race off through the orange and lemon trees of our private oasis. Mark had become so self-reliant out here in the country, I thought.

I took my time with the dishes, enjoying the slow Sunday afternoon, and was just finishing up when I heard the living-room door open. Suddenly our older son, Buddy, yelled, "Mark, what's wrong?" I threw down the dish towel and ran toward the living room just as Mark gasped, "I—I've been rattlesnake-bit—" There was a dull thud. When I got there, Mark was on the floor, unconscious. "Go get your dad. Hurry!" I said to Buddy.

I pulled off Mark's shoe; his foot had already swollen into a large, ugly purple mass. There was a musky odor about him, the same odor we'd noticed the times our animals had been bitten by rattlesnakes. In seconds, Bobby rushed in and grabbed Mark up in his arms. "Come on," he said. "We've got to get him to the emergency center."

We ran and climbed into the cab of Bobby's work truck. I held Mark on my lap, Buddy sat in the middle, and Bobby drove. "O God," I prayed, "help us." It was seventeen miles to the emergency center, and every minute counted.

Mark was unconscious, and convulsions jerked his body. I tried to hold him still, with his face close to mine. As long as I could feel his breath against my cheek, I knew he was still alive. But the soft flutters were becoming weaker and less frequent.

"Hurry, Bobby—please hurry!" I pleaded as he frantically passed car after car. Buddy sat in the center, quietly struggling to hold his brother's legs. None of us dared say it, but we all knew we were in a race with death.

As we neared the business section, steam started to seep out from under the hood of the truck. The motor was overheating. About a mile from the clinic, the motor began to pop and sputter.

I glanced over at Bobby. What would we do if the motor stopped? But before I could get the words out, Bobby had to brake for a slower vehicle and the motor cut off completely. I clutched Mark to me, trying to hold on to whatever life was left. We were right in the middle of traffic. Cars were pulling around us and honking their horns. Bobby jumped out and tried to flag down one of the motorists, but the cars just sped around him. "Why won't they stop?" Buddy sighed.

Desperate by now, Bobby ran over and pulled Mark from my arms. He carried him out to the rear of the car, where the other drivers could see him, but still the cars kept going by. Finally one old compact car stopped. The driver appeared to be a Haitian farm worker, and he didn't understand English. But he could tell we needed help.

"Thank you, thank you . . ." Bobby shouted as he pulled open the door and pushed Buddy in the backseat. Then he laid Mark down beside him and waved the driver off as I jumped in the front.

"We have to get to the emergency center" I cried, but the driver's questioning look told me he didn't understand. I pointed in the direction we should go.

As we pulled away, I glanced back at Bobby standing in the street. There was no room for him in the small car and our truck was blocking traffic, but I wished he could be with me.

At the emergency center, medical technicians started working on Mark immediately, trying to stabilize his condition. They started fluids and began artificial respiration. But soon after Bobby arrived, the emergency technicians told us they had done all they could and were transferring Mark to Naples Community Hospital, where Dr. Michael Nycum would meet us.

By the time we arrived at the hospital, Mark had stopped breathing twice and had gone into a coma. For the next twelve hours we waited and prayed while the doctors and nurses worked constantly with him. We could tell by the looks on their faces that they didn't expect him to make it.

"Folks, about the only thing the little fellow has going for him is his heart—and that's under tremendous strain," Dr. Nycum told us.

We watched helplessly during the next twenty-four hours as the venom attacked every part of his body. His eyes swelled so tight that all we could see were the ends of his eyelashes. His leg was so swollen the doctors had to make long slashes along it to relieve the pressure on the blood vessels. And still they were afraid they might have to amputate.

Then, miraculously, Mark passed the crisis point and began to improve a little. He was still in a coma, and certainly not out of danger, but the swelling began to go down.

After that, each day brought improvement. On Thursday, Bobby and I sat there beside Mark's bed. We were drained, exhausted, prayed out. I was sitting in a chair close to him, holding his hand, when I thought I felt a movement. But no, I told myself, it was probably my imagination. Yet a moment later, there it was again, a faint fluttering of the small hand inside mine.

"Bobby," I said, sitting up and reaching across to him, "Bobby! Mark moved—he moved!"

Bobby summoned the nurses and doctor. Mark was coming out of the coma.

"Mom . . . Mom . . ." he moaned.

"Yes, honey, we're here." The words caught in my throat.

"Dad . . ."

"Yes, Son . . ."

His eyes opened now as he looked over at Bobby. "Dad . . . are you mad at me?"

"What do you mean?" Bobby tried to laugh, but it came out a little ragged. "Of course I'm not mad at you."

"I was afraid you'd be mad at me for being so careless."

Bobby reached over and patted Mark on the head. "We're just thankful you're getting better. But what happened, Son? Do you feel like telling us?"

The nurses and Dr. Nycum moved a little closer.

"Well, Bo and I spotted a bird in a cabbage palm and, well, I guess I wasn't paying too much attention to where I was going. I was looking at the bird and jumped over the ditch . . . and my foot landed on something that moved when I hit it.

"And then it was like something slammed down hard on my foot, and my-leg started getting real hot. When I looked down, I saw a big rattler had hold of my shoe—it was biting on my foot. It was hurting so bad and Bo was barking and jumping at the snake, but it wouldn't let go. Then Bo jumped on the snake and tore into its head. It let go and crawled off into the bushes.

"Dad, I tried to remember what you said to do if we ever got snakebit, but I was hurting so bad, and getting weak and dizzy I was a long way from the house, and I knew none of you would hear if I called..."

"But where were you, Mark?" Bobby asked.

"Out in the field, a long ways from the house. Out there next to the ditch in the field."

"But that's a third of a mile from the house. How did you get to the house?"

Dr. Nycum shook his head. "Medically speaking, it would have been impossible for him to have walked that far."

Bobby and I looked uncertainly at each other. There were also the thirteen steps up to our front door—he'd had to climb those too. I took a deep breath. After everything that had happened, I was almost afraid to ask, but I had to know. "How did you get back to the house, Mark?"

"Well, I remembered you and Dad saying that the more you moved, the quicker the poison would reach your heart, and I knew I couldn't run. But I was so scared, and all I wanted to do was get home. I probably would have run if I could have, but I couldn't because it hurt so bad. And then... Dad, there's something I have to tell you. About the man."

"The man? What man?" Bobby asked. "Was someone out there with you?"

"Yes—I mean, no—I mean, I don't know. All I know is that he carried me..."

"He carried you?"

"Yes, when I couldn't make it to the house. He picked me up." I could feel a tingle on the back of my neck.

"He talked to me in a real deep voice," Mark went on, "and told me that I was going to be real sick, but that I'd be all right."

"What did he look like?" I asked Mark shakily.

"I couldn't see his face, Mom. All I could see was that he had on a white robe, and his arms were real strong. He reached down and picked me up. And I was hurting so bad, I just sort of leaned my head over on him. He carried me to the house and up the steps. When he put me down, I held on to the door and turned around, and—"

His blue eyes stared into mine with an earnestness I'd never seen before. "All I could see was his back."

For a long time, none of us could speak: it was almost more than we could take in. "God is our refuge and strength," I said to myself, "a very present help in trouble" (Psalm 46: 1, RSV).

For most of my life I had believed that passage in the Bible by faith. Now I saw the proof of it.

"Mom...Dad..." Mark said, hesitating. "I know you may not believe me—"

"We believe you," I whispered as Bobby put his arm around me. "We believe you." —*DEBBIE DURRANCE*

Reassurance

Dear Lord:

Could You spare some Guardian Angels
To give me peace of mind
As my children wander from me
And stretch the ties that bind?

You have heavenly legions, Father.
Could you send me just a few
To guide my eager youngsters
As I give them, Lord, to You?

Oh thank You, thank You, Father,
And, oh, my glad heart sings.
I'm certain that just now I heard
The swish of passing wings!
—*BETTY BANNER*

Whose Footprints?

DUSTIN, MY CALIFORNIA BRED GUIDE DOG, was having trouble outside our Long Island apartment. This was his first snowstorm and he was confused. I'm blind, and I wasn't doing so well either. No one was out, so there were no sounds to steer me. Contrary to what many people think, guide dogs do not find the way for a blind person. The blind person directs the dog.

After a harrowing forty-five minutes, Dustin and I finally made it back. But guide dogs must be walked regularly. "Next time why don't you ask God to go with you?" a friend suggested. And so I did. "Lord, go with Dustin and me. The wind is so fierce it's hard to concentrate on our direction. Lead us."

Snow stung our faces and it was difficult to make a path. Dustin whined a little. "Okay, boy," I said to him, "the Lord is with us." And then I gave him a command that a blind person gives only when another person is leading the way: "Dustin, follow!"

Dustin perked up and to my astonishment took off as though he knew exactly where to go. We made it to the street, then headed back to our building—no problem.

A young woman trudged up and offered to walk us to our door. "We'll just follow your footprints," she said. "Yours and the dog's, and that other person's."

"What other person?" I asked.

"There's a dog's prints. And your prints. And a larger person's prints. Wasn't someone with you?"

I paused for a moment and then I answered, "Oh yes, there was Someone with us." There always is. —SANDY SELTZER

Strange Encounters

I WAS EXHAUSTED, numb with grief and shock and fear. The last twenty-four hours had been an unceasing nightmare. I didn't see how God could permit such things to happen to anyone, let alone my little boy, David. I didn't know whether he would survive; the doctors said they couldn't tell me. I didn't know whether the mountain lion that had mauled him was rabid or not. I stood in the hospital corridor and turned my face to the wall and wept silent tears of hopelessness and despair.

Then, although I had heard no one come up behind me, I felt a pair of loving arms enfold me—gentle, supportive, understanding arms. I thought it must be my husband. Chris. Or perhaps some friend or relative who had heard about our trouble and had hurried to the hospital.

But it was not my husband. It was not a friend. It was someone I had never seen before.

And would never see again . . .

* * *

The unbelievable had happened the previous day on a rocky trail in Big Bend National Park on the Texas side of the Mexican border. It was a scorching afternoon, August 2, 1984. As my two sons, David, eight, and Justin, four, raced ahead of us, their stepfather, Chris, called them back, reminding them that the park rangers had told us to stick together. They had said that these piñon-juniper woodlands hid coyote, white-tailed deer, javelina, desert mule, even some mountain lions that occasionally were seen at a distance. But no one had ever been threatened by these. The things to watch out for on the path we were taking, they said, were snakes.

Suddenly, David swung around, his face contorted with fear. He ran toward us screaming, "Mountain lion!"

Before any of us could react, a cougar sprang from the shadow of a tree. Like a tawny streak of lightning it pounced on David's back. The next moment he lay sprawled, not moving, as the huge cat clamped its teeth over his head . . .

There are moments in life that burn themselves into your brain, into your soul. That moment burned into mine. As I stood there in the hospital corridor, I knew it would never go away. And yet, as the gentle arms enfolded me, a soft voice said, "Child, you don't know me. But I know you." I turned and found myself gazing into the face of an elderly black man. He was wearing dark glasses. He wore some kind of old hat. He held a small brown paper bag in one hand, the top crumpled shut. I think—but I'm not absolutely sure of this—he was wearing some sort of brown coveralls.

All this I saw through my tears at a glance. My first reaction was one of astonishment, resistance, almost fright. He must have felt me stiffen, because he said soothingly. "I know all about you and why you are here. God knows too."

I heard these words with incredulity. How could he know about me. No newspaper had published the story. There hadn't been time. And yet, startled and incredulous though I was, I was aware that something remarkable was happening. I have a normal wariness of strangers, but in an instant, it seemed, something melted away that resistance. I no longer felt afraid. I just felt loved. I yielded to the comfort of this stranger's arms. And cried . . .

When the cougar pounced, I watched in horror, unable to move or make a sound. But Chris burst into action. He hurled himself at the lion, trying to kick it away from David. The beast writhed in pain and anger, but did not release its hold on the child. Chris slipped and fell almost on top of them. I screamed, "He's killing him! He's killing him!" Chris seized the cougar by the neck, trying to choke it. Justin was running in circles like a mad thing. When I snatched him to me, he climbed all over me, half crazed with fear. I wanted to calm him, but I couldn't stop screaming.

With colossal effort, Chris wrenched the cougar away from David and flung it aside, but the enraged beast came right back, sinking its claws into his leg. With his free foot, Chris kicked with all his might and the cougar flew backward. Chris snatched up a tiny stick and lunged at the lion with a furious yell. The bluff—and what a courageous bluff it was—worked. The animal sprang into the underbrush and disappeared.

Chris scooped David up in his arms. David's eyes were open but filled with blood. His skull lay exposed; parts of his scalp hung in shreds, bleeding terribly. There were tooth and claw marks all over the upper part of his body. But he was alive.

"Got to stay together!" Chris gasped at me. "Thing might come back!" He tried to hoist David onto his back, but our son was too weak to hold on. So Chris carried him in his arms. After about fifty yards he stopped long enough to rip off his shirt and wrap it tightly around David's head. Then we ran together back toward the lodge and help. But it was more than half an hour away. I didn't see how Chris could make it with a seventy-two pound load of dead weight in his arms. Twice I saw the bushes move on the side of the path. The lion was trailing us.

"Daddy," David murmured weakly, "am I going to die?"

"No, you're not!" Chris assured him. "We're going to pray." And as we stumbled on, we did pray. Chris thanked God for sparing David's life. He asked for healing for David, and for strength for himself to make it back to the lodge. David joined in, and as they prayed together I saw blood running down Chris's leg. I couldn't tell if it was David's blood or my husband's. They both ran together. A short while later, I remembered a phrase from the Bible where another David said that "The Lord delivered me from the paw of the lion" (1 Samuel 17:37). I clung to that . . .

I clung to it just as I was clinging now to my comforting stranger. He said, "God sent me to tell you that your little boy will be restored." Restored. What a strange, archaic word, but one with such healing power in it. And hadn't that other David also used that word in the loveliest of his songs, "He restoreth my soul . . ."? My own soul was being restored. The fear and despair were leaving me.

Now the old man whose arms held me so securely began to pray in a low, musical voice, the most beautiful prayer I ever expect to hear this side of Heaven. He thanked God for saving David's life. He thanked Him for giving Chris and me the strength we needed. Listening to him, I was sure that God was listening too. I knew that David was going to be all right . . .

When at last we stumbled into the lodge, the horrified rangers sprang into action. A paramedic treated David's terrible wounds as best he could. An old park van rushed him to the nearest hospital in the small town of Alpine 110 miles away. We prayed together the whole way. There nurses tried to clean and dress the wounds according to instructions given over the telephone by a trauma team at the Parkland Hospital in Dallas. It was imperative that David be rushed to Parkland for specialized care. The danger was that the exposed skull might dry out and "die," and thus the brain could be affected.

We tried to get an airplane for the five-hundred-mile trip, but ran into nothing but delays and frustrations. Finally in desperation we left in the middle of the night by ambulance and didn't get to Dallas till the next morning. By then David was running a fever; the antibiotics he had received didn't seem to be controlling the infection that had set in. Meanwhile, helicopters and dogs were out tracking the cougar. To be safe, David had to begin the painful series of rabies shots on top of everything else. It seemed more than an eight-year-old body should have to endure . . .

The old man stepped back, his hand still on my arm, and I knew he was about to go. I wanted to ask his name, know how he knew about David, how he knew about our need. But he shook his head and smiled as I formed the first question. "I want you to look at my eyes," he said. He took off the dark glasses. His eyes were white. He was completely blind. "I wanted you to see this." he said, "so that you would understand that God really did send me. Watch!"

He turned and walked unerringly down the long, busy hospital corridor. Straight as an arrow, with no cane to guide him, without touching the walls on either side. He did not bump into anyone or anything. I watched him go, the old hat still on his head, the brown paper bag still clutched in his right hand. He turned a corner and was gone. I never saw him again. And even though I asked around, no one in the hospital knew him—or had even seen him.

Today, a year later, David is almost healed, physically and psychologically. He still has occasional nightmares, but they're less frequent. Two more skin grafts are needed, but his hair has almost covered his scalp now. Doctors are amazed by the rapid progress he is making.

They tracked down the cougar. Small amounts of David's hair and skin were in its stomach, positively identifying it. Surprisingly, tests showed no signs of rabies. No one can guess what made this two-year-old female lion attack. In the fifty years the park has been open, such a thing had never happened before.

And that meeting in the Parkland corridor? If you are invincibly literal-minded I suppose you can choose to believe that the person I met—or the person who came to me—was just some casual visitor to the hospital who had heard about David, and who was remarkably perceptive and kind.

But Chris and I will never believe that. We believe that God heard our prayers and sent one of His messengers, yes, a blind messenger with a funny hat and a brown paper bag, to comfort and strengthen us. We'll believe it forever. And we'll never cease to be thankful.

—KIMETHA BROWN

The Woman from Nowhere

MY PRESCHOOLER SON Marc and I were shopping in a large department store. On our way down to the main floor, Marc hopped on the escalator. I followed. Suddenly Marc screamed. I'd never heard a sound like that before. "Mama! My foot!"

Marc's right foot was wedged between the side of the moving step and the escalator's wall. His body was twisted toward me. He screamed again. The escalator continued downward.

In the panic of the moment, the danger at the bottom of the escalator flashed before me, the thought of the foot being severed—

"Turn off the escalator!" I screamed. "Somebody help!" And then, "Oh, dear God, dear God, help us! Help us!"

Several people at the base of the escalator began a flurry of activity. The escalator stopped! Someone had pressed an emergency button at the bottom of the steps.

Thank You, Father, I prayed.

Marc clutched my arm and cried while I struggled to get a better look at his foot. A chill raced up my spine when I saw the tiny space in which his foot was trapped. It looked no more than a quarter of an inch wide. All I could see of his foot was his heel. The rest had disappeared into the jaws of the machine.

"Someone call the fire department!" I shouted.

Marc looked up at me desperately. "Mama," he said, "pray!"

I crouched next to him, holding him. I prayed. For a moment he quieted. Soon, though, he began crying again. "Daddy! Daddy!" he called out. I shouted out our business phone number, hoping someone would call my husband.

The two of us sat waiting. Marc cried. I patted his head. As the minutes passed I could see dark images of crutches and wheelchairs. I had always taken for granted that our little son would grow up playing baseball and soccer, running on strong legs and sturdy feet. Now, nothing seemed certain.

My prayers were as scattered as my feelings, and I searched my memory for a Bible verse to hold on to.

"And we know that all things work together for good to them that love God, to them who are the called according to his purpose" (Romans 8:28). This was one of the few verses I had memorized.

"You promised, Lord!" I cried. "And we know that all things . . ." Over and over I said that verse. ". . . called according to his purpose."

Marc looked up at me and said, "Mama, my bones feel broken and bleedy."

I clutched his blond head tighter to me, but now it was I who was feeling faint. *I can't faint, Lord,* I prayed. *Marc needs me—O Lord, I know You're here! Where? Help me!*

At that moment I felt warm soft arms enfolding me from behind. A woman's soothing voice said quietly in my ear, "Jesus is here, Jesus is here."

The woman had come down the escalator and sat on the step above me. She gently rocked me from side to side, surrounding my shaking body with a calm embrace. "Tell your son his foot is all right," she said in my ear. There was an assurance in her voice.

"Marc," I said into his ear. "Your foot is all right."

"Tell him you'll buy him a new pair of shoes—whatever kind he wants."

"I'll buy you a new pair of shoes. Any kind you like."

Marc's crying stopped. "Cowboy boots? Like Daddy's?" We were talking about new shoes—new shoes for two healthy feet! For the first time since the ordeal began, I felt hope. Maybe, just maybe, his foot really would be all right.

"Tell him there are no broken bones," she said.

I did.

The firemen arrived. Two men with crowbars pried the step away from the escalator wall, freeing Marc's foot at last. His shoe was in tatters. It took all my courage to watch as the men pulled the shredded sock off Marc's foot, but when they did, they revealed a red, bruised, but whole foot.

I turned to share my joy with my wonderful friend, but all I saw was her leg as she turned the corner at the top of the escalator. I never even saw her face.

My husband, Craig, arrived just as the firemen were setting Marc down on the floor. He was still sobbing, but he could wiggle his toes. Later, X rays confirmed what I already knew: no broken bones, only bruises and swelling.

To this day I do not know who the woman who helped me was, who knew that Jesus was there with us, who knew that the Lord keeps His promises.

Many people have suggested that the woman was an angel of the Lord. I can't be sure about that, but of this I am certain: She was heaven-sent.

—*Laura Z. Sowers*

The Push That Saved Me

THE COACH COMPLIMENTED ME on the great practice I was having at the gym. I went from one event to the next, running through gymnastics routines I wanted to master for competition.

When I got to the uneven bars I was tired and sweaty. But I was still determined to attempt the dismount I'd been practicing in the pit, a rectangle filled with foam that provided a soft landing. This time I was psyched to try it on the mats. "Dear God," I prayed as I climbed up on the bar, "please keep me safe. Amen."

Hanging by my hands, body extended, I swung once around the bar, placed my feet outside my chalked hands and snapped into the air, flipping forward—

But I'd released too early. I didn't have the height to complete a flip and land on my feet. Suddenly, in mid arc, I felt my coach push me so that the upper part of my body landed safely on the mat. The rest of me crashed down on the thin layer of carpet that covered the cement floor.

While Coach iced my back, I remembered my prayer. Why hadn't God helped me as I'd asked?

The pain was excruciating. My fall would probably keep me out of gymnastics for a while, but I realized that I could have been paralyzed if my head and neck hadn't landed on the mat. I thanked my coach for the push that had saved me.

He looked at me, puzzled. "Krissy," he said, "you flew off that bar so fast, no one had time to get anywhere near you."   —KRISTINA SEIDEL

The Man in the Tree

WAKE UP! Water's rising fast!" Somebody was pounding hard on the door of our camper.

When my husband, Earl, and I first fell asleep, rain was hammering on our metal roof like machine-gun fire. Now it was pretty close to midnight, and a ranger outside was hollering that people should move their boats in to shelter.

It was Wednesday, May 27, 1987, and we'd been fishing and camping with some relatives at Chisholm Trail Ridge on Waurika Lake, about twelve miles from where we lived in Comanche, Oklahoma.

By the time I pulled on my jogging pants, Earl had disappeared into the downpour. But in a minute he came back, holding up half a boat key. "Broke off in the ignition," he yelled.

"I'll go for the spare," I yelled back. We had another key at home, and it seemed easy enough to go get it.

I climbed into our yellow pickup and took off, the windshield wipers flapping away but not helping much. I followed the road along the shore, the pickup bouncing over the ruts. Lightning flashed, and in the eerie blue-white light, trees were bent over and the tall grass was almost flattened by the wind.

I pulled into our driveway, grabbed up the boat key, and headed back around the lake, past Beaver Creek bottom.

By now the storm was even worse. I jounced along over potholes, hoping I was still on the road, when . . .

The pickup lurched, then reeled out of control. Something smashed into the pickup and sent it hurtling through the air. I held on to the steering wheel as hard as I could. Then the pickup dropped with a thud.

Icy water poured in everywhere. I threw myself against the door, pushed it open, and fell into churning water that sucked me into the darkness.

Lord help me. I can't swim. I couldn't get my breath. Water stung my eyes, my nose, my throat. I flailed desperately for something, anything, to hold on to.

The water roared like a freight train in a tunnel.

A tree branch! I grabbed it with both hands. The force of the water whipped me around the tree, but I held on. I wrapped my legs around the tree trunk and groped in the darkness for a branch strong enough to climb onto. There! A branch! I hauled myself up and clung to it, shaking.

This couldn't be happening to me—alone. I wanted to cry out for Earl.

Earl! I loved my husband—and totally relied on him. I always had, ever since I came home from the first grade in a one-room schoolhouse in Sugden, Oklahoma, and told Mama I'd be marrying Earl Ralls. Ever since then, when things went wrong, Earl was beside me. I was shy and scared of folks, so Earl always took care of things, protected me.

This time it was just me. And God.

But what a time finally to be thinking of God: when I was in trouble! Why hadn't I been a better Christian? My faith had never wavered, but over the past five years my church attendance hadn't been too regular.

I figured if you were fifty-one years old, unable to swim, sitting in a tree in the middle of the night during a flood, you'd better be prayed up.

I wasn't.

Would God hear me anyhow? I bowed my head against the driving rain and asked for His help.

There was nothing to do now except hold tight and wait. But the rushing water was creeping over my feet and up my legs.

When I was ten, a bunch of us kids were on the lake holding on to the back of a boat, when I got a cramp and had to let go. I'll never forget that feeling of terror as water filled my nose and throat. But Earl's strong arm pulled me out of the water and saved my life. I never did learn to swim, but I learned I could always depend on Earl Ralls.

But Earl wasn't here to tell me what to do in this darkness. Panic-stricken, I reached up for a limb above me . . .

"Don't climb higher until morning."

Was I hearing things? Where did those words come from? I was too terrified to question. I sank back and huddled against the trunk of the tree.

Hour after hour, I held on while the flood roared around me. Gradually light filtered through black clouds. Morning. The water was up to my waist.

I looked up. The branch I'd reached for in the night was dead. It would have cracked under my weight. The strange command I'd heard last night had kept me from falling into the swirling black water. *God, thank You.*

This time I tested each branch beforehand. Little by little I climbed higher. I scanned the horizon for a boat, rooftop, or any sign of life. But only treetops swayed in the rushing flood. There was no sign of my pickup. I opened my mouth to scream for help.

"Save your strength. Don't yell unless you hear something."

Was someone really speaking to me? Or was I imagining those words? I clung to the tree silently.

More hours went by. By now I was desperately thirsty. I tried to sip a handful of the water surging around me, but the flood had washed manure-spotted pastures, flushed out septic tanks, and carried off the carcasses of dead animals. I gagged.

"Lord," I said out loud, "I'm thirsty."

"Suck your shirt."

I looked around in astonishment. And then down at my T-shirt. I lowered my head, gathered the fabric into my mouth, and sucked out fresh rainwater.

The light faded and the temperature dropped. Thursday evening! Could I stand another night shivering in the darkness? Could I stay awake? Or be able to hold on? My fingers were raw and bloody from clutching the rough bark. I was exhausted, limp, and weak. But worst of all, I was lonely.

I blinked, then blinked again.

Sitting on the branch across from me was the largest man I'd ever seen.

I shut my eyes tight, then opened them slowly.

He was still there. Even in the gathering dusk, I could see his eyes clearly. They were incredibly kind.

Neither of us said a word. His presence radiated warmth and comfort. My shivering stopped; I was enveloped in a cocoon of peace. It was like being in a chapel. For the first time, I relaxed and rested.

The hours passed.

At last the man spoke. His voice was gentle but full of authority. "I'm leaving now," he said. "Don't be afraid; I'm going to bring help."

"Don't go!" I begged. "The water's too rough."

"I'm strong," he said. "Don't worry. Everything will be all right."

He disappeared into the darkness as suddenly as he had come.

Soon it was close to dawn. A bone-chilling wind blew up and whipped the rain into a stinging spray. "Lord, I'm so cold!" I said. And at that moment my body warmed. I felt as though I were being enveloped in a soft, warm blanket. I could almost touch it. I stared at my bare arms in astonishment. There was nothing over them. And yet I actually felt cozy, and my shivering stopped.

Friday morning. I couldn't believe I was still holding on. But who was ever going to find me here? Where was the mysterious man? He hadn't come back.

In a flash it hit me. That man wasn't human! But I knew I hadn't imagined him. He'd been there, talked to me. "I'm going to bring help," he had said.

Could he have been an angel? I'd read about them in the Bible. They were called messengers.

But now I was getting weaker. I couldn't hold on much longer. The water was up to my waist again and still rising. I climbed the last few feet to the top of the tree. Then came the voice again.

"Call for help now."

By now I didn't even wonder if it was real or not. "Help!" I shouted as loud as I could. My voice cracked. "Help!"

Only silence. The water was creeping past my waist now, up and up.

Death. So this was it. Then why wasn't I afraid? All I could think of was the warm blanket that had covered me during the night and the stranger who had brought me such peace. I closed my eyes.

Voices! Voices not there right beside me but away in the distance. Voices coming closer and closer. I screamed with all my might.

"Wave!" someone out there called. "Wave so we can see you!"

Out of the haze came a small boat rowed by two men.

I woke up between clean white hospital sheets at Duncan Regional Hospital with Earl sitting right beside me, smiling and holding my hand hard. The rest of my family was there too, and Bob Waitman, pastor of the Patterson Avenue Baptist Church. They told me dozens of people had been over at the church praying that I'd be safe.

Earl and the others had been searching around the Dry Creek bottomland, but I'd been much farther to the west. "You were close to the Youngblood place," Earl told me. "The Youngblood kids went looking for their missing horse and found it in an orchard feeding on some peaches. You must have yelled at just the right moment, because they heard you and ran home, and Mrs. Youngblood radioed for help."

A nurse was turning away folks who had flocked to see me. Earl had told her how shy and scared of people I was, so everybody was surprised when I sat up and said, "Let them in!"

People I'd known all my life, and people I'd never spoken to, put their arms around me; some of them cried. Everybody was amazed at how well I had held up. But I told them, "Don't be thinking I'm Superwoman at fifty-one years of age! The Lord was with me."

For certain, the Lord *had* been with me. And so had that mysterious man. I didn't tell anyone about him then, yet I believe he was an angel.

I'm not so scared of being "out in the world" now. I have a kind of confidence and trust that I didn't have before.

Because I know now that God is always there when I need Him.

His arm is even longer than Earl's. —*DELTA RALLS*

Someone Parked the Car

I WAS DRIVING HOME after visiting my family for Christmas. Traffic on the two-lane road was slow but steady. A fine mist saturated the cold air, and as the temperature dropped, the highway grew slick.

Suddenly my wheels skidded and the brakes locked. The guardrail was coming up fast! I cried out, "God, help me!" The impact of the crash threw me over the seat and I blacked out.

I woke up on the floor in the backseat. A man and a boy were bent over me. "You hit a patch of ice," the man said. "A policeman saw the whole thing. He's radioing for help."

Peering out the window, I realized that my car had been moved to the opposite side of the highway and parked safely on the grass off the shoulder. *How in the world did I get over here?* Before I could ask, another car hit the same patch of ice and spun into the guardrail—at the exact spot I had. The man and his son ran to help.

When trucks arrived to sand the road, father and son returned with the policeman. "By the way," the policeman said, "what happened to your companion?"

I looked at him quizzically: "What companion?"

"He drove the car to this spot," the officer said. "I saw him."

"We saw him too," said the father. "He crossed the lane of oncoming traffic and parked right here. But no one got out. In fact, we had to break a window to get in."

There had been no man in my car. But Someone had been with me.

—DOROTHY HOWARD

Estela's Angel

YOU'LL BE INTERESTED IN THIS," my husband said, handing me the morning paper. Indeed I was interested. There in *The Press-Enterprise* was the story of a fifty-year-old woman named Estela Vera who had lost a leg—and almost her life—after being deliberately run down by a truck on the streets of our own city of Riverside. California. But there was more to the assault than senseless violence, for this was a story of how an angel of the Lord had appeared at the precise moment when the truck was heading down on Estela Vera. "I looked at him," the article reported her saying, "and I knew I wasn't going to die."

I myself believe firmly in angels. I believe they are present among us today, guarding us, warning us, delivering us from danger just as surely. Now as they did in biblical times. Over the years, I have collected a file of stories that people have told me about their encounters with these heavenly beings, and so it was particularly exciting to think that here, close at hand, was another story waiting to be told. But there was something unusual about this angel. It disturbed me that though a woman's life had been spared, this angel had not saved her from physical harm.

Estela Vera had been in the hospital for more than a month by the time I called and asked if I could come see her. Her daughter, Martha, told me I would be welcome. But then I faced the prospect of a visit with mixed emotions: Eager as I was to hear her account of her angel, I was hesitant about asking this sad woman to recall any of the circumstances of such a shocking assault. From what I'd learned in the newspaper, she'd had her fill of tragic times. She'd been raised in severe poverty. Her father was murdered when she was nine. She'd helped educate her brothers and sisters, and she herself had managed to become a registered nurse. But that career ended when a viral infection took away her hearing. Only recently she'd turned to sewing, enrolling in a professional sewing school. Then, two weeks before she graduated, came the accident.

It happened on the day before Easter. Estela went out with Martha and her son Mingo to buy dyes for her grandchildren's Easter eggs. As they drove back from a store in Riverside they saw an ice cream truck parked at the curb on Polk Avenue. The driver had been forced out of the cab by a robber, who had him in a choke hold with a knife at his throat.

Mingo and Martha leaped out and ran across the street. Mingo grabbed the assailant from behind; the man turned, slashing in fury, then jumped into the truck, turned the ignition key and gunned the motor. As Mingo grabbed on to the side of the truck, the robber stepped on the gas, and the truck shot straight across the street toward Estela, who was standing beside her car. The truck slammed into the car, shattering its hubcap spokes and crushing Estela. The man reversed the truck, ran over her again, severing one leg and nearly cutting off the other. Estela went into cardiac arrest. By the time the ambulance arrived, she'd lost seven pints of blood, and the paramedics told Martha and Mingo she probably wouldn't live to reach the emergency room. At the hospital, the doctors continued to give the family little hope. But hour after hour, then day after day, Estela rallied. The medical staff was astounded.

Even on the day I was to meet Estela in the hospital, I remained hesitant. I stood outside her room wondering what kind of a pathetic person I would find. Finally I went in.

A small woman with dark hair looked up from a hospital bed and gave me one of the warmest smiles I'd ever seen. "You're so good to come see me," she said, and I knew immediately that she meant it. Estela's daughter was at her bedside, helping with the conversation, which was a mixture of lipreading and gestures.

For a while it seemed that Estela was asking more questions about me than I was about her. Then I told her of my abiding fascination with angels and her face glowed. Obviously this was something she wanted to talk about. "But first," she said, "do you read the Bible?" I nodded that I did. "Do you know the passage in Psalm 34, 'The angel of the Lord encamps around those who fear him, and delivers them'?" (v. 7, RSV).

"Oh, yes, I do," I assured her.

"How wonderful," she said, "because that's what came into my mind just before the truck hit me." Estela took a deep breath. "That man—his face was filled with hate. He saw me and drove straight at me. It all happened so fast, I couldn't move, I just froze with terror. That's when a prayer went up from my heart and the words from the Psalm shot through my mind. 'The angel of the Lord encamps . . . ' "

I sat spellbound as Estela told how suddenly the form of a man appeared beside the ice cream truck, running toward her. This man was surrounded by a pink glow. He seemed to be all soft, vaporous light. His movements were graceful and fluid; his hands were extended, almost reassuringly, palms open toward her. He had the most loving eyes she'd ever seen, and the kindest smile.

As if in slow motion she saw the truck coming toward her, her daughter screaming, her son hanging on to the side of the truck, trying to stop the robber. But in the same moment she saw the man. And the love radiating from his eyes was more powerful than the hate in the eyes of her assailant. Suddenly she had no fear at all, only peace. Estela knew then that this was an angel from God.

The angel reached her a hairbreadth before the truck did. He cradled her in his arms. She was only vaguely aware of being hit, of being put into an ambulance, of being rushed into surgery. It was like a dream. She remembered whispering the whole of Psalm 34 before she lost consciousness. *The angel of the Lord encamps . . .*

When Estela finished her story she took my hands, as if to emphasize the urgency of what she was saying. "The angel was . . . *so beautiful*," she whispered. "Somehow, without speaking, he promised me that everything would be all right. He was giving me the strength I would need to face the surgeries, to go on with life. Such caring, such peace flowed from him that I knew I would be safe."

Estela sat back, she was at ease. There was no anger in her, no bitterness toward the man who had run her down. She seemed to bask in a glow of serenity, and by the time I left her that day, I too basked in that glow. Nobody could be so close to a miracle without feeling it.

On the way home I thought about how I'd wondered why Estela's angel had not come and lifted her away from danger. Now I knew. This was a *comforting* angel. And in a way he had saved Estela. He transformed her into a person of strength able to rise above pain and hate, truly able to forgive her attacker, and brave enough to triumph over the most terrifying of ordeals.

Then, almost out loud, I said to myself, *Angels don't always rescue people!* In Acts 27 the angel didn't save Paul from shipwreck, but it did take away his fear. In the Garden of Gethsemane, when Jesus prayed,

"Father, if you are willing take this cup from me; yet, not my will but yours be done," God did not stop the crucifixion—but "an angel from heaven appeared to him and gave him strength" (Luke 22:43, NRSV). No, a comforting angel gives succor and the courage to endure.

I see my friend Estela often since our first meeting in her hospital room. She's continuing to do the sewing she loves, making quilts and clothing for underprivileged children. And whenever I speak to groups about angels, I include the thrilling story of Estela Vera. I never get tired of telling it.

My belief in these supernatural creatures has always been firm. But today I'm even more confident that God's angels *are* among us, guiding us, protecting us and giving us comfort. Always comfort.

—*Marilynn Carlson Webber*

Nurse with a Smile

WHEN MY HUSBAND, JOHNNY, ENTERED a hospital in Houston, Texas, two large aneurysms pressed on his heart and spinal cord. Johnny was scared and uncertain. The surgery might leave him paralyzed and he didn't want to live as an invalid. We prayed for God's guidance in this decision. Finally Johnny asked me to leave for a while so he could think.

I went to get a cup of coffee with my brother Jack, who had come with us. "Without that operation," I told him, "Johnny probably won't live out the year."

When Jack and I returned an hour later Johnny was alone in his room, smiling. "You have to meet my nurse, Shu-Lin," he said. "She has convinced me to have the operation."

Shu-Lin had assured Johnny he was in good hands, and promised to pray for him. "Not to worry," she had said. How had she given my husband confidence when the doctors and I couldn't? "You'll understand when you see her smile," Johnny said.

Jack and I met Shu-Lin later that afternoon. She was everything Johnny had described—Asian, warm, caring and cheerful, with a radiant smile.

Johnny's sister Jane arrived to be with us for the surgery, and we went to the waiting room. Shu-Lin accompanied Johnny into surgery. It was her day off, but she said she wanted to be there. During the operation, she returned periodically to let us know how Johnny was doing.

Each time she appeared, we felt relief and optimism. Finally the surgery was over, and Shu-Lin came to give us the good news even before the doctor reported to us.

Johnny spent the next five days in intensive care. Often he woke up to find Shu-Lin wiping his forehead or holding his hand. When he was out of danger, Shu-Lin came to say good-bye. "I must go now," she said. "Others need me."

The following week, Johnny was well enough to go home. We decided I should find Shu-Lin to thank her for being so kind. But when I inquired about her, the nurses on duty just looked at me. They had never heard of her. Johnny and Jack and Jane and I *knew* she had been with us. I went to the administration office, determined to locate Shu-Lin. But I was told there was no such employee.

At that moment I realized: Hospitals don't keep records of guardian angels.

—*Sue Bryson*

Praise Him for His Mighty Acts (and His Lesser Ones, Too)

WOULD YOU BELIEVE four flat tires on one car in one day? Well, listen to this.

Back in 1953 I was planning an easy little trip from my home in Connecticut to Pennsylvania. I had four brand new tires for my car. And that was no ordinary car—it was (and is) the motorized love of my life. It's a 1934 Packard, a tan and chocolate brown beauty, with long sleek lines and highly finished grillwork up front. The top lets down, and there's a sturdy running board on either side of the chassis, which rests on gleaming wire wheels. More about those wheels later.

Life was unsettled for me back at that particular time. Emily McNair, my first wife, had died of cancer. Emily and I had bought that Packard together. It had been an old wreck of a car sold to us by a New Englander with a thick Maine accent.

We had hired a mechanic to restore it, but Emily died before the car was finished. So here I was with our two small children, Nancy, seven, and Efrem III, four. And the Packard.

I withdrew from acting for a while to give myself time to heal, and in the interim, I began composing music. I come from a musical family. Mother was a beautiful soprano known on the opera stage as Alma; and my father, a celebrated violinist and composer, was the director of the Curtis Institute of Music in Philadelphia.

Now *my* first work was going to be performed! It was definitely a thrill, the prospect of going down to Merion, on the Main Line outside of Philadelphia, to hear it presented. I'd written a motet, a choral work sung without instrumental accompaniment. It was based on a sacred text, Psalm 150, an unusual sort of composition for me since I wasn't all that religious. At the time, that is. But I'd put my all into that piece, and it was one of the numbers to be performed on a Sunday afternoon program of religious music by a very distinguished group. My father would be in attendance, too.

The plan that Sunday was for me to drive down to New York, park the Packard, then continue by train to Philadelphia, where I would meet my father. Together we would make the short commute by train to Merion. But if I had known then what awaited me, I might never have ventured out that Sunday. I drove a short distance down Route 202, following the Aspetuck River, then turned off onto Route 37 for a shortcut into New York. There were dark clouds overhead, but the day started off happily.

"Tah, dah, tah, tum, Praise ye the Lord . . . Praise him with the timbrel and dance, dah, dah, dah, dah," I sang, lustily, snatches of my choral work that soon would be magnified by many voices. "Oh, Prai-i-i-se him upo-o-o-on—" *POW!* My left tire. My *new* left tire.

"What in the world?" I exclaimed. "I just *bought* those tires." The flat had come just as I entered the small town of Sherman, Connecticut, and it posed an immediate dilemma for me. There were two spares sitting grandly in the sidewells along the running boards, but they were there mostly for show. They were old and couldn't be trusted. So I ran around trying to find a service station—one open on Sunday. The one I finally found had to call Litchfield, twenty-two miles away, and have a tire delivered.

Well, I figured, *that's okay.* I'd allowed an extra hour and a half traveling time.

Annoyed over the delay but glad that I'd started out early, I drove the Packard back onto the highway. "That tire shouldn't have blown. What bad luck," I brooded. Soon, though, I was humming to myself and fantasizing about the reception I'd get for my motet.

"Praise him with the sound of the trumpet: praise him with the psaltery and harp . . ." *HONK! HONK!* Someone waved at the Packard. (The Packard always gets a lot of attention.)

The dark clouds had now opened up, and rain pelted down. Then I heard a second *Pfffft, flop, flop.* My right rear tire!

"This *can't* be happening!" I said out loud. There I was, in the middle of a downpour on the Saw Mill River Parkway. Straining under the Packard's weight, I began jacking up the car; but the jack broke and splattered me with mud. My temper smoldered.

With good leather shoes sinking in the ooze, I tromped off to find a farmhouse and a phone. A wary woman answered my knock. Through the cracked door, she stared suspiciously at my wet suit, the hair plastered to my forehead, the splotches of mud on my face and clothes.

"Strangers ain't allowed here," she said brusquely. *Slam* went the door. *Click* went the latch. Precious time was lost as I persuaded her through the door to call a service station to come and fix my flat. By this time my head start had eroded.

The tire changed, I was back at the wheel, sitting damply on the leather seat, spinning down the Saw Mill, trying desperately to make up for lost time. And then, the third tire went. The Packard limped into a nearby service station.

Through clenched teeth, I called my father in Philadelphia and told him to go on to the concert without me. I would meet him as soon as I could get there. Dad tried to soothe me, but it was no use.

Back in the car, my blood pressure was boiling. My moment of triumph had been lost, all because of those miserable tires. I no longer puzzled over the oddity of their going flat. I was too infuriated.

And so, when the fourth one blew, I was a dangerous man. I banged shut the door of the Packard. Not even the rain could cool me off. And where was I this time? On the Henry Hudson Parkway. I could *see* the city, but I couldn't get to it. Cars whizzed past, barely missing the Packard, parked precariously on the shoulder just at the end of a curve. No one stopped to help; people only honked and yelled warnings and shook their fists.

But I was too angry to give up. I was going to complete this trip if it killed me! Then I heard it, a *chug-chug-sputter-sputter,* and a jalopy, driven by an old white-haired man, pulled up behind me. Off went the engine, and the man's head slumped against the steering wheel.

Minutes passed, nothing happened. Still seething, I stomped over to the old car and asked gruffly through the window. "Hey, what are you doing here?"

When the old fellow looked up, I caught my breath. I hadn't expected the serene, compassionate gaze that met my angry glare. His face was almost, well, beautiful; and although he must have been near eighty, his eyes seemed ageless.

In a feeble voice, with frequent pauses, he explained, "I'm a little tired, and I thought I'd take a rest."

"A rest!" I yelled. "On the Henry Hudson Parkway?" Could this man be pulling my leg? I wondered. I was beginning to think I was going gaga.

"And what are *you* doing here?" the old man asked in a singsong voice.

"I have a flat tire," I snapped. "In fact, it's my fourth flat tire of the day!"

No reply. Then, after a long wait, he said, "There's a garage a mile and a half down, at the next exit. They'll fix it."

"Don't you understand," I fumed, "I have a flat. I can't drive that far on the rim!" Why, I wondered, was I standing here in the rain talking to this old guy?

After another minute's pause, he asked, "Then why don't *you* fix it?"

I wanted to shake this man until his teeth rattled, I was so mad. "Because my jack broke!" I replied, exasperated by this slow-motion conversation.

Looking at my mud-splattered watch, I realized that the concert would be starting soon.

"I have a jack," said the old man, and he handed me the keys to his trunk.

"Why didn't you say so in the first place?" I said huffily, as I got the jack. As quickly as I could, I changed the tire, then returned the man's jack and keys. Neither of us spoke.

I went back to the Packard, whacked on the hubcap. Then, feeling guilty about my rudeness, I turned back to thank the old gentleman. And I gasped! Jalopy and man had vanished. Without a *sound*. I remembered the sputtering of his engine when he pulled up behind me. There was no way to sneak off in *that* car.

I ran up the Parkway and looked into the distance, cars zooming and screeching around me. No trace of him. "I *am* losing my mind," I said out loud.

Then I began to wonder. Was that man real or wasn't he? The spare tire in place on the front of my car was proof that he'd lent me a jack. But he couldn't have disappeared in those few seconds—twenty at the most—while my back was turned. It was weird. I felt a shiver down my spine.

On the train ride down to Philadelphia, I continued to puzzle over the old man. *Of course,* I thought, *if it hadn't been for him, I'd still be standing helplessly on the parkway. But on the other hand, he wasn't all that helpful. He didn't do anything, in fact, until I told him point-blank what I needed. And yet, he gave it—a jack, that's all I needed. And then he disappeared. Just who was he?*

All those flats, I later found out, occurred because the mechanic failed to put on the boots with the Packard's new tires. The boots would have protected the tires from the Packard's spoked wheels.

But, you know, I never forgot that old man, and years later, when I drew closer to God, I felt—and I believe now—that that old man was sent to help me. As exasperating as he was, he gave me the help I needed. But he made me ask for it.

"Ask, and it shall be given you; seek, and ye shall find." (Matthew 7:7).

But wait, there's more to the story of that day. I walked into the concert in Merion, *two hours* late, just as the choral group burst into "Praise ye the Lord...Praise him for his mighty acts..." The 150th Psalm—*my* motet! Knowing I was delayed, the conductor pushed it back on the program until he felt he could not hold off any longer; and at that moment, I pushed wearily through the doors.

I sat there, muddy and wet, and listened humbly, as the choir's voice swelled at the end: "Let everything that hath breath praise the Lord. Praise ye the Lord."

—*Efrem Zimbalist, Jr., as told to Regina Walker McCally*

The Man on the Rock

W AY BACK IN 1922, when I was in my teens and acting in silent films, I was invited by Tom Mix, one of the great Hollywood cowboys, to a barbecue on the beach at Malibu.

Malibu was then just a slim strip of sand with a few houses on it. During the party that afternoon I foolishly went swimming alone. Not long after I dived into the water, I found myself so far out that I could barely see our group. I tried to swim in, but no matter how hard I stroked, the shore grew farther away. I was caught in the beach's infamous riptide.

Salt water burned my throat, my arms felt as though they carried lead weights and I could barely kick my weary legs. "Dear God," I prayed in desperation, "help me."

At that moment I heard, "Reach up." There on a large rock was a man in a bathing suit holding out his hand. Swiftly he pulled me up beside him. When I could breathe evenly, he said, "You can make it now. Head for the piling that sea gull is on."

It seemed the wrong direction, but I did as he said. As I swam away, I turned around briefly and he raised his hand. The next time I looked he was gone.

At last I made it back to shore and trudged up to the barbecue. Someone asked where I'd been. Exhausted, I replied, "I took a swim out to the rock."

"What rock?" Tom Mix asked. "There's no rock out there." I looked out to sea. Tom was right. I could not find the rock I'd been on. And yet . . .

Today I'm in my eighties. Throughout my long life with all its crosscurrents and contrary tides, I've known there *is* a rock. And a man holding out his hand to me.   —*PATSY RUTH MILLER*

That Blue Toyota Truck

O UR CAR BROKE DOWN in the middle of the West Texas desert, fifty miles from the nearest town. My kids and I tried to flag down some help, but no one stopped. Finally I sat down behind the wheel and prayed to the Lord to help us.

In time a small blue Toyota truck pulled up and an older couple stepped out. Then, to my amazement, the woman said, "We were on another highway and we heard in our prayers that someone needed our help."

The man said he was a mechanic. He looked under the hood of my car and told me that because of a malfunctioning alternator my battery was dead. "We'll take the battery to get it recharged," he said. They left us some sandwiches to eat and a red toolbox full of valuable tools to reassure me of their return.

After two hours they came back with a new battery, which the man installed. Then his wife placed her hands gently on my cheeks and said, "You'll be all right, Cheryl." She turned to my young children and added, "Michael and Janet, be good to your Mommy. See that she gets home safely to Indiana."

They got in their truck. Only after they had driven away did it occur to me: They knew my name. They knew my children's names. They knew where we were going. But we had told them none of these things.   —*CHERYL TOTH*

Friends Angelical

Far beyond the shifting screen
Made of things that can be seen,
Are our friends angelical
Of the Land Celestial.

Thence they come to tend the flowers
That we thought were only ours.
What their toils we may not know,
As they come and as they go.

Only this we know: they see
As we cannot, what shall be,
Watch the hidden buds unfold,
Dream of colour, heart of gold.

Therefore look behind the screen,
Trust the powers of the Unseen.
Neither vague nor mystical
Are our friends angelical.

—AMY CARMICHAEL

This original Guideposts Book was created by the Books and Inspirational Media Division of the company that publishes *Guideposts*, a monthly magazine filled with true stories of hope and inspiration. ¶ *Guideposts* is available by subscription. All you have to do is write to Guideposts, 39 Seminary Hill Road, Carmel, New York 10512. When you subscribe, each month you can count on receiving exciting new evidence of God's presence, His guidance and His limitless love for all of us. ¶ Guideposts Books are available on the World Wide Web at www.guidepostsbooks.com. Follow our popular book of devotionals, *Daily Guideposts*, and read excerpts from some of our best-selling books. You can also send prayer requests to our Monday morning Prayer Fellowship and read stories from recent issues of our magazines, *Guideposts*, *Angels on Earth*, and *Guideposts for Teens*.